世界知名TESOL专家论丛
Foreign Language Teacher Education and Development –
Selected Works of Renowned TESOL Experts

Series Editor: Yilin Sun

U0558910

范式转换:
TESOL与语言变异

Shifting Paradigm:
TESOL and Language Variation

Ahmar Mahboob

上海外语教育出版社
外教社 SHANGHAI FOREIGN LANGUAGE EDUCATION PRESS

图书在版编目（CIP）数据

范式转换：TESOL与语言变异：英文 /（澳）艾哈
迈尔·马赫布卜（Ahmar Mahboob）著. -- 上海：上海
外语教育出版社，2024
（世界知名TESOL专家论丛）
ISBN 978-7-5446-7954-1

Ⅰ.①范… Ⅱ.①艾… Ⅲ.①英语—教学研究—文集
Ⅳ.①H319.3-53

中国国家版本馆CIP数据核字(2024)第026670号

出版发行：**上海外语教育出版社**
（上海外国语大学内） 邮编：200083
电　　话：021-65425300 (总机)
电子邮箱：bookinfo@sflep.com.cn
网　　址：http://www.sflep.com
责任编辑：王晓宇

印　　刷：上海华教印务有限公司
开　　本：635×965　1/16　印张 22.75　字数 415 千字
版　　次：2024 年 9 月第1版　 2024 年 9 月第 1 次印刷

书　　号：**ISBN 978-7-5446-7954-1**
定　　价：**72.00 元**
本版图书如有印装质量问题，可向本社调换
质量服务热线：4008-213-263

世界知名 TESOL 专家论丛

出版说明

"世界知名 TESOL 专家论丛"由上海外语教育出版社约请国际知名英语教育和学术机构——世界英语教师协会（TESOL International Association）的前任主席孙以琳（Yilin Sun）教授担任主编，针对国内教师教育发展的需求，精心策划推出。丛书主编及作者均来自 TESOL 协会，在国际英语教学研究领域颇有建树。这是 TESOL 协会专家首次集中与我国外语界合作，联袂将国际教师教育与发展领域的研究精华向广大读者呈现。

丛书每种致力于教师教育发展的一个研究专题，集萃了作者在该领域的研究成果，既有丰富的理论知识，又有鲜活的课堂实例，从国际范围的广阔视野对英语教师的教学、科研和职业发展等领域的热点话题进行了探讨，展现了该研究领域的发展历程和研究成果。

丛书注重理论联系实际，具有很强的实用性和指导性，可供高校外语教师自学阅读，也可作为教师培训机构的辅助教材或参考读物。相信本套丛书的出版将从教学、科研、职业发展等角度为国内高校外语教师的教育和发展提供切实有效的理论指导和实践借鉴。

Preface

This book, *Shifting Paradigm: TESOL and Language Variation* by Dr. Ahmar Mahboob, is part of the book series *Foreign Language Teacher Education and Development—Selected Works of Renowned TESOL Experts*, published by the Shanghai Academic Publishing Center for Foreign Language Education, Shanghai Foreign Language Education Press.

As we have witnessed, the field of TESOL has transformed itself over the last 50 years, particularly in the last two decades. It has become diverse, complex, multifaceted, and "glocal." The increasing demand for global English has led to an expanded landscape with ever-diversifying profiles of users, uses, and contexts.

This series, titled *Foreign Language Teacher Education and Development—Selected Works of Renowned TESOL Experts*, exemplifies the diversity and complexity of the English language teaching (ELT) field by featuring works from leading researchers and educators in TESOL.

Each book in this series focuses on a specific area within the ELT field, such as critical approaches to English language teaching, second language acquisition research, second language writing research and practice, second language reading research and practice, World Englishes, teacher education, corpus-based grammar/lexical studies, English for specific purposes (ESP), language assessment, bilingual/ multicultural education and language policy, and developing teachers as leaders.

The purpose of each book is to bring together earlier and recent articles to showcase the development of the author's work over their academic career. These articles have been carefully selected to address both theoretical issues and practical implications in English language teaching for in-service and pre-service ELT professionals. This series aims to not only support the professional growth of foreign language teachers but also serve as textbooks or recommended reading in teacher training institutes in China and other parts of Asia.

Each book commences with an autobiographical introduction by the author, in which they identify critical issues within their areas of expertise and discuss how their work has evolved over time. The remainder of the book consists of chapters based on articles published throughout the author's professional career. The book concludes with a chapter in which the author provides a summary of their work, along with predictions and suggestions for the future.

By tracing each author's research and teaching career, which spans a lifetime in some cases, each book offers readers a vivid snapshot of the development of the author's perspectives on the addressed issues. This reflection mirrors the changes in theory, research, and practice within the specific area of inquiry over time. It is our hope that this series will contribute to an extensive knowledge base and foster constructive disciplinary growth within the ELT field.

Ahmar's volume brings together an inspiring collection of representative works that address critical issues in both theory and practice within the areas of language variations in TESOL and Applied Linguistics. Ahmar has dedicated close to 30 years to a successful career as an outstanding scholar and researcher.

This book is divided into three parts. Part One delves into critical issues surrounding non-native English-speaking teachers (NNESTs) in the TESOL field, including the discriminations they face and, more importantly, the unique values, perspectives, and contributions that NNESTs bring to TESOL and Applied Linguistics. Ahmar powerfully demystifies the so-called "native speaker myth," which should not define the ideology of TESOL and Applied Linguistics. He eloquently explores the concept, behaviors, and consequences of "enracement," i.e., the act of making or causing somebody to become (very) raced, according to the author. Racial prejudices are not limited to interactions between members of a majority and a minority group; they can also occur between members of different minority groups. To combat such prejudices, we need to begin by critically examining our own "enraced" behaviors as TESOL professionals.

Part Two of the book focuses on the nature of language, language variation, and their implications for language teaching and education. Using the NNEST perspective, the author introduces the three-dimensional (3D) framework (users, uses, and mode, see Chapter 11) and then presents chapters that critique and expand upon the work on

World Englishes, Language Identity, and Curriculum Studies. The articles in this section challenge the monolingual biases in TESOL and SLA theories and practice, suggesting that a multilingual orientation in TESOL and Applied Linguistics would be more aligned with the mission and context of the TESOL profession.

The final part of the book, Part Three, brings together all the threads that the author has been working on over the years and weaves them into the form of a chapter that reminds readers that TESOL professionals can move beyond theoretical debates and engage in meaningful work that has a demonstrable impact on our learners, ourselves, and our communities. This chapter intentionally includes poetry while eschewing references to make a powerful point about not conforming to typical academic norms. Nonetheless, it convincingly outlines an effective and inspiring path forward to empower our learners and ourselves as TESOL professionals. The author urges us to leave behind the promises marketed by exploitative education and instead retreat to evaluate our circumstances and consider new ways forward.

This powerful collection of articles successfully achieves the author's intention: "to enable people from non-elite backgrounds to thrive in their personal and professional lives." I have known Ahmar for many years, and every time I read his work, I find deep inspiration. I have no doubt that this remarkable volume will inspire and assist all TESOL professionals in embracing Ahmar's vision: "strengthening your own work and doing things that empower you, your community, and the environment." It is truly splendid! Simply splendid!

Yilin Sun
Seattle
October, 2023

Contents

Part III
Moving Forward

Chapter 1

Introduction

Some of my early memories of Pakistan are from 1982, when I was 11 and my parents, siblings, and I visited our relatives and friends in Karachi from the United Arab Emirates.

I remember that we were invited to a large gathering at one of the hotels in Karachi during that visit. At some point, I ventured out and went to one of the stores to buy some candies. What happened during my short interaction with the shopkeeper has impacted my life. For some reason, I don't remember why, I chose to speak in English with the shopkeeper, as opposed to boli (my spoken mother tongue). Being from a foreign environment, my English accent—although not even close to being 'native'—was different enough from the local Pakistani accent to mark me as an outsider. This, in retrospect, put me—a boy of 11—in relative authority over an adult shopkeeper with limited proficiency in English. It was then that I realised the power of language and the authority of English in social and power relations.

This was not a bad discovery for an 11-year-old. And, I am not going to say that I haven't used this to my advantage when I could.

Having grown up with English and having an Honours in English and a Master's in English linguistics, I felt pretty confident with my language and literacy. Things changed for me when I went to the United States of America (USA) to pursue my Master's and then Ph.D. Upon arriving in the USA, all privileges I held because of my proficiency in English instantly eroded. Instead, I was marked as an outsider and a foreigner. My variety of English did not match the dialects of power any longer. From being able to get away with things because of my language, I was now marginalised because of it.

Then, in time, through my professional engagement, my position and authority shifted again with certain groups of peoples. From being another non-native English-speaking teacher (NNEST), I became the co-editor of *TESOL Quarterly*, one of the most prestigious journals in the field. From being an NNEST, I became a student of language and socio-semiotics. And, from being an NNEST, I became the named field leader in the area of English language and literature by *The Australian's Research* magazine in 2019 and was inducted in the Australian Poetry Hall of Fame in 2021.

And, while these recognitions have indeed enabled me, I am always conscious of the scope and limitation of this privilege, which is less than skin deep for me. As soon as I am out of context and people don't know me, I lose all my privileges. These experiences, along with experiences of privilege, and along with my interest in language, socio-semiotics, and the applications of language in society, have allowed me to explore the nature of language along with its uses and implications in society in unique ways.

In this volume, I have included some of my work that focuses on two such issues. In Part I, the focus is on non-native speakers of English who are or want to become teachers of English. The section includes a number of studies that both document the extent of discrimination they face and the reasons behind it. The section ends with a discussion of how NNESTs bring a unique perspective to not just TESOL, but to language studies more broadly. The final chapter in this section, namely Chapter 10, introduces work on language variation, which is the focus of Part II of the book.

In Part II, the focus of the work is on nature of language, language variation, and its implications for language teaching and education. The section starts with an introduction of the 3D framework and then includes chapters that critique and extend work on World Englishes, Language Identity, and Curriculum Studies.

The last section of the book, Part III, pulls all the threads that I have been working on over the years and puts them together in the form of a chapter that shows us how we can leave behind theoretical debates and engage in meaningful work that can have a demonstrable effect on us and our communities. This chapter does not conform to usual academic norms: it includes poetry and excludes references!

In writing these chapters, my intention was to enable people from non-elite backgrounds in their personal and professional lives. It is my hope that this collection of work will help readers in strengthening their own work and do things that empower them, their communities, and the environment.

Part I

NNEST Studies

Chapter 2

Native or Non-Native: What Do Students Enrolled in an Intensive English Program Think?

Mahboob, A. (2004). Native or nonnative: What do the students think? In L. Kamhi-Stein (Ed.), *Learning and teaching from experience: Perspectives on nonnative English-speaking professionals* (pp. 121–147). Ann Arbor: University of Michigan Press.

Most of the work on non-native English-speaking teachers' (NNESTs) issues examines the self-perceptions and personal histories of NNESTs themselves. Recently there has been some work on administrative issues as well (Flynn & Gulikers, 2001; Mahboob et al., 2004). In addition to this work, some articles (Cook, 2000; Liu, 1999; Medgyes, 1992) discuss the underrepresented status of NNESTs within English as a second language (ESL) and English as a foreign language (EFL) programs. These articles point out that program administrators generally prefer hiring native English-speaking teachers (NESTs) to NNESTs because administrators perceive that ESL students do not want NNESTs as their teachers. However, perceptions of ESL students are not well represented in literature on NNEST issues, especially the perceptions of ESL students in the United States.

Mahboob et al. (2004) present the results of a study focusing on the hiring criteria of English language program (ELP) administrators in the United States. The results of their study show that the majority of program administrators agree that the "native English speaker" criterion is important in making hiring decisions. The results also show that the more importance program administrators give to the "native English speaker" criterion, the lower the ratio of NNESTs employed in their programs is. These results support the idea that program administrators perceive "nativeness" to be important and give it significant weight when hiring teachers. These findings, thus, provide empirical support to claims that there is a bias in favor of native English speakers in the profession (Braine,

1999; Cook, 1999; Medgyes, 1992).

As mentioned above, literature on NNESTs suggests that the reason why program administrators stress "nativeness" is that they perceive that students in their programs prefer NESTs over NNESTs. However, administrators' perceptions have not been systematically studied. And there currently are only a few studies of students' perceptions of and preferences for "nativeness" in a teacher (Cook, 2000; Liang, 2002). In one such study, Cook (2000) summarizes his findings and states "nowhere is there an overwhelming preference for NS [native speaker] teachers. Being an NS is only one among many factors that influence students' views of teaching" (p. 331). Cook further states that while program administrators believe that students prefer native speaker teachers, students in various countries themselves do not have an "overwhelming preference" (p. 331) for NESTs. He believes that "nativeness" is not a major factor in influencing students' views. However, Cook does not discuss the reasons for these perceptions.

The purpose of this study is to explore ESL students' perceptions of both NESTs and NNESTs and to investigate what students think about the "native" status. The study also investigates factors that influence students' perceptions of their teachers. Students' perceptions presented in this chapter are, when possible, compared and contrasted with teachers' perceptions of themselves and with other references to related research on NNESTs.

The Study

The purpose of this study is to evaluate ESL students' attitudes towards NESTs and NNESTs. In order to do this, the study relies on qualitative data (Hyrkstedt & Kalaja, 1998). The use of qualitative data to explore students' attitudes is a break away from traditional methods used in attitude studies and has several advantages.

Most studies of language attitudes and perceptions tend to use one of three methods. Ryan, Giles, and Sebastian (1982) present a detailed overview of these methods. According to them, the technique of "content analysis of societal treatment" (p. 7) relies on the use of existing documents that may be available as well as ethnographic observations that do not explicitly solicit information from respondents. In contrast to this technique, the "direct measurement" (p. 7) technique solicits respondents' beliefs and attitudes by using individual or group interviews/questionnaires. A third method used in language attitude studies, the "indirect measurement" (p. 7), became widely used in the 1960s (with the studies of language attitudes towards English and French in Montreal). This indirect method, popularly known as the "matched-guise" approach, uses pre-recorded oral stimulus in different varieties as spoken by a single speaker. Listeners' attitudes towards the various guises (i.e., different varieties that are actually spoken by the same person) are recorded and then analyzed.

Although these three methods have been extensively used in research on language attitudes, their validity and reliability have been questioned. The criticism against the matched-guise technique is particularly severe. In summarizing the problems associated with this technique, Hyrkstedt and Kalaja (1998) state,

> To begin with, the technique has been criticized for its low reliability and validity, as it is difficult to generalize findings from experiments and apply them to real-life situations; second, for its uncritical choice of speech samples and insensitive treatment of subjects. In addition, the technique separates the attitude object from its evaluation. More importantly, the technique forces subjects to respond along dimensions that have been worked out by researchers, instead of along dimensions of their own choice. (p. 346)

In order to avoid these problems, especially the last one listed, Hyrkstedt and Kalaja used a "discourse-analytic" technique to explore the attitudes towards English in Finland. Hyrkstedt and Kalaja gave a "letter-to-the-Editor" to their respondents (80 college students), asking them to write a response to the letter. The response essays were collected by the researchers and coded. In coding the essays, the researchers created categories of responses and counted the distribution of comments in each category. However, instead of categorizing the responses based on predefined categories, the researchers let the categories evolve out of the data. In this sense, they based their analysis on grounded theory (Babchuk, 1997), which also stresses the importance of categories to emerge from data rather than using a priori categories. The findings of the study were then discussed based on the categories that evolved out of the responses and the distribution of the responses (as either positive or negative) among the categories.

Hyrkstedt and Kalaja's technique of studying language attitudes avoids the criticism discussed above that is leveled against other techniques used in studies on language attitudes. In addition, the development of categories based on the data (in contrast to an analysis that uses predefined categories) allows for an exploratory analysis of the data. The current study has adopted the discourse analytic technique in studying and analyzing ESL students' perceptions of NESTs and NNESTs.

Participants

In order to elicit students' perceptions of NNESTs, all students enrolled in an Intensive English Program (IEP) at a large Midwestern university were invited to write an essay on a given topic. Students in this program were provided with classroom instructions for 4–5 hours daily. This IEP had both native and non-native English speakers as language instructors. Thus, the participants in this study were familiar with having NNESTs as teachers in the United States. However, whether the particular student writers in this study had studied with an NNEST in this IEP or not was not explored.

A total of 37 students volunteered to participate in the essay writing. All were adults and came from diverse linguistic backgrounds. The language proficiency of these students varied; based on a holistic evaluation of their essays, the students were either at an intermediate or an advanced level. Because of the small size of the program (the total number of students in the program was approximately 200) and in order to maintain complete confidentiality and anonymity, biographical information about the students was not collected.

Instrument

Following the technique used by Hyrkstedt and Kalaja (1998), participants in this study were given a stimulus topic and asked to write their reactions to the stimulus. The cue given to them stated:

> Some students think that only native speakers can be good language teachers. Others think that nonnatives can also be efficient teachers. What is your opinion about this issue? Please feel free to provide details and examples.

As can be noted in the stimulus above, impartiality was maintained in the statement. Students were therefore free to explore and write their own perceptions regarding this issue. In order not to influence students' essay content, the essay writing was supervised by one of the teachers (native speakers of Anglo-American English) in the program. Neither the researcher, a non-native English speaker, nor any other NNESTs were present during the time the students wrote these essays. The students were informed of the strict confidentiality and anonymity of their essays and were told that their essays would not be used to evaluate them in any way. Students were given 35 minutes to write their essays.

Data Analysis

Out of the 37 essays collected, 4 were discarded because the essays were written entirely on the students' English language learning experience in their own countries, which (although interesting) was not a focus of the current study. One additional essay was disqualified because the student wrote off topic. Thus, the results of the study are based on 32 ESL student essays.

Students' responses to the stimulus were analyzed using a "discourse-analytic" technique, following Hyrkstedt and Kalaja (1998). The 32 essays were coded by four readers (the use of multiple coders has been advocated by Babchuk, 1997). No a priori categories were used in the analysis of the essays; rather, the categories emerged as a result of the analysis. Emphasis on not having a priori categories stemmed from the fear that predetermined categories might perpetuate ideas that did not reflect the students' actual perceptions as well as distract the researcher from observing other uncategorized dynamics in the data.

In the first stage of the analysis, the four readers coded the essays individually. Each individual read and coded the essays using separate colored highlighters for the various types of comments that they found important. Then, the four readers got together and generated a list of categories of students' comments about both NESTs and NNESTs. These categories were then labeled. Any differences in opinion or categorization were resolved after a brief discussion. The total number of comments in each category was counted. This count was distributed within a category based on whether a comment was positive ("+") or negative ("-") in its evaluation. The final stage in the analysis involved sorting the individual categories into major groups and labeling the groups.

Findings

Three broad groups of categories encompassing 10 individual categories emerged from the data analysis. The first group, "linguistic factors," included "oral skills," "literacy skills," "grammar," "vocabulary," and "culture." The second group, "teaching styles," included "ability to answer questions" and "teaching methodology." The third group, "personal factors," included "experience as an ESL learner," "hard-work," and "affect." The following are the results of the analysis.

Linguistic Factors

As noted above, there were 5 linguistic factors that students referred to in their discussion of NESTs and NNESTs. The distribution of comments across these factors is given in Table 1 below.

Table 1   Distribution of Comments for the Linguistic Factors

Linguistic Factors	NESTs		NNESTs	
	Positive Comments	Negative Comments	Positive Comments	Negative Comments
	n	n	n	n
Oral skills	15	0	5	5
Literacy skills	0	0	3	0
Grammar	0	4	12	0
Vocabulary	8	0	4	0
Culture	6	0	4	1
Total	29	4	28	6

Table 1 shows that there were 67 comments distributed over the 5 linguistic categories. There were 29 positive and 4 negative comments about NESTs and 28 positive and 6 negative comments about NNESTs. These results are presented below.

Oral skills

The category of "oral skills" included comments that discussed the teaching of listening and speaking/pronunciation. The teaching of oral skills was considered the forte of the NESTs. There were 25 statements in this category, the highest for any one category. Fifteen of these comments discussed the role of NESTs while the other 10 discussed the role of NNESTs in teaching this skill.

All 15 students' comments related to NESTs were positive. In general, these comments stated that native speakers can provide an ideal model for pronunciation. The following two examples from the essays express students' perceptions of NESTs' ability to teach oral skills:

> The best part of having native speakers as teachers is you can learn natural pronunciation from them. And it is very effective to your listening and speaking. (Student #8)
> ... when native speakers teach, students can learn right rhythem and pronouncation (Student #34)

The two statements above show that NESTs were preferred as teachers of oral skills because "you can learn natural pronunciation from them." This is interesting because research in Second Language Acquisition indicates that pronunciation is one of the hardest linguistic skills to acquire at a native-speaker level for adult ESL students (Dalton-Puffer, Kaltenboeck, & Smit, 1997). However, the results presented above support findings by Arva and Medgyes (2000). In their study of teacher perceptions, they find that the communicative ability of NESTs is perceived to be their strongest attribute by both NESTs and NNESTs. Thus, students' perceptions about NNESTs' oral skills are corroborated by studies focusing on the self-perceptions of EFL teachers.

As compared to NESTs, NNESTs received mixed reviews as teachers of oral skills. Out of the 10 comments that referred to NNESTs, 5 were positive and the other 5 were negative. The positive comments elaborated on the NNESTs' ability to identify the exact problems with their learners' pronunciation and to teach them how to correct it. The following example illustrates this:

> ... non-native speakers try to teach our mistakes ... I think that English pronunciation are difficult for Asian ... he [NNEST] always found my mistakes of English (Student #1)

On the other hand, the negative comments regarding NNESTs' ability to teach oral skills mostly focused on NNESTs' perceived non-standard pronunciation. Students felt that NNESTs were not the best teachers for oral skills because they were themselves non-native-like. The following statement is an example of such comments:

> Although they sometime have problem in pronunciation ... students can get many other from non-natives. (Student #6)

This student stated that NNESTs were not good teachers of oral skills because of their "problematic" pronunciation; however, the student felt that ESL students could learn other skills from NNESTs. Interestingly, some students felt that while NNESTs could be good teachers of listening, they might not be good teachers of speaking. One student discussed this issue at some length and wrote,

> Non-native speakers speak worse than native speakers. But pronunciation is just one part of language. Although non-native speakers cannot speak very well and they have a limit, on the contrary they can teach very well other parts of language: grammar, reading, writing and even listening. (Student #26)

This student, like many others, considered the speech of native speakers standard and all other variations "worse" or less standard.

Another student expressed concern about the prejudice experienced by non-native English speakers who have an accent that differs from what is expected to be the mainstream accent:

> Some people have a prejudice about pronunciation, which mean non-native speaker's pronunciations is a little different, so their teaching is not good. I think that is bad idea. Important thing is teacher's knowledge not pronunciation. If we can understand teacher's pronunciation, it's not a problem. In IEP, some teachers are non-native speaker but I think they have more zeal and wider knowledge. (Student #33)

This student raised a number of important issues. The student pointed out that there was a "prejudice" within the student body against NNESTs' pronunciation. However, this student also suggested that not all students felt this way. For this student, teachers' knowledge instead of their accent or pronunciation was important. The student also pointed out that in the program in which s/he studied, there were a number of NNESTs who had "more zeal and wider knowledge" than NESTs. This reference to NNESTs in his/her own program suggested that this student had been taught by at least one NNEST.

This student's comment suggests the possibility that students' perceptions of NNESTs may be different (and may change) based on whether they have or have not studied with an NNEST in the United States. The comment may be interpreted to suggest that students who have not studied with NNESTs may find pronunciation to be an important factor, while those who have studied with them find teachers' knowledge to be a more important factor.

Though not focusing on students themselves, the results of a study by Reves and Medgyes (1994) in an EFL setting support the notion that EFL teachers from a non-native English-speaking background may feel "deficient" in their language skills. Similarly, in another study, Arva and Medgyes (2000) refer to statements from NNESTs indicating that their oral skills were not very good. Arva and Medgyes quote one non-native English-speaking teacher who felt that "because this is a learnt language, it doesn't come spontaneously" (p. 361). However, in contrast to the current study, Arva and Medgyes' study was conducted in a secondary school EFL setting (Hungary). Furthermore, the NNESTs in their study had lived in an English-speaking country for a very limited time—between two weeks and one and a half years. Thus, it is unclear whether NNESTs in the United States, especially those who have been here for a long time, share the same self-perceptions regarding their oral skills as the NNESTs in Arva and Medgyes' study.

Samimy and Brutt-Griffler (1999) investigate the self-perceptions of non-native teacher trainees enrolled in a master of arts program in teaching English to speakers of other languages (TESOL) in the United States. Samimy and Brutt-Griffler specifically refer to work by Reves and Medgyes and state,

> The present study led us to a different conclusion from that of Reves and Medgyes (1994). Namely, unlike the causal relationship that they established between NNS professional' command of English and impoverished self-image, the results of this study seem to suggest otherwise. In other words … they did not express a sense of inferiority vis-à-vis native speaker professionals. (p. 141)

In yet another study of NNESTs' self-perception in the United States, Mahboob et al. (2002) also report that they did not find any negative self-evaluation based on NNESTs' language skills. Rather, they found that the NNESTs were very confident in their language skills and their ability to teach ESL. One non-native English-speaking teacher in their study said:

> I feel fully integrated; I don't have any doubts about my abilities [to teach English]. … Perhaps I am even more competent than they [my colleagues] are! (Mahboob et al., 2002)

The contrast between the findings for NESTs and NNESTs presented above and the studies by Reves and Medgyes (1994) and Arva and Medgyes (2000) may be a result of the setting. While Reves and Medgyes, and Arva and Medgyes report on data collected in EFL settings, Mahboob et al. (2002), and Samimy and Brutt-Griffler (1999) base their analysis on data collected in the United States. Therefore, the relationship between the instructional settings (EFL vs. ESL) and NNESTs' self-perceptions needs to be further investigated.

Literacy skills

Literacy skills, in this study, included reading and writing. The number of comments for literacy skills was lower as compared to those for oral skills. There were only 3 comments in this category. These comments discussed the positive role of NNESTs in teaching these skills. One student wrote:

> One of the reason I thought non-native speakers can teach English well is the person who came from non-native English country can teach grammar, reading, and listening also. (Student #6)

The statement above shows that this student felt that NNESTs can be good teachers of reading, grammar, and listening. (This statement was also included in the "oral skills" and "grammar" categories because of its reference to those skills.) Another student wrote:

> [NNESTs] could ... be better in writing than native speaker ... (Student #16)

This comment is interesting because not only does it state that NNESTs are good teachers of writing, but it further implies that they are "better" than NESTs.

The positive evaluation of NNESTs as teachers of literacy skills and an absence of any positive comments about NESTs suggest that students find NNESTs to be good at teaching literacy skills (both reading and writing). One reason for this, as given by one of the students, is that to be good writers, both native and non-native speakers need to learn how to write. The statement below shows that some students realize that literacy skills and oral skills are different in nature and that both native and non-native speakers need to develop their reading and writing skills.

> Also, in writing subject ... it is not a matter about pronounciation of language any more. Native speakers also need to know these writing skills when they are writing. So native speakers also are required to take a writing class. (Student #25)

It is interesting to note that the argument presented above mirrors arguments in the literature on NNESTs. Kramsch and Lam (1999) state,

> The controversy surrounding the respective privileges of native speakers (see, for example, Kramsch, 1997) becomes moot when we deal with written language. For no one could argue that people are "born" into reading and writing ... both have to be schooled into literacy and into certain types of academic literacy in order to use language in its written form. (p. 57)

The similarity between Kramsch and Lam's statement and that of the student shows that ESL students are aware of the complexities of literacy acquisition and are sensitive to the equality between NESTs and NNESTs in their literacy achievements.

Grammar

Within the "linguistic factors" group, grammar was the category in which NNESTs received the strongest positive comments. There were 16 comments in this category. 12 were positive comments that discussed the strength of NNESTs in teaching grammar, and 4 were negative comments that described NESTs' weakness in teaching this aspect of the language.

The following is an example of a student's comment elaborating on NNESTs' strength as grammar teachers:

> So ... they [NNESTs] can be good grammar teachers like a TOEFL and TOEIC. (Student #22)

This example shows that students find NNESTs' grammar teaching important for their ability to do well on standardized tests of English, such as the Test of English as a Foreign Language (TOEFL) and the Test of English for International Communication (TOEIC). A pertinent observation here is that NNESTs, especially those who are international teacher trainees in the United States, need to take the TOEFL and/or the Graduate Record Examination (GRE) in order to be admitted to many academic programs across the country. Thus, NNESTs' experience of taking these tests may aid them in their ability to help their students prepare for the tests.

In their study of NNESTs' self-perceptions in the United States, Mahboob et al. (2002) find that NNESTs are aware of their strength in teaching grammar. In addition to showing self-confidence, the NNESTs in the study of Mahboob et al. (2002) also state that their native English-speaking colleagues value their expertise in grammar. Arva and Medgyes (2000) also find that NESTs acknowledge NNESTs' better understanding of grammar. They give the following example from an interview with a native English-speaking teacher:

> The non-native teacher has learnt grammar and is able to convey that to people very clearly with no wastage, whereas I would have to more often look up to find out what it was I was being asked about. (p. 362)

Arva and Medgyes also cite two other NESTs who acknowledge their limitations as grammar teachers:

> This is wrong and this is the correct way you should say it, I know, but I can't explain why it's wrong or right. (p. 361)
> Most native teachers I know never really came across grammar until they started teaching it. So you have to learn it as you go along. (p. 361)

In both examples above, NESTs express their feeling that although they know how to use the language, they are not aware of its rules explicitly. This lack of a grammatical understanding appears to be noticeable to the students. It is probably based on observing this inability of NESTs to satisfactorily explain grammatical concepts that ESL students in the present study labeled NESTs as not being good teachers of grammar. While discussing this perceived weakness, one student stated:

> Sometimes native speakers are not structure teachers, because even they speak the language perfectly, and understand the structure very well, they do not know what is the pain, because they did not have the pain. (Student #8)

It is interesting to note that the student's comment supports the perceptions of the native English-speaking teacher in the study by Arva and Medgyes (2000). The student quoted above states that while native speakers can "speak the language perfectly," they are not good at teaching its grammatical structure. This statement also attributes the NESTs' inability to teach structure to their lack of experience of explicitly learning it.

Vocabulary

Students stated that both NESTs and NNESTs can be good teachers of vocabulary. There were 12 statements in this category and all of them were positive. There were more statements that supported the idea that NESTs are better teachers of vocabulary than NNESTs. An example statement that showes that NESTs are good vocabulary teachers is given below:

> Many slang words and new vocabulary. Native speakers can explain it easily. (Student #19)

The following is an example of a statement that supports the idea that NNESTs are good vocabulary teachers:

> Next, non-native English teacher can give the definitions of the words that we cannot understand. (Student #12)

There were no negative comments in this category. Thus, both NESTs and NNESTs were considered to be effective teachers of vocabulary, though NESTs received more positive comments than NNESTs.

Culture

A number of students discussed the teaching of culture in relation to NESTs and NNESTs. There were 6 comments supporting the idea that NESTs have the ability to teach culture. An example of such a comment is given below:

> By the conversation with Americans, I can learn some pronunciation, slang and American culture. (Student #5)

The above example shows that some students perceive that they can acquire an understanding of U.S. culture from NESTs.

Four comments also supported the notion that NNESTs can be a source of cultural knowledge. This view was expressed by 1 student in the following statement:

> Sometimes, we [students] cannot understand some specific words because we do not have cultural background. For these situation, they [NNEST] can explain the word's definitions more easily than explaining of native speaker. (Student #12)

In contrast to the 4 comments supporting the idea that NNESTs were a good source of cultural knowledge, 1 comment disagreed with the notion. The following is the comment reflecting this idea:

> You can learn a foreign language perfectly, but you will always keep your conception of the world ... (Student #35)

This quotation shows that, for some students, no matter how well one learns a new language, one will always maintain their cultural heritage and this will influence their teaching ability.

Teaching Styles

As already noted, the second group of categories was labeled "teaching styles." There were two categories of comments that were placed in this group: "ability to answer questions" and "teaching methodology." Table 2 below presents the distribution of comments across categories.

Table 2   Distribution of Comments for the "Teaching Styles"

	NESTs		NNESTs	
Teaching Styles	Positive Comments	Negative Comments	Positive Comments	Negative Comments
	n	n	n	n
Ability to answer questions	0	3	4	0
Teaching methodology	0	1	5	0
Total	0	4	9	0

As the table shows, there were a total of 13 comments in this category. Four of them, all negative, described NESTs; while the other 9, all positive, described NNESTs. The following are the results of the analysis.

Ability to answer questions

This category included statements that described students' satisfaction or dissatisfaction with the explanations or answers that teachers provided. There were 7 comments in this category. Interestingly, all comments about NESTs were negative while all comments about NNESTs were positive. The following statement from one of the students exemplifies the case:

> In my opinion, I can get sufficient answer from non-native rather than natives in some questions ... (Student #22)

This statement suggests that while NESTs cannot provide "sufficient answer" to students' questions, NNESTs' response satisfies them. The following comment supports the same idea:

> Sometimes I have questions ... non-native speakers are better teachers than native speakers. (Student #5)

Teaching methodology

Similar to the previous category, titled "ability to answer questions," students found that NNESTs employed teaching methodologies that promoted enhanced learning. One student stated:

And they [NNEST] can teach the most efficient way to study the language for foreigners. (Student #33)

… The non-native teacher who also might have same experience and situations as me. So they knew how I could feel … And they also knew the way they taught effctly. (Student #28)

In contrast to the positive evaluation of NNESTs' teaching skills, the same student felt that NESTs did not use appropriate teaching methodologies and stated:

[NESTs] don't have patience about hearing the other countries' speakers' stories. (Student #28)

One possible explanation for students' positive evaluation of NNESTs' methodology is that their teaching styles may match their students' learning styles. In a study on learning styles, Peacock (2001) finds that students express discomfort when their EFL teachers' teaching styles do not match their learning styles. He finds that China's Hong Kong EFL students prefer "kinesthetic" and "auditory" learning styles and disfavor "individual" and "group" styles. In comparison, he observes that local NNESTs favor "kinesthetic," "group" and "auditory" styles while Western NESTs only favor "kinesthetic" and "group" styles. Peacock concludes that EFL teachers should implement a balanced approach to instruction as a means to accommodate a variety of learning styles. A study of NNESTs' self-perceptions also reveals that they are very confident of their teaching abilities (Kamhi-Stein et al., 2004). In their study of NESTs and NNESTs in K-12 program in California, Kamhi-Stein et al. suggest that the NNESTs' strong sense of cultural awareness and empathy may contribute to the teachers' positive self-perceptions about their instructional practices. It is interesting to note that these two characteristics, cultural awareness and empathy, were also found to be categories that emerged in the analysis of students' perceptions. However, it should be noted that Kamhi-Stein et al. conducted their study in a K-12 setting. Teachers' perceptions regarding their teaching methodology in adult ESL programs may differ.

Personal Factors

3 categories of comments were grouped together as "personal factors." There were a total of 30 comments in this group. The distribution of these comments is provided in Table 3.

Table 3   Distribution of Comments for the Personal Factors

Personal Factors	NESTs		NNESTs	
	Positive Comments	Negative Comments	Positive Comments	Negative Comments
	n	n	n	n
Experience as an ESL learner	0	4	15	0
Hard-work	0	0	5	0
Affect	0	0	6	0
Total	0	4	26	0

Table 3 shows that, much like in the case of "teaching styles" group, NESTs only received negative comments, if any, while NNESTs received positive comments.

Experience as an ESL learner

This category received the second largest number of comments (n = 19). 15 of these comments support the idea that NNESTs are better teachers because they have had the experience of learning English themselves, while the other 4 stated that NESTs are not good teachers because they have not had the experience of learning English.

A number of issues discussed in the essays, for example, NESTs' perceived weakness and NNESTs' perceived strength in teaching grammar and answering students' questions, were attributed to teachers' experience, or a lack of experience, as ESL learners. The following statement by one of the students exemplifies this:

> Because they [NNESTs] learned the language which they teach now, they know what problems do students have in learning language. For example, native speakers have never learned grammar, so most of them don't know how to teach grammar. (Student #9)

Almost half of the ESL students (15 out of 32) in this study felt that NNESTs' experience of learning English as a second language makes them aware of the problems that ESL learners may face. The students therefore felt that NNESTs are better equipped to help them. They also felt that NNESTs have more empathy for them because of this experience. Discussing this point, one student stated:

> Non-native teachers also have studied the language as foreigner, so, the teachers have many experiences about the language. During the teachers' study they realized many problems that can't be found by native teachers. (Student #3)

It is interesting to note that in studies of NNESTs' self-perceptions, NNESTs seem to be aware of this advantage. Lee and Lew (2001) report that teacher trainees enrolled in a master of arts program in TESOL "unanimously agreed that the most valuable asset is their experience as learners of English" (p. 146). They present the following quotation from one of their participants who shared her advantage of having had the experience of learning English.

> I can understand and feel what the professor is saying about the theories, and I can put myself into the learners' shoes when I am preparing a lesson plan. (p. 146)

This quotation shows that the participant in Lee and Lew's study was able to extract the appropriate message from her graduate TESOL classes and applied this understanding to her own teaching.

In addition to this self-awareness, in another study of NNESTs' self-perceptions, Liu (1999) quotes one of his participants, Ms. I,

> I also briefly mention my experience learning English so that they realize that I went through the same process that they are going through now. I want them to feel that I have also experienced learning English as a second language ... [Ms. I then explains the reason for doing this and adds] it is important not only having had experience teaching languages but more importantly having been a student of a second/foreign language. This creates and establishes trust and rapport with the students at their level of experience. (p. 171)

This quotation further confirms that not only are NNESTs aware of their advantage of having been ESL learners, but they also utilize this benefit to their advantage in their teaching.

An interesting observation in relation to this category is that many TESOL programs in the United States have a foreign language requirement for their teacher trainees. This suggests that many ESL teachers have had at least some experience of learning a second/foreign language. However, the ESL students in this study did not show awareness of this fact.

Hard-work

There were 5 comments in this category and all of them supported the idea that NNESTs were hard-workers. Some students felt that to be a non-native English speaker and a teacher of English in the United States, NNESTs have to work very hard. One student wrote:

> I felt that the people who study very hard for another language can be speaker without any problem ... Non-native speaker can do ... teaching easily. (Student #32)

Another student forwarded the same idea when s/he stated:

> I think non-natives can be a good teacher they try to study and practice hardly. (Student #4)

In contrast to the comments describing NNESTs as hard workers, there were no comments that described NESTs as hard workers. An absence of comments about NESTs in this category should not necessarily be taken as a sign that students do not consider them hard workers; rather, the absence of comments may be interpreted as a factor of the category itself: Native English speakers do not need to work hard to be good speakers of English.

Hard-work also comes out as a marker in several studies that look at NNESTs' self-perceptions (Kamhi-Stein, 1999; Lee & Lew, 2001). Kamhi-Stein (1999) refers to a former student who "found herself working twice as hard as any of her [NEST] colleagues in order to gain acceptance of her ESL students" (p. 150). This reference shows that NNESTs feel that they need to work harder to prove themselves. Regardless of the reason for this hard-work, a study of students' perceptions shows that ESL students recognize this hard-work and appreciate their NNESTs for it.

Affect

Six statements were placed in this category. All of these were positive statements about NNESTs. This category was related to NNESTs' "experience as an ESL learner." Some students felt that NNESTs could empathize with them and provide them with emotional support because they had gone through the process themselves and knew how it felt. One student stated:

> The non-native teacher who also might have same experience and situations as me. So they knew how I could feel ... (Student #28)

Another student specifically stated that NNESTs are more empathetic and wrote:

> I think non-native speakers can be better language teachers because of their empathy and diverse culture. (Student #21)

Arva and Medgyes (2000) explain that NESTs themselves realize their shortcoming in being unable to appreciate the process that their students go through. They cite the following statement from a native English-speaking teacher:

> Being a native speaker, it is difficult for you to appreciate what the students are going through when they are learning English. (p. 362)

The reference to Arva and Medgyes' study provides support and validity to this study of ESL students' perceptions. It also shows that ESL students have a keen observation and are sensitive to their teachers' (both NESTs or NNESTs) relative strengths and weaknesses.

One student focused on the relationship between language proficiency and affect at some length by sharing a story about two of his friends who were piano teachers. This student wrote:

> When I lived in Japan. I had a friend who is a piano teacher. She learned playing the piano at University. But her playing quarity is not good. On the other hand, I had another friend who is also piano teacher. She graduated a very famous music university. So, she is a really good piano player. Both of them teached piano to children. They were completely different because teacher who is a good player could teach a high level tequnick but the another teacher couldn't teach a high level teq. But the result was strange. Students who were taught by a good player teacher couldn't improve their play, but another students could improve. I considered well about this result. The teacher who can teach high level teq. to children couldn't teach how playing piano is interesting, but the teacher who can't teach high level teq. could teach how playing piano is interesting, also she couldn't show high level playing but could teach how to learn.
>
> In this case, the teacher who is not high level can be a good teacher. I think it is same as English teacher. If an English teacher is not a native

speakers, he can teach how to enjoy English and learn English. And also he can teach a correct answer to his students. (Student #33)

For this student, the skills that a person has do not necessarily translate into teaching ability. The student felt that NNESTs could teach language learners how to "enjoy" English as well as be able to provide appropriate answers to their questions. While this student believes that NESTs have a higher level of language proficiency, he suggests that NNESTs can be effective too since they can teach learners how to "enjoy" the language learning process.

Summary of Findings and Discussion

Data for this study were collected using a "discourse-analytic" technique. The advantage of using this technique was that the analysis and findings were grounded in qualitative data rather than based on a priori categories. The findings of this study are collated in Table 4 below.

Table 4   Distribution of Positive and Negative Comments for NESTs and NNESTs.

Categories	NESTs		NNESTs	
	Positive Comments n	Negative Comments n	Positive Comments n	Negative Comments n
Linguistic Factors				
Oral skills	15	0	5	5
Literacy skills	0	0	3	0
Grammar	0	4	12	0
Vocabulary	8	0	4	0
Culture	6	0	4	1
Teaching Styles				
Ability to answer questions	0	3	4	0
Teaching methodology	0	1	5	0
Personal Factors				
Experience as an ESL learner	0	4	15	0
Hard-work	0	0	5	0
Affect	0	0	6	0
Total	29	12	63	6

Table 4 shows that the distribution of perceived strengths for the two groups of teachers is complementary. Thus, while NESTs are seen as good at teaching oral skills, NNESTs are seen as good at teaching literacy skills and grammar. Table 4 also shows how NNESTs' experience of having studied the language themselves is perceived as their strongest characteristic.

The results of this study support several of Medgyes' (2001) assumptions regarding the "bright side of being a non-NEST" (p. 436). Although the focus of his work is on EFL settings, a comparison of his assumptions with the results of this study is informative. The data collected in this study support Medgyes' assumption that "non-NESTs can teach learning strategies more effectively" (p. 436). This assumption is supported by the students' belief that their NNESTs' understanding of ESL teaching comes from their own learning experience. As a result of this experience, learners felt that NNESTs were able to anticipate and explain concepts better than NESTs. They felt that explanations given by NNESTs were more satisfactory than those provided by NESTs.

The students' preference for NNESTs' teaching methodology is especially interesting when considered in light of the research conducted in the 1980s. In the 1980s there was a perception that to become good teachers, NNESTs should not only improve their linguistic skills to match those of native speakers, but they should also adopt the teaching practices and methods of NESTs. The following extract from Sheorey (1986), himself a NNEST, illustrates this point:

> the study gives an indication of which errors are most irritating to native ESL teachers, a finding which we can use to bring our own error-evaluation practices in line with those of native teachers. I am assuming here that acquiring a native-like sensitivity to errors is a proper goal (however elusive it might be) for non-native ESL teachers, and that we should seek to adjust our error-evaluation practices accordingly. (p. 310)

This reference supports the idea that the goal of NNESTs should be to acquire native-like teaching sensitivity. The results from the present survey of students' perceptions not only negate the need for NNESTs to become native-like in their pedagogical practices, but indeed suggest that they have unique characteristics that students find lacking in NESTs, especially in the teaching of grammar and the ability to answer questions. Thus, statements from earlier studies, such as Sheorey (1986), need to be reanalyzed in light of the findings discussed here that suggest that "acquiring a native-like sensitivity" is not "a proper goal" for NNESTs. Rather, the unique teaching abilities of both NESTs and NNESTs complement each other and together provide a better learning environment for ESL students.

Students also perceived NNESTs to be more understanding and empathetic towards them. They felt that NNESTs, again based on their ESL learning experience, could provide affective support that NESTs were not equipped to do. As a result of NNESTs' experience of being ESL learners, it is possible that their teaching methodology fits their students' expectations. McCargar (1993) reports that students come to a class with a number of expectations and that they feel disappointed if these expectations are not met. In this study, students' reference to NNESTs' ability to answer questions satisfactorily and to provide empathy suggests that NNESTs have a first-hand understanding of how to meet their students' expectations.

The perception that NESTs are more skilled in their language competence was shared by a majority of the students in their essays. The students perceived NNESTs to be good at teaching all skills except speaking and pronunciation. This perception of NNESTs' "less-than-native-like" pronunciation is one possible reason why the students in this study do not share Medgyes' idea that NNESTs provide their students with an imitable model. In fact, none of the students' essays in this study discuss the role of NNESTs as providing good learner models. Students only refer to NNESTs' experience as ESL learners in relation to their ability to better answer students' questions, provide empathy, and use appropriate teaching methodologies. They do not feel, or at least explicitly state, that NNESTs provide them with good learner models.

Students feel that NNESTs' English is not perfect and therefore they are not the ideal "language models" (Medgyes, 2001, p. 436) for them. This negative perception of NNESTs' oral skills is also supported by a number of attitudinal studies that evaluate perceptions of individuals from various countries and language backgrounds towards different varieties of English. For example, Forde (1996) studies the attitudes of Chinese elementary school children towards different varieties of English and reports that the respondents preferred native varieties of English (both American and British) over local models. Forde also finds that the respondents linked teachers' variety of English to their ability to teach. In other studies of language attitudes, Chiba, Matsuura, and Yamamoto (1995), Dalton-Puffer et al. (1997) and Jarvella, Bang, Jakobsen, and Mees (2001) find attitudes towards Japanese, Austrian and Dutch varieties of English, respectively, to be less favorable as compared to a native variety of English. The results of the current study, focusing on an ESL setting, support the findings in EFL settings. The students in the current study view that NESTs are their "language models" (Medgyes, 2001, p. 436). As one of the students put it, "... I want the *truth* [emphasis added] pronunciation which non-natives teachers can't speak or use voice like native speakers ..." This student's use of "truth pronunciation" reflects the views of students who may feel that there is an "ideal," "true," and/or "correct" pronunciation of English. Bhatt (2002), in his discussion of the historical influences on the TESOL field, points out that the Chomskyan notion of an "ideal native speaker" has permeated the field and is responsible for such perceptions. This perceived importance of an "ideal native speaker" model is especially interesting in ESL because there is ample linguistic evidence that adult ESL learners cannot achieve native-like pronunciation. Dalton-Puffer et al. (1997) raise a similar point and argue that "the prominence of native speaker in language teaching has obscured the distinctive nature of the successful L2 user and created an unattainable goal for L2 learners" (p. 185). However, regardless of an understanding of the weaknesses of a native-speaker model by academics, it is perceived to be the eventual goal by ESL learners in this study.

This emphasis on pronunciation by the students may be one factor that influences administrators' perception that students do not want non-native teachers and may be one cause of program administrators' ranking of the criterion "accent" as important in making hiring decisions (Mahboob et al., 2004). This understanding of students' preference for a "native" accent might also be a reason that Flynn and Gulikers (2001) list "accent" to be an important criterion in hiring NNESTs.

Medgyes' (2001) assumption regarding the benefit students might have from NNESTs sharing their mother tongue was not supported by the results of this study. However, this may be because the essays focused on students' experience of learning English in the United States and not their home countries. The nature of ESL classes in the United States is such that students from multiple mother tongues take the same class. Thus, even if NNESTs share the mother tongue with one group of students in their classes, they may not be able to use it for instructional purposes in a multilingual class. It is also possible that the students had not had the experience of having an NNEST who shared their mother tongue in their stay in the United States. A future study of NNESTs in an EFL setting or in an ESL setting where their students share their mother tongue will be better able to evaluate the validity of this assumption.

Conclusions

The strongest finding of this study is that NESTs are perceived to be best for teaching oral skills. In addition to oral skills, NESTs are also perceived as being stronger in their ability to teach vocabulary and culture. However, some students perceive them as being weak in their ability to teach grammar. Furthermore, some students also perceive that NESTs are not always able to answer their questions well.

There were a number of characteristics mentioned in the essays that favored NNESTs. These included: "linguistic factors" such as the NNESTs' ability to teach literacy skills and grammar; "teaching styles" including their ability to use appropriate teaching methodologies and to satisfy students' questions. NNESTs were also perceived to have strengths related to "personal factors," including their experience of being ESL learners, being hard-working, and providing affective and emotional support. In contrast to their strengths, NNESTs were criticized by some students as being unable to teach oral communication skills. This weakness appeared to be rooted in students' belief that in order for them to acquire a "true" and "correct" pronunciation, they must have native speaker models.

In summary, the results of this study show that ESL students in the United States do not have a clear preference for either NESTs or NNESTs; rather, they feel that both types of teachers have unique attributes. Students find that there are strengths in the way NNESTs teach them when compared to NESTs. This is an important finding and shows that students are not naive and do not necessarily buy into the "native speaker fallacy" (Phillipson, 1992) that only native speakers can be good language teachers. The findings of this study clearly demonstrate that the importance given to the "native English speaker" hiring criterion by program administrators (Mahboob et al., 2004) is not shared by students. Both NESTs and NNESTs working collaboratively can provide a better learning environment for ESL students. This is best exemplified in the following quotation from one student:

> In my opinion, learning language have various ways and skills. You can't learn a language well just use one skill. Therefore, the different experiences from native and non-native speakers also can be your teacher when you learn a foreign language. You can get wonderful linguistical learning skills from different people and ways. (Student #5)

However, it should be noted that the present study was based on only 32 essays. A future study with a larger number of essays may reveal additional dimensions of students' perceptions of NESTs and NNESTs. A future study should also incorporate a secondary data collection task. In this way, it will be possible to add to the reliability of the results. Furthermore, biographical data should be collected from the participants in order to explore whether personal backgrounds make a difference in students' perceptions. Finally, a future study should include students in programs other than college-level IEPs. Other types of programs, such as community colleges and K-12, should be the focus of future research. It is possible that students' attitudes in these institutions may be different.

Implications for Classroom Teaching

The result of the study of students' perceptions has implications for classroom teaching for both NNESTs and NESTs. One of the primary implications is that NNESTs should feel confident about their teaching methodology. The results of this study show that students appreciate their teaching methods and the emotional support that they provide for their students. NNESTs should also actively reflect on and use their own language learning experiences to develop techniques and methods that they believe will help their students. An important implication of this study is that NNESTs should realize that, even though they may not sound like native speakers, students do not necessarily hold that against them. Students will appreciate teachers who work hard on their lesson plans and use their experience to teach their classes. Another implication of this study is that students, in general, do not share the assumption that many administrators have: that ESL students prefer NESTs. Students are perceptive of the positive qualities that NNESTs possess and the contributions that they make.

The results of the study also have instructional implications for NESTs. Students find that NESTs can help them understand the culture of the host environment. NESTs should use this positive evaluation and build on it. However, at the same time, the negative evaluations of their ability to teach grammar and answer students' questions should lead them to reflect on how they can improve these aspects of their teaching. They might want to consider using varied teaching methods and styles and rethink the way they respond to students' questions. They may also consider team-teaching, collaborating, or exchanging ideas and experiences with NNESTs. Such collaboration will be mutually beneficial to both NNESTs and NESTs.

Implications for ESL Teacher Education Programs

The findings give support to a collaborative model of teacher education (Matsuda, 1999). Recent work in teacher preparation (e.g., de Oliveira & Richardson, 2004; Matsuda, 1999; Matsuda & Matsuda, 2004) suggests that, with the current demographics of the graduate student population in TESOL programs, the model of teacher education that is most beneficial to all students is a collaborative one. In this collaborative model, native and non-native teacher trainees exchange notes and have a continuous dialogue which allows them to develop the skills that the other group excels in. Such a model of teacher education seems to be supported by the findings discussed in this chapter. With the complementary distribution of skills and attributes of NESTs and NNESTs, as perceived by the ESL students in this investigation, collaboration between the two will promote a better teaching-learning setting for ESL students.

NNESTs in the United States may discuss issues about the teaching of oral skills and culture with NESTs. Similarly, NESTs can benefit from discussing how NNESTs present and teach various grammatical points and what methods they use to explain problematic issues to their students. NESTs can also benefit from talking to NNESTs about their experiences as English language learners. This might include a discussion of linguistics and other areas that NNESTs have found problematic in their own learning of the language and ways in which they overcame these problems. A discussion of these issues will provide an opportunity for NNESTs to reflect on their learning experiences and use them more actively in their own teaching.

Collaboration between native and non-native teacher trainees can be achieved using various techniques. For example, TESOL program faculty may choose to use journal exchange as part of their course requirements (Matsuda & Matsuda, 2004). Faculty may also assign groups or pairs to write reports or complete assignments focusing on topics that require collaboration between native and non-native speakers. Faculty teaching practicum courses may consider pairing native and non-native speakers as team teachers. They may also consider having both NESTs and NNESTs observe each others' classes (Brady & Gulikers, 2004).

Finally, TESOL programs may consider developing a "buddy-teacher program," in which native and non-native teacher trainees are paired as "buddies." In addition to having an educational purpose, such a program may also provide emotional and other support for non-native students who may be international students and new to the United States (Brady & Gulikers, 2004).

Implications for Program Administrators

The results of this study have a number of implications for administrators of IEPs in the United States. In particular, the results of this study have implications for program administrators who do not hire NNESTs because of their perception that ESL students only want NESTs. The results of this study show that ESL students do not prefer NESTs. Rather, this study reveals that students value both NESTs and NNESTs. This study shows that students feel that both NESTs and NNESTs contribute uniquely to their ESL learning experience in the United States and that together they can provide the best learning environment.

Based on these results, program administrators should consider making hiring decisions based on language and teaching expertise and not on the teachers' native or non-native status. It should be noted that being a native speaker does not guarantee linguistic expertise (Pasternak & Bailey, 2004; Rampton, 1990). By focusing on teachers' teaching abilities and teachers' professional qualifications rather than their native or non-native status, program administrators will create a context of learning for their students that will be more supportive of not only their needs as language learners but also as individual human beings.

References

Arva, V., & Medgyes, P. (2000). Native and non-native teachers in the classroom. *System*, 28(3), 355–372.

Babchuk, W. A. (1997, October). *Glaser or Strauss?: Grounded theory and adult education.* Paper presented at the Midwest Research-to-Practice Conference in Adult, Continuing and Community Education, Michigan State University, MI.

Bhatt, R. M. (2002). Experts, dialects, and discourse. *International Journal of Applied Linguistics, 12*(1), 74–109.

Brady, B., & Gulikers, G. (2004). Enhancing the MA in TESOL practicum course for nonnative English-speaking student teachers. In L. Kamhi-Stein (Ed.), *Learning and teaching from experience: Perspectives on nonnative English-speaking professionals* (pp. 206–229). Ann Arbor: University of Michigan Press.

Braine, G. (1999). From the periphery to the center: One teacher's journey. In G. Braine

(Ed.), *Non-native educators in English language teaching* (pp. 15–28). Mahwah, NJ: Erlbaum.

Chiba, R., Matsuura, H., & Yamamoto, A. (1995). Japanese attitudes toward English accents. *World Englishes, 14*(1), 77–86.

Cook, V. (1999). Going beyond the native speaker in language teaching. *TESOL Quarterly, 33*(2), 185–209.

Cook, V. (2000). The author responds ... *TESOL Quarterly, 34*(2), 329–332.

Dalton-Puffer, C., Kaltenboeck, G., & Smit, U. (1997). Learner attitudes and L2 pronunciation in Austria. *World Englishes, 16*(1), 115–128.

de Oliveira, L., & Richardson, S. (2004). Collaboration between native and nonnative English-speaking educators. In L. Kamhi-Stein (Ed.), *Learning and teaching from experience: Perspectives on nonnative English-speaking professionals* (pp. 123–134). Ann Arbor: University of Michigan Press.

Flynn, K., & Gulikers, G. (2001). Issues in hiring nonnative English-speaking professionals to teach English as a second language. *CATESOL Journal, 13*(1), 151–161.

Forde, K. (1996). A study of learner attitudes towards accents of English. *Hong Kong Polytechnic University Working Papers in ELT and Applied Linguistics, 1*(2), 59–76.

Hyrkstedt, I., & Kalaja, P. (1998). Attitudes toward English and its functions in Finland: A discourse-analytic study. *World Englishes, 17*(3), 345–357.

Jarvella, R. J., Bang, E., Jakobsen, A. L., & Mees, I. (2001). Of mouths and men: Non-native listeners' identification and evaluation of varieties of English. *International Journal of Applied Linguistics, 11*(1), 37–56.

Kamhi-Stein, L. D. (1999). Preparing non-native professionals in TESOL: Implications for teacher education programs. In G. Braine (Ed.), *Non-native educators in English language teaching* (pp. 145–158). Mahwah, NJ: Erlbaum.

Kamhi-Stein, L., Aagard, A., Ching, A., Paik, M.-S. A., & Sasser L. (2004). Teaching in Kindergarten Through Grade 12 Programs: Perceptions of Native and Nonnative English-Speaking Practitioners. In L. Kamhi-Stein (Ed.), *Learning and teaching from experience: Perspectives on nonnative English-speaking professionals* (pp. 69–88). Ann Arbor: University of Michigan Press.

Kramsch, C., & Lam, W. S. E. (1999). Textual identities: The importance of being non-native. In G. Braine (Ed.), *Non-native educators in English language teaching* (pp. 57–72). Mahwah, NJ: Erlbaum.

Lee, E., & Lew, L. (2001). Diary studies: The voices of nonnative English speakers in a master of arts program in teaching English to speakers of other languages. *CATESOL Journal, 13*(1), 135–149.

Liang, K. Y. (2002). *English as a second language (ESL) students' attitudes towards non-native English-speaking teachers' accentedness.* Unpublished master's thesis, California State University, Los Angeles.

Liu, J. (1999). Nonnative-English-speaking professionals in TESOL. *TESOL Quarterly, 33*(1), 85–102.

Mahboob, A., Uhrig, K., Newman, K., & Hartford, B. (2002, April). *Perceptions of non-native speaking teachers.* Paper presented at the 36th meeting of the Teachers of English to Speakers of Other Languages, Salt Lake City, UT.

Mahboob, A., Uhrig, K., Newman, K., & Hartford, B. (2004). Children of a lesser English: Nonnative English speakers as ESL teachers in English language programs in the United States. In L. Kamhi-Stein (Ed.), *Learning and teaching from experience: Perspectives on nonnative English-speaking professionals* (pp. 100–120). Ann Arbor: University of Michigan Press.

Matsuda, A., & Matsuda, P. K. (2004). Autonomy and collaboration in teacher education: Journal sharing among native and nonnative English-speaking teachers. In L. Kamhi-Stein (Ed.), *Learning and teaching from experience: Perspectives on nonnative English-speaking professionals* (pp. 176–189). Ann Arbor: University of Michigan Press.

Matsuda, P. K. (1999). Teacher development through native speaker-nonnative speaker collaboration. *TESOL Matters, 9*(5), 1 & 10.

McCargar, D. F. (1993). Teacher and student role expectations: Cross-cultural differences and implications. *The Modern Language Journal, 77*(2), 192–207.

Medgyes, P. (1992). Native or non-native: Who's worth more? *ELT Journal, 46*(4), 340–349.

Medgyes, P. (2001). When the teacher is a non-native speaker. In M. Celce-Murcia (Ed.), *Teaching English as a second or foreign language* (pp. 429–442). Boston: Heinle & Heinle.

Pasternak, M., & Bailey, K. M. (2004). Preparing nonnative and native English-speaking teachers: Issues of professionalism and proficiency. In L. Kamhi-Stein (Ed.), *Learning and teaching from experience: Perspectives on nonnative English-speaking professionals* (pp. 155–175). Ann Arbor: University of Michigan Press.

Peacock, M. (2001). Match or mismatch? Learning styles and teaching styles in EFL. *International Journal of Applied Linguistics, 11*(1), 1–20.

Phillipson, R. (1992). *Linguistic imperialism.* Oxford, England: Oxford University Press.

Rampton, M. B. H. (1990). Displacing the "native speaker": Expertise, affiliation, and inheritance. *ELT Journal, 44*(2), 97–101.

Reves, T., & Medgyes, P. (1994). The non-native English speaking EFL/ESL teacher's self image: An international survey. *System, 22*(3), 353–367.

Ryan, E., Giles, H., & Sebastian, R. (1982). An integrative perspective for the study of attitudes toward language variation. In E. Ryan & H. Giles (Eds.), *Attitudes towards language variations: Social and applied contexts* (pp. 1–19). London: Arnold.

Samimy, K. K., & Brutt-Griffler, J. (1999). To be a native or non-native speaker: Perceptions of "non-native" students in a graduate TESOL program. In G. Braine (Ed.), *Non-native educators in English language teaching* (pp. 127–144). Mahwah, NJ: Erlbaum.

Sheorey, R. (1986). Error perceptions of native-speaking and non-native-speaking teachers of ESL. *ELT Journal, 40*(4), 306–312.

Chapter 3

Children of a Lesser English: Status of Non-Native English Speakers as College-Level English as a Second Language Teachers in the United States[1]

Mahboob, A., Uhrig, K., Newman, K., & Hartford, B. (2004). Children of a lesser English: Nonnative English speakers as ESL teachers in English language programs in the United States. In L. Kamhi-Stein (Ed.), *Learning and teaching from experience: Perspectives on nonnative English-speaking professionals* (pp. 100–120). Ann Arbor: University of Michigan Press.

Today, it is an uncontested fact that English is the fastest-growing language in the world. It is also accepted that there are more non-native speakers of English than native speakers (Alatis & Straehle, 1997). According to a British Council (1986) report, there are as many as two billion people learning English globally and who have "some awareness of English" (p. 4). More recently, Kachru (1996) writes, "there are now at least four non-native speakers of English for every native speaker" (p. 241). Keeping these facts in mind, it can be concluded that the large majority of English language teachers around the world are non-native speakers. In fact, Reves and Medgyes (1994), based on a survey of 216 English as a second language (ESL) and English as a foreign language (EFL) teachers in 10 countries, report that "in two-thirds of the schools there were no NESTs [native English-speaking teachers], while only one third of the schools employed both NEST and non-NESTs" (p. 356). Canagarajah (1999) also states that up to 80% of the English language teachers globally are non-native speakers of English.

As a consequence of the high demand for learning English and the corresponding cadre of English language teachers and specialists, a

---

[1] An earlier version of this study was presented at the 36th annual meeting of the Teachers of English to Speakers of Other Languages, Salt Lake City, UT, April 2002.

large number of teachers (both pre- and in- service) come to countries where English is a native language to be trained as teachers of English. According to one study that looks at 173 graduate programs in North America (including the United States and Canada), 40% of the students preparing to be English teachers in Teaching English to Speakers of Other Languages (TESOL) and Applied Linguistics programs are non-native speakers (Liu, 1999). Kamhi-Stein (1999) reports that the number of non-native English speakers from either an international or a U.S. background, in at least one U.S.-based institution, is as high as 70%. These figures provide evidence that programs that prepare ESL/EFL teachers in North America (specifically the United States) attract a high number of non-native speakers of English.

While the literature on non-native English-speaking teachers (NNESTs) (Braine, 1999; Cook, 2000; Medgyes, 1992; Tang, 1997) suggests—and in fact presupposes—that the number of NNESTs working in English language programs (ELPs) in native English-speaking countries is disproportionate to the number of NESTs (and to the number of non-native English-speaking graduate students in TESOL programs, Applied Linguistics, and/or Language Education programs), and that there are no empirical studies that report the proportion of NNESTs to NESTs working in ELPs. The present study is designed to fill this gap in the literature by presenting the results of a survey of college-level ELPs in the United States.[2]

In addition to investigating the numerical status of NNESTs in relation to NESTs, the survey results also evaluate the weight which program administrators give to various hiring criteria, including the native and non-native English speaker status of potential teachers. Medgyes (1992), focusing on the United Kingdom, states that program administrators prefer native speakers because they are "aware that international students studying in Britain preferred to be taught by native-speaking English teachers. This demand would have to be satisfied by the school principal ..." (p. 344). However, Medgyes' report is based on an informal "straw poll" (p. 343). The current study provides empirical evidence to evaluate such claims on the issues of hiring/non-hiring of NNESTs in college-level ELPs in the United States.

---

[2] All four authors contributed to the design of the survey instrument used for this study. However, the first author was responsible for the analysis presented in this chapter (see Mahboob, 2003, for a complete version of the study).

The Study

Participants

The participants in this study were 503 college-level ELPs listed in a publication entitled "English Language and Orientation Programs in the United States," published by the Institute of International Education in 1997. The ELPs listed in this publication were spread throughout the 52 states of the United States. All the programs in this study were college-level Intensive English Programs (IEPs); thus, all discussion in this study is limited to college-level ELPs and should not be extended or generalized to K-12 or other types of programs.

One hundred and twenty-two surveys were completed, and 24 surveys were returned unopened because of "unknown addressee" status. Thus, the response rate, based on a total of 479 ELPs that received the survey, was 25.5%. The geographical distribution of the programs that responded was not tracked.

The surveys were addressed to program administrators. Teachers, regardless of language status, were not asked to complete any surveys for this study. Thus, the results of this study are based on feedback from program administrators only.

Survey

The survey developed for the purposes of this study consists of three sections (see Appendix A for a copy of the survey). The first section contains questions that pertain to the criteria that administrators use to hire and evaluate English language teachers in their programs. There are 10 criteria that the program administrators rate on a 6-point Likert scale (ranging from "0" to "5," where "0" implied "least important" and "5" implied "most important"). The 10 criteria listed are: "accent," "U.S. citizenship," "U.S. nationality," "dialect," "educational experience," "enrollment in associated academic program," "ethnicity," "native English speaker," "recommendation," and "teaching experience." In addition to the question on hiring criteria, a number of other questions related to the programs are also included in this section. These questions are used as distractors and will not be analyzed in this chapter.

The second section contains questions about teacher demographics, including whether they are native or non-native English speakers, male or female, and graduate or undergraduate students in an affiliated teacher preparation program. The information collected in this section also looks at the total number of international students in their affiliated graduate programs. It should be kept in mind that the results from the question on international students do not include non-native English-speaking graduate students who are U.S. citizens.

The third section contains questions about the demographics of the students in the ELPs, such as how many students there are in each program, which countries/regions they represent, and what proportion of them go on to study at a university or college in the U.S. This last section is not important for the current study and therefore will not be discussed in this chapter.

Data Analysis

Once the completed surveys were received by the researchers, the data were entered using the *Statistical Package for the Social Sciences* (Version 10.0.7, 2000). Subsequent analysis was performed with the aid of this statistical software. Teacher demographics were studied using descriptive statistics, including totals, percentages, and means. The hiring criteria were analyzed using a variety of statistical methods. In order to study the importance of each individual criterion, the mean, mode, and standard deviation for the various criteria were calculated. The relationships among the various criteria were explored using a hierarchical cluster analysis, designed to allow the identification of relatively homogeneous groups of variables. The hierarchical cluster analysis used Pearson correlations to measure the relationship between the various criteria (for a complete description of hierarchical cluster analysis, see Mahboob, 2003). In order to understand which criterion best explains the ratio of NNESTs employed in a program, a multivariate linear regression analysis using the stepwise method was conducted. In this case, the dependent variable was the ratio of NNESTs employed in a program, and the independent variables included the 10 hiring criteria rated by program administrators.

Results and Discussion

The two sections of the survey relevant to the present chapter are the instructor section and the administrative section. Within these sections, there are a number of questions that are utilized to keep the survey broad-based and to divert the attention of the respondents from the sensitive issue of NESTs and NNESTs. Before discussing the results of specific sections of the survey, the demographic information of the teachers will be presented.

The results of the survey analysis show that out of the 122 respondents,

115 program administrators provided information about the gender of the teachers employed in their programs. There were a total of 1,394 teachers in these 115 programs. Of these teachers, 1,016 were female and 378 were male. Thus, 72.8% of the teachers in the 115 ELPs were female and 27.2% were male. This figure implies that the majority of ESL teachers, approximately three-fourths, are female.

Table 1 below provides a list of all the countries/regions represented in the study and the number of teachers from each of these countries/

Table 1   Distribution of NNESTs Based on Their Countries/Regions of Origin

Countries/Regions of Origin	n	Countries/Regions of Origin	n
Chinese Taiwan	8	Austria	1
Chinese mainland	6	Bulgaria	1
Brazil	5	Cambodia	1
Germany	5	Croatia	1
Russia	5	Ghana	1
Turkey	5	Greece	1
Japan	4	Guyana	1
Korea	4	Holland	1
Mexico	4	Italy	1
Morocco	4	Kenya	1
Poland	4	Kuwait	1
Czech	3	Latvia	1
Finland	3	Middle Eastern	1
Iran	3	Nepal	1
Lebanon	3	Nicaragua	1
Chile	2	Norway	1
Colombia	2	Pakistan	1
Egypt	2	Palestine	1
India	2	Romania	1
Israel	2	Spain	1
South Africa	2	Switzerland	1
Vietnam	2	Thailand	1
Angola	1	The Philippines	1
Argentina	1	Ukraine	1
Asian	1		

Total = 107

regions. The distribution of the countries/regions in Table 1 suggests that there is no preference in hiring NNESTs based on their countries/regions of origin. By extension, it further suggests that Kachru's (1992) distinction between countries of the "expanding circle" (where English has a long history because of a colonial past and where it is used as an official language, e.g., Pakistan, India, Singapore) and countries of the "outer circle" (where English has recently gained popularity and where it is not used as an official language, e. g., Japan, China, Brazil) does not impact the distribution of NNESTs working in the ELPs.

The results presented in Table 1 also show that none of the program administrators listed the U.S. as a country/region of origin for any of their NNESTs. However, teachers who were born in the U.S. but who are not native speakers of English do exist. Therefore, it is possible that the program administrators failed to report the NNESTs who were born in the U.S., or they might have reported information by country/region of heritage rather than origin. However, the current data do not provide any evidence to support either hypothesis. This issue needs to be further explored in a follow-up study.

Administrators were also asked to provide information on the teachers' language status. The results of the survey analysis show that the 118 program administrators (out of the 122 respondents) provided answers to the relevant questions and reported having 1,313 NESTs and 112 NNESTs on their staff. These numbers mean that out of a total of 1,425 teachers, 7.86% were NNESTs and 92.14% were NESTs. The 112 NNESTs were hired by 50 of the 118 ELPs. Therefore, at the time of the survey, 68 ELPs (57.6%) employed only NESTs and 42.4% employed both NESTs and NNESTs. These results show that college-level ELPs in the U.S. do not have an equal representation of NNESTs and NESTs.

Program administrators were also asked to provide detailed information about the total number of teachers employed by their program and the distribution of these teachers based on their status as "native" or "non-native" speakers of English and—in their capacity as instructors—as "full-time," "part-time," "graduate students," and/or "others." The results of the analysis are given in Table 2 below.

Table 2 below shows that there were a higher number of NESTs in each category. There were 634 full-time NESTs compared to 25 full-time NNESTs. This implies that only 3.8% of the full-time staff was comprised of NNESTs. The percentage of full-time NNESTs was the lowest among

Table 2   Distribution of NESTs and NNESTs by Position

Type of Position	NESTs n	Percent %	NNESTs n	Percent %
Full-time (with benefits)	634	96.20	25	3.80
Part-time (not graduate students)	550	91.00	54	9.00
Graduate students	110	79.00	29	21.00
Others (please specify)	19	83.00	4	17.00
Total	1313	92.14	112	7.86

the four categories of teachers listed. In addition to the full-time teachers, there were 550 part-time NESTs compared to 54 NNESTs. This implies that 9% of the part-time instructors were NNESTs. There were 110 native English-speaking graduate students teaching in the ELPs as compared to 29 non-native English-speaking graduate students. Thus, 21% of the graduate student teacher population was comprised of NNESTs. This was the highest percentage of NNESTs in any category. The last category of teachers was listed as "others." There were 19 NESTs in this category and 4 NNESTs, meaning that 17% of teachers in the "others" category were NNESTs.

The total number of teachers in each of the ELPs surveyed ranged from 1 to 74, with the total number of NESTs in each of the various programs ranging from 1 to 68 and the total number of NNESTs ranging from 0 to 14. Thus, the highest number of NNESTs in any of the programs was 14 (out of a total of 37 teachers). In order to understand the relationship between the number of NESTs and NNESTs in a program, ratios were calculated. However, before presenting the results of the ratio analysis, it is important to understand the function and the properties of the ratio. Ratios are used to display information about frequencies in relation to each other. Thus, theoretically, the ratio of NNESTs will be "0" if there are no NNESTs in a program, and it will be "1" if all the teachers in a program are NNESTs.

The actual distribution of the ratio in the 118 programs that provided information regarding the number of teachers in their program ranged between 0 and .4. As already noted, the majority of the programs (n = 68) did not have any NNESTs at the time of the survey. Therefore, they had a ratio of 0. In addition, among the 50 ELPs that did hire NNESTs, a high number of ELPs had a low ratio, implying that the proportion of NNESTs in these programs was low. The program with the highest ratio had a ratio of .4, implying that 40% of the teachers in this program were NNESTs. This program had a total of five teachers, of which three were NESTs and the other two NNESTs. The program with 14 NNESTs had a ratio of .378 (the second highest ratio). There were 16 ELPs with a ratio of .2 (meaning that at least 20% of the teachers in these programs were NNESTs). The majority of the programs (24 of them), had a ratio of less than .2 (meaning that less than 20% of the teachers in these programs were NNESTs). This last finding shows that, in general, college-level ELPs in the U.S. that have hired NNESTs have similar proportions of NNESTs and NESTs in their programs (assuming, of course, that there are similar proportions of NNESTs seeking such jobs).

The survey also asked the program administrators to provide information about any undergraduate or graduate programs with which they were affiliated. One hundred and twenty program administrators responded to this question; out of these, 26 indicated that their program was affiliated with a department of Applied Linguistics, TESOL, or Language Education, and only 21 program administrators provided detailed information on the distribution of their undergraduate/graduate student population. Thus, the results given in Table 3 below are based on 21 programs only.

Table 3   Distribution of Student Population in the Program with Which the ELPs Are Affiliated

Type of Students Enrolled in the Program Affiliated with the English Language Program	Total Number of Students	Average Number of Students per Program (n = 21)
Undergraduate students	297	14.14
Graduate students	356	16.95
International graduate students	173	8.23

As Table 3 shows, the number of undergraduate students enrolled in the programs with which the 21 ELPs were affiliated was 297. The number of graduate students was 356, and out of these, 173 were international students. These results mean that of 356 graduate students in 21 programs, 48.59% are international students. This figure is comparable to that found elsewhere in the relevant literature (see Kamhi-Stein, 1999; Liu, 1999).

In this study, the respondents were not asked to provide the number of non-native English-speaking graduate students who are U.S. citizens. According to Kamhi-Stein (personal communication), there may be a substantial number of graduate students who are U.S. citizens and consider themselves non-native speakers of English. Thus, the 48.59% in this study only represents the percentage of international graduate students in the 21 programs that provided information on their visa status and may not reflect the total percentage of non-native English-speaking graduate students in the programs. It is possible that the actual number of non-native graduate students is higher than the 48.59% presented above.

The number of international graduate students in a program was correlated with the ratio of NNESTs employed in the affiliated English language program (ELP). The results of this analysis show that no significant correlation was found between the ratio of NNESTs in an ELP and the number of international graduate students in its affiliated teacher preparation program. This lack of a correlation implies that the number of international (non-native) students in a graduate program is not related to the number of NNESTs employed in an affiliated ELP. This result supports the idea that the ELP administrators do not place much emphasis on "enrollment in an associated academic program" as a criterion for hiring prospective instructors.

The ratio of NNESTs who were also graduate students in an affiliated program was correlated with the number of international graduate students (if any) in those programs. This was done to verify the above-mentioned lack of a significant correlation between the number of international graduate students and the ratio of NNESTs in a program. There were 10 ELPs that employed graduate students enrolled in the programs with which they were affiliated. The result of the analysis for the 10 ELPs that hired graduate students shows that there is not a significant correlation between the number of international graduate students enrolled in a program and the ratio of graduate students from a non-native English-speaking background teaching in an affiliated program ($p = .57$). This lack of a significant correlation supports the earlier finding that there is not a relationship between the ratio of NNESTs employed in an ELP and the presence or absence of international students in an affiliated program.

Administrative Questions

This part of the study asked the respondents to rank 10 criteria in making hiring decisions: "accent," "citizenship," "nationality," "dialect," "education," "enrollment in an affiliated educational program," "native English speaker," "recommendation," "ethnicity," and "teaching experience." The results for this question, presented in Table 4 below, are based on 122 responses (100% of the surveys that were received). Table 4 provides a ranking of the mean ratings, as well as the mode and standard deviation for each criterion.

Table 4   **Ranking of Mean Ratings, Standard Deviation, and Mode for the Various Hiring Criteria**

Hiring Criteria	Mean Ratings		
	M	SD	Mode
Teaching experience	4.28	1.35	5
Educational experience	4.15	1.35	5
Recommendation	3.55	1.37	4
Native English speaker	2.86	1.83	5
Accent	2.86	1.66	4
Dialect	1.93	1.69	0
Citizenship	1.24	1.61	0
Nationality	1.13	1.47	0
Enrollment in associated academic program	1.08	1.54	0
Ethnicity	0.74	1.08	0

Note: Scale 0 = not important at all, 1 = not very important, 2 = slightly important, 3 = somewhat important, 4 = moderately important, 5 = very important

As shown in Table 4, "teaching experience" receives the highest mean rating among the 10 hiring criteria ($M = 4.28$). In addition, the standard deviation for this criterion is relatively low ($SD = 1.35$) when compared to standard deviations for other criteria, indicating that the respondents are in general agreement with one another about the importance of this criterion in their hiring decisions. "Educational experience" is the second highest ranked criterion. Its mean rating is 4.15 with a standard deviation of 1.35. Moreover, the mode is 5, suggesting that a high number of respondents believe that educational experience is a key criterion in making hiring decisions.

Table 4 also shows that program administrators find the "recommendation" criterion to be important in making hiring decisions. It receives a moderately high mean rating of 3.55 and a standard deviation of 1.37. The mean rating for the "native English speaker" criterion is 2.86. However, when viewing this mean rating in light of a mode of 5 and a standard deviation of 1.83 (the highest for any of the criteria listed), it can be seen that program administrators are, in fact, split in their rating of this criterion. Table 5 below shows this split in the ELP administrators' rating of this criterion. As can be seen in the table, 45.9% of the respondents indicate that this criterion is moderately to highly important in making hiring decisions, while 29.5% of the respondents feel that this criterion is not very important or not important at all.

Figure 1 below illustrates the results presented in Table 5. As can be noted in the figure, the bars form a U curve. This U curve, also known as an inverted bell curve, is indicative of bi-modalism, implying that most respondents prefer to rank this criterion at either the lower end (0–1) or the higher end (4–5). This also accounts for the high standard deviation of this criterion.

Table 5   Importance in Hiring: Relative Weight Given to the "Native English Speaker" Criterion

Relative Weight Given to the "Native English Speaker" Criterion	Frequency n	Percent %
Not important at all	20	16.4
Not very important	16	13.1
Slightly important	13	10.7
Somewhat important	17	13.9
Moderately important	24	19.7
Highly important	32	26.2
Total	122	100.00

Note: Scale 0 = not important at all, 1 = not very important, 2 = slightly important, 3 = somewhat important, 4 = moderately important, 5 = very important

Figure 1   Relative Weight, in Percentage, Given to the "Native English Speaker" Criterion

As Table 5 and Figure 1 suggest, the native and non-native status of a potential teacher is an issue in the field: administrators either consider it very important or not important at all. The high mode of 5 (see Table 4) suggests that being a native speaker is an important criterion for a majority of the administrators (59.8% of the respondents consider it at least somewhat important). The importance given to the criterion suggests one reason why NNESTs seem to be under-represented in ELPs in the U.S.

The results presented in Table 4 also show that the mean rating received by the hiring criterion entitled "accent" is 2.86 with a standard deviation of 1.66 and a mode of 4. This relatively high mean rating considered in the light of the high mode suggests that "accent" forms an important criterion for making hiring decisions for quite a number of programs. A question that will be of interest here, although not asked in the current survey, will be about administrators' preference for specific accents and how they define accent in general.

Table 4 also shows that "dialect" receives a mean rating of 1.93 and a mode of 0, but has one of the highest standard deviations among the criteria ($SD = 1.69$). Clearly, this result shows that there is notable variation among the respondents regarding the importance of dialect in making hiring decisions, but since the mean rank remains low, overall, this criterion is not very important for most program administrators.

"Citizenship" is ranked low, with a mean rating of 1.24. Since the mode for this criterion is 0, the implication is that most administrators think that it is not of much importance in making hiring decisions. Like citizenship, "nationality" is rated low by the respondents. The mean rating for this criterion is 1.13 with a relatively low standard deviation of 1.47. The mode for this criterion was also 0, implying that many respondents do not find it useful in making hiring decisions.

The results of the study also show that the criterion titled "enrollment in associated academic program" is not considered very important by most of the program administrators (see Table 4). The majority of the respondents find this criterion of little value in making hiring decisions. The mean rating for this criterion is 1.08 with a standard deviation of 1.54. The mode for this criterion is 0. The lack of importance given to this criterion is an important finding. As documented in relevant literature cited earlier (Kamhi-Stein, 1999; Liu, 1999), there are a high number of international students in academic programs in TESOL and Applied Linguistics. A lack of importance given to potential teachers' affiliations to associated degree/professional programs suggests that non-native graduate and undergraduate students enrolled in such programs do not necessarily receive any special consideration just because of their links to affiliated programs. Thus, it seems, there may not be a notable relationship between an ELP being affiliated to a graduate degree program and the number of NNESTs that the ELP hires.

As shown in Table 4, "ethnicity" receives the lowest mean rating among all the criteria ($M = .74$). The standard deviation, also the lowest, is 1.08. The mode for this criterion is 0. Taking all these figures into account, these results suggest that ethnicity is of very little value to most of the respondents when they make hiring decisions. A lack of emphasis on "ethnicity" is interesting. According to Amin (1999), an unmarked ESL teacher is an Anglo-white male native speaker of English. Amin's comment suggests that "ethnicity," as well as "gender," may play an important role in making hiring decisions. However, the present data are not sufficient to evaluate the role of these two criteria as suggested by Amin.

Relationship and Hierarchy Between Various Criteria

In order to understand the relationship between various criteria, a hierarchical cluster analysis was conducted. This analysis allows the identification of relatively homogeneous groups of variables. The hierarchical cluster analysis performed in this study uses Pearson correlations to measure the relationship between various criteria.

The results of the hierarchical cluster analysis show that the 10 criteria fall into three major clusters. These three clusters have been labeled: "professional background," "linguistic background," and "personal background." This classification is important because it groups together the different criteria. The order in which these three clusters are described below represents the average importance given to the criteria in each cluster.

Three criteria, "educational experience," "teaching experience," and "recommendation," fall into the "professional background" cluster. All of these criteria deal with professional qualifications of teachers. There is a very close relationship between "educational experience" and "teaching experience" ($r = .77$, $p < .001$) and these two criteria are also related to "recommendation." Another three criteria, "accent," "dialect," and "native English speaker," fall into the "linguistic background" cluster. Within this cluster, "accent" and "dialect" are more closely (but not highly) related to each other (r = .509, p< .001) than to "native English speaker." The last cluster, "personal background," is formed by four criteria, "U.S. citizenship," "U.S. nationality," "ethnicity" and "enrollment in an associated academic program." These criteria deal with various aspects of teachers' personal background. Within this cluster, "U.S. citizenship" and "U.S. nationality," perhaps unsurprisingly (because of the similarity in their meaning), form the closest relationship (r = .806, p< .001). These two criteria are also related to "ethnicity" and to teachers' "enrollment in an associated academic program."

Relationship Between Total Number of NNESTs and Criteria for Hiring

In this section, the relationship between various criteria and the ratio of NNESTs in a program is reported. This relationship is first presented through a correlation between the 10 criteria and the ratio of NNESTs working in a program. The results based on this correlation analysis help identify significant relationships between any of the criteria and the ratio. Table 6 below presents the results of the analysis.

Table 6   Correlation of the Ratio of NNESTs and NESTs in a Program and the 10 Hiring Criteria

Hiring Criteria	Pearson Correlation	Sig. (2-tailed)
Accent	−.014	.899
U.S. citizenship	−.141	.204
U.S. nationality	−.071	.526
Dialect	−.036	.750
Educational experience	−.103	.356
Enrollment in associated academic program	.016	.884
Ethnicity	−.138	.215
Native English speaker	−.375*	.001
Recommendation	.09	.419
Teaching experience	−.022	.842

* Correlation is significant at the .01 level (2-tailed).

Table 6 shows that the "native English speaker" criterion had the highest (negative) correlation with the ratio of NNESTs in a program. In addition, this is the only significant correlation found between any of the 10 criteria and the ratio of NNESTs in an ELP ($r = -.375$, p< .001). The negative value of the correlation is important. It implies that the less importance the administrators give to the "native English speaker" criterion, the higher the number of NNESTs in an ELP. Conversely, the more importance the administrators give to the "native English speaker" criterion, the lower the number of NNESTs in that ELP.

It is important to point out that while "educational experience," "teaching experience" and "recommendation" had a higher mean rating than "native English speaker," they do not correlate with the actual ratio of NNESTs in a program. This observation suggests that, in making hiring decisions, the importance given to being a "native English speaker" is more significant than the professional background of teachers.

A correlation analysis only studies two variables at a time. Therefore, in addition to the correlation analysis, a multivariate linear regression using the stepwise method is conducted in order to explain the ratio of NNESTs in a program. A linear, stepwise regression is used to find the independent variables that best explain the dependent variable. In this case, the dependent variable is the ratio of NNESTs employed in a program, and the independent variables include the 10 hiring criteria rated by program administrators. Table 7 below presents the results of the regression analysis.

Table 7   Results of the Regression Analysis

Hiring Criteria	Unstandardized Coefficients		Standardized Coefficients	t	Level of Significance
	B	Std. Error	Beta		
Recommendation	1.83E-02	.007	.579	2.659	.009
Native English speaker	−2.20E-02	.005	−.617	−4.498	.001
Teaching experience	1.42E-02	.006	.525	2.383	.019

The results presented in Table 7 above show that the dependent variable, the ratio of NNESTs in a program, may be explained by focusing on three independent variables, i.e., three criteria. The three independent variables that significantly explain the dependent variable are "recommendation," "native English speaker," and "teaching experience." Among these, the most significant independent variable is "native English speaker" with the highest t-value of −4.498 (p< .001). The second statistically significant independent variable is "recommendation" with a t-value of 2.659 (p< .01), and the third statistically significant independent variable is "teaching experience" with a t-value of 2.383 (p< .05).

The negative t-value of "native English speaker" implies that the ratio of NNESTs in a program will be higher if the program administrator of that program ranks "native English speaker" as an unimportant criterion. Thus, there may be a greater number of NNESTs in a program if the administrator of that program places a low emphasis on the "native speaker" criterion. This finding is also supported by the negative correlation discussed earlier and shows that there is a relationship between the importance given to the "native English speaker" factor and the actual ratio of NNESTs in a program.

In addition to the "native English speaker" criterion, "recommendation" is found to be a significant independent variable that explains the ratio of NNESTs in an ELP. This result means that administrators who place emphasis on recommendation letters are more likely to hire NNESTs in their program, given that all other variables are equal. This finding suggests that for NNESTs to be hired, they must provide strong references.

The last important result of the regression analysis shows that "educational experience" also explains the ratio of NNESTs in a program. This finding implies that administrators who may hire NNESTs look for high educational qualifications in their teachers (all other variables being equal). Thus, NNESTs who are hired must have high educational qualifications in a related field.

In summary, the results of the regression analysis suggest that if the administrator considers "native English speaker" to be an important criterion for hiring, and if not much weight is given to "recommendation" and "educational experience," that program will have a low ratio of NNESTs. In other words, these results may be interpreted to suggest that for NNESTs to obtain a job in a particular college-level ELP in the U.S., they must have strong recommendation letters, high educational qualifications in TESOL or Applied Linguistics or a related field, and most importantly, they must apply to a program whose administrators do not believe that being a native speaker is an important characteristic of an ESL teacher.

It should be noted that the three significant variables belong to either the "professional background" cluster or the "linguistic background" cluster. The variables in the "personal background" cluster are not found to be significant. This lack of importance given to personal background by program administrators when making hiring decisions is also observed earlier in the discussion of the mean ratings of the 10 criteria. This confirmation of results based on different analytical procedures adds reliability to the findings.

The finding that administrators favor the hiring criterion titled "native English speaker," taken together with the low number of NNESTs in the 118 ELPs surveyed (7.9%), provides empirical evidence to support Cook's (2000) and Medgyes' (1992) observations that administrators prefer to hire native speakers over non-native speakers.

Summary of Findings and Conclusion

The results of the college-level ELPs' survey, based on data collected from 118 ELP administrators throughout the U.S., show that out of a total of 1,425 ESL teachers in these programs, only 112 are NNESTs. Thus, it can be concluded that the number of NESTs working in ELPs is substantially higher than the number of NNESTs.

The correlation analysis shows that the number of international students in a graduate program is not related to the number of NNESTs working in an affiliated ELP. The lack of a significant correlation suggests that the presence or absence of international graduate students in a graduate degree program is not related to the number of NNESTs who teach in the affiliated ELP. The results of the analysis of the survey also show that more program administrators consider "native English speaker" an important criterion than do not (59.8% of the respondents consider it at least "somewhat important"). A correlation analysis between the various hiring criteria and the ratio of NNESTs working in a program further suggests that there is a link between a low number of NNESTs in ELPs and administrators' emphasis on "native English status." A negative correlation is found between the relative importance given to "native English speaker" in the hiring process and the ratio of NNESTs in a program. This negative correlation suggests that the more importance a program administrator gives to a teacher's status as a native speaker, the smaller the ratio of NNESTs in that program. In addition to the correlation, a regression analysis with the ratio of NNESTs being the dependent variable and the 10 criteria being the independent variables is conducted. The results of this regression analysis show that the criterion "native English speaker" most significantly explains the ratio of NNESTs in a program. Two other significant independent variables that significantly explain the ratio of NNESTs in a program are "recommendation" and "teaching experience."

In summary, an analysis of the surveys collected from 122 college-level ELPs reveals the following:

1. Most program administrators give a rating of "somewhat important" to teachers' "native English speaker" status.
2. There is a significant negative correlation between the relative importance given to the "native English speaker" hiring criterion and the ratio of NNESTs in that program (this is the only criterion that significantly correlates with the ratio); that is, the more importance program administrators give to the "native English speaker" criterion, the smaller the number of NNESTs employed in their programs will be.
3. There is a lower proportion of NNESTs to NESTs in actual practice in U.S.-based ELPs.
4. There is a lack of a significant correlation between the number of NNESTs employed in an ELP and the number of international graduate students in an affiliated program.
5. The criteria "native English speaker," "recommendation" and "teaching experience" are found to be the only three significant independent variables (out of a total of 10 independent variables) that significantly explain the ratio of NNESTs in a program.

While the response rate in this study was respectable, future studies relying on mailed surveys should consider including a second mailing or sending the survey to a randomly selected subset of the total number of ELPs to increase their response rate. Also, future studies should give respondents an opportunity to list additional criteria that they might use in making hiring decisions. This might reveal factors that administrators consider important in hiring that were not included in the survey. Finally, in addition to collecting data from college-level ELPs, future studies should collect data from ELPs associated with various community colleges across the U.S. as well as K-12 educational institutions.

At this time, based on the results of this investigation, it can be concluded that the "native English speaker" status is an important factor in the hiring of teachers at college-level ELPs. Regardless of other qualifications that NNESTs might have, they are not equally represented in U.S.-based ELPs, even though NNESTs comprise a majority of the world's English teachers and a substantial number of graduate students in TESOL graduate classes in the U. S. Taking into consideration the results of this study, it can be said that non-native speakers of English are treated as "children of a lesser English" in the profession of English language teaching in the U.S. Should

U.S.-based ELPs seek to offer their international students exemplary role models of non-native English-speaking teachers, and should they seek to reflect a realistic and inclusive picture of the diversity represented by World Englishes, then ELPs would do well to examine their hiring practices and include increasing numbers of NNESTs among their staff.

Appendix A
ENGLISH LANGUAGE PROGRAMS SURVEY

I. Administrative Questions

1. On a scale of 0 to 5 (0 being the least important and 5 being the most important), please rank each of the following criteria for hiring ESL instructors in your English Language Program.

   ____ Accent   ____ Enrollment in associated academic program
   ____ American citizenship   ____ Ethnicity
   ____ American nationality   ____ Native English speaker
   ____ Dialect   ____ Recommendation
   ____ Educational experience   ____ Teaching experience

2. What professional development opportunities (seminars, workshops, classes, etc.) are available on a pre-service or an ongoing basis to your instructors?

3. Which of the following criteria do you use to evaluate instructors in your English Language Program? (You may mark one or more of the following.)
   ____ Student evaluations
   ____ Classroom observations
   ____ Other (please specify)

4. Do you use an integrated/holistic approach to language teaching or do you teach skills (listening, speaking, reading, writing, and grammar) in separate classes?

5. How many ability levels (e. g. Three: 1 = beginning, 2 = intermediate, 3 = advanced) are there in your English Language Program?

6. Which of the following criteria do you use when placing students into various levels in your English Language Program? (You may mark one or more of the following.)
   ____ TOEFL score
   ____ In-house placement exam

_____ Class grades
_____ Michigan Test
_____ Others (please specify)

II. Instructor Questions

7. Do you have an undergraduate or a graduate program affiliated with your English Language Program? (e. g., Applied Linguistics, TESOL, Language Education, etc.)

   Yes   No

   If "yes," please answer the following questions:
   - a. How many undergraduate students do you have in the program?
   - b. How many graduate students do you have in the program?
   - c. How many of those graduate students are international students?

8. How many instructors are there in your English Language Program?
   - a. How many are females?
   - b. How many are males?

9. How many of your English Language Program instructors are:

Full-time (with benefits):	Native speakers[3]	_____
	Non-native speakers	_____
Part-time (not graduate students):	Native speakers	_____
	Non-native speakers	_____
Graduate students:	Native speakers	_____
	Non-native speakers	_____
Others (please specify):	Native speakers	_____
	Non-native speakers	_____

10. Do all your instructors have specific training in English as a Second Language (ESL), linguistics, Foreign Language Teaching (FLT), etc.?

    Yes   No

    If you answered "no," what are the minimum required educational qualifications for instructors in your English Language Program?

11. Do your graduate students teach as paid instructors, or do they teach as part of a practicum experience?

12. If you have any instructors who are non-native speakers, which countries/

---

[3] The term "native" here includes American, Australian, and British English, and so on.

regions are they from?

III. *Student Questions*

13. How many students are currently enrolled in your English language program?

14. Which countries/regions are represented among your students? Which countries/regions have the highest representation?

15. Approximately what proportion of your students go on to study at a university or college in the United States?

_____	5–10%
_____	10–25%
_____	25–50%
_____	50–75%
_____	75–100%
_____	Unknown

References

Alatis, J., & Straehle, C. (1997). The universe of English: Imperialism, chauvinism, and paranoia. In L. Smith & M. Forman (Eds.), *World Englishes 2000* (pp. 1–20). Honolulu: University of Hawaii.

Amin, N. (1999). Minority women teachers of ESL: Negotiating white English. In G. Braine (Ed.), *Non-native educators in English language teaching* (pp. 93–104). Mahwah, NJ: Erlbaum.

Braine, G., editor. (1999). *Non-native educators in English language teaching.* Mahwah, NJ: Erlbaum.

British Council. (1986). *English language and literature [Activity Report No 4].* London: Author.

Canagarajah, A. S. (1999). Interrogating the "native speaker fallacy": Non-linguistic roots, non-pedagogical results. In G. Braine (Ed.), *Non-native educators in English language teaching* (pp. 77–92). Mahwah, NJ: Erlbaum.

Cook, V. (2000). The author responds ... *TESOL Quarterly, 34*(2), 329–332.

Institute of International Education. (1997). *English language and orientation programs in the United States.* Annapolis, MD: Author.

Kachru, B. B. (1992). Teaching world Englishes. In B. B. Kachru (Ed.), *The other tongue: English across cultures* (2nd ed., pp. 355–365). Chicago: University of Illinois Press.

Kachru, B. B. (1996). The paradigms of marginality. *World Englishes, 15*(3), 241–255.

Kamhi-Stein, L. D. (1999). Preparing non-native professionals in TESOL: Implications for teacher education programs. In G. Braine (Ed.), *Non-native educators in English language teaching* (pp. 145–158). Mahwah, NJ: Erlbaum.

Liu, D. (1999). Training non-native TESOL students: Challenges for TESOL teacher education in the West. In G. Braine (Ed.), *Non-native educators in English language teaching* (pp. 197–210). Mahwah, NJ: Erlbaum.

Mahboob, A. (2003). *Status of nonnative English speakers as ESL teachers in the United States.* Unpublished doctoral dissertation, Indiana University, Bloomington.

Medgyes, P. (1992). Native or non-native: Who's worth more? *ELT Journal, 46*(4), 340–349.

Reves, T., & Medgyes, P. (1994). The non-native English speaking EFL/ESL teacher's self-image: An international survey. *System, 22*(3), 353–367.

Statistical package for the social sciences (version 10.0.7, 2000). Chicago: SPSS.

Tang, C. (1997). On the power and status of nonnative ESL teachers. *TESOL Quarterly, 31*(3), 577–580.

Chapter 4

Beyond the Native Speaker in TESOL

Mahboob, A. (2005). Beyond the native speaker in TESOL. In S. Zafar (Ed.), *Culture, Context, & Communication* (pp. 60–93). Abu Dhabi: Center of Excellence for Applied Research and Training & The Military Language Institute.

Introduction

I still remember the words of one of my good friends who called me one evening in the winter of 1996 after she was told that she could not be hired as an English as a second language (ESL) teacher in the language program affiliated to her department:

> Now, this is what gets me so mad: I am here—a student in their MA program, but they refuse to hire me because they say that students only want native speakers as their teachers. You know what: I don't believe them. They only want to hire their own people. They only want me for my money. I am so mad. I want to sue them. I am good enough to be getting straight "A"s; I am good enough to be paying a hell of a lot of money; I am good to leave here and teach English in my country; but, I am not good enough to teach in the program. Is this crazy or what?

Although I remember this case very vividly, this is not the only person that I know who was refused an English language teaching (ELT) job based on their status as a non-native speaker of English in the United States. Stories such as my friend's are, unfortunately, much too common. These stories are not only based in the English-speaking western countries, but all across the globe. I have met a number of young bright and qualified Asians who find it hard to get suitable employment after returning home from the US/UK/Australia with an MA in TESOL/Applied Linguistics. One of the factors behind not being hired is a belief shared by many employers (Mahboob et al., 2004) that native speakers are better teachers than non native teachers and that students prefer native speakers. What are the causes behind such beliefs? What evidence is available to support or contradict them?

These are some of the questions that will be discussed in this chapter. The issue of discrimination based on the way one speaks is not a new one. Neither is the gate-keeping power of accent/pronunciation a recent discovery. These issues have been talked about both in popular literature as well as in linguistic research. In literature, a well-known example is that of Eliza Doolittle in George Bernard Shaw's "Pygmalion". Eliza's desire to learn to speak better is rooted in her dream to open her own flower shop. She knows that she will not be able to successfully operate her own business if she speaks with an East End accent (an accent that is marked as that of uneducated and uncultured people). Thus, she is willing to pay to learn her own tongue. Discussing a similar theme, Halliday (1968) writes:

> A speaker who is made ashamed of his own language habits suffers a basic injury as a human being: to make anyone, especially a child, feel so ashamed is as indefensible as to make him feel ashamed of the color of his skin. (p. 165)

This statement explicitly reflects on discrimination based on language and speech and compares it to racism. On a similar note, Labov (1969) stresses that the language of one group should not be measured against that of another. For example, the language of Afro-Americans should not be compared to or evaluated in terms of the norm of the Anglo-Americans. Labov argues that such comparisons are ethnocentric and therefore unjustifiable. In contrast to the fairness of these arguments, in practice (as evidenced in my friend's frustrated remarks), these philosophies of equality based on linguistic backgrounds seem to be often ignored in the profession of teaching English as a second language.

In this chapter, I will first present some key findings of studies that indicate how these philosophies are violated in the ESL profession. I will then present an overview of studies that discuss various historical influences on the profession and how these influences centralized the role of the native speaker in TESOL and applied linguistics. After exploring the ways in which the native speaker has been mythologized, we will look at research that demystifies them. The chapter will end with a reevaluation of the role of non-native speakers and will direct us to look beyond the native speaker in TESOL.

The Status of Non-Native English Speakers in TESOL

Today, it is an uncontested fact that English is the fastest-growing language in the world. It is also accepted that there are more non-native speakers of English than native speakers (Alatis & Straehle, 1997). According to a British Council report (1986), there were as many as two billion people learning English globally and who have "some awareness of English" (p. 4). Keeping these facts in mind and considering that there are a limited number of native speakers who choose to be English teachers, it can be concluded that the large majority of English language teachers are non-native speakers. In fact, Reves and Medgyes (1994), based on a survey of 216 ESL/EFL (English as a foreign language) teachers in ten countries, report that "in two-thirds of the schools there were no NESTs [Native English Speaking Teachers], while only one third of the schools employed both NEST and non-NESTs" (p. 356). Canagarajah (1999) states that up to 80% of the English language teachers globally are non-native speakers of English.

Although a majority of English language teachers are non-native speakers of the language, they have been treated as step-children (Mahboob et al., 2004). And, in many places (where equally qualified native and non-native speakers are both available), preference is given to native English-speaking teachers. In a study that explores hiring practices in college-level English language programs (ELPs) in the United States, Mahboob et al. (2004) show that out of a total of 1,425 ESL teachers in 118 programs only 112 are NNESTs (non-native English-speaking teachers). Thus, the number of NESTs working in ELPs is found to be substantially higher than the number of NNESTs. The results of this study also show that more program administrators consider "native English speaker" an important criterion than not (59.8% of the respondents consider it at least "somewhat important"). The results of a correlation analysis between the various hiring criteria and the ratio of NNESTs working in a program further suggest that there is a link between a low number of NNESTs in ELPs and administrators' emphasis on "native English status". A negative correlation is reported between the relative importance given to "native English speaker" in the hiring process and the ratio of NNESTs in a program. This negative correlation suggests that the more importance a program administrator gives to a teacher's status as a native speaker, the smaller the ratio of NNESTs is in that program. In addition to the correlation, a regression analysis with the ratio of NNESTs being the dependent variable and 10 potential hiring criteria being the independent variables is conducted. The results of this regression analysis show that the criterion "native English speaker" most significantly explains the ratio of NNESTs in a program. Two other independent variables that significantly explain the ratio of NNESTs in a program are "recommendation" and "teaching experience". However, the single most important criterion in making hiring decisions is "nativeness."

Mahboob et al.'s (2004) work is the first study that statistically shows the importance of being native in the job market; earlier studies assume such a bias against non-native speakers and explore possible reasons behind it. For example, Medgyes (1992), focusing on the United Kingdom, states that program administrators prefer native speakers because they are "aware that international students studying in Britain preferred to be taught by native-speaking English teachers. This demand would have to be satisfied by the school principal …" (p. 344). Cook (2000) agrees with Medgyes and believes that the main reason for program administrators not hiring NNESTs is their perception that ESL students who enroll in their ELPs expect NESTs. Thus, according to these papers, NNESTs are not hired because program administrators believe that students do not want them.

While the literature on NEST-NNEST issues suggests that administrators' belief that students prefer NESTs over NNESTs, studies of ESL students' perceptions do not corroborate these beliefs. In one study of students' perceptions, Cook (2000), using data collected through a questionnaire survey, reports,

> The NS teacher was preferred by 18% of Belgian 15-year-olds, 44% of English children, and 45% of Polish children. Looked at in reverse, 47% of Belgian, 32% of English, and 25% of Polish children preferred nonnatives, the rest having no preference. (p. 331)

In discussing these results, he states, "No where is there an overwhelming preference for NS teachers. Being an NS is only one among many factors that influence students' views of teaching" (p. 331). Thus, his study shows that students do not simply prefer teachers based on their status as a native or a non-native speaker, but rather their preferences are more complex. However, while Cook's work shows that students may not have a clear preference for either NESTs or NNESTs, his work does not explore the reasons for these diverse views. In another study of students' perceptions, Mahboob (2004) finds that ESL students in his study (based in the United States) do not have a clear preference for either NESTs or NNESTs; rather, they feel that both types of teachers have unique attributes. Based on an analysis of students' essays, he reports that students find strengths in the way NNESTs teach them when compared to NESTs. This is an important finding and shows that students are not naive and do not necessarily buy into the "native speaker fallacy" (Phillipson,

1992) that only native speakers can be good language teachers. The findings of this study demonstrate that the importance given to the "native English speaker" hiring criterion by program administrators (Mahboob et al., 2004) is not shared by students. Mahboob concludes by stating that both NESTs and NNESTs working collaboratively can provide a better learning environment for ESL students. [This study will be discussed at greater length in a later section.]

With current research revealing that native speakers are not better teachers than non-native speakers (Cook, 2000; Mahboob, 2004), the question that we need to ask is: how and why did the notion of "native speaker" gain prominence in TESOL and applied linguistics and how has it been maintained? This question will be discussed at length in the following section when we look at ways in which the "native speaker" has been mythologized in applied linguistics and TESOL literature.

Mythologizing the Native Speaker

Chomsky's use of the "idealized native speaker-hearer" (Chomsky, 1986) as an abstraction for theoretical linguistic research has been extensively used in second language acquisition (SLA) research. The influence of the Chomskyan paradigm on SLA can be measured by the following statement from Gregg (1993), "in SLA ... the overall explanandum is the acquisition (or non-acquisition) of L2 competence, in the Chomskyan sense of the term" (p. 278). Bhatt (2002) evaluates the influence of Chomsky in applied linguistics in detail and states,

> Most of the constructs used in second language acquisition (SLA) theories, especially the cognitivist approaches, derive their meaning from the epistemology and methodology of the Chomskyan paradigm—the study of language as a cognitive system. Leading experts in the SLA field, such as Coder (1967, 1973), Selinker (1972) and Dulay, Burt and Krashen (1982), embraced this view uncritically.

We will return to discuss Bhatt's work in more detail later on in this section. Let us first examine how cognitivists, such as Selinker and others, use the Chomskyan paradigm to centralize the role of the native speaker in TESOL and Applied Linguistics. Selinker's theory of fossilization implies that learners of a second language are unable to achieve "native" proficiency in a second language. Inherent to this theory is a journey in which a second language learner begins with their L1 and their ultimate goal is to achieve native-like proficiency in L2. At any given stage during this process of language learning, a learner's language is labeled as "interlanguage". Selinker (1969) defines this as following,

> An "interlanguage" may be linguistically described using as data the observable output resulting from a *speaker's attempt to produce a foreign norm*, i.e., both his errors and non-errors. [emphasis added]

Intrinsic in this definition of "interlanguage" is a learner's "attempt to produce a foreign norm". However, it is worth questioning this assumption: do learners of a language want to achieve native proficiency? This question has not been sufficiently addressed in research and needs to be taken up.

In addition to "interlanguage", Selinker (1972) also introduces and defines the term "fossilization",

> ... the real phenomenon of the permanent non-learning of TL structures, of the cessation of IL learning (in most cases) far from expected TL norms.

This definition of "fossilization" defines learners' language in terms of their shortcomings in relation to native speaker (or target language) norms. In addition, he states that "fossilization" is the end result of most of the learners-implying that most language learners are unable to achieve native proficiency in their second language. A critical examination of the terms "interlanguage" and "fossilization" reveals a hidden ideology in these terms which privileges the native speaker. The terms "interlanguage" and "fossilization" imply that the goal of a second language learner is to be just like a native speaker and that if one does not achieve this goal then s/he has "fossilized".

Regardless of the ideological and attitudinal loading of these terms, they have gained status in applied linguistics and TESOL. This status and authority of the terms "interlanguage" and "fossilization" can be measured by their inclusion in the *Unabridged Random House Dictionary*. This dictionary defines the two terms as following:

> Interlanguage: "... the linguistic system characterizing the output of a nonnative speaker at any stage prior to full acquisition of the target language." (p. 995)
> Fossilization: "... to become permanently established in the interlanguage of a second-language learner in a form that is deviant from the target-language norm and that continues to appear in performance regardless of further exposure to the target language." (p. 775)

As can be seen, the dictionary definitions of these terms also use the reference to the "acquisition of the target language" and "deviance from the target language". The inclusion of these terms and definitions in a dictionary legitimizes the terms in general and gives authority to these views.

As a result of the focus on the "target language" norm in the operational definitions of "interlanguage" and "fossilization", Selinker's work has given authority to the native-speaker model in SLA and, by extension, in language teaching models (this will be discussed in more detail later). Thus, a majority of research in second language acquisition evaluates learners in terms of how well they have acquired "native-speaker" norms. For example, in his overview of SLA research, Ellis (1994) writes: "Learners often failed initially to produce correct sentences and instead displayed language that was markedly *deviant from target language norms.*" (p. 15) [italics added] This description of learner language clearly reflects Selinker's hypothesis. Long's (1981) stress on the role of native speakers in their ability to provide ideal language input is another example of the influence of the native speaker model in SLA. Long states, "participation in conversation with NS ... is the necessary and sufficient condition for SLA" (p. 275). Cook (1999) in his evaluation of the use of native speakers norm in SLA states that the native speaker model may have some use as a "temporary" measure but must not be used to measure final achievement. He states,

> An unknown object is often described in terms of one that is already known (Poulisse, 1996); someone who has never seen a tomato before might describe it as a rather soft apple with a large number of pips. But this description is no more than a temporary expedient until the individual has understood the unique properties of the object itself. The learner's language is an unknown object, so SLA research can justifiably use native speakers' language as one perspective on the language of L2 learners, provided it does not make native speakers' language the measure of final achievement in the L2. (p. 190)

In addition to the description of learner language in terms of native norms, SLA methodologies themselves seem to be influenced by this "comparative fallacy" (Bley-Vroman, 1983). Some of the most widely used research methodologies in second language acquisition, including grammaticality judgments and error analysis, by definition, require a comparison of learner language to native speaker norms.

This importance of native speakers as being the model and native-like language being the goal of a language learner is not restricted to theoretical research in SLA and applied linguistics, but has also been expressed by language teacher educators. In one such work, Stern (1983) states,

> The native speaker's "competence" or "proficiency" or "knowledge of the language" is a *necessary point of reference for the second language proficiency* concept used in language teaching (p. 341). [emphasis added]

More interestingly, Medgyes (1986) in one of his earlier papers in which he discusses the problems with the communicative approach in an EFL setting states,

> For all their goodwill, native speakers are basically unaware of the whole *complexity of difficulties that non-native speakers have to tackle*. Native-speaking teachers tend to ignore, among other things, the fact that a great proportion of the energy of their non-native colleagues is inevitably used up in the constant struggle with *their own language deficiencies*, leaving only a small fraction attending to their students' problems. (p. 112) [emphasis added]

Medgyes' use of the term "language deficiencies" shows that he had fallen into the trap of the "comparative fallacy". [However, to be fair to Medgyes, his later work shows a different positioning on this issue. These later papers will be discussed in the following section.] In another paper Reves and Medgyes (1994) state,

> Because of their relative English language deficiencies, non-NESTs are in a difficult situation: *by definition they are not on a par with NESTs* in terms of language proficiency. Their deficit is greater if they work in *less privileged teaching situations, cut off from NESTs or any native speakers.* (p. 364) [emphasis added]

This quote shows that Reves and Medgyes not only buy into the "comparative fallacy", but they also believe that NESTs provide a better teaching and learning model and the NNESTs may not perform well if they are not in contact with NESTs. This agreement of Medgyes with the "native speaker model" may be interpreted in light of the findings from language attitudes studies. Lambert et al. (1960) find that in their study of attitudes towards English and French in Montreal both English-speaking (high status) and French-speaking (low status) respondents gave favorable and positive ratings to the English guises. Lambert et al. call this the "minority group reaction" and state that individuals who are members of low status group may assume and accept the values promoted by members of the high status group. Based on this understanding, it is possible to classify Reves and Medgyes' acceptance of the "comparative fallacy" as a "minority group reaction".

In a recent paper, Bhatt (2002) presents an extensive analysis of discourse in applied linguistics and TESOL to show how the native speaker myth has become the ideological reality for TESOL and applied linguistics. Bhatt states that the purpose of his paper is to,

> ... demonstrate how the pronouncements of the ESL/ELT experts contribute to "regimes of truth" around the legitimization of Standard English ideology. These regimes establish as fundamentally unquestionable the propositions that there has to be a single "correct" standard of usage for the English language. (p. 75)

Bhatt argues that in order to establish the authority of standard or native English, the field has evolved a number of axioms. These axioms, he argues, are held "above debate; the assumptions shared are not propositions to be defended or attacked" (p. 75). He lists three such axioms in TESOL and applied linguistics:

1. There is a standard language that provides access to knowledge.
2. Only those few who speak the standard can command linguistic authority over non-standard speakers.
3. Myth and history are indistinguishable. (pp. 76–77)

Bhatt (2002) discusses six ways in which the "native speaker norm" is maintained and promoted in English language teaching practices. In doing this he critically examines Quirk (1990). Bhatt states that his choice of using Quirk is based on Quirk's status in the field as an "expert". Bhatt also attempts to show how these six arguments promoted to maintain the "native speaker norm" are controversial and have been challenged by other applied linguists.

Bhatt believes that one of the ways in which the native speaker norm is projected in the teaching of English is "strategic discoveries" (p. 88). Bhatt states that experts in the field, e.g. Quirk (1990), refer to work that supports their point of view and refers to it as being "interesting" and "sophisticated". Bhatt uses the following quote from Quirk (1990, p. 6) to illustrate his point, "In a range of interesting and sophisticated elicitation tests [referring to Coppieters' (1987) work], the success rate of the non-natives fell not merely below but outside the range of native success ..." (p. 88). He argues that the use of the terms "interesting and sophisticated" raises the status of these findings and marks them as prominent and "strategic discoveries". Bhatt further states that the "interesting" and the "sophisticated" work in Quirk's statement has been challenged on several grounds in the field. He specifically refers to Birdsong's (1992) study that replicated Coppieters' work and found that there were no significant differences in the performance of fluent non-native speakers and native speakers.

A second strategy used to maintain the "native speaker norm" in English language teaching is the "deficit discourse" argument. Bhatt once again cites Quirk (1990) who states that the teaching of English in non-English dominant countries is a problem because the teachers themselves are not proficient users of English. Bhatt refers to work in "The Other Tongue" (Kachru, 1992) which documents that English in different parts of the world has been indigenized with their own local norms. In fact, in some of these countries, only a minority of people prefer Standard British English (2% in India; Kachru, 1977). This aspect of "deficit discourse" is manifested in a number of studies that discuss the role of NNESTs (e.g. Sheorey, 1986).

A third strategy that Bhatt discusses is the "ideological intoxication argument". Bhatt states,

> ... Quirk (1990; 9) argues against the efforts of those—"ideologically intoxicated"—members of the linguistic discourse community who have attempted to democratize language use ... Quirk makes oblique reference to alternative ideologies—like liberation linguistics and language variation—but denigrates them to the benefit of the standard language ideology, using the moral *fiber* argument. (p. 90) [emphasis original]

Bhatt labels a fourth strategy used by Quirk as "the discourse of nostalgia". He states that this strategy of promoting a "standard" and "native speaker" norm is a recurrent one. He also states that the argument that the standards of the English language are falling has been advanced since the eighteenth century. Based on claims that suggest that the standards of English are falling, the argument presented by Quirk (1990) is that unless a standard is maintained, the various varieties will get out of hand and will blind "both teachers and taught of the *central linguistic structure* from which the varieties might be seen as varying" (p. 4) [emphasis original].

"The discourse of tutelage" is a fifth strategy that Bhatt recognizes in Quirk's (1990) argument in favor of standard native speaker norms. Based on his discussion of Coppieters' (1987) work [discussed earlier], Quirk argues that "the implications for foreign language teaching are clear: the need for native teacher support and the need for non-native teachers to be in constant touch with the native language" (p. 7). In this statement, Quirk explicitly gives status to the native speaker and sets the role of a non-native speaker subservient to that of a native speaker. Reves and Medgyes' (1994) work discussed earlier is one example in which academics use the "discourse of tutelage" to state that NNESTs need to be in constant touch with native speaker models.

Bhatt states that a last strategy used by Quirk is to make the above arguments "obvious and self-evident". Quirk argues that since native speakers are more proficient than non-native speakers (by referring to Coppieter, 1987), they provide better pedagogical models for English language learners.

Bhatt argues that as a result of using these six strategies productively, the Chomskyan paradigm has dominated the applied linguistics and TESOL discourse. He further argues that the power yielded to the cognitivists may be defined in Foucault's (1980) notion of regimes of truth. Bhatt defines regimes of truth as "sets of understandings that legitimize particular sociolinguistic attitudes and practices" (p. 79). Thus, in terms of this paper, the "particular sociolinguistic attitudes and practices" that hold the native speaker as the ideal model for language acquisition and learning are forwarded and maintained through references to and an understanding of the Chomskyan paradigm in applied linguistics. The emphasis on the cognitive approaches and the focus on the ideal-native speaker model in applied linguistics has resulted in what Firth and Wagner (1997) call "a skewed perspective" (p. 295). They define this "skewed perspective" as one

> … that is accompanied by an analytic mindset that conceives of the FL [foreign language] speaker as a deficient communicator struggling to overcome an underdeveloped L2 [second language] competence, striving to reach the "target" competence of an idealized NS. (pp. 295–296)

This emphasis on "striving to reach" the native-speaker norm creates a situation in which an L2 user, regardless of their proficiency or ability to communicate, is compelled to match the native-speaker norm (parallels "deficit discourse" and "discourse of tutelage" arguments above). This generous and approving attitude towards native speakers at the cost of non-native speakers has negative effects on the creativity and confidence of

NNESTs. It discourages them and makes them feel unappreciated. Tollefson (1995) also discusses this issue and states that this imbalance in socio-linguistic power results in a life long apprenticeship for the L2 speaker in which s/he has no hope of enunciation. Kachru and Nelson (1996) also raise a similar issue when they write,

> When we say "English as a second (or even third or fourth) language", we must do so with reference to something, and that standard of measure must, given the nature of the label, be English as someone's first language. This automatically creates attitudinal problems, for it is almost unavoidable that anyone would take "second" as less worthy, in the sense, for example, that coming in second in a race is not as good as coming in first. (p. 79)

This statement reflects an awareness that terms like "first language" and "second language" are not neutral but attitudinally loaded (as is the term "native speaker"). It is this attitudinal loading of terms such as "first language speaker", "mother tongue speaker", or "native speaker" that has translated into a preference for such speakers as language teachers/models in TESOL. However, the exposing of these attitudinal and political loadings in recent years as well as the questioning of assumptions behind terms like "interlanguage" and "fossilization", is leading to a demythologizing of the native speaker. The following section looks at this demythologizing in more detail.

Demythologizing the Native Speaker

The acceptance of "native speaker norms" as the model to be acquired and as the model that students should be exposed to has recently been challenged by a number of academics. For example, Phillipson (1992) challenges the notion that native speakers make better teachers. While he concedes that native speakers might be able to make instinctively better grammatical judgments, he argues that they are at a disadvantage when trying to explain specific questions about their native language unless they have received training to do so. He refers to the importance given to native speaking models as the "native speaker fallacy" (p. 194).

Phillipson sees the spread of English and the focus on native norms of usage and culture as a symbol of a new form of imperialism, "linguistic imperialism". In his book, Phillipson argues that motivations behind the post-colonial spread of English are economic, political and cultural.

Referring to a director of an international chain of English language schools, he writes,

> As the director of a dynamic worldwide chain of English language schools puts it, "Once we used to send gunboats and diplomats abroad; now we are sending English teachers" (p. 8).

Other sociolinguists have also raised the issues of culture and identity in regard to language standards. Crystal (1985) writes that all "discussion of standards ceases very quickly to be a linguistic discussion, and becomes instead an issue of social identity" (p. 9). Thus, these experts argue that the issue of being native is not simply a linguistic issue, but rooted in economic, political and cultural issues.

In a different, but powerful take on this issue, Rampton (1990) problematizes the term "native speaker". He suggests that the term "native speaker" should be dropped from usage and replaced by other more inclusive terminology. He argues that the concept of a native speaker as it is currently used includes three aspects and that each of these is non-overlapping and therefore needs to be referred to separately. The three aspects that he refers to are language expertise, language affiliation, and language inheritance. The difference between language expertise and language affiliation and inheritance can be understood if we place them on a continuum that uses an individual's identification with the language as a measure. Thus, language expertise is different from inheritance and affiliation in that a language expert does "not have to feel close to what they know a lot about. Expertise is different from identification" (p. 98). The difference between language affiliation and inheritance can be explained in terms of heritage. In language affiliation, a person may identify with the language or the group of people who speak that language, but has not inherited it from her/his parents. Rampton states,

> The crucial difference between them [language affiliation and inheritance] is that affiliation refers to a connection between people and groups that are considered to be separate or different, whereas inheritance is concerned with the continuity between people and groups who are felt to be closely linked. Inheritance occurs within social boundaries, while affiliation takes place across them. (p. 99)

Rampton further argues that expertise is learned and is relative to other experts' knowledge. Two other characteristics of a language expert are that "expertise is partial. People can be expert in several fields, but they are never omniscient"; and "to achieve expertise, one goes through processes of certification, in which one is judged by other people" (p. 99). Rampton argues that because of these characteristics of a language "expert" it is "fairer to both learners and teachers" (p. 99).

A use of Rampton's terminology helps in clarifying different issues that are clouded by the terms "native" or "mother tongue" speaker. In using this terminology, it is possible to differentiate a person who may not be a "native" speaker of a language, but may have more "expertise" in the language than a "native" speaker and may or may not "affiliate" him/herself with the language. The term "native" in this case loses its use. Language inheritance, the aspect that is most closely associated with the "native" or "mother tongue" speaker, becomes only one of the three aspects that need to be considered in evaluating a person's skills in a language. In this sense, the title of Paikeday's (1985) book "The Native Speaker is Dead" is very symbolic. In this book, Paikeday argues,

> I am convinced that "native speaker" in the sense of the sole arbiter of grammaticality or one whose intuitions of a proprietary nature about his or her mother tongue and which are shared only by others of his own tribe is a myth propagated by linguists, that the true meaning of the lexeme "native speaker" is a proficient user of a specified language, and that this meaning satisfies all contexts in which linguists, anthropologists, psychologists, educators, and others use it, except when it directly refers to the speaker's mother tongue or first-acquired language without any assumptions about the speaker's linguistic competence (p. 87).

In contrast to Rampton and Paikeday, Cook (1999) takes a somewhat different approach to this issue. He argues that there is a "qualitative difference" between the minds of monolingual and bilingual speakers. He believes that the two are different in their language competencies, both of their L1 and L2. Cook writes that while the effects of L1 on L2 are easy to identify and have been studied extensively, "the effects of the L2 on the L1 have been little discussed" (p. 191). Cook uses the term "multicompetencies" and defines it as:

> A neutral term for the knowledge of more than one language, free from evaluation against an outside standard ... the term multicompetencies implies that at some level the sum of the language knowledge in the mind is relevant, not just the portions dedicated to the L1 and the L2. (pp. 190–191).

He argues that the mind of a multicompetent person is different in both its "language processing" and "thought processes". These differences between monolingual and multicompetent people imply that people who learn English as a second language and users of English who learn a second language are both qualitatively different from monolingual English speakers. Based on these differences, Cook argues, "L2 users have to be looked at in their own right as genuine L2 users, not as imitation native speakers" (p. 195).

By problematizing the concept of a native speaker and by unpacking the various dimensions of this term, the literature discussed here has contributed to the demythologizing of the native speaker. This problematizing and demythologizing of the native speaker has generated (and is generating) research that reevaluates the role that being native plays in TESOL. Some of this research is presented in the following section.

Reevaluating the Native Speaker in TESOL

After a discussion of the various aspects of native/non-native issues presented in the previous sections, we will look at some research that reevaluates the role of the non-native speaker in TESOL.

As has been discussed, the blind acceptance of the native speaker norm in English language teaching has come into question. Liu (1999) refers to several studies in reference to pedagogical implications of being an NNEST:

1. D'Annunzio (1991)—attributes the success of his program to the hiring of bilingual tutors 'who shared the students' experiences' (p. 52).
2. Philipson (1992)—posits that they have gone through 'the laborious process of acquiring English as a second language and ... have insight into the linguistic and cultural needs of their learners' (p.195).
3. Auerback (1993)—argues that 'it is not just the experience as a language learner, but the experience of sharing the struggles as a newcomer that is critical' (p. 26) and that ESL programs therefore benefit greatly from hiring nonnative-English-speaking professionals.

In addition to the work cited in Liu, Medgyes (1992, 2001) argues that based on their unique experiences, NNESTs can make positive contributions to the field. He lists 6 unique assets that NNESTs have and that NESTs cannot offer:

1. Only non-NESTs can serve as imitable models of the successful learner of English.
2. Non-NESTs can teach learning strategies more effectively.
3. Non-NESTs can provide learners with more information about the English language.
4. Non-NESTs are more able to anticipate language difficulties.
5. Non-NESTs can be more empathetic to the needs and problems of their learners.
6. Only non-NESTs can benefit from sharing the learners' mother tongue. (pp. 346–347)

Based on these six unique assets, Medgyes argues that ESL/EFL students benefit from NNESTs in ways that they cannot from NESTs.

In a recent study, Mahboob (2003, 2004) examines Medgyes' assumptions in light of attitudinal data collected from adult ESL learners in the United States. Although most of Medgyes' assumptions are supported by Mahboob, one of them is partly contradicted (#1). Participants in Mahboob's study believe that NNESTs' pronunciation is not perfect and therefore they are not the ideal "language models" for spoken language (Medgyes, 2001, p. 436). The negative perception of NNESTs' oral skills in Mahboob's study is also supported by a number of other attitudinal studies that evaluate perceptions of individuals from various countries and language backgrounds towards varieties of English. For example, Forde (1995) studies the attitudes of Chinese elementary school children towards different varieties of English and reports that the respondents prefer native varieties of English (both American and British) over local models. Forde also finds that the respondents link teachers' variety of English to their ability to teach. In other studies of language attitudes, Chiba et al. (1995), Dalton-Puffer et al. (1997) and Jarvella et al. (2001) find attitudes towards Japanese, Austrian and Dutch varieties of English, respectively, to be less favorable as compared to American/British varieties of English. Thus, the results of Mahboob's study, focusing on an ESL setting, support these findings in EFL settings.

The participants in Mahboob's study view that NESTs are better "language models" when it comes to pronunciation. One of the participants in Mahboob's study states,

> I want the *truth pronunciation* [emphasis added] which non-natives teachers can't speak or use voice like native speakers ...

This individual's use of "truth pronunciation" reflects the belief that there is an "ideal", "true", and/or "correct" pronunciation of English and reminds us of the influence of the Chomskyan (1986) notion of an "ideal native speaker" in TESOL (as discussed in an earlier section). This perceived importance of an "ideal native speaker" model for pronunciation is especially interesting because there is ample evidence in SLA studies that adult ESL learners cannot achieve native-like pronunciation. Thus, the goal to learn the "truth pronunciation" is one that needs to be critically examined in the classroom. It's difficult for adult learners to learn to speak like native speakers and there is substantial evidence that most of them will not set up expectations that cannot be fulfilled. Dalton-Puffer et al. (1997) raise a similar point and argue that "the prominence of native speaker in language teaching has obscured the distinctive nature of the successful L2 user and created an unattainable goal for L2 learners" (p. 185).

Returning to a discussion of Medgyes' list of NNEST assets, Mahboob's (2004) study (as pointed out earlier) supports most of them. Participants in this study believe that NNESTs' understanding of L2 teaching is based on their own L2 learning experience and results in their ability to anticipate and explain concepts better than NESTs. This positive evaluation of NNEST teaching methodology is especially interesting when considered in light of the research conducted in the 1980s. In the 1980s there was a perception that to become good teachers, NNESTs should not only improve their linguistic skills to match those of native speakers, but they should also adopt the teaching practices and methods of NESTS. The following extract from Sheorey (1986), himself a NNEST, illustrates this point:

> the study gives an indication of which errors are most irritating to native ESL teachers, a finding which we can use to bring our own error-evaluation practices in line with those of native teachers. I am assuming here that acquiring a native-like sensitivity to errors is a proper goal (however elusive it might be) for non-native ESL teachers, and that we should seek to adjust our error-evaluation practices accordingly (p. 310).

This quote suggests that the goal of NNESTs' should be to acquire native-like teaching sensitivity. The results from Mahboob's study of student perceptions not only negate the need for NNESTs to become native-like in their pedagogical practices, but indeed suggest that they have unique characteristics that students find lacking in NESTs, especially in the teaching of grammar and the ability to answer questions. Thus, statements from earlier studies, such as Sheorey, need to be reexamined in light of new findings. "Acquiring a native-like sensitivity" is not "a proper goal" for NNESTs; rather, the unique teaching abilities of both NESTs and NNESTs complement each other and together provide a better learning environment for language learners. Providing a positive learning environment for our students is not a question of choosing between native or non-native speakers, but of looking beyond the concept of nativeness in TESOL.

Conclusion

The chapter argues that the native speaker was centralized in applied linguistics and TESOL as a result of the Chomskyan paradigm. Early applied linguists and SLA researchers used the "native speaker" norm as being the goal of all language learners. And, any learner language that fell short of this norm was considered interlanguage. Furthermore, if an individual did not show "improvement" in the interlanguage over time, they were considered to have fossilized. Such terminology and its inclusion in reference books led to a general belief that language learners should speak a language like native speakers and therefore only native speakers can serve as genuine and worthy models/teachers.

However, starting in the early 1990s a body of literature questioned these assumptions and unpacked the various factors that are glossed over and merged into the term "native speaker". Rampton (1990) presents a strong argument that we need to consider at least three aspects that are lumped together in this term: language expertise, language affiliation, and language inheritance. He argues that it would be more beneficial for the field if we consider language expertise over language inheritance when it comes to language teaching.

This chapter also shows that there is now a large and growing body of literature that has demonstrated that being "native" is not a sufficient or necessary condition for becoming a successful and effective teacher. There is evidence that ESL/EFL learners do not have a preference for NESTs and that they are perceptive to the strengths of both NESTs and NNESTs. Research has documented that NNESTs have some unique attributes that NESTs do not have and that many of these emerge from NNESTs' experience of having learned English as an additional language.

This chapter begins with the comments of one of my friends who was frustrated and angry at not being hired as an ESL teacher because of her status as a non-native speaker of English. It was my conversations with her and other friends who were in a similar position that led me into working on this aspect of applied linguistics and TESOL. In pursuing this issue, I investigated and questioned the nature of arguments that were presented to glorify the native speaker. The present chapter is a result of this study of the literature and shows that current literature stresses the need for expertise (both in language and pedagogy) and professional credentials over linguistic inheritance. And, in this, I hope, we have gone beyond the native speaker.

References

Alatis, J., & Straehle, C. (1997). The universe of English: Imperialism, chauvinism, and paranoia. In L. Smith & M. Forman (Eds.), *World Englishes 2000* (pp. 1–20). Honolulu: University of Hawaii.

Baumgardner, R. J. (Ed.). (1993). *The English Language in Pakistan*. Karachi: Oxford University Press.

Bhatt, R. M. (2002). Experts, dialects, and discourse. *International Journal of Applied Linguistics, 12*(1), 74–109.

Birdsong, D. (1992). Ultimate attainment in second language acquisition. *Language, 68*, 706–755.

Bley-Vroman, R. (1983). The comparative fallacy in interlanguage studies: The case of systematicity. *Language Learning, 33*, 1–17.

British Council. (1986). *English Language and Literature [Activity Report No4]*. London: Author.

Canagarajah, A. S. (1999). Interrogating the "native speaker fallacy": Non-linguistic roots, non-pedagogical results. In G. Braine (Ed.), *Non-Native Educators in English Language Teaching* (pp. 77–92). Mahwah, New Jersey: Lawrence Erlbaum Associates.

Chiba, R., Matsuura, H., & Yamamoto, A. (1995). Japanese attitudes towards English accents. *World Englishes, 14*(1), 77–86.

Chomsky, N. (1986). *Barriers*. Cambridge, MA: MIT Press.

Cook, V. (1999). Going beyond the native speaker in language teaching. *TESOL Quarterly, 33*(2). 185–209.

Cook, V. (2000). The author responds ... *TESOL Quarterly, 34*(2), 329–332.

Coppieters, R. (1987). Competence differences between native and fluent non-native speakers. *Language, 63*, 544–573.

Crystal, D. (1985). How many millions? The statistics of English. *English Today, 1*(1), 7–9.

Dalton-Puffer, C., Kaltenboeck, G., & Smit, U. (1997). Learner attitudes and L2 pronunciation in Austria. *World Englishes, 16*(1), 115–128.

Ellis, R. (1994). *Second Language Acquisition*. Oxford: Oxford University Press.

Firth, A., & Wagner, J. (1997). On discourse, communications, and (some) fundamental concepts in SLA research. *The Modern Language Journal, 81*(3), 285–300.

Forde, K. (1995). A study of learner attitudes towards accents of English. *Hong-Kong Polytechnic University Working Papers in ELT & Applied Linguistics, 1,* 59–76.

Foucault, M. (1980). *Power/Knowledge: Selected Interviews and Other Writings 1971–1977.* New York: PantheonBooks.

Gregg, K. (1993). Taking explanation seriously; or, let a couple of flowers bloom. *Applied Linguistics, 14,* 276–294.

Halliday, M. (1968). The users and uses of language. In J. Fishman (Ed.), *Readings in the Sociology of Language.* The Hague: Mouton.

Jarvella, R., Bang, E., Jakobsen, A., & Mees, I. (2001). Of mouths and men: non-native listeners' identification and evaluation of varieties of English. *International Journal of Applied Linguistics, 11*(1), 37–55.

Kachru, B. (1977). The new Englishes and old models. *English Language Forum, 15*(3), 29–35.

Kachru, B. (1992). *The Other Tongue* (2nd ed.). Urbana: University of Illinois Press.

Kachru, B., & Nelson, C. (1996). World Englishes. In S. L. McKay & N. H. Hornberger (Eds.), *Sociolinguistics and Language Teaching* (pp. 71–102). Cambridge: Cambridge University Press.

Labov, W. (1969). The logic of non-standard English. *Georgetown Monographs on Language and Linguistics, 22,* 1–44.

Lambert, W. W., Hodgson, R., Gardner, R. C., & Fillenbaum, S. (1960). Evaluational reactions to spoken languages. *Journal of Abnormal and Social Psychology, 60,* 44–51.

Liu, J. (1999). Nonnative-English-speaking professionals in TESOL. *TESOL Quarterly, 33*(1), 85–102.

Long, M. (1981). Input, interaction and second language acquisition. In H. Winitz (Ed.), *Native Language and Foreign Acquisition. Annals of the New York Academy of Sciences, 379*(1), 259–278.

Mahboob, A. (2003). *Status of nonnative English speaking teachers in the United States.* Unpublished Ph.D. Dissertation, Indiana University, Bloomington.

Mahboob, A. (2004). Native or non-native: What do the students think? In L. Kamhi-Stein (Ed.), *Learning and Teaching from Experience: Perspectives on Nonnative English-Speaking Professionals* (pp. 121–147). Michigan: University of Michigan Press.

Mahboob, A., Uhrig, K., Hartford, B., & Newman, K. (2004). Children of a lesser English: Nonnative English speakers as ESL teachers in English language programs in the United States. In L. Kamhi-Stein (Ed.), *Learning and Teaching from Experience: Perspectives on Nonnative English-Speaking Professionals* (pp. 100–120). Michigan: University of Michigan Press.

Medgyes, P. (1986). Queries from a communicative teacher. *ELT Journal, 40*(2) 107–112.

Medgyes, P. (1992). Native or non-native: Who's worth more? *ELT Journal, 46*(4), 340–349.

Medgyes, P. (2001). When the teacher is a non-native speaker. In M. Celce-Murcia (Ed.),

Teaching English as a Second or Foreign Language (pp. 429−442). Boston: Heinle & Heinle.

Paikeday, T. M. (1985). *The Native Speaker Is Dead!* Toronto: Paikeday Press.

Phillipson, R. (1992). *Linguistic Imperialism*. Oxford University Press.

Quirk, R. (1990). Language varieties and standard language. *English Today, 21*, 3−10.

Rampton, M. B. H. (1990). Displacing the 'native speaker': Expertise, affiliation and inheritance. *ELT Journal, 44*(2), 97−101.

Reves, T., & Medgyes, P. (1994). The non-native English speaking EFL/ESL teacher's self image: An international survey. *System, 22*(3), 353−367.

Selinker, L. (1969). Language transfer. *General Linguistics, 9*, 67−92.

Selinker, L. (1972). Interlanguage. *International Review of Applied Linguistics, 10*, 209−231.

Sheorey, R. (1986). Error perceptions of native-speaking and non-native-speaking teachers of ESL. *ELT Journal, 40*(4), 306−312.

Stern, H. H. (1983). *Fundamental Concepts of Language Teaching*. Oxford: Oxford University Press.

TESOL. (1991). *Statement on non-native speakers of English and hiring practices*. Washington, D.C.: TESOL.

Tollefson, J. (1995). *Power and Inequality in Language Education*. Cambridge: Cambridge University Press.

Chapter 5

Confessions of an Enraced TESOL Professional

Mahboob, A. (2006). Confessions of an enraced TESOL professional. In A. Curtis & M. Romney (Eds.), *Shades of meaning: Articulating the experiences of TESOL professionals of color* (pp. 173–188). Mahwah, New Jersey: Lawrence Erlbaum Associates.

Personal History

I am a child of the diaspora—a model product of the postcolonial world. My parents were born in British India in the 1930s: my mother in Bhopal and my father in Gorakhpur, Uttar Pradesh (U.P.). Both sets of my grandparents migrated to Karachi in the late 1940s as British India was splintered into two antagonistic nation-states. Having moved to a "new" country, my grandparents struggled to make a life for themselves and their children. I am lucky in that my grandparents considered education to be of extreme importance and took all steps to make sure that their children (my parents) were educated. For my mother, this meant that she had to travel to Lahore (with her elder sister) to take her matric examination. For my father, it meant that he had to travel to and live in Peshawar to complete his bachelor of arts degree. They both earned their master's degrees from Karachi University: my mother in psychology and my father in English literature. This was in the early 1960s. My parents, like many other young, educated urbanites of the time, were actively involved in left-wing politics. However, the government was turning sharply to the right. Thus, with growing political instability and a violent crackdown on left-wing politics, my family decided to move to the United Arab Emirates (UAE) in January 1975. I was 39 months old.

My formal schooling started in the UAE. I attended a school for Pakistani expatriates in Sharjah (Pakistan College Sharjah—since then it has changed its name due to new UAE government regulations). The medium of instruction in this school was English, which meant that all subjects were taught in English. At school, we were actively discouraged from using any language other than English. At home and in other contexts, I grew up speaking a mixture of English and Urdu—depending on the domain of the conversation and the people involved. The series of migrations that started with my grandparents had yet to settle. From the UAE, I moved back to Karachi for 1 year (1985–1986). Not being able to settle down in General Zia-ul-Haq's Islamicized Pakistan, my parents decided to move back to the UAE. We lived there for another 2 years and then moved back to Pakistan—this time we moved to Gilgit (a small city in the mountains of northern Pakistan), where my parents taught English to children at a local school. In addition to my parents, there was a British couple who were also teaching English at this school. This couple was one of my early professional inspirations—I, like them, wanted to travel the world and support my travels through teaching English. Of course, this was rather naïve of me; I later discovered that they could do this because they were "native" speakers of the language, and they were White and in demand. I did not qualify for the jobs that came naturally to them.

My year in Gilgit was a series of unforgettable experiences. Just to give you an impression, we lived without running water or electricity—and this was in the late 1980s! I enrolled in a local intermediate college (equivalent to U.S. high school) in Gilgit. During one vacation, I went to Karachi to visit my brothers who were going to college there. On the way back, I was trapped in a landslide and was unable to return to Gilgit. With the winter approaching and the school back in session, it was decided that I would transfer to an intermediate college in Karachi. After graduating from the intermediate college, I found a job as an English teacher—my only qualification being that I was proficient in the language and had always scored high grades in the subject. For a year, I taught English to elementary and secondary school children, but I felt unqualified. In November 1990, I began attending Karachi University. I completed my bachelor's degree (Hons) in English literature in 1994, and my master's degree in linguistics in 1995. This stay in Karachi, from 1989 to 1995, marks the longest period that I continuously lived in one city—6 years!

Feeling unsatisfied with my academic qualifications and with a thirst to learn more, I arrived in the United States on June 19, 1995, to continue my higher education. This was a major move for me. Although I had lived in various places, this was my first exposure to the West. I soon learnt that I had to retool myself to survive in this society.

I lived in Bloomington, Indiana, from 1995 to 2002. However, I did not live there continuously. I was only there during the school year; in the summers (for at least 3 months each year), I would either travel to another country to teach English, or visit my family in Pakistan. On these trips to Pakistan, I worked/volunteered at local educational institutions as an educator or a researcher.

My experiences and exposure at Indiana University, some of which I share in this chapter, have shaped my academic life. My interest in and focus on NNEST (nonnative English speaking teacher) issues, World Englishes, and teacher education developed during my stay there. In addition to my academic understanding, my work that visits to various countries during the summers helped me develop a localized understanding of these issues.

As a graduate student at Indiana University, I was also quite active in the local TESOL affiliate. I was elected the vice president of INTESOL (Indiana Teachers of English to Speakers of Other Languages) in 2001, and the president of this organization in 2002. In July 2002, before I completed my doctorate, I was offered a tenure-track position at East Carolina University, NC, and left Indiana. Although I found the department and the university very supportive, I felt the political atmosphere in the United States in general, and in Greenville, NC, in specific, to be increasingly suffocating, especially for a person with my South Asian Muslim heritage. I soon started looking for jobs outside the United States and was offered a position in the department of linguistics at the University of Sydney. I arrived in Sydney on June 28, 2004. At the time of writing, I plan to live in Sydney—however, with my history, I cannot guarantee how long I will stay here or where I will go next. Such is a story of a child of the diaspora.

The Concept of Enracement

Let me start the formal part of this chapter by reflecting on the chapter's title: "Confessions of an *Enraced* TESOL Professional." *Enraced*, as you know, is not a word that you will find in your dictionaries. *Race* as defined in my student-time (Pakistani) copy of *Oxford Advanced Learner's Dictionary* (Cowie, 1989) is a noun that means: "any of several large subdivisions of mankind sharing physical characteristics, e.g. colour of skin, colour and type of hair, shape of eyes and nose" (p. 1030). However, to me, *race* is not only something that describes us, but is also something that is performed to and by us—it is a verb. And so, based on the analogy of *rage*, namely *enrage* ("make (sb) very angry"; *Oxford Advanced Learner's Dictionary*, p. 400), I have created the word *enrace*: to make or cause somebody to become (very) raced. The verb *enrace* represents actions/negotiations through which we acquire our awareness of race. The verb *enrace* does not only mean that we are enraced by others—that others cause us to construct our racial identity—but, also that we enrace others—that our actions, behaviors, and/or discourses lead to a (re) negotiation of other people's racial awareness. This process of enracement is a result of our negotiations and interactions with people (both of our own race and other races) and is partly grounded in how other people view, experience, and/or stereotype our race and how we view, experience, and/or stereotype them. This form of negotiation and identity building is, of course, not restricted to the issue of race, but extends to other forms of human stereotypes, beliefs, and/or orientations (e.g., gender, ethnicity, language [including accent], creed, sexual orientation, and so on). However, in this chapter, I restrict myself to reflecting on issues of race (with some discussion of language as it relates to race).

The process of enracement may or may not be a positive one. It is possible that our negotiations with individuals may result in a positive reflection of our racial identity, but it is also possible that they may result in a negative experience. It is also very possible that racial identity is not a subject of a particular negotiation at all. Similarly, our own actions and behavior may also lead to a positive or a negative evaluation of other peoples' racial identities. However, in many instances, we tend not to focus on our own actions/behaviors toward others as acts of enracement. We prefer to talk about how our racial identities are negotiated through our (unfortunate) experiences and tend to forget how our actions might impact others. In the narratives that follow, I include incidents that helped me define and evaluate my own racial identity, and episodes in which I feel that I caused others to enrace their identities. Let me start with two episodes that exemplify this.

Narrative 1: On Being Enraced

When I first came to the United States as an international student in the mid-1990s and entered my first class, I could sense that everyone turned around to look at me. I felt as if I were guilty of something and had transgressed an unmarked boundary. Although it is possible that I was being overly sensitive about other students' gazes, I felt insecure at that moment in time. I felt that they were looking at me because I was the only one in the room with dark skin color (and a sing-song South Asian accent). It wasn't that the people in this instance were rude or anything, it was just the way they looked at me. It marked me as an outsider—an other. This feeling impacted my behavior and confidence: Every time I opened my mouth to say one thing, I uttered the opposite. I felt that I said the absolute wrong thing every time I opened my mouth: I wanted to say one thing, but uttered the opposite. I was also very conscious of my accent/language. Although a proficient speaker of Pakistani English, I suddenly felt that my English was not good enough. I lost all confidence. It was not until a few weeks into the semester that I regained my confidence and redeveloped a positive self-identity.

Narrative 2: On Enracing Others

During the same time as that of Narrative 1, I noticed that most of the international students in the class were from Asia—many with very marked accents and ungrammatical English. They were what many *desis* (people from South Asia) call *chaptas* or *chinkas*, and there are not many positive stereotypes about them. I therefore subconsciously maintained a distance from them and focused my energies to make friends with the Anglo Americans—people whom I considered to be cool. I did not attempt to make friends with the Asian students and they made no attempts to befriend me. It was not until a few weeks into the semester that a casual comment from a classmate made me realize what I was doing: I was letting my own racial stereotypes influence my behavior with the others in my class. This realization helped me reflect on and change my behavior. I actively developed friendships with several of my Asian classmates, a few of which we still maintain via e-mail and phone calls. However, I often wonder and feel guilty about how I might have enraced some of them and how my behavior might have made them feel about their race and their English language proficiency.

These two contrasting but overlapping events define the scope of this chapter. The simultaneity of time and place of these two narratives shows how we can enrace and be enraced by others at the same time. Another aspect of enracement that these two brief narratives show is that racial prejudices do not only come into play between members of a majority and a minority group, but also between members of different minority groups (the Asian students and I were both members of visible minority groups in the United States). Additionally, they show that a narrative on race does not only relate to critical incidents in which one describes how one's race becomes an issue for others, but also is a reflection of how one's own stereotypes and racial prejudices impact one's relationships with others. Finally, the narratives suggest a link between race and language (that is explored later in the chapter).

At this point, I would also like to admit that this sharing of my experiences about race is neither comfortable nor easy. Although it is hard to revisit events when my racial identity was given precedence over my professional abilities, it is even harder to admit my own past biases and prejudices and how they colored my behavior. It is in sharing this racial misbehavior that I use the term *confessions* in the title of this chapter. I am greatly ashamed of how I might have behaved in the past and apologize to those whom I might have offended.

On Being Enraced in TESOL

In Narrative 1, I recalled how I was the only student with a dark skin color in my initial graduate courses in the United States. Although this was of surprise to me then, it is an even greater surprise to note that in my 6 years as a graduate student and now 3 years as a university-based educator, I have come across only one graduate student who was Black and none with my own skin color (although I have met and seen a few at conferences). This observation leads me to think that there is something about race that relates to our chosen profession. However, when we take in the larger global picture, this race—TESOL relationship cannot be sustained: Most English teachers in West Africa (and other parts of Africa) are Black; most English teachers in South Asia are of my skin color. Thus, a claim that race is intrinsically tied to the TESOL profession is not really accurate. Nevertheless, the fact remains that people with these racial/cultural backgrounds are a minority in applied linguistics and TESOL programs in the United States (and, in my recent experience, in Australia as well). I believe that the reason for this low representation lies in other places: limited access to economic resources to pursue education in the West, low status of social sciences in their home countries, and visa policies and regulations that control the entry of people from these countries into the United States. Although these (and other) factors can explain the low proportion of people from African and South Asian countries in TESOL in the global North, they do not explain the extremely low proportion of African Americans and people of other U.S.-based racial minorities in the profession. It is here that race becomes relevant again. It is my understanding, based on my research on NNESTs (e.g., see Mahboob, Uhrig, Newman & Hartford, 2004), that part of this has to do with hiring practices and administrators' perceptions of what the students want. There is a widely held perception that EAL (English as an Additional Language) students want native speakers as their teachers (Braine, 1999; Cook, 1999; Mahboob et al., 2004; Medgyes, 1992), and that a native speaker is of an Anglo (White) origin (Amin, 1999, 2004; Paikeday, 1985). This perception results in a hiring bias that, in turn, translates into a lack of enthusiasm of non-Anglos to enter this profession.

These critical conditions have now persisted over such a length of time that people who are victims of these conditions themselves reflect and emulate them. Lambert, Hodgson, Gardner, and Fillenbaum (1960) have termed such acceptance of low status by members of a minority group as "minority group reaction." This minority group reaction subdues the minorities and helps them accept their unprivileged status. However, the recent critical movement in applied linguistics and TESOL has questioned these power dynamics (this book being an example of such work) and is raising our awareness of the issues.

Narrative 1 is, in many ways, a benign narrative. It is one in which I was enraced not as much through what other people said or did, but rather through what I felt they did or did not do. It was partly, I believe, due to my own heightened sensitivity of being different. Most students in the room might not even have looked at me, but I felt that they were all staring at me. This suggests that enracement may happen in absence of any specific actions and can be a consequence of one's own sensitivities. However, not all narratives of enracement are benign. Let me share another story in which I felt that race was of central concern.

Narrative 3: Where Race Matters

A person I know quite well and who in 1996 earned her master's degree in applied linguistics with straight As wanted to go on for a doctorate. However, being an international student (who is not allowed to work off campus in the United States) from a middle-class background, she could not afford to pay her way through the program. Her only hope of pursuing her dreams was to be given a job at the affiliated English language program (ELP) as an ESL teacher. She set up an appointment to see the program director. During the interview, the program administrator said:

> While I have no problems with your grades or language skills or letters of support, I do have concerns about how you look. Now don't get me wrong, dear, but as you know our students pay a lot of money to come and study with Americans. Although I would like to hire you, how will I be able to justify this to our students? They will not be happy to see a person with your appearance as their teacher.

These were words that neither my friend nor I have ever been able to forget. Needless to say, she did not get this job—it was offered instead to an Anglo American graduate student who was not as qualified as my friend was (his GPA was not as high and he did not have any previous teaching experience). With this refusal, my friend lost all faith in being accepted as an equal in a profession in which she had invested so much (money and time). Her dreams shattered and she returned to her country.

Every time I recall this story, it makes me really angry and frustrated: angry because the director of the ELP was so overtly racist about their hiring policies, and frustrated because there is not much that we can realistically do about such behavior.

Narrative 3 supports the claim that hiring decisions are made based on administrators' perceptions of who students want or do not want as their teachers (Braine, 1999). It is interesting to note that current research suggests that administrators' perceptions of students' beliefs are not always accurate (Mahboob, 2003, 2004). We also know that even if some students have biases, exposure to trained professionals of different races/accents educates and changes these perceptions. In addition, we cannot be sure if the administrator in Narrative 3 referred to the issue of students' beliefs because she truly believed in it or because using students' beliefs was an easy excuse for not hiring my friend, a person of color. Regardless, this incident not only enraced my friend, but also greatly affected me. It is coincidental (or maybe not, because it occurred in the same critical conditions that I described earlier) that I had a very similar experience shortly after my friend went through this rejection.

Narrative 4: Accent and Race

When my friend was going through these difficult times, I had only been in the United States for about a year. I was nearly finished working on my master's degree in applied linguistics and was transitioning into the doctoral program. I considered myself, in some ways, very lucky, because I was one of the few international students in the master's program (in fact, if I remember correctly, I was the only one) who had an AI position (associate instructor, for which the department covered my tuition and gave me a small allowance to apply to my living expenses). I was (and still am) very appreciative of this support, because without it I would not have been able to pursue my doctoral education. However, my particular AIship setup was also a dilemma for me. Whereas all other AIs in the department taught ESL at an affiliated ELP, I was given the task by one of the ELP directors to help out the office staff. Thus, while my colleagues were gaining valuable experience (and training) in teaching ESL, I—who was studying for the same degree in the same program—was not considered good enough to teach. I can't help but to view this through the lens of my colonized (South Asian) history and see a reflection of the White officers walking freely and the dark coolies (luggage carriers) carrying their luggage for them.

Although I learnt a lot working in the office and made some good friends amongst the office staff, I was never satisfied with my position. I wanted to teach. I wanted to get the same experience and training as my colleagues were getting. When I approached one of the directors of the ELP, I was told that they could not let me teach unless I "changed my accent." And, once again (this time in person), I heard the now eerily familiar structure "You know we would love to have you join the teaching team, but ..." The director followed the "but" with a reference to students' desires. She said something like "... the students come here to study with Americans and will complain." As she said this, I kept thinking of my friend who was given an almost identical response—the difference being that with her the issue was not her language but instead her race. I left the office sad, but not as devastated as my friend. I still had an AIship that supported my doctoral work, unlike my friend and many other people I knew. Before ending this narrative, I should mention that, over time, I was allowed to teach in this ELP. Once given an opportunity to prove myself, I was asked to teach every session until I left to take up my first tenure-track position.

What I did not include in Narrative 4 is that after I left the office and thought about what had happened, I realized that the administrator was being less than totally honest: There were at least two British speakers of English and one nonnative speaker of English with a European background.

Thus, it was not true that they hired only Americans or speakers of American English. However, one thing that was terribly true about this was that the three non-Americans were all White. I wonder if it was my skin color rather than my accent that was really the issue. Race was definitely an issue in Narrative 3—it was clearly articulated as such. In my case, however, it was camouflaged and couched in terms of "accent." To me, this episode implied that although non-American White accents were acceptable, non-American non-White accents were not. It wasn't so much that I had an accent that I refuse(d) to give up (it is who I am, it is part of my identity), as it was that even if I did not have that accent, I would be marked by the color of my skin. Narratives 3 and 4 have made me realize that race and accent in TESOL are closely tied together.

So far, I have shared narratives that I experienced/witnessed. However, the real-life consequences of the relationship among race, nativeness (accent), and TESOL are quite widespread. One good way of evaluating the scope of this relationship is to look at job advertisements that explicitly ask for "White native speakers." These ads exemplify the relationship that is raised in the literature on NNESTs (e.g., Amin, 2004; Braine, 1999; Paikeday, 1985). Although there has been a decrease in the number of ads that state this openly, it is not uncommon to find them (and ads that specify the need for "native speakers" are still very common). A quick google search with the key terms *White native ESL teacher job* will lead you to some very interesting posts. Although there are a larger number of employers who specify race as a factor in their hiring policies, there are also some prospective teachers who market themselves as "White." Three ads that specifically request "White native speakers" are reproduced in Appendixes A, B, and C, and one ad placed by a prospective "White" teacher is shown in Appendix D. In addition to these ads, there are numerous websites that document first-hand experiences of people who found themselves victims of this racism in TESOL (Appendix E). The following quote is taken from the website of The TEFL Academy on April 15, 2005 and shares the lament of one non-White, nonnative ESL teacher who wanted to find a teaching position in China:

> I have tried for five months to contact the schools directly, but the only replies I got so far were "Sorry, your qualifications are great, but the school headmaster wants white native speakers." I am getting depressed.

This poster clearly articulated the discrimination that he or she had experienced in multiple attempts to find suitable employment. Browsing through this and other similar web pages situates Narratives 3 and 4 in a larger critical context—where White native speakers are preferred over non-White nonnative professionals. They show that these narratives, although personally relevant to me because they enraced me, are not uncommon.

In this section, I focused on two overlapping (in terms of time) critical incidents that enraced me in terms of my skin color and my "non-White" accent (and situated them in a larger critical context). However, I must sadly acknowledge that while I was being enraced, I was simultaneously enracing others. These narratives are the focus of the following section.

On Enracing Others in TESOL

As I stated in Narrative 4, I was a privileged international graduate student in that I was offered an AIship soon after I began my master's program. None of the other international students in the MA program at that time had this opportunity. Maybe, as a result of this privileged status, or maybe simply because I was insensitive, I sometimes, uncritically, behaved in ways that I cannot justify—and, in doing so, enraced others. I offer the following unpleasant narrative to exemplify one such instance.

Narrative 5

It was during my second semester as a graduate student and an AI that I was working with a group of students on a set of questions in our language testing class. During the course of the discussion, I wanted to make my voice heard and therefore said something to the effect that "I know this better because I have studied English all my life and people from 'your' background do not know this." Although I won the argument that day and our group presentation went really well, I have often reflected on this episode and I feel that there were better ways of getting my point across.

This short episode has stuck with me. Although I'm not sure if people in my group found my comment racist or discriminatory, or if they accepted it as being a statement that described and compared our two backgrounds, to me, in retrospect, it was a racist comment. It was racist in the sense that I considered myself to be better than others because of my background/status (which the others in my group did not share). In a very ironic way, I was using my country's British colonial history to elevate my status and inferring that those whose countries had not been colonized by English speakers were somehow inferior. By making them conscious of their non-English-based background, I was enracing them—whether they were conscious of it or not. Although I am ashamed of what I said, in one way I am glad that it did happen. The incident foregrounded what I must have been feeling for a long time—it brought to the surface and exposed the stereotypes and prejudices under which I was functioning. Through this explicit display of my prejudice, I was able to reflect on my behavior and evolve.

Narrative 6

I have been actively involved in the NNEST Caucus in TESOL for several years. As part of our vision, the NNEST Caucus wants to foster an environment in which nativeness and race are taken out of the equation in TESOL. Therefore, it came as a blow to me when one of the presenters at the 2005 TESOL convention said that she felt that she did not really belong in the NNEST community. She said that when she attended the NNEST Caucus meetings, she was the only Black professional and felt isolated and left out. She said that the Caucus was dominated by people from an Asian background who did not always welcome her amongst them. Her presentation really moved me, and afterward I went up to her and, as the chair of the Caucus, formally apologized and told her that I would take active steps to reduce such unintended alienation.

As I noted earlier, I was shocked to hear these comments because we actively encourage diversity in the Caucus. However, regardless of our attempts, it appears that our members are enraced within the Caucus. This was extremely revealing to me. On reflection, I was able to appreciate the woman's comments and was able to see that this member's experience of being enraced by another member of a minority group was similar to those related in Narratives 2 and 5. In their attempt to gain equal status and recognition, members of one minority group at times fail to recognize their power of enracing members of another minority group. This is seen in Narrative 6, when the presenter felt that she was not included in the NNEST discourse at the various Caucus meetings (here the enracement occurred not because of a specific action by the members of the community, but rather the lack of any action). In order to redress this situation, I brought up her presentation/feelings at the Caucus open meeting and led a discussion on ways of integrating all voices into the Caucus. This episode showed me that it is not only an individual, but also an organization/institution (even those that are designed to counter discrimination), that can enrace people. As members of these organizations, we need to monitor our actions (and nonactions) to reduce any negative enracement that may occur within them.

These narratives reflect how we need to continuously examine our own behavior and how it might contribute to the enracement of others. It is through this critically reflective journey that we can better understand the construct of enracement and how we (both individually and collectively) at once enrace and are enraced through our interactions with others. This journey, although painful and difficult at times, reveals that there is yet some hope in focusing on enracement.

Concluding Remarks: On Hope in Enracement

This chapter has been a reflective journey in which I shared several narratives to show how race is not just a noun, but also a verb. My goal was to show how, through our actions (and sometimes nonactions), we enrace and are enraced by others. In this concluding section of the chapter, I would like to expand the scope of this discussion and address how we can use the notion of enracement in other work in TESOL. I would specifically like to do two things:

1. Consider how this notion of enracement may be used to study different aspects of race and TESOL.

2. Talk about how we can use this notion of enracement to begin a dialogue with ourselves and with others to create a more informed and tolerant society.

So far in this chapter, I have focused on how enracement is a result of our interactions with other individuals. Although this is still a ripe area for future research/reflection, the notion of enracement can also be used in other areas of interest to professionals in TESOL and applied linguistics. For example, we could look at how various EAL textbooks and material represent people of different races. We can ask questions like: Is there a pattern in which people of different races are identified as being native or nonnative speakers of English (e.g., through pictures in textbooks, etc.), and is there a pattern in the various social and/or professional roles assigned to people of different races in the textbooks? If such patterns are discovered, we could continue our research into how such patterns are developed/represented. This research will suit the critical discourse framework (Fairclough, 1995) and lend itself to multimodal discourse analysis (Baldry & Thibault, 2006).

In addition to applying the notion of enracement to future research, we could also use it to educate ourselves and others. Throughout this chapter, I have attempted to encourage us to reflect on the various processes of enracement and to consider not only how other peoples' behavior enraces us, but also to monitor how our behavior might enrace others. We could use this understanding of enracement to educate (ourselves and) others and to sensitize people to how their actions might affect others. It is through such reflection on enracement that we can find hope for a more equitable future.

Appendix A[1]

We urgent want 2 white native English teachers in our Xi'an Kingdergartin,we will offer rmb 3500–4500 a month and one year round ticket, rmb 2000 summer holiday travel allowance, free accommodation, health insurance, etc.

You're freely welcomed to contact us soon!

Appendix B[2]

If you are a responsible, creative, hardworking, punctual, organized and easy going individual, than we may have the right opportunity for you. We are one of the fastest growing schools in Indonesia. We are currently hiring for the 2005/2006 school year. We have immediate openings for pre-school, kindergarten, elementary and high school teachers.

Position requirements:

1. Due to new government policies, we can only accept resumes from applicants from Canada, United States, Australia, New Zealand, and the United Kingdom.
2. Be under the age of 35 years old.
3. Have a TEFL or TESOL certificate from an accredited education institution.
4. Have a college or university degree from an accredited institution (any field of study).
5. Have a minimum of six months to one-year actual teaching experience.
6. Have a proven track record of success and contract completion.
7. Applicants cannot have facial hair (men), i.e. mustaches or beards, visible

---

[1] Source: http://marksesl.com/china_jobs/webbbs_files/index.cgi?read=200712

[2] Source: http://www.esljunction.com/jobs/about5520.html

tattoos, or piercing other than the ears (women only and only one hole).

8. No history of drug or substance abuse (all teachers will be tested).

9. No history of mental illness.

All utilities and other expenses are the personal responsibility of the employee.

Application procedure:

1. Please email all relevant documents in JPEG or PDF format.

2. CV/resume

3. A recent color photo

4. University/college degree

5. TEFL or TESOL certificate

6. Two letters of references from previous employers (all references will be contacted)

Please do not apply, if you do not meet the requirements stated on job posting. Only a short list of applicants will be contacted. Thank you.

Email address: XXX

Deadline to submit all documents: June 15, 2005.

Appendix C[3]

White Native English Teacher Available in Shanghai

ESL-EFL Teaching Job Wanted

Experienced business teacher capable of lecturing on management, e-commerce, finance, accounting, sales & marketing, communication.

Looking for position to begin in September some where in Asia. I have a degree, TEFL certificate and 15 years of international business experience.

Email me at: XYZ.

Appendix D[4]

I'm an Australian born chinese and I have been applying for a few jobs teaching english in Hong Kong. I have a degree and a teaching diploma. However, when I applied for a job I got an email from a prospective employer who told me they were interested in my application. When he found out that I was asian (my surname) he told me that even though I had an Aussie accent it didn't matter because it was the fact that I was asian that stopped him from employing me. He also told me that it was going to be very difficult to become employed because of my 'face'. Has this happened to anyone else? And is it really that difficult for Western born asians to become employed as Teachers of english?

---

[3] Source: http://www.englishschoolwatch.org
[4] Source: http://hongkong.asiaxpat.com/forums/speakerscorner/threads/59469.asp

Appendix E[5]

Post: ... but would anyone on this list be familiar with how an Asian-American or Asian-Canadian or ANY female with obviously Asian ethnic blood (but who grew up in the West) would be treated in the Middle East? Would I be at a disadvantage in the hiring process (since we're required to send photos) because I don't have the Western "look" despite my Western credentials and upbringing?

Response: In almost all of the top TESL jobs in the UAE, recruitment decisions are taken by Western expats .... Without the luxury of anti-racist legislation in the West, you may very soon become appalled by attitudes of fellow Western expats.

Response: As for getting a teaching job, well let me put it like this: it would be perfectly normal for a white Brit with mediocre experience and qualifications to be preferred over a non-white native-speaker of English with excellent qualifications and extensive experience. Sad, but unfortunately very true. Sadder still: it's normally Westerners making these decisions NOT locals!

References

Amin, N. (1999). Minority women teachers of ESL: Negotiating White English. In G. Braine (Ed.), *Non-native educators in English language teaching* (pp. 93–104). Mahwah, NJ: Lawrence Erlbaum Associates.

Amin, N. (2004). Nativism, the native speaker construct, and minority immigrant women teachers of English as a second language. In L. Kamhi-Stein (Ed.), *Learning and teaching from experience: Perspectives on nonnative English-speaking professionals* (pp. 61–80). Ann Arbor: University of Michigan Press.

Baldry, A., & Thibault, P. (2006). *Multimodal transcription and text analysis.* London: Equinox.

Braine, G. (Ed.). (1999). *Non-native educators in English language teaching.* Mahwah, NJ: Lawrence Erlbaum Associates.

Cook, V. (1999). Going beyond the native speaker in language teaching. *TESOL Quarterly,* 33(2), 185–210.

Cowie, A. P. (Ed.). (1989). *Oxford advanced learner's dictionary* (4th ed.). Oxford, UK: Oxford University Press.

Fairclough, N. (1995). *Critical discourse.* London: Longman.

Kamhi-Stein, L. (Ed.). (2004). *Learning and teaching from experience: Perspectives on nonnative English-speaking professionals.* Ann Arbor: University of Michigan Press.

Lambert, W. W., Hodgson, R., Gardner, R. C., & Fillenbaum, S. (1960). Evaluational reactions to spoken languages. *Journal of Abnormal and Social Psychology,* 60, 44–51.

---

[5] Source: http://www.eslcafe.com/forums/job/viewtopic.php?t=3461

Mahboob, A. (2003). *Status of nonnative English speaking teachers in the United States.* Unpublished doctoral dissertation, Indian University, Bloomington.

Mahboob, A. (2004). Native or nonnative: What do the students think? In L. Kamhi-Stein (Ed.), *Learning and teaching from experience: Perspectives on nonnative English-speaking professionals* (pp.121–147). Ann Arbor: University of Michigan Press.

Mahboob, A., Uhrig, K., Newman, K., & Hartford, B. (2004). Children of a lesser English: Nonnative English speakers as ESL teachers in English language programs in the United States. In L. Kamhi-Stein (Ed.), *Learning and teaching from experience: Perspectives on nonnative English-speaking professionals* (pp. 100–120). Ann Arbor: University of Michigan Press.

Medgyes, P. (1992). Native or non-native: Who's worth more? *ELT Journal, 46*(4), 340–349.

Paikeday, T. M. (1985). *The native speaker is dead!* Toronto: Paikeday Publications.

Chapter 6

Racism in the English Language Teaching Industry

Mahboob, A. (2009). Racism in the ELT industry. In *Studies in Applied Linguistics and Language Learning*, ed. A. Mahboob & C. Lipovsky, 29–40. Newcastle upon Tyne: Cambridge Scholars Press.

Introduction

This chapter argues that the English Language Teaching (ELT) industry often does not treat all speakers of English as equal in its hiring practices. Rather, it gives preferential treatment to White native speakers of English. That one's race may play a role in hiring decisions is not news. In fact, the social and political movements that make discrimination in employment on the basis of race legally unacceptable are quite recent. For example, the Civil Rights movement in the United States that led to desegregation of Black and White people is still less than 50 years old. However, such laws do not exist globally. The lack of anti-discrimination policies can impact who is hired, as well as the terms and conditions under which they are hired. In countries such as the U.S., where anti-discrimination laws do exist, employers have developed ways of abiding by the laws, yet still maintaining discriminatory practices in their hiring policies (see Mahboob 2003; Moussu 2006). In the ELT industry, this often happens through a preference for native speakers of English, who are positioned as the referent of the EAL (English as an Additional Language) classroom. A common assumption in describing a native speaker of English is that a native speaker is White, and speaks a variety of English associated with the UK, Canada, the USA or Australia. Non-White people who speak a variety of English associated with a South country, for example, India, Nigeria, or Singapore, are constructed as non-native speakers of English. In addition to positioning people based on their accents and language histories, the preference for native speakers conceals a bias in favor of White teachers (Amin 2000; Golombek and Jordan 2005; Leung, Harris, and Rampton 1997; Paikeday 1985; Rampton 1990). While there are no published studies that document the extent of bias against non-White non-native ELT teachers, there is ample anecdotal evidence that employers in the ELT industry prefer to hire White native speakers to other speakers as language teachers. Current studies also convincingly show that there is a preference for hiring native English-speaking teachers over non-native ones (Mahboob 2003; Mahboob, Uhrig, Newman, and Hartford 2004). The results of Mahboob's study indicate that, all other factors being equal, a native speaker will have a higher chance of being hired than a non-native speaker.

The current chapter explores the complex relationship between non-Native English-Speaking Teachers (NNESTs), race, and ELT hiring practices and is divided into three sections. The first section examines the perceived racism in the ELT industry and its employment policies. In the following section, Mahboob's (2003) data is reanalyzed to explore how expert discourses in TESOL and Applied Linguistics have evolved to give prominence to White native speakers. After studying the relationship between the construct of a native speaker and Whiteness, the chapter adopts van Dijk's (1993) understanding of 'elite discourses of racism', and identifies and examines specific terms and concepts that are used in Applied Linguistics to study phenomena that operate to privilege native speakers. The chapter ends by identifying additional questions that need to be studied.

Perceived Racism in ELT Employment

Much of the current understanding of racism in TESOL and Applied Linguistics is based on the narratives of non-White teachers (see for example Braine 1999; Curtis and Romney 2006). In addition to such narratives, numerous websites that are focused on ELT issues include anecdotes that represent perceived racism. In this chapter, two such web posts are discussed: the first one comprises selected portions of a lengthy online discussion on race and the second one is an online job advertisement.

The first excerpt, from a web discussion quoted below, revolves around a question from an Asian-Canadian woman who wants to know what her chances are of getting a job in the Middle East.

> Quote 1: Post: ... but would anyone on this list be familiar with how an Asian-American or Asian-Canadian or ANY female with obviously Asian ethnic

blood (but who grew up in the West) would be treated in the Middle East? Would I be at a disadvantage in the hiring process (since we're required to send photos) because I don't have the Western 'look' despite my Western credentials and upbringing?

Response: In almost all of the top TESL jobs in the UAE [United Arab Emirates], recruitment decisions are taken by Western expats ... Without the luxury of anti-racist legislation in the West, you may very soon become appalled by attitudes of fellow Western expats.

Response: As for getting a teaching job, well let me put it like this: it would be perfectly normal for a white Brit with mediocre experience and qualifications to be preferred over a non-white native-speaker of English with excellent qualifications and extensive experience. Sad, but unfortunately very true. Sadder still: it's normally Westerners making these decisions NOT locals! (Source: ESL-Café)

This quote was selected for several reasons: 1) the racial dimension in employment is clearly articulated by those who have personal experience, 2) it is a discussion that takes place over a number of days, 3) there are several contributors, and 4) all the contributors agree with a racial reading of the hiring process (providing some internal triangulation). The web discussion suggests that having appropriate ELT credentials and being raised in the West are not seen as sufficient qualifications and that being White is perceived to be the most privileged credential by the discussants. In this, the quote validates Lee's (2010) study in which she adds her voice as a non-White native speaker of English who grew up in Canada, but faces (racial) discrimination in the ELT industry when it comes to employment opportunities. This interpretation of the web discussion also corroborates Lee's experiences in that the preference for native speakers in ELT camouflages a racial prejudice as well.

In discussing a racial dimension in ELT, it needs to be clarified that the argument is not that all White ELT practitioners are racist, but rather that being White is an advantage in the field and one that does not relate to professional needs. Furthermore, as the web discussion illustrates, it is not simply non-White people complaining about racist behavior by White people, but rather, there are many White people in the field who find their colleagues' attitudes towards other speakers discriminatory. Furthermore, non-White individuals are also seen to discriminate against other non-White individuals in the field (Mahboob 2006).

The next piece of data to be examined comes from a different category of web postings. The following is an online advertisement that specifies that the employers are looking for an English language teacher who is 'white and not too old'.

> Quote 2: we are a school in beijing shijingshan district and looking for a native english speaker who is white and not too old. it is very urgent because the new teachers are supposed to work from September 1st. the salary is 7000rmb per month. the working time is 3 to 6 from monday to friday. please contact me at XXX. (Source: China-Daily)

The clearly articulated preference for 'White' teachers (note that no other qualification/experience requirements are listed) in this ad supports the perceptions cited in the previous quote that some employers will hire only White native speakers. In addition, it raises the issue of ageism, which is beyond the scope of this paper and is, therefore, not taken up here (for a discussion of this issue, see Templer 2003).

These quotes suggest that there are at least two dimensions of prejudice in ELT: Whiteness and native speakerism[1]; and that both these factors contribute to the status given to various teachers. In fact, as will be argued in the following sections, the two factors are linked. An unmarked native speaker is White and a preference for native speakers as employees is usually a polite and politically correct (or at least acceptable) way of saying that only White candidates need apply.

Survey of Adult EAL Programs in the United States

In the previous section, we examined some anecdotal evidence that showed that White native speakers are perceived to be favored by employers in the field of ELT. In this section, we will reexamine data from a previously published research project to further explore the relationship between race and NNESTs. Based on a survey of 122 adult English Language Professionals (ELPs) in the United States, Mahboob (2003), and Mahboob, Uhrig, Newman, and Hartford (2004), report that employers consider being a native speaker to be an important criterion when making hiring decisions. The instrument used in this study invited participants to rate 10 possible hiring criteria on a 6-point Likert scale. The study showed

---

[1] Two other factors that were raised in the web postings that were surveyed include 'ageism' and 'expatriateness'. These factors are, however, not discussed here.

that the more importance program administrators gave to the 'native English speaker' criterion, the fewer the number of NNESTs employed in their programs. More importantly, based on a regression analysis, the study found that three criteria, 'native English speaker', 'recommendation' and 'teaching experience', explain the ratio of NNESTs in a program. Of these, the most significant independent variable was 'native English speaker'. Thus, the results of this study indicated that all other factors being equal, a person's status as a 'native speaker' can make a difference to whether they will be hired or not.

Although not fully analyzed in these studies, the data included administrators' evaluation of the role of ethnicity and national origin in making hiring decisions. In re-examining this data with a focus on race, it was noted that while being a 'native speaker' was considered an important factor, 'ethnicity' and 'nationality' were perceived as having low importance. The mean ranking for 'ethnicity' was the lowest amongst the 10 criteria listed. The mean ranking for 'nationality' was also amongst the lowest. The mode for both these criteria was '0', implying that most respondents claimed that they do not find these criteria relevant in making hiring decisions. However, it was noted that these ratings are not consistent with the actual distribution of teachers in these programs when sorted based on their national and ethnic origins.

The survey reported that out of the 1425 teachers listed, only 107 (7.86%) were NNESTs. While these NNESTs represented a wide range of countries (48), a quick reanalysis of the data based on ethnic and racial origins points to a preference for White teachers. Of the 107 NNESTs, 56 (52.3%) were White, 28 (26.2%) were Asian, 3 (2.8%) were of (Black) African origin, and 20 (18.7%) comprised the 'other' category. This distribution of the teachers shows a majority of White teachers within a non-native minority. While this majority of White non-native speakers does not necessarily mean that the hiring decisions were racially motivated (to argue this, one must study these numbers in relation to the applicant pool in order to evaluate such a claim), it does highlight a dominance of White teachers among the already small pool of NNESTs.

The relatively high number of White NNESTs with contrasting low importance given to ethnic and national origin in the survey may be partly explained by the cautiousness that influences employers' decisions when completing surveys. Being conscious of what is and is not potentially disadvantaging may impact how people respond to survey questionnaires.

To say that one takes ethnicity and nationality into consideration when making hiring decisions is implicitly stating that one is being discriminatory—which is both politically incorrect and legally prohibited in many situations in the United States. Thus, the safe response in a survey is to give such criteria a low or no rating, which represents a shortcoming of the research method. However, a careful study of the survey data can show inconsistencies to help identify issues that need further investigation. In this reanalysis of the survey data, such a discrepancy was observed— the low ratings of ethnicity and nationality appear to be in contrast with the majority of White teachers in the NNEST pool that are employed by these schools. It is revealing that when NNESTs are hired, there is a disproportionately high representation of White teachers compared to non-White teachers. This finding suggests that being White is an unmarked feature of being an ESL teacher.

An Unmarked EAL Teacher

In the survey discussed here, it was observed that 'ethnicity' and 'nationality' are considered politically unmarked and therefore listed as being not important in making hiring decisions. On the other hand, 'native speaker' is marked and is listed as an important criterion in making hiring decisions. It was argued that this is perhaps a reflection of participants' understanding of what they consider to be safe answers. It was also observed that regardless of the administrators' responses, there is a majority of White teachers within the NNEST pool. One important question to ask here is: Why was native speaker listed as an important criterion whereas ethnicity was not? This is perhaps a trick question because, in many ways, as will be argued here, the concept of a native speaker of English has always included a specific ethnic and racial identity. Davies (1991) emphasized this point when he wrote that the first recorded use of the term 'native speaker' is in the following definition by the American linguist Leonard Bloomfield: 'The first language a human being learns to speak is his native language, he is a native speaker of this language' (Bloomfield 1933 cited in Davies 1991). In defining the characteristics of a native speaker and native language, traits such as birth, heredity, and innateness of linguistic qualities have always been emphasized. These traits form the backbone of how the term native speaker is understood. For example, the *Oxford Advanced Learner's Dictionary* (1989, 84) defines a native speaker as a 'person who has spoken (a particular language) since birth, rather than learning it later'. The inclusion of such terms in dictionaries underscores their widespread use. Based on such an understanding, the native speaker of English is seen as American, Australian, English or Canadian. More importantly, a native speaker of English is seen as a White person who was born and raised in these countries. People of other races are not identified as native speakers of English; rather they are seen as speakers of, for example, Black English/ Ebonics, Pakistani English, or Chinese English. Such an understanding of how race relates to native speaker status is relevant in TESOL. For example, the specific requirement of 'white' native speakers in job ads (e.g., quote 2 above), requirements of submitting colored photographs, and narratives of discrimination against non-White speakers of English (e.g., quote 1 above), all provide evidence of how EAL programs accept the construct that being a White native speaker is an important aspect of being a teacher in the field of TESOL (also see Leung, Harris, and Rampton 1997; Rampton 1990).

The use of the 'native speaker' construct to veil a preference for hiring White native speakers in EAL is also influenced by recent developments in Linguistics and Applied Linguistics. One of the most influential of these developments has been Chomsky's use of the 'idealized native speaker-hearer' concept (Chomsky 1986) as an abstraction for theoretical linguistic research. For English, this 'idealized native speaker-hearer' is seen as a White person and this notion has been extensively used in Applied Linguistics and Second Language Acquisition (SLA) research. The influence of the Chomskyan paradigm on SLA can be measured by the following statement from Gregg (1993, 278), who states that the purpose of SLA is to study 'the acquisition (or non-acquisition) of L2 competence, in the Chomskyan sense of the term'. One result of this influence is that non-White native and non-native speakers of English are seen as life-long learners of English.

An understanding of the preference for native speakers of English and a non-recognition by White TESOL practitioners of race and ethnicity as factors in the hiring process in EAL programs can also be developed by using van Dijk's (1993) framework of elite discourses of racism. van Dijk argues that liberal discourses of elite racism tend to deny racism. He refers to a 'worldwide system of military, economic and cultural power of the *white* West over the Rest' [emphasis added] (van Dijk 1993, x), in which the elites—political, media, educational, corporate and academic—play a role in the enactment, legitimation and reproduction of racism through the ages. He posits that ethnic dominance and racism are still a reality in Western societies and that elite discourses continue to play a primary role in the reproduction of contemporary ethnic and racial inequalities. The racism of the elites is predominantly discursive; through their influential text and talk, they 'manufacture the consent' (van Dijk 1993, 8) needed for the legitimation of their own power in general, and for their leadership in maintaining the dominance of the White group in particular. Popular racism, concludes van Dijk, can be effective only when it is spread through the population by the mass media and similar forms of public discourse controlled by the elites. One such powerful public discourse is that of academia. This chapter will therefore now outline how academic discourses of TESOL and second language acquisition research shape the public mind to consider White native speaker models as being the target norm for English language acquisition.

There are a number of ways that academic discourses of TESOL contribute to the view that native speakers of English are ideal teachers. These include couching a preference for native speaker norms of language and cultural practices in expert scientific and research-based arguments. The use of an 'idealized native speaker' discussed earlier can, in fact, be understood as an example of such liberal discourse of elite racism— White native speakers are privileged through academic discourses and their language is identified as the target language for English language learners worldwide. Bhatt (2002) posits that expert discourses in Applied Linguistics perpetuate inequality by using terms such as 'interlanguage' and 'fossilization', which give prominence to White native speakers by assuming that the goal of language learners is to acquire native-like proficiency. These terms suggest that since most learners fail to sound like White native speakers, they are 'fossilized' at a certain point in their 'interlanguage'. Such interpretations and assumptions of learner goals and failure to sound like native speakers have been promoted by many TESOL experts and are accepted by the larger population. This acceptance of the underlying principles behind these terms by the non-experts can be judged by their inclusion in dictionaries. The mainstream literature in SLA, which uses terms such as 'interlanguage' and 'fossilization', offers an example of how, perhaps unwittingly, experts in Applied Linguistics and TESOL contribute to and reflect a racial understanding of the world—one where White native speakers are model users of the English language and Non-

White native speakers of Non-White Englishes aim to achieve competency in the 'standard' or White English. These assumptions then contribute to a discourse that gives higher status to White native speakers and portrays other speakers as lifelong learners (see also Mahboob 2005). Thus, it can be argued that Lee (2010) and other non-White speakers of standard/ White English are complimented on their language ability because they are considered to be model language learners—they look foreign, but speak English like White native speakers. Kachru's (1991, 1992) work on World Englishes is worth discussing here as well as its main point is that speakers of English from the Inner Circle countries—England, Canada, the US, and Australia—are constructed as the model, while the varieties of English from the Outer Circle (e.g., Singapore, Ghana, and Sri Lanka) and Expanding Circle (e.g., Brazil, China) are marked as being not only different, but deficient. Although the varieties of English from regions other than the Inner Circle produce a sizeable literature in English and use the language for both internal and external communication, they are studied in terms of their deviations and differences from White Englishes[2]. Although World Englishes are growing as an area of focal research, there are experts who dismiss World Englishes as being 'ideologically intoxicated' (Quirk 1990, 9).

In summary, a critical understanding of the term native speaker and the current literature in Linguistics and Applied Linguistics suggests that Whiteness and First World status are essential characteristics in being considered native speakers of English and that this unmarked 'native speaker' is framed in the literature as being the ideal English language teacher.

Concluding Remarks

This chapter has attempted to show that hegemonic discourses of the White native speaker teacher's superiority ensure that he/she continues to be the referent in ELT. The chapter suggests that employers seem to think that they should hire native speakers over non-native speakers because native speakers are better teachers; and that native speakers are imagined as White. A reanalysis of Mahboob, Uhrig, Newman, and Hartford's

---

[2] At one level, World Englishes offer a pluralistic paradigm that is largely ignored in Applied Linguistics and TESOL literature. However, it can be argued that there is a hierarchy among World Englishes on the basis of race: White Englishes are constructed as Inner Circle English varieties while the Outer Circle Englishes are seen as non-White varieties.

(2004) survey further indicates that even in ELT institutions that hire non-native speakers, there is a majority of White non-native teachers. What can ELT experts do to address this imbalance in hiring practices in both North and South countries? First of all, more empirical research should be conducted in order to further document such practices. As has been illustrated, this is not a simple task, as respondents are aware of what are 'safe' and 'unsafe' answers, and give safe answers, which may not necessarily reflect their hiring preferences. Hence more sophisticated data collection instruments have to be developed in order to triangulate employers' responses. The more difficult challenge is for TESOL to unravel and demystify the discourses that construct White native speakers as the best teachers. Questions that need to be addressed include: For what professional reasons do White native speakers continue to be privileged? As teaching is an activity which has to be learned, what value should be put on someone who is born in a White English-speaking family? Here, it needs to be pointed out that non-White teachers may also be born in an English-dominant family. Another point worth addressing is that proficiency in language can be learned/developed in a formal setting, that is, in a school, so that being born in an English-dominant family may not be relevant.

In addition to these questions, a discussion of the goals of language teaching is also needed: Should a White native speaker model continue to be the goal of language learning/teaching? And if so, why? In the 21st century, the role of English as the world language appears to be taking a different direction than in the latter half of the 20th century, which was characterized by colonialism, immigration from South to North countries, and American imperialism, whereby South speakers of English felt they needed to communicate with North speakers of English in North varieties of English. It appears that the future of English is that of an intralanguage, that is, of an additional language between speakers who have different first languages, say Chinese, Urdu, and Ibu, and hence the native speaker of English may be less and less relevant as a model for language teaching and learning.

Finally, it needs to be stressed that if ELT wants to develop into a profession rather than remaining a largely unlegislated industry, then it should aim to eradicate all forms of discrimination. To evolve into a profession, the ELT community needs to challenge and remove from its belief system the notion that 'some speakers are more equal than others', to give all members of the TESOL community the justice and equality that they deserve.

References

Amin, N. (2000). *Negotiating nativism: Minority immigrant women ESL teachers and the native speaker construct.* Ph. D. dissertation, University of Toronto, Toronto. (Unpublished.)

Bhatt, R. (2002). Experts, dialects, and discourse. *International Journal of Applied Linguistics, 12* (1), 74–109.

Braine, G. (ed.) (1999). *Non-native educators in English language teaching.* Mahwah, New Jersey: Lawrence Erlbaum Associates.

China-Daily. Retrieved May 15, 2005, from: http://bbs.chinadaily.com.cn/forumpost. shtml?toppid=167112.

Chomsky, N. (1986). *Barriers.* Cambridge, Massachusetts: MIT Press.

Curtis, A., & Romney, M. (2006). *Shades of meaning: Articulating the experiences of TESOL professionals of color.* Mahwah, New Jersey: Lawrence Erlbaum Associates.

Davies, A. (1991). *The native speaker in applied linguistics.* Edinburgh: Edinburgh University Press.

ESL-Cafe. Retrieved May 15, 2005, from: http://www.eslcafe.com/forums/job/viewtopic. php?t=3461.

Golombek, P., & Jordan, S. (2005). Becoming "black lambs" not "parrots": A poststructuralist orientation to intelligibility and identity. *TESOL Quarterly, 39*(3), 513–533.

Gregg, K. (1993). Taking explanation seriously; or, let a couple of flowers bloom. *Applied Linguistics, 14*(3), 276–294.

Kachru, B. (1991). Liberation linguistics and the Quirk concern. *English Today, 7*(1), 1–13.

Kachru, B. (1992). The other tongue: *English across cultures.* (2nd ed.). Urbana and Chicago: University of Illinois Press.

Lee, C.-J. (2010). Native versus nonnative: A literacy teacher educator's story. *Language and Literacy, 12*(1), 46–56.

Leung, C., Harris, R., & Rampton, B. (1997). The idealised native speaker, reified ethnicities, and classroom realities. *TESOL Quarterly, 31,* 543–560.

Mahboob, A. (2003). *Status of nonnative English speaking teachers in the United States.* Ph. D. dissertation, Indiana University, Bloomington. (Unpublished.)

Mahboob, A. (2005). Beyond the native speaker in TESOL. In *Culture, context, and communication,* ed. S. Zafar, 60–93. Abu Dhabi, UAE: Center of Excellence for Applied Research and Training & The Military Language Institute.

Mahboob, A. (2006). Confessions of an enraced TESOL professional. In *Shades of meaning: Articulating the experiences of TESOL professionals of color,* eds. A. Curtis and M. Romney, 173–188. Mahwah, New Jersey: Lawrence Erlbaum Associates.

Mahboob, A., Uhrig, K., Newman, K., & Hartford, B. (2004). Children of a lesser English: Nonnative English speakers as ESL teachers in English language programs in the United States. In *Learning and teaching from experience: Perspectives on nonnative English-speaking professionals,* ed. L. Kamhi-Stein, 100–120. Ann Arbor: University of Michigan Press.

Moussu, L. (2006). *Native and non-native English-speaking English as a second language teachers: Student attitudes, teacher self-perceptions, and intensive English program administrator beliefs and practices*. Ph.D. dissertation, Purdue University, West Lafayette. (ERIC Document Reproduction Service No. ED 492 599.)

Oxford Advanced Learner's Dictionary. (1989). Oxford: Oxford University Press.

Paikeday, T. (1985). *The native speaker is dead!* Toronto: Paikeday Publishing.

Quirk, R. (1990). Language varieties and standard language. *English Today*, 6(1), 3–10.

Rampton, B. (1990). Displacing the 'native speaker': Expertise, affiliation and inheritance. *ELT Journal*, 44(2), 97–101.

Templer, B. (2003). Ageism in TEFL: Time for concerted action. *TESL Reporter*, 36(1), 1–22.

van Dijk, T. (1993). *Elite discourse and racism*. London: Sage Publications.

Chapter 7

Students' Appraisal of Their Native and Non-Native English-Speaking Teachers

Lipovsky, C., & Mahboob, A. (2010). Students' appraisal of their native and non-native English speaking teachers. In B. Brady (Ed.), *The WATESOL NNEST Caucus Annual Review*, Vol. 1.

Introduction

In recent years, a number of studies have explored attitudes toward and perceptions of non-native English-speaking teachers (NNESTs). However, most of these studies, not unlike other work on language attitudes, have used surveys (Benke & Medgyes, 2005; Lasagabaster & Sierra, 2005; Moussu, 2006) and/or qualitative data that focus on emerging themes/content (Mahboob, 2004; Mahboob & Griffin, 2006). While survey data provide a statistical analysis of participants' attitudes (based on a predetermined set of comments and/or criteria) and the qualitative data document participants' attitudes in terms of the categories of comments that emerge from the data, the actual language used by students to project their perceptions is left unanalyzed. The results of the existing studies that do look at qualitative data are presented in terms of categories of comments that were recorded in favor of or against teachers' native-speaker status. The actual discourse of evaluation is not analyzed. Thus, missing from the current literature is an analysis of the actual language used to comment on native English-speaking teachers (NESTs) and NNESTs in interviews and other qualitative data. It is our contention that an analysis of students' language of appraisal will add to the richness of our understanding of perceptions. The goal of the present study is therefore to examine students' perceptions of NESTs and NNESTs by conducting a linguistic analysis of students' texts.

Background and Methodology

Data for this project come from essays written by 19 Japanese high school students attending a four-month English as a second language (ESL) orientation program at the beginning of a year-long study abroad program in the United States. The program was taught by two TESOL professionals: one an NEST and the other an NNEST. Program participants were asked to write a diagnostic essay at the beginning (T1) and end (T2) of the program on the following topic:

> Some students think that only native speakers can be good language teachers. Others think that non-natives can also be efficient teachers. What is your opinion about this issue? Please feel free to provide details and examples.

These essays were collected with two goals in mind: (1) to evaluate students' writing and grammar, and (2) to explore any shift in students' perceptions of native and non-native English-speaking TESOL professionals. The essay task was based on Mahboob (2003), in which the essays written by ESL students in an intensive English language program in the United States were studied for their attitudes toward NNESTs. Mahboob (2003) used the grounded approach to study these data and observed that ESL students did not prefer native or non-native speakers but rather found them to bring unique attributes to their classes. Following Mahboob (2003), Mahboob and Griffin (2006) also applied the grounded approach to their study. Corroborating earlier findings, they found that students' comments could be placed into three broad categories: linguistic factors, teaching styles, and personal factors. The first group, linguistic factors, includes "oral skills", "literacy skills", "grammar", "vocabulary", and "culture"; the second group, teaching styles, includes "ability to answer questions" and "teaching methodology"; and the third group, personal factors, includes "experience as an ESL learner", "hard work", and "affect". Within each of these categories, students reported both positive and negative comments (examples of these categories are provided in the appendix). The results of the study showed that the trends in student responses did not change over time—e.g. NESTs were still considered strong in teaching oral skills and NNESTs were considered strong teachers of literacy skills. The results also indicated that ESL students in this study found the distinction between NESTs and NNESTs less relevant after being exposed to both in an ESL setting. However, as in previous work in this area, students' language of appraisal was not studied. It is here that the present study adds a fresh perspective to this body of work.

Theoretical Framework

The Appraisal Framework is an extension of M. A. K. Halliday's Systemic Functional Linguistics (SFL) theory (Halliday, 1994). The model emerged from work by functional linguists on the role of evaluation in narrative in the context of secondary school and workplace literacy. Their concern was to build a comprehensive framework of evaluative meanings that could be used systematically in discourse analysis (Martin, 2000, 2003). As Martin (2000) contends, "What ha[d] tended to be elided in SFL approaches [until then] ... is the semantics of evaluation—how the interlocutors are feeling, the judgements they make, and the value they place on the various phenomena of their experience" (p. 144). Since its inception, the Appraisal Framework has been applied to the analysis of spoken and written texts across a wide range of areas, including conversation (Eggins & Slade, 1997; Precht, 2003), institutional talk (Lipovsky, 2008), spoken academic discourse (Hood & Forey, 2005), academic writing (Hood, 2004a, 2004b, 2005, 2006), literacy (Rothery & Stenglin, 2000), media discourse (e.g. White, 1997, 1998, 2006; Martin, 2004), medical discourse (Jordens, 2002), and so on.

The Appraisal Framework describes the linguistic means by which individuals encode their feelings and beliefs (or attitudes), how they grade the strength of these feelings and sharpen or blur their utterances, and how they position themselves with regards to these values and possible respondents, hence the three sub-systems of Attitude, Graduation, and Engagement (see Figure 1). The system of Attitude especially is concerned with all types of evaluative assessments, both positive and negative (see Martin, 2000; White, 2002; Martin & Rose, 2003; Martin & White, 2005; or White, 2005, for further description). More specifically, it might entail how individuals share their feelings (e.g. how happy or unhappy, or satisfied or dissatisfied they are), assess people's behavior (their capacity, tenacity, and so on) and appraise the value of things and performances (e.g. how significant something is), hence the three categories of Affect for presenting emotional responses, Judgement for evaluating human behavior, and Appreciation for evaluating products and performances. These three categories are illustrated in the examples below (Attitudes are in bold):

- Affect: He **likes** teaching English.
- Judgement: He is a **brilliant** teacher.
- Appreciation: His classes are **exciting**.

Figure 1 System of Appraisal (adapted from Martin & Rose, 2003)

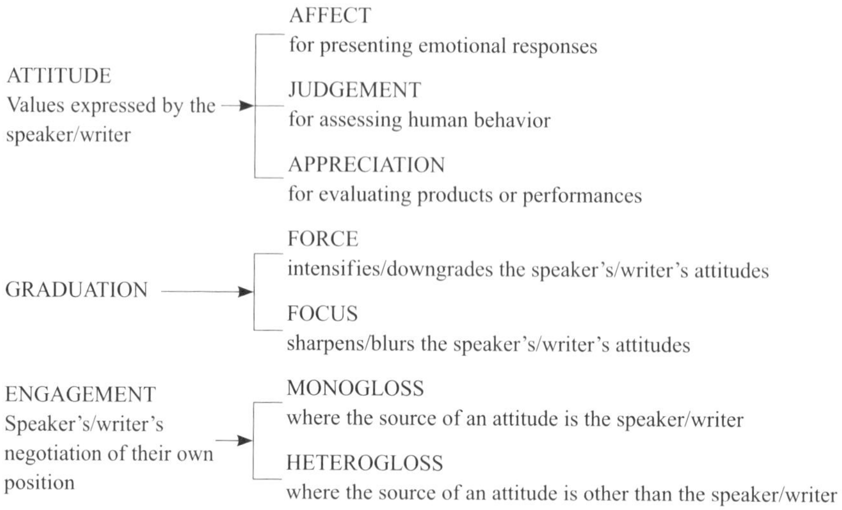

ATTITUDE
Values expressed by the
speaker/writer →

AFFECT
for presenting emotional responses

JUDGEMENT
for assessing human behavior

APPRECIATION
for evaluating products or performances

GRADUATION →

FORCE
intensifies/downgrades the speaker's/writer's attitudes

FOCUS
sharpens/blurs the speaker's/writer's attitudes

ENGAGEMENT
Speaker's/writer's
negotiation of their own
position →

MONOGLOSS
where the source of an attitude is the speaker/writer

HETEROGLOSS
where the source of an attitude is other than the speaker/writer

Each category of Attitude in turn includes a variety of subcategories. They are summarised in Figure 2. These categories will be drawn upon hereafter as required in the course of our analysis.

The system further distinguishes feelings that involve reactions to a "realis" stimulus (e.g. "she **liked** English") from intentions toward an "irrealis" stimulus (e.g. "she **wanted** to learn English"). It also differentiates "inscribed" Attitudes that are made explicitly, using attitudinal lexis (e.g. "a **knowledgeable** teacher"), from "invoked" Attitudes or "tokens" that are evoked through descriptions of one's experience (e.g. "a teacher who could answer all the questions that I asked").

Performance and the capacity of the performer are of course strongly connected. So a positive or negative Appreciation of a performance may imply a positive or negative Judgement of the performer, as in the following example:

Her pronunciation is **good** [+APPRECIATION: Valuation] [t, +JUDGEMENT: Capacity].

In this statement, "good" realizes the student's Valuation of her NNEST's pronunciation. In so doing, though, the student also provides a positive Judgement of her teacher's oral skills.

Lastly, Attitudes are gradable, so they can be amplified (as in "a <u>very</u> good teacher") or downgraded (as in "a teacher <u>a bit</u> boring"). Utterances

Figure 2   Subcategories of Attitude (adapted from Martin, 2000)

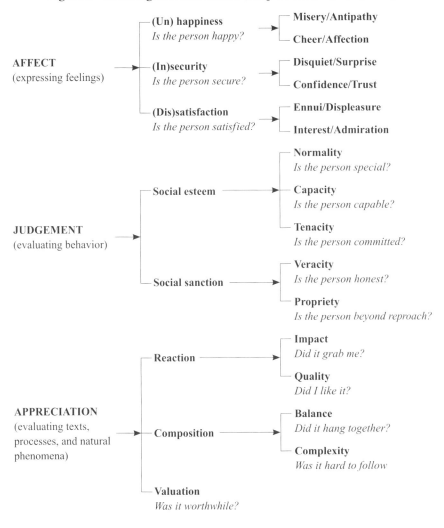

can also be sharpened (e.g. "a <u>real</u> teacher") or blurred (e.g. "<u>some kind of</u> teacher"). In the Appraisal system, this is referred to as Graduation (see Figure 3). Hood (2004a), Martin and White (2005), and Hood and Martin (2006) provide detailed descriptions of Graduation. The system thus provides an effective tool for analyzing attitudinal meanings. In the context of the present study, it is effectively used to investigate students' attitudes toward their NESTs and NNESTs.

Figure 3   System of Graduation (adapted from Martin & Rose, 2003)

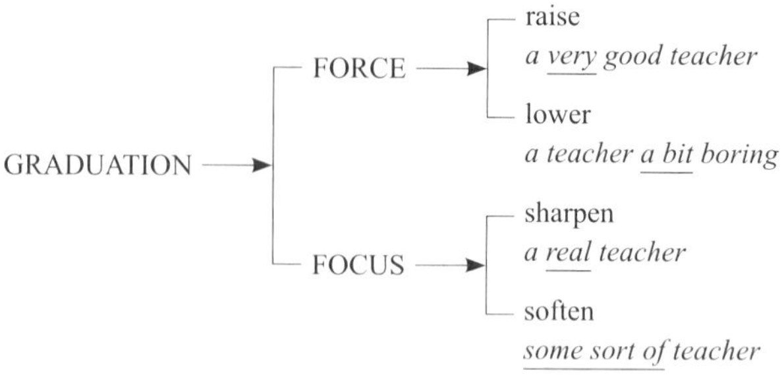

Results

The T1 and T2 essays were coded, counting every instance of Attitude (Affect, Judgement, and Appreciation) and Graduation (Force and Focus). Some students included in their essays narratives on non-native speakers who were not teachers or related their own experience of teaching Japanese to foreigners. These examples were not included in the analysis, and only evaluations pertaining to teachers and ALTs (Assistant Language Teachers, that is, native speakers of English who teach conversation classes in Japanese schools) were accounted for. Then, to give a better representation of the students' evaluations of their teachers, we found it necessary to differentiate instances of Judgement (Capacity). Thus, we distinguish in our discussion teachers' linguistic competence (in both Japanese and English) from their teaching ability.

The Appraisal analysis gave a detailed representation of the students' attitudes toward their NESTs and NNESTs. In the students' essays, emotional responses were infrequent, and most evaluations were applied to either the N/NESTs themselves (i.e. Judgements) or their performance (i.e. Appreciations). In the next section, we discuss their linguistic competences and teaching methodology, as well as some personal factors, presenting various examples taken from the students' essays.

Linguistic Competences

In their Judgements and Appreciations of NESTs' and NNESTs' linguistic competences, the students commented on their teachers' oral skills (listening and speaking/pronunciation), literacy skills (reading and writing), grammar, vocabulary, and knowledge of culture. Some students also commented on their N/NESTs' competence (or lack of competence) in the native language of their students.

Oral skills

We included in this category the teaching of listening and speaking/ pronunciation, as well as conversational skills. All the evaluations of the NESTs were positive, e.g.:

(1) Native speaker has **good** [+APP Valuation] sound of language [t, +JUD Capacity]. Student #9/T1[1]

(2) Of course her [NEST's] pronusation was <u>much</u> [GRA: Force: intensity] **better** [GRA: Force: intensity/+APP Valuation] than Japanese teachers [t, +JUD Capacity]. Student #18/T2

(3) Their conversations [NESTs'] are <u>so</u> [GRA: Force: intensity] **cool** [+APP Valuation]! [GRA: Force: intensity] Student #19/T1

NESTs' oral skills were viewed as "good", "natural", "real"—even "cool"! This view is supported by comment (2), which seems to imply that native speakers possess ideal skills (see "of course"). Note, however, that NESTs are evaluated through a comparative ("her pronusation was much **better**"), which does not preclude NNESTs' good pronunciation (see Mahboob & Lipovsky, 2007, for further discussion).

NNESTs, in contrast, received both positive and negative evaluations, e.g.:

(4) Her pronouncitation is <u>really</u> [GRA: Force: intensity] **good** [+APP Valuation] [t, +JUD Capacity]. Student #15/T1

This student valued her NNEST's pronunciation highly, as shown by the intensifier "really". A number of students, however, viewed their NNESTs' oral skills negatively, e.g.:

(5) They [NNESTs] sometimes speak like Japanese pronanciation [t, -JUD Incapacity]. Student #6/T2

(6) In Japanese school, we are tought English by non-natives teachers. Their pronanciation is <u>so</u> [GRA: Force: intensity] **bad** [-APP Reaction/t, -JUD

---

[1] The extracts from the essays are shown as written by the students. Numbers refer to students. *T1* refers to the first set of essays, *T2* to the second set. The coding for Attitudes is indicated in the brackets. *AFF* stands for *Affect*, *JUD* for *Judgement*, *APP* for *Appreciation*, and *GRA* for *Graduation*. "+" indicates a positive Attitude whereas "-" indicates a negative Attitude. The letter *t* for *token* indicates an evoked or non-explicit Attitude. Attitudes are marked in bold; Graduations are underlined.

Incapacity]. And we can't learn [t, -JUD Incapacity] listening, we are not used to listen from natives teachers [t, -JUD Incapacity]. so it is **hard** [-APP Reaction/t, -AFF Unhappiness] for us. When I came to U.S, I couldn't listen <u>a lot of</u> [GRA: Force: quantity: amount] words [t, -JUD Incapacity]. Student #4/T2

Example (6) highlights the connection between performance and ability, as the student's negative Appreciation of NNESTs' pronunciation of English ("their pronanciation is so bad") entailed a negative Judgement of their speaking skills. This in turn resulted in a series of negative Judgements of the student's listening skills ("we can't learn listening"; "we are not used to listen from natives teachers"; and "when I came to U.S, I couldn't listen a lot of words"). This also occasioned negative feelings on the part of the student ("it is hard for us"). This exemplifies how an Appraisal analysis provides more fine-tuned information than a Thematic analysis by bringing to light the impact of N/NESTs' competences on their students' competences, even highlighting students' feelings over the process.

Competence in the learners' native language

A number of comments dealt with N/NESTs' competence (or lack of competence) in their students' native tongue. Some students viewed this as an incentive for practicing their conversation skills in English, e.g.:

(7) This teacher [NEST] doesn't speak our language and understand what I say [t, -JUD Incapacity] so I must speak teacher's language and I'll become a **good** [+APP Valuation] speaker! [GRA: Force: intensity] Student #6/T1

This aspect did not emerge in Mahboob's (2003) study, since the essays that discussed the learners' experience in their own country were discarded. What is of particular interest to us within the scope of the present study, though, is that what would have been picked up as a deficiency in the Thematic analysis (NESTs do *not* speak Japanese and therefore *cannot* communicate in this language with their students) turns out to be an advantage, since it obliges learners to communicate exclusively in English, thus contributing to their progress. Note that the negative Judgement on the NEST ("this teacher doesn't speak our language and understand what I say") is explicitly linked to a positive Appreciation of the learner's skills ("so I must speak teacher's language and I'll become a good speaker!").

Conversely, some students viewed NESTs' lack of knowledge in their students' native language as an obstacle to learners' comprehension, e.g.:

(8) It is a **problem** [-APP Valuation] that we sometimes cannot figure it out only with explaining from native speakers [t, -JUD Incapacity] … So we need our mother tongue, Japanese to understand the meaning of words more clearly. Also, if we asked some questions to native speakers, they didn't answer them clearly [t, -JUD Incapacity]. Student #5/T2

This student appreciated negatively the fact that NESTs cannot provide explanations in the learners' native language, especially as far as the learning of vocabulary is concerned. NESTs' answers to their students' questions were also considered unclear, possibly because of the language difference. In effect, NESTs' inability to speak their students' tongue and answer their questions in that language puts the onus on the students. Mahboob (2003) does not discuss this aspect, since the participants in his study are intermediate and advanced students. Examples (7) and (8) also show the advantage of an Appraisal analysis over a Thematic analysis, as these examples highlight how some students can view a factor as an advantage, while others view the very same factor as a disadvantage.

Likewise, NNESTs' ability in their students' tongue was viewed as either impeding students' speaking skills, or, on the contrary, as facilitating their learning and understanding of English, as the two examples below illustrate:

(9) The best [GRA: Force: intensity] of **good** [+APP Valuation] things [about NNESTs] is to be able to speak same language with students [t, +JUD Capacity]. If we have a question, we can ask English or first language [t, +JUD Capacity]. If we cannot speak [t, -JUD Incapacity], first language is **better** [+APP Valuation/GRA: Force: intensity] than English. Student #6/T2

(10) When I talked to non-natives in no our language, and I found the language, I speaked our language and teacher may **help** [+JUD Capacity] us. but this help is **far** [GRA: Force: intensity] **from good** [-APP Valuation] speakers, I think. Student #6/T1

In example (9), NNESTs' ability in the students' native language is viewed as an advantage for language learning. However, in example (10), this ability is viewed as a disadvantage, since it might hinder learners' progress. Examples (9) and (10) highlight another instance when the Appraisal analysis proves more fine-tuned than the Thematic analysis, as it shows how the same factor can generate either a positive or a negative Appreciation.

Literacy skills

Students evaluated NNESTs' literacy skills (reading and writing) positively, e.g.;

   (11) He [NNEST] has **mastered** [JUD Cap/GRA: Force: Intensity] speaking, writing, and listening [t, +JUD Capacity]. Student #12/T1

   (12) My high school's English teacher can't speak English well [t, -JUD Incapacity]. But, I can learn **good** [+APP Valuation] writing at his class [t, +JUD Capacity]. Student #7/T1

This latter comment suggests that NNESTs can have good literacy teaching skills, independently of their ability in other skills. Another student wrote:

   (13) Some Americans cannot write in English in formal style or are confused between expressions for speaking and for writing [t, -JUD Incapacity]. Student #5/T2

These comments illustrate students' awareness that literacy skills are learned, and thus independent of other skills.

Grammar

     Students valued NNESTs' knowledge and teaching of grammar positively, e.g.:

   (14) His [NNEST's] grammer is **better** [GRA: Force: intensity/+APP Valuation] than native speaker in his university [t, +JUD Capacity]. Student #12/T1

   (15) I think it [NNEST's class]'s **good** [+APP Valuation] for us to teach grammer. Student #6/T2

Example (14) highlights the fact that NNESTs' linguistic competences can even surpass the NESTs'. Grammar is also the category in which NNESTs received the strongest comments in Mahboob's (2003) study.

     In the following extract, a student reflected on her NEST's teaching skills for grammar:

   (16) Someday I asked her [ALT] to teach grammar. But she said 'I don't know what should I teach you [t, -JUD Incapacity]'. I was very [GRA: Force: intensity] **surprised** [-AFF Insecurity] because I was thinking that people from English spoken country, they all can teach us perfectly [t, +JUD Capacity]. Student #18/T2

This comment illustrates that native speakers actually may not know about grammar until they learn how to teach it.

Vocabulary

Students stated that NESTs were good for learning vocabulary, e.g.:

(17) If native speakers teacher teaches English to students, they can learn English slang [t, +APP Valuation]. Student #17/T2

Example (8) above, however, highlights the fact that students may find it difficult to learn vocabulary from their NESTs because of NESTs' inability to explain the words in the students' native language. This of course is specific to an EFL context.

In contrast, evaluations of NNESTs were mixed, e.g.:

(18) She [NNEST] knows many [GRA: Force: quantity: amount] words which are very [GRA: Force: intensity] **difficult** [-APP Composition] [t, +JUD Capacity] therefore even natives don't know. Student #15/T2

(19) Certainly, if we **want** [AFF Desire] to be a **good** [+JUD Capacity] English speaker, it is **effective** [+APP Valuation] that we learn speaking English with native speakers. That is because there are a lot of [GRA: Force: quantity: amount] idioms or expressions that non-natives don't know in their English [t, -JUD Incapacity]. Student #5/T2

These comments exemplify how that the knowledge of slang and idioms distinguished NESTs from NNESTs.

Culture

A few comments dealt with the teaching of culture. Both NESTs and NNESTs received positive evaluations in this category, e.g.:

(20) They [NESTs] know any them histry and country very [GRA: Force: intensity] **good** [+APP Valuation] [t, +JUD Capacity]. so [GRA: Force: intensity] **good** [+APP Valuation]. Student #13/T1

(21) They [NNESTs] know about other country's cultures or their country's culture [t, +JUD Capacity]. Student #7/T2

Interestingly, two students viewed NNESTs' classes as an opportunity to learn about a third culture.

Teaching Methodology

Some students also commented on their teachers' teaching methodology. Only NNESTs were appraised in this category, always positively, e.g.:

(22) They [NNESTs] know which word we learned fast [t, +JUD Capacity]. Student #2/T2

(23) Non-natives teachers teach me how to learn second language, how to make friend in the country I don't know anything, and many other things [GRA: Force: quantity: amount] [t, +JUD Capacity]. Student #4/T2

(24) Non-natives have some **great** [GRA: Force: Intensity/+APP Valuation] necks [knacks] they prooted because they became the language teachers by doing their own necks, not learned when they were babies like native speakers do [t, +JUD Capacity]. And then, they can tell their students about that [t, +JUD Capacity]! [GRA: Force: intensity]. Student #19/T2

These comments show that NNESTs were attributed specific skills that stem from their own experience as language learners, and how students perceived that they can benefit from these skills.

Personal Factors

Students also commented on personal factors related to their teachers. Interestingly, all these comments are in support of NNESTs. Factors include NNESTs' empathy with their students and their tenacity in learning English.

Empathy with the students

Students perceived their NNESTs as having empathy with them, since they had experienced the same difficulties as them in learning English. The following comments illustrate this point:

(25) I think that non-natives teachers is **better** [+JUD: Capacity/GRA: Force: intensity] than natives teachers. Because non-natives teachers are knowing that we can not understand language which we are learning easy [t, +JUD Capacity]. Student #4/T1

(26) Non-native speakers [...] know which word we learned fast [+JUD Capacity]. They know what kind of words we can use [t, +JUD Capacity]. They **understand** [+JUD Capacity] us. Student #2/T2

(27) I also think someone who study language very [GRA: Force: intensity] **hard** [+JUD Tenacity], they can teach [t, +JUD Capacity] it very [GRA: Force: intensity] **well** [+APP Valuation]. Because, they know how to learn it is **the best** [+JUD Capacity/GRA: Force: intensity]. And they also know students feeling [t, +JUD Capacity]. #20T1

These comments highlight students' perception that NNESTs' empathy vis-à-vis their students impacts their teaching. However, students also seemed to value the feeling of empathy itself (c.f. "they also know students feeling"; "they understand us").

Tenacity

A number of students commented on their teachers' hard work. Some recognized that proficiency in the language is not sufficient to make a good teacher. In the following example, the student states that tenacity is a characteristic of both NESTs and NNESTs who are good teachers:

(28) The most [GRA: Force: intensity] **important** [+APP Valuation] thing is not native or non-native. If you **want** [AFF Desire] to be a **good** [+JUD Capacity] language teacher, you have to spent a lot of time [GRA: Force: Extent: Scope: Time] on studying [t, +JUD Tenacity] language. What you need is **efforts** [+JUD Tenacity]. Student #15/T1

Students recognized though that greater effort and tenacity were necessary on the part of NNESTs, as shown in the following comment:

(29) I think that if we [NNESTs] **effort** [+JUD Tenacity] to learn English, we can teach [t, +JUD Capacity]. It may be so [GRA: Force: intensity] **hard** [-APP Reaction] [t, -AFF Unhappiness] but I think it is **important** [+APP Valuation] for non-natives speaker to try [GRA: Focus: Fulfilment] **their best** [+JUD Tenacity/GRA: Force: intensity]. Student #12/T1

This evaluation not only underlines the need for tenacity, but also highlights the emotional impact on NNESTs through a token of Affect, stressed by an intensifier ("It may be so hard"). Again, this is additional information gained from an Appraisal analysis over a Thematic analysis.

A number of students wrote narratives in their essays highlighting their NNESTs' tenacity to exemplify how they had become proficient in English, hence good teachers. The extract below presents an example of a text where Tenacity is strongly represented. In this extract, the student provides a particular example of an NNEST whom she is familiar with to illustrate how non-natives can achieve proficiency in their non-native language (exemplified by the NNEST receiving a scholarship to study abroad, being first in her English class in Great Britain, and eventually becoming a teacher of English in Japan):

(30) I have a **good** [+JUD Capacity] English teacher ho is non-native speaker in my high school. She speaks very [GRA: Force: intensity] **well** [+APP

Valuation] even though she is non-native speaker [t, +JUD Capacity]. One day, she talked me about her exchange student's life in British. She has been to British for only three months as an exchange student. when she was twenty years old. She has **wanted** [AFF Desire] to go abroad since she was in junior high school. But **sadly** [-AFF Unhappiness], she was so [GRA: Force: intensity] **poor** [-JUD Normality] that she couldn't go abroad. When she was in university, she study English very [GRA: Force: intensity] **hard** [+JUD Tenacity] she found an information which said that if she pass the examination, she could be an exchange student for free. She was very [GRA: Force: intensity] **good** [+APP Valuation] at writing in English [t, +JUD Capacity] at that time. But she had one big [GRA: Force: quantity] **problem** [-APP Valuation], "speaking English" [t, -JUD Incapacity]. She has never talked native English speakers. "I tried to speak to foreign people when I found them at the station, park and even at the hospital [GRA: Force: Extent: Scope: Space] [t, +JUD Tenacity]." She said. She passed the examination [t, +JUD Capacity] with these great [GRA: Force: quantity: amount] **efforts** [+JUD Tenacity]. But she had only three months. She kept studying very [GRA: Force: intensity] **hard** [+JUD Tenacity]. In British university, she got first prise in English class [t, +JUD Capacity]. After she went abroad, she took an examination to be an English teacher. But she didn't stop [GRA: Force: Extent: Scope: Time] studying [t, +JUD Tenacity]. She studied English **harder and harder** [GRA: Force: intensity] [+JUD Tenacity]. She knows many [GRA: Force: quantity: amount] words which are very [GRA: Force: intensity] **difficult** [-APP Composition] therefore even natives don't know [t, +JUD Capacity]. She showed me that everybody can be a **good** [+JUD Capacity] teacher with great [GRA: Force: Quantity: Amount] **efforts** [+JUD Tenacity]. Student #15/T2

Our coding of inscribed Attitude, that is, using explicit attitudinal lexis, is outlined in Table 1: Evaluations Focus on the NNEST's Linguistic Skills and Her Determination to Improve Her English.

Instances of invoked Attitude are outlined in Table 2 (with "t" marking ideational tokens/evoked evaluations). These ideational tokens extend the positive prosody of Tenacity and Capacity inscribed through the explicit attitudinal lexis. It culminates in the evaluation that "everybody can be a good teacher with great efforts". Note also that the student uses Graduation to either intensify the Judgements of Tenacity (e.g. "study English very hard"; "great efforts"; "kept studying very hard"; "studied English harder and harder"), or to evoke Attitude through the grading of non-attitudinal terms ("I tried to speak to foreign people when I

Table 1 Inscribed Attitude in Extract 30

Appraising items	Affect	Judgement	Appreciation	Appraised
good		+capacity		English teacher
very well			+valuation	NNEST's speaking skills
wanted	+desire			go abroad
sadly	-happiness			being too poor to afford going abroad
so poor		-normality		being too poor to afford going abroad
very hard		+tenacity		NNEST's studying
very good			+valuation	NNEST's writing skills
big problem			-valuation	NNEST's speaking skills
great efforts		+tenacity		passing the examination
very hard		+tenacity		NNEST's studying
harder and harder		+tenacity		NNEST's studying
very difficult			-composition	words
good		+capacity		teacher
great efforts		+tenacity		NNEST's studying

Table 2 Invoked Attitude in Extract 30

Appraising items	Affect	Judgement	Appreciation	Appraised
speaks very well		t, +capacity		NNEST
very good at writing in English		t, +capacity		NNEST
she had one big problem "speaking English"		t, -capacity		NNEST
I tried to speak to foreign people [...] at the hospital		t, +tenacity		NNEST
she passed the examination		t, +capacity		NNEST
she got first prise		t, +capacity		NNEST
she didn't stop studying		t, +tenacity		NNEST
she knows many words which are very difficult		t, +capacity		NNEST

found them at the station, park and even at the hospital"; "she didn't stop studying") (see Lipovsky & Mahboob, 2008, for further discussion of the students' use of Graduation). Thus, the NNEST is construed as determined to improve her English and rewarded in her efforts as she becomes quite competent in the language, knowing "many words which are very difficult therefore even natives don't know". The student assumes her reader(s) to align with the idea that native speakers are more proficient in their own tongue than non-native speakers. The word "even" challenges this view, and thereby sets out to demonstrate that tenacity is rewarded: "everybody can be a good teacher with great efforts".

NNESTs as role models

An effect of NNESTs' success in their language learning is that it inspires their students. The following comment illustrates this point:

> (31) They [NNESTs] became **great** [GRA: Force: intensity/+JUD Capacity] speakers of the specific [GRA: focus] language even they are not native speakers. To learn the language which is not first language for students by the teachers who are not native, students can be **encouraged** [+AFF Happiness]. Student #19/T2

Likewise, NNESTs' tenacity is a model that their students are keen to follow:

> (32) I learned her if we think we **want** [AFF Desire] to be something and study **hard** [+JUD Tenacity], our **dream** [AFF: Desire] come **true** [+APP Valuation]. Student #1/T1

Enjoyment

The last category of comments concerns the pleasure or enjoyment that can derive from learning a language. The following evaluation exemplifies this point:

> (33) I think that non-natives are also **good** [+JUD Capacity] teachers. Because they can teach us the **pleasure** [+APP Reaction] of learning new language! [GRA: Force: intensity] If there had not been Japanese English teacher, I would never know **the pleasure** [+APP Reaction] of learning English. Student #19/T1

The absence of similar comments about NESTs does not mean that no pleasure can be derived from attending their classes:

(34) We [NEST and student] had <u>really</u> [GRA: Force: intensity] **good** [APP Val] time together. Student #18/T2

Discussion

This study highlighted that students perceive NESTs and NNESTs as having complementary strengths. NESTs were usually praised for their oral skills (in particular their pronunciation and conversation) and knowledge of vocabulary (including slang and idioms). However, this did not preclude a number of NNESTs from being praised for these skills as well. Conversely, NNESTs attracted positive evaluations for their teaching of literacy skills and knowledge and teaching of grammar, highlighting the fact that these skills are independent of linguistic skills, as they can be learned. NNESTs were also appraised positively for their teaching methodology, stemming from their own experience and skills acquired as language learners, from which their students could benefit. Likewise, students felt that their NNESTs had empathy for them, since they had experienced the difficulties of learning English, and their tenacity to master the language became a model some students were keen to emulate. N/NESTs' competence (or lack of competence) in their students' native tongue (L1) was viewed as either an advantage or a liability. Some students viewed their teacher's lack of knowledge in their L1 as an incentive for honing their own speaking skills in English, while other students viewed it as impeding comprehension, as the teacher's explanations were at all times provided in English. The availability of L1 use could either deter students from asking questions in English and prevent them from progressing in their L2 or facilitate their comprehension of their teacher's explanations. Significantly, the Appraisal analysis highlighted the strong link that students perceive between their teachers' linguistic skills (pronunciation and knowledge of students' L1) and their own performance.

Regarding the language of evaluation specifically, in their essays the students generally shunned negative evaluations to favor positive evaluations of their N/NESTs. The data contain few explicit negative Attitudes. When they do, negative Judgements and Appreciations often derive from negations; that is, the student negates a positive performance, rather than stating directly that it is bad, e.g.:

(35) My high school's English teacher can't speak English well [t, -JUD Capacity].

(36) My English teacher does **not good** [-APP Valuation] accent [t, -JUD Capacity].

In (35), the student states that her teacher "can't speak English well", rather than writing that s/he speaks English badly. Likewise in (36), the student states that her teacher "does not good accent", rather than stating that her accent is bad. This mitigation denotes some reticence on the part of the students to be critical of their teachers, although there are a few exceptions (as in example (6) above). Another way students mitigated their evaluations was to use invoked Appraisal, as in the following example:

> (37) They [NNESTs] sometimes speak like Japanese pronanciation [t, -JUD Incapacity].

In this example, rather than criticizing NNESTs directly through explicit negative lexis, the student chose to invoke her criticism through a comparison. Note also that this token of Judgement actually only states that NNESTs' pronunciation is non-native. Students' use of invoked Attitudes through the expression of ideational meanings also demonstrates an attempt to be objective rather than subjective.

Example (37) highlights another particularity of students' Appraisal of their N/NESTs in that it was commonly comparative. Here is another example:

> (38) Of course her [NEST's] pronusation was much [GRA: Force: intensity] **better** [GRA: Force: intensity/+APP Valuation] than Japanese teachers [t, +JUD Capacity].

In (38), the NEST's pronunciation is qualified as "much better than Japanese teachers", rather than "good". The Valuation "much better" points at a criticism against NNESTs' pronunciation, although the fact that criticism is merely implied makes it impossible to determine whether the NNESTs' pronunciation is bad or just not as good as NESTs'. Of course, this tendency to compare NESTs' with NNESTs' skills could be attributed to the nature of the task that the students were given.

Students' evaluations of their N/NESTs were not only mostly positive but also highly graduated, e.g.:

> (39) Her pronounceation is very [GRA: Force: intensity] **good** [+APP Valuation]
> (40) They became **great** [GRA: Force: intensity/+JUD Capacity] speakers of the specific language even they are not native speakers.
> (41) Their conversations [NESTs'] are so [GRA: Force: intensity] **cool** [+APP Valuation]! [GRA: Force: intensity] Student #19/T1

In (39), the pre-modifying intensifier "very" amplifies the positive Valuation of the teacher's pronunciation; alternatively, the teacher's pronunciation could have been described as "good" or "kind of good". In (40), the intensifier is fused within a lexical item that also serves a semantic function, as "great" can be unpacked as "very" + "good". In (41), the intensification is realized through the pre-modifying intensifier "so" as well as the exclamation point. Thus, the students not only positively appraised their teachers but often also amplified their positive evaluations of them (see Lipovsky & Mahboob, 2008, for further discussion of students' use of Graduation).

This analysis also revealed the advantage of an Appraisal analysis over a Thematic analysis, as the former appeared more fine-tuned than the latter. For instance, the Appraisal analysis highlighted aspects of N/NESTs' (lack of) knowledge that are doubled-sided, such as when it showed that NESTs' lack of knowledge in their students' L1 and NNESTs' knowledge in their L1 could each be viewed either as an advantage or a drawback.

The Appraisal analysis also highlighted affective issues that had been downplayed by the Thematic analysis. Students in examples (6) and (29) above reported that learning a foreign language can be "hard". This explicit negative Valuation actually brings to light more private affective issues, as shown by the double-coding as a token of Unhappiness, highlighting how daunting mastering a foreign language can at times appear. Examples (31) and (32), in contrast, highlighted that students can be encouraged by their NNEST's success in learning another language.

Another benefit of the Appraisal analysis comes from the fact that it takes into account the co-text of the evaluations. Students' evaluations about their N/NESTs did not come in a void. They were often attached to narratives (as in example (31)). The analysis highlighted that students' Appraisals of their NESTs and NNESTs often recurred throughout their essays, with long strings of text devoted to a given evaluation, with the result of an ongoing cumulative effect. Furthermore, the students often amplified their evaluations through intensifications or repetitions. In other words, "the volume is turned up so that the prosody makes a bigger splash which reverberates through the surrounding discourse" (Martin & White, 2005, p. 20). This highlights the advantage of Appraisal over Thematic analysis, as Appraisal "unfolds dynamically to engage us, to get us on side, not with one appeal, but through a spectrum of manoeuvres that work themselves out phase by phase" (Martin & Rose, 2003, p. 56). As such, the analysis of extended units of meanings underlined the semantic prosody of the students' essays and provided more fine-tuned information.

Conclusion

The present study supports other studies that found that students do not necessarily prefer being taught by NESTs or NNESTs but rather value the combination of their qualities, as shown in this comment:

> (42) It is not that natives teachers know **better** [JUD: Capacity/GRA: Force: intensity] than non-natives teachers. So I think that theaching to each teachers is **important** [APP Valuation] things for us. Student #4/T1

At a time when communication in English more often concerns L2 speakers than L1 speakers and the status of the native speaker of English becomes less significant, this analysis challenges the view that solely a native speaker model should be the goal of language learning and teaching. Importantly, the analysis of students' language of Appraisal in their evaluations of their N/NESTs also brought a new perspective to the existing body of literature, as it highlighted not only *what* the students said and thought about their N/NESTs, but also *how* they said it, providing an added fine-tuned perspective on the topic.

Appendix

Examples of categories from Mahboob and Griffin (2006):

Linguistic Factors

Oral Skills

Positive Comment NEST
I wanna learn English by native speakers because I wanna be like a native speakers. Their conversations are so cool! Non-native's conversations are not real ... (TS: T1)

Negative Comment NNEST
And non-native speakers is dificult. I think non-native speakers no beautiful. I think native speakers is natural. non-native speakers is no natural ... (MT: T1)

Grammar

Positive Comment NNEST
... It we want to learn grammatical English, non-natives are better ... (ES: T1)

Writing

Positive Comment NNEST

My high school's English teacher can't speak English well but, I can learn good writing at his class ... (ME: T1)

Negative Comment NEST
... And, my English school's teachers are all American and Canadian. They teach me writing not so much ... (ME: T1)

Culture

Positive Comment NEST
... natives teachers teach me many slangs, American culture, and about American ... (AKA: T2)

Teaching Styles

Ability to Answer Questions:

Negative Comment NEST
... if we asked some questions to native speakers, they didn't answer them clearly ... (ES: T2)

Teaching Methodology

Positive Comment NNEST
I think that non-natives are also good teachers because they can teach us the pleasure of learning new language! If there had not been Japanese English teacher, I would never know the pleasure of learning English ... (TS: T1)

Personal Factors

Experience as an L2 Learner

Positive Comment NNEST
I think that non-natives can also be efficient teachers. Because this four month, we learned with non-native and native. Sometimes our accent were not correct, but non-native understood what we want to say more than native. When we talked, they understood more than hostfamily. Non-native speakers know how to learn English from teacher. They know which word we learned fast. They know what kind of words we can use. They understand us.(AM: T2)

Hard Work

Positive Comment NNEST
I think that non-native speaker can be also be efficient teachers. Because. I think that if we effort to learn English, we can teach. It may be so hard but I think

it is important for non-natives speaker to try their best. My high school English teacher is non-native speaker, but he have tried his best for twenty years. So he is as good as native speaker ... (MHO: T1)

> Negative Comment NEST
> For example, if you native teachers, you haven't to study English very hard. Because they were born in America. That's they have spoken English ... (SK: T1)

Affect

> Positive Comment NNEST
> ... how to make friend in the country I don't know anything, and many other things. And non-natives teachers support us, when we have homesich or something ... (AKA: T2)

References

Benke, E., & Medgyes, P. (2005). Differences in teaching behaviour between native and non-native speaker teachers: As seen by the learners. In E. Llurda (Ed.), *Non-native language teachers: Perceptions, challenges, and contributions to the profession* (pp. 195–216). New York: Springer.

Eggins, S., & Slade, D. (1997). *Analysing casual conversation.* London: Cassell.

Halliday, M. A. K (1994). *An introduction to functional grammar* (2nd edition). London: Edward Arnold.

Hood, S. (2004a). Appraising research: Taking a stance in academic writing. Unpublished doctoral dissertation, University of Technology, Sydney.

Hood, S. (2004b). Managing attitude in undergraduate academic writing: A focus on the introductions to research reports. In L. Ravelli & R. Ellis (Eds). *Analysing academic writing: Contextualised frameworks* (pp. 24–44). London: Continuum.

Hood, S. (2005). What is evaluated and how in academic research writing?: The co-patterning of attitude and field. *Australian Review of Applied Linguistics Series, 19,* 23–40.

Hood, S. (2006). The persuasive power of prosodies: Radiating values in academic writing. *Journal of English for Academic Purposes, 5*(1), 37–49.

Hood, S., & Forey, G. (2005). Introducing a conference paper: Getting interpersonal with your audience. *Journal of English for Academic Purposes, 4,* 291–306.

Hood, S., & Martin, J. R. (2006). Invoking attitude: The play of graduation in appraising discourse. In R. Hasan, C. Matthiessen & J. Webster (Eds.), *Continuing discourse on language: A functional perspective* (pp. 737–762). London: Equinox.

Jordens, C. F. C. (2002). Reading spoken stories for values: A discursive study of cancer survivors and their professional carers. Unpublished doctoral dissertation, University of Sydney, Sydney.

Lasagabaster, D., & Sierra, J. M. (2005). What do students think about the pros and cons of having a native speaker teacher? In E. Llurda (Ed.) *Non-native language teachers: Perceptions, challenges, and contributions to the profession* (pp. 217–242). New York: Springer.

Lipovsky, C. (2008). Constructing affiliation and solidarity in job interviews. *Discourse and Communication, 2*(4), 411–432.

Lipovsky, C., & Mahboob, A. (2008). The semantics of graduation: Examining ESL learners' use of graduation over time. In A. Mahboob & N. Knight (Eds.), *Questioning linguistics* (pp. 224–240). Newcastle: Cambridge Scholars Publishing.

Mahboob, A. (2003). Status of nonnative English speaking teachers in the United States. Unpublished doctoral dissertation, Indiana University, Bloomington.

Mahboob, A. (2004). Native or nonnative: What do the students think? In L. Kamhi-Stein (Ed.), *Learning and teaching from experience: Perspectives on nonnative English-speaking professionals* (pp. 121–147). Ann Arbor: University of Michigan Press.

Mahboob, A., & Griffin, R. B. (March, 2006). *Learner perspectives of native and non-native teachers*. Presentation given at the Annual TESOL Convention, Tampa, FL.

Mahboob, A., & Lipovsky, C. (2007). Examining attitudes towards NNESTs: A comparison of a thematic vs. an appraisal analysis. In C. Gitsaki (Ed.), *Language and languages: Global and local tensions* (pp. 292–306). Newcastle: Cambridge Scholars Publishing.

Martin, J. R. (2000). Beyond exchange: APPRAISAL systems in English. In S. Hunston & G. Thompson (Eds.), *Evaluation in text: Authorial stance and the construction of discourse* (pp. 142–175). Oxford: Oxford University Press.

Martin, J. R. (2003). Introduction. In M. Macken-Horarik & J. R. Martin (Eds.), *Text, special issue—Negotiating heteroglossia: Social perspectives on evaluation* (pp. 171–182). Berlin & New York: Mouton de Gruyter.

Martin, J. R. (2004). Mourning: How we get aligned. *Discourse & Society, 15*(2–3), 321–344.

Martin, J. R., & Rose, D. (2003). *Working with discourse: Meaning beyond the clause*. London & New York: Continuum.

Martin, J. R., & White, P. R. R. (2005). *The language of evaluation: Appraisal in English*. New York: Palgrave Macmillan.

Moussu, L. (2006). *Native and non-native English-speaking English as a second language teachers: Student attitudes, teacher self-perceptions, and intensive English program administrator beliefs and practices*. Unpublished doctoral dissertation, Purdue University, West Lafayette.

Precht, K. (2003). Stance moods in spoken English: Evidentiality and affect in British and American conversation. *Text, 23*, 239–257.

Rothery, J., & Stenglin, M. (2000). Interpreting literature: The role of APPRAISAL. In L. Unsworth (Ed.), *Researching language in schools and functional linguistic perspectives* (pp. 222–244). London: Cassell.

White, P. R. R. (1997). Death, disruption and the moral order: The narrative impulse in massmedia 'hard news' reporting. In F. Christie & J. Martin (Eds.), *Genres and institutions: Social processes in the workplace and school* (pp. 101–133). London: Cassell.

White, P. R. R. (1998). Telling media tales: The news story as rhetoric. Unpublished doctoral dissertation, University of Sydney, Sydney.

White, P. R. R. (2002). Appraisal—The language of evaluation and stance. In J. Verschueren, J.-O. Oestman, J. Blommaert & C. Bulcaen (Eds.), *The handbook of pragmatics* (pp. 1–26). Amsterdam & Philadelphia: John Benjamins.

White, P. R. R. (2005). *Appraisal website.* http://www.grammatics.com/appraisal/. Accessed 20 March 2009.

White, P. R. R. (2006). Evaluative semantics and ideological positioning in journalistic discourse: A new framework for analysis. In I. Lassen, J. Strunck, & T. Vestergaard (Eds.), *Mediating ideology in text and image: Ten critical studies* (pp. 37–67). Amsterdam: John Benjamins.

Chapter 8

English: The Industry

Mahboob, A. (2011). English: The industry. *Journal of Postcolonial Cultures and Societies*, 2(4), 46–61.

Introduction

One might wonder what the title of this chapter implies. What does one mean when one says English—the industry? Most people know English as a language, perhaps as a global language. Why industry, then? As this chapter will outline, English is not only a language. There are a range of commercial, economic, and industrial interests that are affiliated to it. It is these interests that we will call 'industry' in this paper. In particular, this chapter will focus on how the English language relates to the interests of corporations and governments, who use the language to make money and to promote certain beliefs and practices. The chapter will also highlight some of the politics that arise as a result of this 'marketing' and 'industrialization' of English. The chapter will consider how various nationalistic and political agendas are related to English, the industry, and how they work in tandem to create a particular linguistic hegemony (i.e., dominance that is mistaken by most, including the dominated, to be fair and natural).

Before we look at the development and establishment of English as an industry, it is important to share a broad introduction to the rise of English as a global language. This broad introduction will serve to help us understand some of the industrial interests tied to the language in later parts of this chapter. While the history of the English language can be traced back to well over 1,000 years, English started becoming a global language over the last 400 years or so as the English people started conquering and colonizing different parts of the world. As English expanded its geographical presence, it was adopted in different parts of the world in different ways. In certain parts of the world, for example, Australia, Canada, New Zealand, and the United States of America, English-speaking people settled in large numbers, killed and/or removed the local inhabitants, and formed their own societies. These settled varieties of English, along with British English, are what we now consider 'native' varieties of English. Next, we have places where the English colonized the people and governed the lands through a group of locals. The English language, in these contexts, was seen as the language of power and locals who aspired to work for the government (British) or to achieve official recognition strived to learn it. In the postcolonial era, many of these countries maintained English as an official language. Examples of current nation states where English was introduced through colonization and has been maintained include: Bangladesh, India, Kenya, Pakistan, the Philippines, Singapore, etc. The English language has been used for hundreds of years in these countries and has become 'nativized' or 'indigenized' (Kachru, 1992). Then, we have countries that were settled by the English and became hubs for slave trade and settlement. For example, many Caribbean islands served as destination for slaves brought in from various parts of Africa, who spoke different languages. These people developed new languages over time and used English as the lexifier language (the language that supplies a large proportion of the vocabulary). These languages are referred to as creole languages, but (when lexified by English) can be considered varieties of English. Finally, with the current political and economic power of the English-speaking countries, English is being learnt in most countries as a foreign language. Each of these processes that accompanied the spread of English has had an impact on the language and has contributed to the recognition of English as a global language. With this growth and recognition of English, a range of industries that contribute to and support the English language have emerged. In this paper, we will explore what this English industry is and how it relates to various economic, socio-political and educational issues.

English—the Industry

In the previous section, we outlined a short history of the evolution of the English language into a global language. It was pointed out that English is now learnt and used pretty much all around the world. As English was (and is) learnt in many parts of the world as an additional language, the learners need teachers, teaching material, and language tests, etc. This need for teachers and material has led to a development of a large number of local, national, and multinational corporations that train and produce these human and material resources. In addition to the export of these resources, there are large numbers of non-English-speaking migrants who move to English-speaking countries: as students, workers, or refugees. These individuals need to have appropriate English language skills to be able to operate effectively in their new English-dominant environments. This contributes to the demand for an English language industry. Estimates suggest that this English industry is worth billions of dollars. According to estimates, the English language textbook industry alone is worth over £5 billion. Note that this figure is ten years old. Since then, the number of English language learners has increased considerably and the age at which English is introduced to children in schools has been lowered in several countries (e.g., in Japan, South Korea, Saudi Arabia). This has resulted in additional demands for English language teaching materials. It also suggests that the amount quoted above would have multiplied over the last decade. Note also that this amount does not include the worth of the English language testing and teaching/teacher development industries, which would add a considerable amount to the figures quoted.

As we consider the rise of the English language and its use across the world, one of the factors that has supported and fuelled this is the assumption that English is the language of modernization and development. As English was the language of the empire and is the language of some of the most powerful, industrialized, and developed nations (USA and the UK), it is assumed that one must learn the language of these countries to understand how these developed countries operate and succeed. The goal, as people from the developing nations see it, is to become 'developed' by learning from these countries. This desire to develop leads to the need to access the literature and research being produced in these countries. This requires the ability to read, write and communicate in English, which, in turn, leads to a belief that English is 'the' language of science, technology, and development. This belief is fuelled by the fact that the language in which access to the needed literature is available is English. Over time, this belief has become an assumption, perhaps even an axiom, that everyone shares and accepts as a given—something that does not need to be questioned or challenged. The extent of this belief can be gauged by looking at the results of a study that I conducted in Pakistan a few years ago (Mahboob, 2002). 98.8% of the participants in the study stated that it was important to study English. When prodded, they gave the following reasons for wanting to learn English: English is the language of education, science, technology, and development; English is essential for professional growth; and English is a global language. In contrast to this, only 89.4% of the participants believed that it was important to study Urdu (the national language of Pakistan) and only 44% of the participants stated that it was important to study their mother tongue (if other than Urdu). The results document how the participants' belief that English is 'the' language for education and that other languages (including their national language and/or mother tongue) are not as important in education. A further result from the same study indicates that while 94.4% of the participants stated that English should be the medium of instruction for university education, only 26.5% of the participants supported Urdu and 0% (no one) supported mother tongues (other than Urdu). These figures further support the argument being presented in this chapter that there is an assumption that English is the language of development, which is accessed through (higher) education.

The belief that development comes through modelling developed nations leads people to learn through the literature being produced in English by the developed nations. In fact, not only do English-speaking countries produce literature in English, but also other non-English speakers in the 'developed' and 'developing' countries publish in English. In many universities around the world, academic performance of researchers is measured by their publications in 'international' journals—journals that tend to be published in English. As a result of this large body of research and other academic material being published in English, there is not only a demand for English language textbooks, but also books and material on other subjects in English. This contributes to the status of English and opens up additional markets for publishers. The importance of this industry can be gauged if we note how multinational publishers produce 'global' editions of their books for international markets (such as for India or China). One reason that these publishers produce cheaper editions to cater to international markets (that cannot afford American or European prices) is to make sure that their revenues are not threatened by copyright violations. Since these markets are very large, selling the books at a reduced price can still result in large profits because of the volume of sales. This global demand for textbooks in English (and of English) shows how deeply embedded the value of English is around the world. Given that this belief leads to considerable profits for the publishing companies that are based in English-speaking countries, it serves their interests to perpetuate the myth that Western knowledge is the road to development and that development and English are intrinsically related. And, to further maintain the power of Anglo-Englishes (and speakers of these dialects), they contribute to myths that suggest that only Standard English can be used for global communication and publications, as local variations may lead to incomprehensibility and miscommunication.

The Politics of a 'Standard' Language

In addition to the myth that the road to development lies through English, a second myth that is perpetuated through the English industry is the myth of a 'standard' English language. This can be seen by examining a number of key products in the field, including grammar books, textbooks, and language tests. This section of the chapter will consider each of these in some detail. This myth also serves the interests of a small group of people who use this 'standardized' dialect of English as their 'native' language, as will be noted in this section and then developed in the following one.

The current language teaching practices aim to teach learners of English—in all contexts—to reflect the patterns of language as used by native speakers of the language. This is done through codifying a particular dialect of the language and calling it 'standard' English. It is important to note that in linguistics, there is no technical difference between a dialect and a standard language. Nor is there any linguistic difference that makes one dialect better than another. A standard language is a dialect that is recognized as an 'official' representation of a range of dialects that collectively form a language. What we call a standard language is a dialect that has been selected, studied, and codified for education, media, and other official purposes. The recognition of a particular dialect for these purposes is usually a political decision and is given on the basis of some political or socio-economic factors (relating to the speakers of that dialect). No particular dialect (or language for that matter) is linguistically better or worse than any other. All languages can carry the meanings that their speakers intend to make through them, and, if necessary, can evolve to make new meanings. However, regardless of this observation by linguists, the English language industry markets Standard English as the 'correct' way of using English (and English as being 'the' language of science and development). It ignores evidence that indicates that even monolingual mother tongue speakers of English speak the language using a range of dialects that may or may not reflect the usage prescribed through 'standard' English. While these variations are labeled as dialects in the case of native speakers, the same (or other) variations used by English language learners and those who speak a different variety of English (e.g., Pakistani English or Nigerian English) are marked as wrong.

The codification and teaching of Standard English is carried out through grammar books and other textbooks and teaching resources.

The grammar books and textbooks employed to teach Standard English use what we call a prescriptive (or pedagogical) grammar. Prescriptive grammars tell us what 'correct' and 'incorrect' usage of language are and how to use language 'properly'. To understand this better, let us consider the following example: prescriptive grammars state that we should not split infinitives, i.e., we should not insert an adverb in between a word group such as '*to conclude*'. This rule is taught in schools around the world. However, if we look at how language is actually used by people, we will note that this rule cannot be supported by actual language data. We often come across constructions such as: '*to quickly conclude*', '*to boldly conclude*', and '*to finally conclude*'. In all three of the examples just cited, the to-infinitives are broken up by an insertion of an adverb. Prescriptive grammars prohibit this; however, language samples collected from users of English do not support this rule. This shows that prescriptive grammars do not necessarily reflect how language is used by the speakers of that language.

The example above is based on data from 'native' speakers. As was outlined in the introduction to this chapter, English today is actually used around the world and in some contexts, e.g., ex-British colonies and English-based creoles, has a very long tradition of usage. The English used in these contexts reflects a wide range of deviations from Standard English. For example, the following two examples from my work on Pakistani English show how Pakistani English differs from Standard British English:

> Pakistani English: I am seeing the sky from here.
> British English: I can see the sky from here.
>
> Pakistani English: Public-dealing office
> British English: An office which deals with the public

Both examples show syntactic variations between Pakistani and Standard British English. Research from other varieties of English also documents such variation at all linguistic levels: phonology, morphology, lexis, syntax, semantics, and pragmatics. Thus, although the evidence overwhelmingly shows that language variation is a natural linguistic characteristic, grammar and other textbooks present language as a set of static structures—something that even 'native' speaker data cannot always support.

Another notable observation about the construction of the native speaker myth is that it reflects English as spoken by middle-class White speakers of the language. Being the politically dominant group in BANA

(Britain, Australia, and North America) countries, their dialect is used to 'codify' and 'standardize' the language. Other speakers of English are marginalized. For example, the English spoken by Afro-Americans or the Chicano speakers in the United States is not used for the purposes of codification of Standard American English. One example of the difference between Standard English and Afro-American English is in the use of double negatives. Double negatives (I ain't gonna do nothing.) are considered inappropriate in Standard English; however, this linguistic feature is quite common in Afro-American English.

Another very powerful tool that feeds the 'standard' language myth is language testing. Language tests are used for a number of purposes: admission to universities, jobs, immigration, etc. and therefore carry significant consequences. These tests, for example, the TOEFL and IELTS, use standard American or standard British English as the norm. While these 'high stake' tests are used as gatekeepers to the universities in the United States, the United Kingdom, and Australia, current research shows that they do not determine student performance in academic courses (Dooey & Oliver, 2002; Phakiti, 2008). These studies therefore question the validity of the tests. Although a lengthy discussion of the tests (and their reliability/validity) is not appropriate here, it is important to note that the tests reinforce the myth that there is a 'standard' language that is used in these countries and that students who want to come to these countries must speak this variety of English.

Now, while it is possible to argue that in an academic context, access to standard English is crucial—in order for the students to read texts (written in Standard English) and to write for an audience using language considered appropriate in academic contexts, the use of the same tests for immigration purposes has different agendas. In some countries, for example in Australia, prospective immigrants must secure a minimal score in IELTS (in Australia, this varies between 6.5–7, depending on the immigration category) before they are permitted. This language score carries considerable weight in the point system that is used to determine whether an applicant is eligible to be granted immigration or not. One purpose of this test is that English is considered the national language of Australia and therefore all immigrants are expected to have competence in the language. While this expectation might look appropriate to some on the surface, there are a number of issues related to it. One of the most crucial issues with such testing is that only people who have a particular educational and socio economic background can get the required scores. People who were not educated in English in their home countries and/

or who cannot afford to pay for the test (which costs quite a lot—especially for people living in the developing countries where incomes are low) are excluded from entering the country based on their inability to produce appropriate language documentation. McNamara (2009) points out the discriminatory policies and practices that the use of such tests supports. He suggests that this policy, in some ways, reflects a linguistic apartheid—where people who can use a particular language in a particular way (as measured by a test designed by the dominant group) are allowed entry, while others are denied it. This use of language tests, based on Standard English, shows how language can be used for political purposes. This, of course, is not just happening in Australia. Language and other sorts of tests are being used for similar gatekeeping purposes in the Netherlands, Sweden, Denmark, France, Germany, Estonia, Latvia, the UK, and the US (McNamara & Shohamy, 2008). In the context of the present paper, the preference for standard language for immigration purposes shows how the use of the notion of a 'standard language' supports both the industry (since people must take the expensive tests, perhaps multiple times—in order to qualify for immigration) and the government (which wants only a certain group of people to migrate).

The use of a standard language is also critical in the development of a native-speaker myth—someone who is seen as an ideal user of the language. This issue is taken up in the next section.

The Construction of the Native and Non-Native Speaker Identities in the English Language Teaching (ELT) Industry

The standard language myth ties into another myth: native speakers are the ideal language teachers of English. The assumption here is that native speakers are the ideal users of the language and serve as the best models for language learners. In many cases, especially in non-English-speaking countries, this leads to hiring practices in language schools that privilege any native-English speaker over a non-native speaker, even if the native speaker has no credentials in English language teaching. The assumption that native speakers provide the best models of the language and serve as the best teachers is what has been labelled as the 'native speaker myth' in the literature. The notion of a native speaker is further tied in with issues of 'racism' in the ELT profession. This issue has been discussed in several books and journal articles and will be discussed in some detail in this section.

The concept of a native speaker evolved as the new world order was being established after the Second World War, decolonization was in full gear, and concerns about who is 'native' to a nation state (in the context of migration) were being flagged. It was in this context that English language experts debated the importance of maintaining and promoting Standard English. Linguists such as Randolph Quirk, among others, argued that mutual communication could only be maintained through English between people in different parts of the world. This position of promoting a particular variety of English worldwide worked well with the myth of a standard language and supported the 'native speaker myth'.

Applied linguists' definitions of the native speaker have emphasized traits such as birth, heredity, and innateness of linguistic qualities (see Amin, 2000). Rampton (1990) points out that one of the connotations of being a native speaker of English is that English is inherited either through genetic endowment or through birth into the social group that is stereotypically associated with it. Leung, Harris, and Rampton (1997), building on Rampton's (1990) research, also discuss the issue of the race of the idealized native speaker. They argue that there is an 'abstracted notion of an idealized native speaker of English from which ethnic and linguistic minorities are automatically excluded' (p. 546). Leung, Harris, and Rampton appear to be saying that even non-White people who are born and have grown up in the First World are not seen as native speakers. One source of evidence of such discriminatory practices is found in job ads and teachers' anecdotes posted on various blogs and websites. Consider the following examples:

> Post: ... but would anyone on this list be familiar with how an Asian-American or Asian-Canadian or ANY female with obviously Asian ethnic blood (but who grew up in the West) would be treated in the Middle East? Would I be at a disadvantage in the hiring process (since we're required to send photos) because I don't have the Western "look" despite my Western credentials and upbringing?
> Response: In almost all of the top TESL jobs in the UAE, recruitment decisions are taken by Western expats ... Without the luxury of anti-racist legislation in the West, you may very soon become appalled by attitudes of fellow Western expats.
> Response: As for getting a teaching job, well let me put it like this: it would be perfectly normal for a white Brit with mediocre experience and qualifications to be preferred over a non-white native-speaker of English with excellent qualifications and extensive experience. Sad, but unfortunately very true. Sadder still: it's normally Westerners making these decisions NOT locals!
> (Source: ESL-Café)

The quote above comprises selected portions of a lengthy discussion on race, gender and employment opportunities for the 'visible' minorities. The discussion revolves around a question from a female Asian-Canadian who is curious about her chances of getting a job in the Middle East. The responses reveal how ESL teachers working in the region perceive the relevance of race in hiring decisions. Among the various issues raised in this online discussion, the two that I would like to draw your attention to are: 1) White applicants may be preferred over non-White applicants regardless of their qualifications and/or experience, and 2) it is not only the local people that discriminate on the basis of race, but also the White expatriates who are responsible for recruiting new staff.

The experiences shared in the discussion above are corroborated when we look at job ads posted for English language teachers. One such example is shared below:

> Job ad: we are a school in beijing shijingshan district and looking for a native english speaker who is white and not too old. it is very urgent because the new teachers are supposed to work from september 1st. the salary is 7000 rmb per month. the working time is 3 to 6 from monday to friday. please contact me at XXX. (Source: China-Daily) [This add has not been modified: the non-capitalization is in the original]

This job advertisement categorically asks for 'a native English speaker who is white and not too old'. This quote corroborates the perceptions cited in the previous quotes. In addition, it specifies that the applicants be 'not too old'. The issue of ageism is out of the scope of this paper, but for those interested in this issue, see Templer (2003).

The impact of these prevalent discourses of White native speaker is strong in both the BANA and other countries. In the non-English-speaking countries, the prejudice against non-White non-native ESL teachers is shared by both expatriate and local program administrators, which leads to the question: Why do non-native speakers discriminate against other non-native speakers? This question can partly be explained by looking at Gramsci's (1971) concept of hegemony, whereby the dominant group uses ideological control to subordinate other groups. The notion of popular 'consensus' is key to Gramsci's concept of hegemony, as people come to assume that certain ideas and discursive positions are natural and universal. Gramsci's arguments are supported by early language attitude studies. For example, in their study of attitudes towards English and French in Montreal, Lambert, Hodgson, Gardner, and Fillenbaum (1960) found that both English-speaking (high status) and French-speaking (low status) respondents gave favourable and positive ratings to the English guises. Lambert et al. called this the minority group reaction and stated that members of a low-status group may assume and accept the values promoted by members of the high-status group. Regarding the native speaker, as Nayar (1994) puts it: 'Generations of applied linguistic mythmaking in the indubitable superiority and the impregnable infallibility of the "native speaker" has created stereotypes that die hard' (p. 4). Applied linguists have exported their messages globally through ESL texts, teacher education literature, and through their teaching. If the world of English speakers can be convinced that White native speakers are best qualified to teach ESL/EFL, then employers of colour can justify to themselves that in hiring White native speakers they are hiring the most suitable candidates.

In addition to web posts and other anecdotal data, Mahboob, Uhrig, Newman, and Hartford (2004), based on statistical evidence, show that being a native speaker is an important criterion in hiring teachers in adult English language programs in the United States. The results of a survey of 118 English language program administrators throughout the United States showed that out of a total of 1,425 ESL teachers in these programs only 112 (7.9%) were non-native speakers of English. Thus, the number of NESTs (native English speakers in TESOL) is substantially higher than the number of NNESTs (non-native English speakers in TESOL) in English language programs in the United States. In contrast to the low proportion of NNESTs, the survey results showed that 48.59% of the graduate students in TESOL, Applied Linguistics, and/or Language Education programs were international students who were non-native speakers of English. This contrast between the ratio of graduate students and ESL teachers (in associated programs) is telling of an unfair distribution of teaching positions. The results of the survey also showed that 59.8% of the respondents considered 'native speaker' as at least 'somewhat important' in making hiring decisions. A correlation study between ten hiring criteria and the ratio of NNESTs indicated that there was a link between the low number of NNESTs in ESL programs in the United States and administrators' emphasis on 'native English status'. In addition to the correlation, a regression analysis with the ratio of NNESTs being the dependent variable and the ten criteria being the independent variables showed that the criterion, 'native English speaker', most significantly explained the ratio of NNESTs in a program (t=−4.498, p< .001).

This statistical study showed that being a native speaker of English plays an important role in hiring decisions; and that, regardless of other qualifications that NNESTs might have, they are not proportionally represented in the profession. At this point, no comparable studies are available for other countries; however, the anecdotal and attitudinal studies available suggest that the preference for 'native' speakers is widespread and not only limited to the United States.

So far in this section, we have documented how native and non-native teachers are treated differentially. This, of course, has an economic dimension as well. The preference of native speakers, who come from English-speaking Western countries means that these people are given jobs as teachers and local teachers (who may be well qualified) are left unemployed. The low status given to NNESTs also results in differences in the pay scales and benefits of these teachers in comparison to NESTs. While the issues surrounding NNESTs are still current, there is a growing NNEST movement that is creating awareness of the problems and attempting to address the problems.

The NNEST movement has created space for questioning the native speaker myths in TESOL and Applied Linguistics. However, this movement is still in its early stages. This movement can be traced back to the 1996 TESOL Convention where George Braine organized a colloquium 'In their own voices: Non-native speaker professionals in TESOL' which resulted in a drive to set up the NNEST Caucus in the TESOL association. The NNEST Caucus was established in 1998 and in 2008 the NNEST Caucus became the NNEST Interest Section. The specific goals of the NNEST Caucus/Interest Section are:

- to create a non-discriminatory professional environment for all TESOL members regardless of native language and place of birth,
- to encourage the formal and informal gatherings of non-native speakers at TESOL and affiliate conferences,
- to encourage research and publications on the role of non-native speaker teachers in ESL and EFL contexts, and
- to promote the role of non-native speaker members in TESOL and affiliate leadership positions.

Two of these goals are related to the status and position of NNESTs within the field, and the other two have to do with issues of advocacy. Since its establishment, the Caucus/Interest Section has made significant contributions to achieve these goals, however, all is not yet well. There is still ample evidence of discriminatory hiring and advertising practices against NNESTs around the world and more needs to be done to make TESOL an equitable profession.

In this section, we related the preference of NESTs in terms of their access to 'standard' language. However, there are other cultural and political agendas that privilege NESTs. One of these is the relationship between English and Christianity and the proselytizing that is packaged with English language teaching. This will be discussed in the next section.

The Missionary Role of English

Discourses of Christianity have been strongly enmeshed in the field of English language teaching. These links go back to the times of colonization. Colonization, while a wealth generator for the colonizers, was locally marketed (in the West) in the name of religion, virtue, and civilization. The non-Christian world was seen as being barbarous and a place that needed to be saved and rescued from their imminent doom. The English poet, Rudyard Kipling (1865–1936) writing about colonization, argued that it was the 'white man's burden' to enlighten the 'new-caught, sullen peoples, Half-devil and half-child'. In the context of American colonization of the Philippines, Rafael's (2000) names the same agenda, 'White love'. By White love, Rafael refers to the need of the West to save the savages by converting them to Christianity, replacing their native languages with English, and by changing their native cultures. However, the purpose of colonization was not only grounded in Western moral values. The goals of colonization were economic. In exposing these hidden agendas, Spring (1998) cites Charles Grant who said, 'to introduce the language of the conquerors, seems to be an obvious means of assimilating a conquered people to them ... this is the noblest species of conquest, and wherever, we may venture to say, our principles and language are introduced, our commerce will follow [stress added]' (p. 15). The documents from colonial times indicate that even from the earliest colonial history, Christianity, language and commerce were tied together. This relationship has not been broken. What has changed is the form that colonization now takes. Instead of colonizing lands, the neo-colonial powers use English and knowledge constructed through English (as discussed in an earlier section) to colonize the minds of the people.

Discourses of Christianity are still strong in the field of TESOL.

Karmani (2005a, 2005b) points out that Billy Graham and his son, along with many other missionaries, are openly proselytizing in Iraq in English as a second language (ESL) classes. Similarly, there are a large number of missionaries who take up jobs as English teachers to go to other parts of the world to proselytize. A recent example of a job posting that both discriminates against NNESTs and has a strong Christian Service element serves to exemplify this point. This ad was posted (posting date: 2/27/2007) on the Eastern Mennonite University's Career Services page. The job description from this ad is copied below:

WANTED: Teachers who want to make an eternal impact: Full Time Job Description: All Nations Christian Academy (ANCA) (Grades K-9) Native English Speaking Preschool/Elementary/Middle School Teachers wanted Do you want to make an eternal impact for Christ's kingdom? Do you want to make your life count? Do you want to take part in a dynamic school ministry of training the next generation of Korean missionaries and discipling servant leaders to be shining beacons of light in this world? Here's your chance to make a significant and lasting impact in our next Joshua generation's lives as we disciple and teach our future global servant leaders.

1. About our school and the ministry Our school's mission is to train up young people, especially Korean missionary kids (MKs), in the way they should go according to God's Word. We also have an after school English academy (grades 1–9) which reaches out to the community that we serve with the gospel of Jesus. We seek to provide the best well-rounded Christian education and to disciple students to become fully devoted followers of Christ and to equip them to be "radical world changers." We believe that teachers are disciplers as well as teachers. We come alongside the Christian parents to assist them in providing the necessary discipleship for each student. We offer Preschool/Kindergarten through 4th grade in the International School, which uses mainly curriculum from Christian publishers such as ABeka, Bob Jones, and other reputable educational providers. The classes are taught mainly in English. We believe in close, personal, individual interaction and relationship building discipleship, so classes are small. Our team has worked hard to create a unique learning environment which differentiates ANCA from other schools. We don't just impart knowledge, but we impart a Godly life. We don't just grow the heads of the students with knowledge, but grow the hearts with wisdom.

2. Qualifications—Believe in Jesus as Lord and Savior and have a personal relationship with Him everyday—Have a mission/discipleship mind—Hold at least a Bachelor's degree or equivalent.—DON'T need a teacher's certificate or other ESL certificates, but preferably have professional classroom teaching experience. (Early-childhood Development or a Kindergarten teaching license is favored)—A native speaker of American English—Retired people are welcome

Source: EMU Career Center—Jobs Data. Accessed: 4/27/2007

Among other things, a reader will note that the ad does not require training in TESOL. The key qualifications for the job are 1) being a believer in Jesus as Lord and Savior, and 2) being a native speaker of American English. Not only is TESL certification not required; but also, the need to have one is discounted by an explicit statement that emphasizes that candidates 'DON'T need' one [emphasis in original]. This ad ties the discussion of nativeness (discussed in the previous section) to Christianity and shows how native speakers who are Christians are recruited to be sent abroad to proselytize. Among other things, the discounting of the educational training for these people is troubling as it undermines the profession of English language teaching that sees professional training and development as a key requirement for English language teachers. This advertisement and the goals behind it reflect some of the current literature on Christianity and English language education being produced by Christian educators. These teachers are often trained in what Edge (2003) has termed 'stealth evangelism'. We will look at the reasoning that supports such evangelism next.

Robison (2009) believes that all tactics are fair in trying to convert people to Christianity and that it is acceptable to use English language teaching to disguise these intentions. Robison grounds his discussion of TESOL and Christianity on the belief that 'truth originates in God and is revealed in the person of Jesus Christ'. He argues that as long as this 'truth' is upheld, other truths or lies are relative and may be placed on a scale based on whether or not they cause 'unjustifiable' damage to others. Robison builds his arguments by showing that truth and lies, openness and concealment are all relative terms and need to be seen in terms of the absolute truth—which is Jesus Christ. His beliefs—and those of many other evangelical English language teachers—lead them to use any tactic that can help them achieve their purpose. This situation appears to be a continuation of the era of English expansion when missionaries saw it as their duty to spread Christianity, and did so in the ESL classroom.

While some people use English language industry to further their religious agendas, it is also worth noting that given the 'nativization' processes of English, people in various parts of the world have resisted and, in fact, changed the language to reflect their own religious and cultural values. In a study of 'English as an Islamic language' (Mahboob, 2009), I have shown how the lexical, semantic, and pragmatic structures in Pakistani English have been adapted to reflect local cultural and religious beliefs and practices.

To understand this, let us look at some examples of lexico-semantic adaptation and extension in Pakistani English. Words that are commonly used in Pakistani English that represent Islamic values include greetings Assalam-o-Alaikum, and words of praise and appreciation Maasha-Allah and Alhumd-o-Lillah. These phrases are not only found in personal exchanges, but also in public discourse, e.g., on radio and television shows as well as political and other speeches. In an earlier study, Baumgardner, Kennedy, and Shamim (1993) list 54 lexical categories in Pakistani English that have been influenced by local languages and cultures and noted that one of the most productive categories is religion. In fact, they sub-categorize Islamic borrowings in Pakistani English into 44 groups, for example, administrative posts (amir, nazim, etc.), concepts (hadith, zina, etc.), education (iqra, maktab, etc.), and marriage (halala, nikah, etc.). Baumgardner, Kennedy, and Shamim (1993) base their categorization on examples they collected from English language newspapers. One such example is:

> I may be a devout believer of purdah [segregation] system but ...
> (Baumgardner, Kennedy, & Shamim, 1993)

In this example, Baumgardner, Kennedy, and Shamim (1993) show that the term 'purdah' is borrowed from Urdu and means 'segregation' in English. However, in my work, I argue that this meaning of purdah, 'segregation', is only one of the meanings of the word as it is used in Pakistani English. 'Purdah' has been both semantically and metaphorically extended in Pakistani English and is used with at least two additional meanings. The examples below show how users of Pakistani English extend the meaning of 'purdah':

> A lot has been made of the women being forced to observe purdah. (Dawn, October 15, 2001)
> The delegates took care to draw the purdah over quarrels. (Dawn, May 30, 2004)
> This is with reference to Mr. Hafizur Rahman's article "Urdu: 'in purdah'" ...
> (Dawn, April, 11, 2005).

While the first example above is similar to Baumgardner et. al.'s example where the word is used in a traditional sense of 'segregation', the other two show how the term is used metaphorically in unique contexts: in the second example the term is used for 'cover-up' or 'conceal', and in third example it is used to mean 'disempowered' or 'retreat'. Both these uses represent a semantic extension of the concept of 'purdah'. They also exemplify how Pakistani English reflects a Muslim cultural identity where terms from Islamic heritage are borrowed and semantically extended to carry a unique Pakistani sensitivity. In addition to these three meanings of 'purdah', a fourth meaning attested both in Pakistani/South Asian newspapers and some international sources is that of 'ban'. This use of 'purdah' can be seen in the example below.

> Twelve-year-old Kiran Khan will swim at the Commonwealth Games this week as Pakistan's female swimmers emerge from "sporting purdah". (http://www.dailyexcelsior.com/, July 31, 2002; accessed May 24, 2008)

The news story about the 'sporting purdah', in the context of the lifting of the ban against female Pakistani swimmers contesting in international sports tournaments, was also picked up by the international media. In many instances, such as in the example below, the term 'sporting purdah' was adopted without any changes:

> When Sana Abdul Wahid took the plunge in the 50 metres butterfly at the Commonwealth Games yesterday, she did so in a bodysuit that took Pakistani women "out of sporting purdah". (http://www.timesonline.co.uk/tol/sport/article798105.ece, July 31, 2002; accessed May 24, 2008)

The examples shared in this section show how lexical items related to Islamic concepts and terms are borrowed into English. Some of these terms, over time, extend their semantic range and are used in new contexts. This process demonstrates how local cultural concepts influence the English language and give it a local flavour. The process also shows how local communities are not passive recipients of Western knowledge and language, but they resist these by adapting and changing the language to suit their own purposes.

Conclusion

This chapter has attempted to show how globalization of English has served a number of mutually related interests. In specific, we have noted how the English language industry profits from selling English as the language of science and development. Hidden in this marketing of English, we have observed, are agendas of 'colonization of the mind', which are achieved by normalizing beliefs that Western values, sciences, and practices are the road to success and development. However, while we observe the role of the English industry in creating and maintaining Western hegemonic interests, we have also examined ways in which communities engage with and resist these interests. How these contrasting interests and values play out in the long term—especially with the rise of China as a global power—are yet to be seen and something that is worthy of ongoing research and study.

References

Amin, N. (2000). *Negotiating nativism: Minority immigrant women ESL teachers and the native speaker construct*. Unpublished doctoral dissertation, University of Toronto, Toronto, Canada.

Baumgardner, Robert J., Kennedy, Audrey E. H., & Shamim, Fauzia (1993). The Urduization of English in Pakistan. In Robert J. Baumgardner (Ed.), *The English Language in Pakistan*. Karachi: Oxford University Press.

Dooey, P., & Oliver, R. (2002). An investigation into the predictive validity of the IELTS test. *Prospect, 17*(1), 36–54.

Edge, J. (2003). Imperial troopers and servants of the Lord: A vision of TESOL for the 21st century. *TESOL Quarterly, 47*(4), 701–708.

Gramsci, A. (1971). *Selections from the prison notebooks*. Translated by Q. Hoare & G. N. Smith. New York: International Publishers.

Kachru, B. (ed.) (1992) *The other tongue: English across cultures*. Urbana, IL: University of Illinois Press. [2nd edition; 1st edition 1982].

Karmani, S. (2005a). TESOL in a time of terror: Toward an Islamic perspective on applied linguistics. *TESOL Quarterly, 39*(4), 738–748.

Karmani, S. (2005b). English, "Terror," and Islam. *Applied Linguistics, 26*(2), 282–287.

Lambert, W. W., Hodgson, R., Gardner, R. C., & Fillenbaum, S. (1960). Evaluational reactions to spoken languages. *Journal of Abnormal and Social Psychology, 60*, 44–51.

Leung, C., Harris, R., & Rampton, B. (1997). The idealised native speaker, reified ethnicities, and classroom realities. *TESOL Quarterly, 31*(3), 543–560.

Mahboob, A. (2002) "No English, no future!" Language policy in Pakistan. In S. Obeng & B. Hartford (Eds.) *Political Independence with Linguistic Servitude: The politics about languages in the developing world*. New York: NOVA Science.

Mahboob, A. (2009). English as an Islamic language. *World Englishes, 28*(2), 175–189.

Mahboob, A., Uhrig, K., Newman, K., & Hartford, B. (2004). Children of a lesser English: Nonnative English speakers as ESL teachers in English language programs in the United States. In L. Kamhi-Stein (Ed.) *Learning and Teaching from Experience: Perspectives on Nonnative English-Speaking Professionals*. Ann Arbor: Michigan University Press.

McNamara, T. (2009). Australia: The dictation test redux? *Language Assessment Quarterly, 6*(1), 106–111.

McNamara, T., & Shohamy, E. (2008). Language tests and human rights. *International Journal of Applied Linguistics, 18*(1), 89–95.

Nayar, P. B. (1994). Whose English is it? [16 paragraphs]. TESL-EJ [*On-line serial*] Retrieved: February 14, 2001, from http://www-writing.berkeley.edu/TESL-EJ/ej01/f.1.html.

Phakiti A. (2008). Predicting NESB international postgraduate students' academic achievement: A structural equation modeling approach. *International Journal of Applied Educational Studies*, 3(1), 18–38.

Rafael, V. (2000). *White Love and Other Events in Filipino History*. Duham: Duke University Press.

Rampton, M. B. H. (1990). Displacing the "native speaker": Expertise, affiliation, and inheritance. *ELT Journal*, 44(2), 97–101.

Robison, R. (2009). Truth in Teaching English. In M. Wong & S. Canagarajah (Eds.) *Christian and Critical English Language Educators in Dialogue: Pedagogical and Ethical Dilemmas*. New York: Routledge.

Spring, J. (1998). *Education and the rise of the global economy*. London: Lawrence Erlbaum Associates.

Chapter 9

Looking for Native Speakers of English: Discrimination in English Language Teaching Job Advertisements

Mahboob, A., & Golden, R. (2013). Looking for Native Speakers of English: Discrimination in English Language Teaching Job Advertisements. *Voices in Asia Journal, 1(1)*, 72–81.

Introduction

Over the last 20 years, research interest in issues of non-native English-speaking teachers (NNESTs) has grown tremendously. This research has looked at the perceptions of students towards NNESTs (e.g., Mahboob, 2004; Moussu, 2006; Nemtchinova, 2010), at issues of teaching (e.g., Cots & Diaz, 2005; Forman, 2010), at issues of training NNESTs (e.g., Barratt, 2010; Nemtchinova, 2010), and at issues of hiring and discrimination (e.g., Braine, 1999; Clark & Paran, 2007; Mahboob et. al., 2004; Selvi, 2010). This body of work documents that being a native speaker of English is not an essential factor in being an effective teacher. It advocates against discrimination against NNESTs and recommends that hiring decisions be based on candidates' professional qualifications. In support of this research and professionalization of the field, TESOL International has published two statements regarding discriminatory hiring practices in the English Language Teaching (ELT) profession. The first, in 1992, was the "Statement on non-native speakers of English and hiring practices", and the second, in 2006, was the "Position statement against discrimination of non-native speakers of English in the field of TESOL". Despite this work, research shows that many employers consider a candidate's nativeness to be an important criterion in making employment decisions (Clark & Paran, 2007; Mahboob et al., 2004; Selvi, 2010). This chapter builds on this body of research and investigates how job advertisements can discriminate against candidates with particular backgrounds.

Kubota and Lin (2006: 481) support this work by stating that "focussing on non-nativeness in employment discrimination is absolutely necessary when seeking social justice in this globalized era as more English language teachers are recruited in many communities around the world". In spite of this call, there has been little research to date on such discriminatory practices in job advertisements. One study that does look at this is Selvi (2010), who found that the job advertisements privileged people who were native speakers of English and, often, were citizens of certain countries. This chapter extends this research agenda and examines what criteria employers advertise when hiring English language teachers, and how these practices differ across two regions (Middle East and East Asia). The findings of this study suggest that the discriminatory practices that the field has been trying to eliminate are still visible and that more work needs to be carried out to make TESOL an equitable profession.

Methodology

To investigate what qualities ELT employers look for in potential job candidates, this study collected 103 job advertisements from the website *ESL Jobs World*. Of these, 53 were for jobs in the Middle East and 50 for jobs in East Asia. The job advertisements were taken from a single online source in order to reduce the possibility of duplicate advertisements and make comparisons between the two regions, without having to worry about whether the website policies might have impacted the nature of the job advertisements. In reviewing these 103 job advertisements, we found a number of duplicate job advertisements. We removed all duplicate advertisements from the corpus and were left with 77 advertisements: 42 from East Asia and 35 from the Middle East. The 77 advertisements were then analyzed for the selection criteria included in the body of the advertisements.

Results

A content analysis of the 77 advertisements showed that they listed up to seven factors as key requirements for potential candidates. These factors included: age, educational qualifications, gender, nationality, nativeness, race, and teaching experience. These factors can be classified as either professional (educational qualifications and teaching experience) or biographical (age, gender, nationality, nativeness and race). Each advertisement varied in terms of the criteria it included. Below we will first present an overview of our findings (Table 1) and will then look at each of the factors in some detail. Table 1 provides a count of times (tokens) that each factor was included in the advertisements—across the two regions and in total.

Table 1   Biographical and Professional Factors by Region

	Factors	Middle East	East Asia	Total
Biographical	Age	3	18	21
	Gender	3	1	4
	Nationality	18	20	38
	Nativeness	27	34	61
	Race	0	2	2
Professional	Education	31	22	53
	Experience	31	19	50

Table 1 above gives the frequency of each of the seven criteria mentioned in the advertisements. The Table shows the frequency count for each feature for the two regions as well as for the 77 advertisements together. These results show that "nativeness" was the single most frequent criterion mentioned in the advertisements across the two regions (61 tokens), followed by education (53 tokens), experience (50 tokens), nationality (38 tokens), age (21 tokens), gender (4 tokens), and finally race (2 tokens). Table 1 also shows some differences across the two regions. While nativeness (34 tokens) and nationality (20 tokens) were the two most frequently mentioned factors in the advertisements for East Asia, the advertisements for the Middle East listed the two professional factors, education and experience (31 tokens each), more frequently (note that nativeness was still a commonly included requirement). The table also shows that age as a requirement was mentioned more often in advertisements for East Asia (18 tokens) than for the Middle East (3 tokens). Gender was slightly more frequently mentioned in the advertisements for jobs in the Middle East (3 tokens) as compared to those for East Asia (1 token). And, finally, race was included only in 2 advertisements—both for jobs in East Asia.

Having provided an overview of the findings, we will now look at each of the factors in more detail below. In presenting the findings of the study, we will first look at the professional factors and then biographical factors.

Professional Factors

There were two main types of professional factors included in the advertisements: educational qualifications and teaching experience.

Educational Qualifications

Of all 77 advertisements, 59 (77%) included education requirements. Forty-seven of these 59 advertisements required at least a bachelor's degree. In the Middle East, 74% of advertisements included minimum educational requirements (either a university degree or an ELT certification) while in East Asia the figure was 63%. There were differences between the advertisements collected from the two regions in terms of the types of educational qualifications required. Of the advertisements that required specific educational qualifications, 89% from the Middle East required a university education; whereas, only 52% from East Asia mentioned this requirement. Thirteen percent of advertisements in the Middle East required at least a master's degree, while there was no minimum requirement of a master's degree in the advertisements from East Asia. Of the advertisements from the Middle East, 32% required bachelor's degrees in English, Linguistics, Education or related fields. Two advertisements specifically stated that Americans must have English- or education-related degrees. None of the advertisements from East Asia specified the field of study for potential candidates.

There was a disparity in the ELT certificate requirements across the two regions as well. In all, 34% of the advertisements from the Middle East required some form of ELT certificate (e.g., TESOL, TEFL, CELTA), while only 24% of the advertisements from East Asia had such a requirement. The results indicate that the advertisers placed a higher value on university degrees than on ELT qualifications in general across both regions.

Some advertisements showed further restrictions on the educational qualifications of the candidates. For example, one advertisement from the Middle East, which did not specify any particular countries from which the candidates should come, stated that the candidates' qualifications should have been obtained in the UK, Ireland, Australia, NZ, USA, Canada or South Africa. Another stated that online, weekend, or correspondence TEFL courses would not be accepted.

Teaching Experience

There was further dissimilarity between the two regions when it came to required teaching experience of the candidates. For example, 89% of advertisements from the Middle East stated that teaching experience was either required or preferred; while, in East Asia, this figure was 45%. Furthermore, when teaching experience was mentioned as a criterion in the advertisements, 40% of the advertisements from East Asia did not specify the length of experience required; 47% required one-to-two years of experience; and only 14% required three or more years of experience. On the other hand, only 7% of advertisements from the Middle East did not specify the length of experience; 47% required one-to-two years; and 46% required three or more years of experience.

Biographical Factors

In contrast to the two professionally oriented criteria, there were five types of hiring criteria specified in the advertisements related to personal or biographical factors. Eighty-eight percent of all the advertisements analyzed mentioned at least one—if not more—biographical factors. There was some difference between the two regions, but not a very large one: 93% of the advertisements from the Asian corpus and 83% of the advertisements from the Middle East included specific biographical requirements. These biographical factors include age, gender, nationality, nativeness, and race. None of the factors have any clear professional relevance and their inclusion as essential criteria for the jobs advertised raises the question: if biographical factors are used in determining an applicant's suitability for a role, could this result in discrimination?

Age

Of the advertisements from the Middle East, eleven (26%) included specific age requirements for the applicants. Of the remaining eighteen advertisements, the minimum required age was 20 and the maximum was 60. The average lowest acceptable age was 23 years, while the average highest acceptable age was 48 years. One advertisement simply stated that "older persons" were preferred.

In East Asia, only three advertisements included age requirements for the applicants. Of those remaining, two had "under 60" as the requirement, and the third had "30+".

Gender

Of the seventy-seven advertisements, four (5%) referred to gender, with one in East Asia requiring a female teacher and three in the Middle East requiring male teachers.

Nationality

Thirty-eight (49%) of the advertisements listed specific countries from which the applicants must come. Of these, 95% of the advertisements named the US, 89% named the UK, 84% named Canada, 66% named Australia, 55% named New Zealand, 37% named Ireland, and 24% named South Africa. While both regions showed preferences for candidates from North America and the UK, there were differences when it came to other countries. The advertisements from East Asia showed more of a preference for applicants from Australia and New Zealand, while those from the Middle East mentioned Ireland and South Africa more frequently. No advertisements from East Asia listed South Africa as a desired native-speaker country. One advertisement from the Middle East mentioned that it was due to "visa blocks" that only US, UK and Canada passport holders would be considered. No advertisements from East Asia mentioned any such immigration policies. Two advertisements, both from the Middle East, named the required countries in the title: "ESL—Instructor—UK/Irish Candidates" and "ESL—Instructors—UK/Irish/USA/Canadian Citizens". One advertisement, which did not mention required countries from which the "native speaker" candidates should come, did however state that interviews would be held in the UK, Australia and New Zealand.

Nativeness

Nativeness was the most common biographical variable in the data set. Eight advertisements (10%) used the word "native" in the title for the job advertisement. Two other advertisements, both from the Middle East, did not use the word native, but instead specified the names of countries from which they required applicants in the title for the job advertisement.

Of the seventy-seven advertisements, only ten (13%) did NOT have any mention of "native speaker" or "nationality" requirement. This represented 9.5% of all advertisements from East Asia and 17% of those from the Middle East. In terms of "nativeness", 79% of all advertisements specifically used the term native speaker. Two of these, both from East Asia, named possible exceptions to the rule. One allowed for "overseas Chinese from the UK, USA or Australia". The second stated that "exceptions may sometimes be made in cases of non-native speakers who have no discernable accent".

One advertisement from East Asia with no "native speaker" requirement did however state that one of the job's duties would be to tell students about what life is like overseas. While this may not necessarily mean that the employer required only overseas applicants, it does seem to exclude locally qualified English language teachers who may not have spent time abroad.

Race

Two advertisements, both from East Asia, referred to the race of the candidate. In the first, a position specified "white native speakers" stating that they must be from the USA, UK, Australia, Canada, New Zealand or Ireland. The second listed "Caucasian" as a position requirement along with being a native speaker from the US or Canada. This advertisement also referred to nativeness in its title.

Discussion

The results of this study show that there remains a distinction between NESTs and NNESTs, with a strong preference for NESTs as candidates for English teaching positions. It is also important to note that an absence of certain criteria in a job advertisement does not necessarily mean that they won't be used in the recruitment decision-making process. This study highlights an association between native English speakers and Inner Circle Englishes as no Outer Circle countries were specifically mentioned as possible places from which native speakers would be accepted.

Our research also shows a gap between the results from East Asia and those from the Middle East when it came to nativeness as an important hiring criterion. This may be partly due to the histories of each region. Many countries that comprise East Asia were subject to colonialism and therefore might place a higher perceived value on the English spoken and taught by Western teachers. Butler (2007) also suggests a reason why there may be more requirements for native speakers in East Asia. In her paper, she states that governments in East Asia have recently highlighted the importance of oral communication skills in the teaching of English at the elementary school level, leading to an increased concern about the accents and pronunciation of local teachers having a negative impact on students. On the other hand, the first waves of migrants into the Middle East were workers from South and South East Asia and therefore it is possible that program directors in the Middle East would have a higher recognition of the abilities and qualifications of teachers from that region. However, given the nature of the present study, it is difficult to hypothesize about the possible reasons for the varying levels of discriminatory advertisements across the two regions. The motives and ideologies underlying the beliefs around nativeness would be worthy of further investigation in an attempt to understand and counter discrimination in the field.

It has been almost twenty years since the first research into issues surrounding non-native English teachers (Phillipson, 1992), and yet discriminatory practices continue to exist. Alongside the native speaker fallacy is an assumption that students prefer to be taught by native speakers. Studies such as Mahboob (2004), Moussu (2006), Moussu and Llurda (2008) amongst many others have consistently shown that both NESTs and NNESTs have (perceived) strengths and weaknesses when it comes to English language teaching. For example, research has shown that while NESTs are seen to have better vocabulary and pronunciation, students perceive NNESTs as having a better understanding of how English grammar works. NNESTs are also perceived to be better role models in the learning of English as they have already been through the process of learning English themselves: they are more familiar with the needs of learning the language. Similarly, Butler's 2007 study showed that accent had no impact on student performance, despite government concerns about local teachers. Unfortunately, as the results of the present study show, there is little evidence of the impact of research on NNESTs in the advertisements analyzed in this paper. Given all the research and calls for NEST-NNEST collaboration (Matsuda & Matsuda, 2001), one is still left with the question: why are native speakers still seen as the ideal model for teachers?

One factor that needs to be considered here is the definition of non-native speaker. Braine (1999: xiv) states that by its very definition a non-native speaker is classified against a native speaker—but the classification of native speakers is not without debate. It would be of interest to know if those advertisements which required a native speaker but did not specify a country from which the teacher should come would be happy to offer the job to a Singaporean native speaker, for example. Moussu & Llurda (2008) believe that there are many people who cannot be classified as either. They question how, for example, an Indian person for whom English is a first language would be categorized. They suggest that such a person would be a native speaker of a "non-native variety". This, however, maintains the distinction between native and non-native varieties of the language, and raises the question of how important the variety of English spoken by a teacher might or might not be.

As more people globally continue to learn and use English, and different varieties become accepted into the family of World Englishes, so-called native varieties may no longer be seen as standard forms of the language to which all speakers must aspire. In fact the growing research around, and acceptance of, English as an International Language (EIL) could mean that one day native speakers may join supposed non-native speakers in a shared language. Llurda (2004) believes that, as there are now more people who speak English as an L2 than those who speak it as an L1, the onus will be on the native speaker to adapt to the principles of EIL and the needs of EIL speakers, rather than teaching a native variety of the language. He states that as English is becoming a global language across many cultures, NNESTs should also value the multicultural contribution that they are able to bring to L2 and L3 learners. The impact that these discriminatory practices may have on the confidence, self-belief and motivation of NNESTs must be taken into account as the ELT profession needs to access their experience in learning English as a second language and the different cultural perspective they can provide for students (see also Mahboob, 2010).

A worrisome trend across the advertisements analyzed is a preference for native speakerness over teaching or educational qualifications. This impacts both the students who, as future English speakers, may be taught by individuals who are not qualified to do so, and teacher education and training institutions that train English language teachers. If these qualifications are not seen as relevant to getting a teaching position, then one may ask: what future is there for those taking these courses? And, by extension, of the institutions and programs that offer these courses?

The results of this study show that despite TESOL's two position statements on discrimination in the industry as well as other advocacy initiatives, discrimination against NNESTs in hiring remains rampant. A further step could be to encourage all TESOL members not to accept any positions of employment where the advertisement is deemed discriminatory and possibly contact the employer telling them their reasons in the hope that this will filter through over time. In his 2009 article, Selvi argues that there are three "A's" required in order to move away from the preference for native speakers. They are awareness, advocacy and activism. This would require an awareness-raising campaign in publications by recognized individuals and institutions in the field. The results of the current study were in line with those found by Selvi in his 2010 paper and reconfirm his conviction that underlying norms and practices in the ELT profession need to be reconstructed to value professionalism over "native speakerism".

Further study of interest could also look at whether or not special status is given to native speaker teachers of other international languages such as Arabic, Chinese, Spanish, etc. Moussu and Llurda (2008) highlight how little research has been done on this to date, suggesting that this may be due to the position of English as a global lingua franca.

Conclusion

The results of this study suggest that the concern about discriminatory practices in employment is justified. Eighty-eight percent of all advertisements looked at in this study had a discriminatory element to them. It would be of interest to draw a further implication from Mahboob et al.'s (2004) study and look at whether the discrimination in the job advertisements is manifesting itself in the actual employment of English language teachers in these regions. A future study might also consider analyzing the advertisements by employer type (for example, university or training center) and using this to further focus the analysis of the actual employment of NESTs versus NNESTs in these institutions.

While further study into this is needed, twenty years of research has shown that discrimination does exist. Therefore, it is now time to look forward and find ways to eradicate these practices. It may not be necessary to eliminate the distinction between native and non-native speakers altogether but rather utilize the strengths of both through further research in the area of collaborative teaching. The value and strengths of all English language teachers must be recognized based on their qualifications and experience and not on their mother tongue, race, or country of birth. Employment discrimination has been prohibited by law since as early as the 1960s in some countries. We must ask then why it is so prevalent in the ELT industry and why, despite awareness raising and discussion on the topic, it still continues.

References

Barratt, L. (2010). Strategies to Prepare Teachers Equally for Equity. In A. Mahboob (Ed.), *The NNEST Lens: Non Native English Speakers in TESOL*. Newcastle upon Tyne: Cambridge Scholars Press. 180−201.

Braine, G. (Ed.). (1999). *Non-Native Educators in English Language Teaching*. Mahwah, NJ: Lawrence Erlbaum Associates.

Butler, Y. G. (2007). How are Nonnative-English-Speaking Teachers Perceived by Young Learners? *TESOL Quarterly, 41*(4), 731−755.

Clark, E., & Paran, A. (2007). The Employability of Non-Native-Speaker Teachers of EFL: A UK Survey. *System, 35* (4), 407−430.

Cots, J. M., & Díaz, J. M. (2005). Constructing Social Relationships and Linguistic Knowledge Through Non-Native-Speaking Teacher Talk. In E. Llurda (ed.), *Non-Native Language Teachers: Perceptions, Challenges and Contributions to the Profession*. New York: Springer. 85−105.

Forman. R. (2010). Ten Principles of Bilingual Pedagogy in EFL. In A. Mahboob (ed.), *The NNEST Lens: Non Native English Speakers in TESOL*. Newcastle upon Tyne: Cambridge Scholars Publishing. 54−86.

Kubota, R., & Lin, A. (2006). Race and TESOL: Introduction to Concepts and Theories. *TESOL Quarterly, 40*(3), 471−493.

Llurda, E. (2004). Non-Native-Speaker Teachers and English as an International Language. *International Journal of Applied Linguistics, 14*(3), 314−323.

Mahboob, A. (2004). Native or Nonnative: What Do Students Enrolled in an Intensive English Program Think? In L. Kamhi-Stein (Ed.), *Learning and Teaching from Experience: Perspectives on Nonnative English-Speaking Professionals*. Ann Arbor: University of Michigan Press. 121−147.

Mahboob, A. (2010). *The NNEST Lens: Non Native English Speakers in TESOL*. Newcastle upon Tyne: Cambridge Scholars Press.

Mahboob, A., Uhrig, K., Newman, K., & Hartford, B. S. (2004). Children of a Lesser English: Status of Nonnative English Speakers as College-Level English as a Second Language Teachers in the United States. In L. Kamhi-Stein (Ed.), *Learning and Teaching from Experience: Perspectives on Nonnative English-Speaking Professionals*. Ann Arbor: University of Michigan Press. 100−120.

Matsuda, A., & Matsuda, P. K. (2001). Autonomy and Collaboration in Teacher Education: Journal Sharing Among Native and Nonnative English-Speaking Teachers. *CATESOL Journal, 13*(1), 109−121.

Moussu, L. (2006). *Native and Non-Native English-Speaking English as a Second Language Teachers: Student Attitudes, Teacher Self-Perceptions, and Intensive English Program Administrator Beliefs and Practices*. Ph.D. dissertation, Purdue University. (ERIC Document Reproduction Services No. ED 468 879.)

Moussu, L., & Llurda, E. (2008). Non-Native English-Speaking English Language Teachers:

History and Research. *Language Teaching, 41*(3), 315–348.

Nemtchinova, E. (2010). The "Who's Worth More?" Question Revisited: MA TESOL Practicum Host Teachers' Perceptions of NES and NNES Teacher Trainees. In A. Mahboob (ed.), *The NNEST Lens: Non Native English Speakers in TESOL*. Newcastle upon Tyne: Cambridge Scholars Publishing. 129–153.

Phillipson, R. (1992). *Linguistic Imperialism*. Oxford: Oxford University Press.

Selvi, A. F. (2009). *And Justice for All: Building Local Efforts on NNEST Issues*. Retrieved April 9, 2011 from http://www.tesol.org/NewsletterSite/view.asp?nid=2982.

Selvi, A. F. (2010). All Teachers Are Equal, But Some Teachers Are More Equal Than Others: Trend Analysis of Job Advertisements in English Language Teaching. *WATESOL NNEST Caucus Annual Review, Vol 1.*

Teachers of English to Speakers of Other Languages. (1992). A TESOL Statement of Non-Native Speakers of English and Hiring Practices. *TESOL Matters*, 2(4), 23.

Teachers of English to Speakers of Other Languages. (2006). *Position Statement Against Discrimination of Nonnative Speakers of English in the Field of TESOL*. Retrieved April 9, 2011 from http://www.tesol.org/s_tesol/seccss.asp?CID=32&DID=37.

Chapter 10

The NNEST Lens: Implications and Directions

Mahboob, A. (2018). The NNEST Lens: Implications and directions.
In A. F. Selvi (Ed.) *The TESOL Encyclopedia of English Language Teaching*.
New Jersey: Wiley-Blackwell, 1–7.

Framing the Issue

The term, *NNEST Lens*, comes from the title of an edited volume, *The NNEST Lens: Nonnative English Speakers in TESOL* (Mahboob, 2010) and is defined as "a lens of multilingualism, multinationalism, and multiculturalism through which NNESTs—as classroom practitioners, researchers, and teacher educators—take diversity as a starting point, rather than as a result" (p. 1). While the coinage, NNEST (non-native English-speaking teachers) Lens, is new, the ideas that it draws from and consolidates have been discussed and debated in TESOL and associated fields of study for a number of years. The value of the NNEST Lens lies in its ability to critically review and consolidate this work and highlight its relevance to the field. The NNEST Lens encourages further research in areas that can contribute to ethical and equitable professionalization of TESOL.

By questioning the monolingual assumptions and power relationships between native and non-native English speakers, the NNEST Lens, in a broader context, can be understood as one aspect of a much larger critical movement that has focussed on questions of power, equity, and access in social sciences. And, in our particular context, the NNEST Lens is a way of understanding and supporting the development of theory and practice in linguistics, applied linguistics, and TESOL which questions and responds to a monolingual bias in the discipline and associated professions. This critical and multilingual orientation promotes research and practice that aims to break monolingual and/or native-speaker biases in the field. This implication of the NNEST Lens is reflected in the concluding remarks of a recent review of literature on NNESTs, where Llurda (2015) states that the NNEST Lens "entails a new way of approaching recurrent problems in language, language teaching, and language-based research" (p. 113). This entry explores some of the implications of the NNEST Lens on theory and practice in linguistics, applied linguistics and TESOL, and identifies some of the directions that this work is taking. In specific, it considers how the NNEST Lens is and can be used by teachers, practitioners, material writers, and researchers amongst others to critically review and encourage anti-discrimination-oriented research in TESOL, teacher education, linguistics, and applied linguistics.

Making the Case

Research on what can be termed *NNEST studies* started off with a focus on issues of discrimination against NNESTs; for example, Medgyes (1992, 1994) discussed differences between NESTs and NNESTs and identified potential benefits that NNESTs can bring to the profession. Following this early research, a landmark contribution to the field was Braine's (1999) edited volume, which included a number of auto-ethnographic studies investigating factors that perpetuated discriminatory practices in TESOL. In order to dispel the myth that native English-speaking teachers (NESTs) were inherently better teachers than NNESTs, a number of studies explored the attitudes and perceptions of students towards NESTs and NNESTs and showed that students did not have a categorical preference for either. This research provided substantial evidence that both NESTs and NNESTs can be good teachers, if they were trained and had a strong understanding of declarative and procedural knowledge of language and language teaching. Thus, what was important was expertise, training, and professional development, rather than nativeness (see, for example, contributions to Kamhi-Stein, 2004).

While this thread of research on attitudes of various stakeholders towards NESTs and NNESTs is probably the single largest body of research in the area of NNEST studies, there are at least three reasons that scholars working in this area need to reassess the focus and methodology used in this work: 1) we have numerous studies now that all essentially say the same thing, regardless of the context in which they were carried out; thus, unless, a study includes a new angle to their survey or reports something new, additional studies do not contribute to building our knowledge about NNEST issues; 2) most of this research uses surveys; useful as these surveys are, they have a number of limitations and survey-based NNEST research needs to respond to these limitations; and 3) this research, while extremely useful in the early days of NNEST studies, has served its purpose, which was to raise awareness of the unsupported assumptions and biases in the field; that purpose has now been sufficiently addressed and researchers need to focus their work on other issues (some of which will be identified later on in this chapter).

A related set of research projects has explored biases in hiring policies and procedures. Early research on this issue, based on a regression analysis, showed that all other factors being equal, being a native speaker of English was a significant factor in making hiring decisions in English language centers in the United States. The findings of this research provided statistical evidence of discrimination in the ELT profession in the United States of America. Research in other contexts also showed that NNESTs faced discriminatory policies in hiring, and, if hired, were given a lower salary and fewer benefits than NESTs. In 2010, Selvi reported on a systemic study of job advertisements posted on two well-known ELT recruitment websites and noted that almost 75% of the advertisements reviewed in EFL contexts required prospective candidates to be native speakers of English. In another study of job advertisements for English teachers in the Middle East and East Asia, Mahboob and Golden (2013) found that 88% of the advertisements analyzed had some discriminatory feature (including age, gender, nationality, nativeness, and race) and 79% of the advertisements required "native speakers". These relatively recent findings raise the question as to why research on NNESTs has not had a greater impact on hiring and recruitment practices (Kumaravadivelu, 2016).

There are at least two possible reasons for an apparent low impact of NNEST research on hiring policies. First, NNEST research has been dominated by attitudinal and politically oriented research. This research has an advocacy agenda, i.e., its main purpose is to advocate for NNESTs. It does this by highlighting the strengths of NNESTs and questioning discriminatory practices in hiring and recruitment practices. What it does not do as well is to provide resources and strategies that can overcome such discriminatory practices. One way of doing this, which will be discussed in the following section, is to contribute more to literature that can be used in teacher education courses and by practicing teachers in their professional lives. This work can be developed by adopting an NNEST Lens. Second, the impact of advocacy takes time. The literature on NNESTs is still relatively new and tends to reach people who are actively engaged in the academic dimensions of TESOL and Applied Linguistics (e.g., graduate students, academics). This literature may not have yet reached program directors and managers. The impact of the NNEST literature will develop slowly over time as new graduates, who in many contexts are more aware of NNEST issues, take on key administrative positions in the ELT industry. In addition, it may be useful for people interested in this issue to write to the general public (via op-ed pieces etc.) to develop a wider awareness of the issues.

Implications

As identified above, the NNEST Lens has resulted in and can further contribute to teacher education and teaching resources. This work is of considerable importance to NNEST studies as it influences both in-service and pre-service TESOL educators and therefore impacts classroom practices and teaching behavior. For example, among other things, contributions to Mahboob (2010) include chapters that take the concept of the NNEST Lens to raise awareness about inequities and to encourage strategic advocacy; to develop strategies for teacher preparation programs; to discuss the role of mother tongue in classroom teaching; as well as to discuss ways in which NESTs and NNESTs can collaborate to create better learning environments for their students.

Research on teaching and teacher education that looks through an NNEST Lens is critically important for making ELT a more equitable profession. In a recent paper, Kumaravadivelu (2016) argues "... All the center-based methods are clearly linked to native speakerism. That is, they promote the native speaker's presumed language competence, learning styles, communication patterns, conversational maxims, cultural beliefs, and even accent as the norm to be learned and taught" (p. 8). In arguing this, Kumaravadivelu stresses, amongst other things, the importance of NNESTs to reconsider the politics of current dominant teaching methodologies and develop approaches that "take into account the local historical, political, social, cultural, and educational exigencies" (p. 16).

In addition to work on teaching and teacher education, the NNEST Lens also raises questions about some of the core ideas in (English) linguistics. For example, research on World Englishes, which, by definition takes an NNES perspective, has challenged how English is described only in terms of native English varieties. Work on English as a Lingua Franca provides evidence of how language is negotiated in context by people engaged in the interaction. Recent work on language has also questioned the limitation of studies based on their focus on a single semiotic mode and ignoring how meanings are construed and represented multimodally. Mahboob (2014) presents a 3-dimensional model that attempts to explain how language variation can be understood in terms of three interrelated factors: relationship between participants (users of language), register (purpose/use of language), and mode (channel of communication); along with a fourth dimension, time. Figure 1 below provides a visual representation of the 3-dimensional framework:

Figure 1   3-dimensional model of language variation

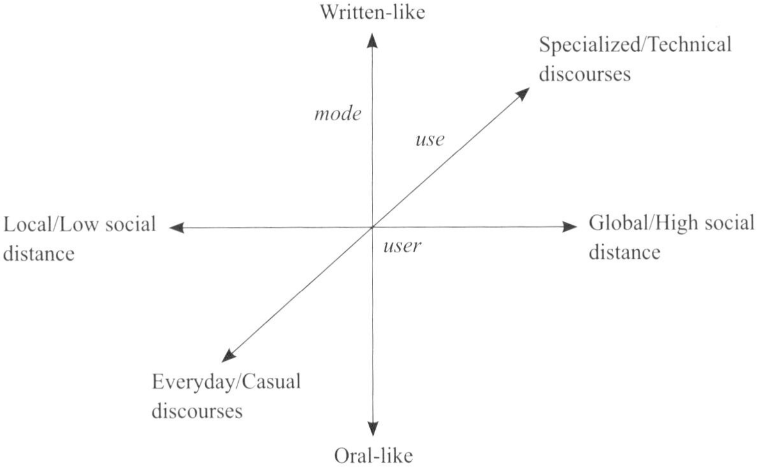

The works identified above are also closely aligned with research on translanguaging and transculturalism that questions the traditional static models of and boundaries between languages. These works have also led to the questioning of the notion of "language proficiency" in recent years; for example, Mahboob and Dutcher (2014) argue that models of language proficiency need to respond to criticisms of the static nature of language and engage with dynamic models. Presenting their Dynamic Approach to Language Proficiency (DALP), see Figure 2 below, they posit that "being proficient in a language implies that we are sensitive to the setting of the communicative event, and have the ability to select, adapt, negotiate, and use a range of linguistic resources that are appropriate in the context" (p. 117).

Figure 2   Zones and metaphors of the DALP model

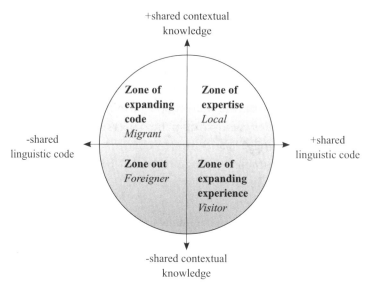

The questions about language and language proficiency raised in the theoretical work sketched out above have numerous implications for Applied Linguistics and TESOL research and practice. For example, rethinking the nature of language and language policy has implications for work in the area of language assessment, identity research, and second language development studies. Mahboob and Dutcher (2014) discuss the implications of DALP on language assessment. They suggest that tests of language proficiency should investigate an individual's (both native and non-native speakers) ability to negotiate meaning in diverse contexts rather than responding to discrete test items based on a static model of language.

Research on identity in TESOL and Applied Linguistics looks at identity as fluid and dynamic and is closely related to NNEST issues. For example, contributors to Curtis and Romney (2006) illustrate how identity in TESOL may be racialised and related to non-nativeness. More recently, other researchers use narrative analysis to discuss how teachers' identities impact their pedagogical practices and also how NNESTs (as well as other teachers) can draw from their identities as pedagogical resources.

Finally, research on language development has changed radically over the last decade. With a sustained questioning of the native speaker as the norm for language acquisition, debates on the nature of language learning, and a questioning of the nature of the language itself, there have been significant shifts in second language development studies. A growing number of research projects in this area now use alternative theoretical and research models to explore language development. Some of these include language as complex adaptive system, narrative research, conversation analysis, critical theory, and socio-cultural theory. All of these approaches challenge the notion of language as a static native-speaker-oriented product and therefore are relevant to NNESTs.

This brief chapter has attempted to show how the NNEST Lens is a useful tool that helps consolidate work that challenges monolingual native-speaker norms in TESOL and Applied Linguistics research. While a number of the papers cited in this chapter were not designed to specifically explore NNEST issues, these works relate to and align with questions that are at the core of NNEST studies. Together, this work responds to both theoretical and practice-oriented issues which need to be addressed in the field to change the underlying conditions that lead to discrimination against NNESTs.

In concluding, let us consider another quote from Kumaravadivelu's (2016):

> A critical appraisal ... of discourse on the NS/NNS inequity in our field leads me to a sobering conclusion: Seldom in the annals of an academic discipline have so many people toiled so hard, for so long, and achieved so little ... The subaltern can speak; the subaltern can write. The question is: Can the subaltern act?

My answer to Kumaravadivelu, based on this broad-brush review of literature, is: yes, we can and we have been. The NNEST community and colleagues are currently engaged in the kind of research that leads to a paradigm shift. This work, in time, will change the nature of language studies and impact professional practices.

References

Braine, G. (Ed.). (1999). *Non-native Educators in English Language Teaching*. Hillsdale, NJ: Erlbaum.

Curtis, A., & Romney, M. (Eds.). (2006). *Color, Race, and English Teaching Language Teaching*. Mahwah, NJ: Lawrence Erlbaum Associates.

Kamhi-Stein, L. (2004). *Learning and Teaching from Experience: Perspectives on Nonnative English-Speaking Professionals*. Ann Arbor, MI: University of Michigan Press.

Kumaravadivelu, B. (2016) The decolonial option in English teaching: Can the subaltern act? *TESOL Quarterly*, 50(1), 66–85.

Llurda, E. (2015). Non-native teachers and advocacy. In M. Bigelow & J. Ennser-Kananen (Eds.) *The Routledge Handbook of Educational Linguistics*. New York: Routledge, 105–116.

Mahboob, A. (2010). *The NNEST Lens: Nonnative English Speakers in TESOL*. Newcastle: Cambridge Scholars Press.

Mahboob, A. (2014). Understanding language variation: Implications for EIL pedagogy. In R. Marlina & R. Giri (Eds.) *The Pedagogy of English as an International Language: Perspectives from Scholars, Teachers, and Students*. London: Springer, 14–32.

Mahboob, A., & Dutcher, L. (2014). Dynamic approach to language proficiency: A model. In A. Mahboob & L. Barratt (Eds.) *Englishes in Multilingual Contexts: Language Variation and Education*. London: Springer. 117–136.

Mahboob, A., & Golden, R. (2013). Looking for native speakers of English: Discrimination in English language teaching job advertisements. *Voices in Asia Journal*, 1(1), 72–81.

Medgyes, P. (1992). Native or non-native: Who's worth more? *ELT Journal*, 46(4), 340–349.

Medgyes, P. (1994). *The Non-native Teacher*. London: Macmillan.

Selvi, A. F. (2010). "All teachers are equal, but some teachers are more equal than others": Trend analysis of job advertisements in English language teaching. *WATESOL NNEST Caucus Annual Review*, 1, 156–181.

Part II

Language Variation

Chapter 11

Understanding Language Variation: Implications of the NNEST Lens for TESOL Teacher Education Programs

Mahboob, A. (2018). Understanding language variation: Implications of the NNEST lens for TESOL teacher education programs. In Juan de Dios Martínez Agudo (Ed.) *Native and Non-Native Speakers in English Language Teaching: Implications and Challenges for Teacher Education*. Boston: De Gruyter Mouton.

Introduction

All NNESTs (non-native English speaking teachers) share one aspect about their linguistic repertoire: they all speak at least one other language in addition to English. This shared feature of the NNESTs has a number of implications and is the main argument for what Mahboob (2010) calls 'The NNEST Lens'. The NNEST lens is defined as 'a lens of multilingualism, multinationalism, and multiculturalism through which NNESTs—as classroom practitioners, researchers, and teacher educators—take diversity as a starting point, rather than as a result' (Mahboob 2010, p. 1). The NNEST lens challenges the monolingual bias (Kachru 1994) in TESOL theory and practice and suggests that having a multilingual orientation in TESOL would be much better aligned with the needs and context of NNESTs. In this chapter, we will examine some of the implications of the NNEST lens for teacher education programs. In particular, we will consider the implications of the NNEST lens in developing an understanding of language and about the use of local languages in teaching.

Understanding Language and Language Variation

In numerous casual surveys—at conferences and in classes—I asked in-service and pre-service teachers how they would define the following terms: language and grammar. The responses that I got are almost always the same: language is a form of communication; and, grammar is a set of rules that tell us how language works. Both of these are common-sense understanding of the terms and are quite limited for language educators. Given that the key role of English language teachers (ELTs) is to teach 'language', it is essential that language teachers have a more technical understanding of what language and grammar are. And, more specifically, since NNESTs are teachers of English, teacher education programs need to help pre- and in-service teachers develop an understanding of 'English' in today's world.

While it is true that language is used for communication, language *is not* communication. Language, as defined by Halliday (2009), is a semogenic system: a system that creates meaning. Language is not the only semogenic system—there are others such as music, colours, etc.—but language is arguably one of the most important ones and it plays a key role in how we learn to create and represent meaning. We are able to use language to create and communicate meaning because language is patterned. As humans, we notice, recognise, interpret and use a range of patterns to understand, to mean and to communicate. The study of these patterns of language is grammar. Grammar is not a set of rules; grammar is a way of understanding how language works. Language, we can say, is data and grammar is the way in which we make sense of the data. Thus, it is possible for us to have different grammars: each influenced by the limitation/extent of data and the purpose of explaining the data. Thus, depending on the corpus and our purpose, we can have different grammars. If we take 'native-speaker' language and describe it in terms of structural rules that can be taught to students, then we will develop traditional prescriptive grammars. If we take 'native-speaker' language and describe it in terms of its structural features, then we develop a traditional descriptive grammar. If we take 'native-speaker' language and describe it in terms of how the human mind transforms the deep structure of the language into surface structures, then we are developing a transformative grammar. If we take 'native-speaker' language and describe it in terms of what choices speakers have available and how they make specific choices in particular contexts, then we are moving towards a functional grammar. In each of the examples here, the end grammar that we develop is a response to the data that we have and the purpose of developing the grammar. Grammar itself, broadly speaking, is a theory of language—a theory that helps us organise, make sense of, describe, explain and predict language. The last element here, prediction, is a key aspect and worth some more discussion.

If we think of grammar as a theory of language, then, as a theory, a grammar should be able to predict language use. This means that a strong grammar should not only describe how language works in the corpus that it is based on, but it should be able to predict—with some level of certainty—how language can/will be used in instances not included in the corpus. This is an important test for a grammar and one that shows that most of the grammars that we learn and teach in teacher education programs are not strong grammars (in that they are unable to predict language use).

Traditional descriptive/prescriptive grammars are perhaps the most common type of grammars that teachers and students of English are familiar with in most parts of the world. These grammars have evolved out of earlier grammars of English (which, some argue, were not based on English data but modelled on Latin) and are based on written samples of English by monolingual speakers of the language. Most ELTs are familiar with such grammars and the rules associated with such grammars, even if they may not agree with some of them. For example, while rules such as 'do not split infinitives' etc. are now considered myths, they were included in grammar books and taught as 'rules'. These rules lost their validity (in some contexts) because they were not predictive: there were/are hundreds of examples that demonstrate that even monolingual speakers of English split infinitives (e.g., the introductory text from *Star Trek*, 'to boldly go where no man has gone before'). However, there are many other rules that are not questioned and continue to be taught. For example, one of the key rules taught about English is that an English sentence must minimally have a subject and a verb. While this 'rule' is valid in many contexts, it does not apply to procedural texts where the subject is often elided and clauses start with a verb. Thus, traditional grammars are not always able to predict actual language use.

This issue becomes even more complex when we consider non-native varieties of English, also known as World Englishes, and contexts where English is not used as a local/community language. One reason for this is that these traditional grammars do not draw on data from non-native users of the language when abstracting grammatical principles. Thus, traditional grammars are not drawn on in explaining non-native use of language. While this may not be an issue in itself, problems arise when the native-user-based grammars are seen as 'correct' or 'standard' language and other uses of the language are measured against them (and found lacking). One might ask the question: if traditional grammars cannot even always predict language use within other native contexts, how valid or appropriate is it to use them for non-native contexts?

The problem of documenting and using native-user-based grammar books as reference points becomes a bigger issue in contexts where English is not used as a community/local language. In such contexts, people do not always have access to samples of language use that they can draw on or learn from. In these contexts, people depend on grammar books as a source of information about appropriate use of language. In many contexts, the books readily available are traditional grammar books. As we have noted above, these grammars have limitations. But, since there are no other recognised sources available locally, people (including local ELTs) use these reference books as 'authority' and follow the traditional descriptions of language in these books. Things can get even worse in situations where local publishers/authors republish or plagiarise a selection of the grammar 'rules' found in primary sources without fully realising how the whole grammar works or the implications of picking and choosing some of the 'rules' from one book and combining them with those found in others. These locally produced books have a considerable impact on learners who buy and use them. Among other things, this creates problems in terms of peoples' understanding of grammar—as a set of rules—and perpetuates myths about language. These myths need to be challenged in TESOL teacher education programs through focussed and informed discussions about the nature of language, grammar, and language variation (see Mahboob 2014). Descriptions of language need to be based on data that reflects its use by both native and non-native users of the language (note that I'm not saying learners of the language—whether native or non-native—but users).

Research on World Englishes, which studies the spread of English worldwide, has challenged monolingual descriptions of English. World Englishes scholars (see, for example, Jenkins 2015; Kirkpatrick 2010; and contributions to journals such as *World Englishes*, *English World-Wide* and *English Today*) look at how English is used (and how it changes) in different contexts—including those where English is not a 'native' language. These scholars have demonstrated that the English language is not a monolithic entity and that it varies greatly based on who is using it, how and where it is used, and for what purpose. These scholars have also shown that these variations exist across all strata of language: grapho-phonology, lexico-grammar, and discourse-semantics.

For example, at grapho-phonological strata, we notice differences between spellings in British and American English, as in 'colour' (British) and 'color' (American); we also hear phonological differences between speakers of English from differing parts of the world, as in the word 'bar': '/baː/' (British) and '/baːr/' (American). At the lexico-grammatical strata, we observe how certain things are called by different names in different parts of the world, as in 'boot of a car' (British), 'trunk of a car' (American), and 'dickie of a car' (Pakistani); and how sentences and clauses are put together in different ways, as in 'What time is it?' (British) and 'What is the time?' (Pakistani). Finally, the way that information is put together and how and what things are said in different contexts can also be different across varieties of English; for example, letters to editors published in Pakistani English newspapers sometimes include a note of thanks to the editors as well as a praise of the newspaper—moves which are absent from editorials published in other parts of the world (Hartford & Mahboob 2004).

The World Englishes examples shared above show how Englishes can diverge in many contexts and how an NNEST lens, one that is not limited to monolingual native speaker data, can expand our gaze and show us other possibilities of explaining and describing language use. However, as has been discussed in Krishnaswamy and Burde (1998), Pennycook (2002), Bruthiaux (2003), Mahboob and Szenes (2010) and Mahboob and Liang (2014), using national labels in describing languages and Englishes is quite problematic. As pointed out in Mahboob and Szenes (2010), this is problematic because it leads World Englishes researchers into describing discrete linguistic features that are used to contrast one national variety with another and that do not necessarily contribute to a theory of language or of how meaning is construed or communicated in and across these varieties. In such cases, these researchers argue, linguistics becomes a tool for nationalistic agendas and loses focus on understanding language and how it works (without consideration to national borders).

While it is important for ELTs to understand language variation, nation-state based understandings of language are not necessarily productive. Instead, we need to think of language variation across a range of continua (or dimensions). In previous work (Mahboob 2014), I have identified four continua: users, uses, mode, and time that help us understand how language varies based on who is using it, for what purposes, with what resources, and when to use it. In this work, I have mapped three dimensions (users, uses, and mode) to develop a three-dimensional (3D) framework of language

Figure 1   The 3D framework of language variation

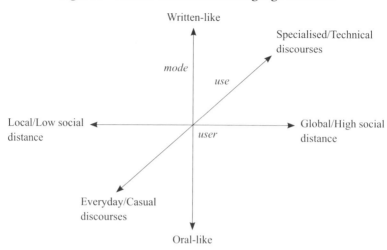

variation (see Figure 1 above). Above, I have included some of the relevant points from my previous work (Mahboob 2014/2015) to explain the three dimensions.

The first dimension of variation in language in the framework relates to who we are as 'users' of the language and with whom we are interacting. The user cline of language variation can be based on 'low' vs. 'high' social distance. People who have low social distance (i.e., they have many shared social factors, e.g., age, gender, origin, location, socio-economic status, ethnicity, religion, family, school, etc.) may have unique ways of using language that reflect their relationship and this language may not always be transparent to others (see, for example, Wolfram 2014). The indicator 'low social distance' helps us understand why people use 'local' forms of language, with their local denotations and connotations. On the other hand, when interacting with people with whom one has a higher social distance, one tends to use a more 'standard' or 'global' language—one that minimises 'local' idioms, forms, and features and is thus less prone to miscommunication. The indicator 'high social distance' helps us explain why people use 'global' forms of language, minimising local forms and features, and facilitating communication with people who speak a different 'local' variety of the language.

The second dimension of variation in language is related to the purpose or 'use' of the language. To understand this dimension of language variation, we consider whether the language being used is about 'everyday/

casual' discourses or about 'specialised/technical' discourses. For example, one could talk about music using specialised/technical language; or one could talk about music in everyday/casual language. In both cases, the topic remains the same; however, the specific linguistic choices vary based on the purpose of the exchange. In linguistic terms, this variation is understood as register variation, a concept used extensively in literature in genre and ESP (English for Special Purpose) studies.

The third dimension of language variation is 'mode' (Martin 1985; Derewianka 2014). Modes of communication include aural, visual, and mixed channels of communication. The way we use language varies based on whether we are speaking, writing, or—as is becoming common today—combining these two modalities (for example, in online chats, blogs, etc.). Note that the framework uses 'written-like' and 'oral-like' as the two end points. These labels acknowledge that language may be transcribed through a writing system, but may be more similar to oral language in terms of its linguistic characteristics than to written language, e.g., a dialogue included in a textbook or a novel, or a personal travel blog that includes images and texts. Similarly, language can be more written-like even when it is spoken, e.g., a plenary talk at a conference. It also needs to be noted that texts can be multimodal, i.e., they can draw on various modalities simultaneously (e.g., a talk which uses a PowerPoint that includes images and text).

These three dimensions are plotted together in Figure 1 to provide the basic framework of language variation. The framework helps identify eight domains (Table 1 below), with each domain including a range of variations, based on varying combinations of users, uses, and mode. Table 1 below lists the eight domains[1], identifying areas of linguistic study that focus on that domain, and examples of where one would find such language.

The fourth dimension, time, is not plotted in Figure 1, nor represented in Table 1. This is because time relates to each of the other three dimensions and every one of the eight domains that emerge from the framework. Thus, for example, language varies across time on the user dimension: language in all communities shifts and changes over time. While the impact of time is acknowledged in this model, we will not focus on it in this chapter.

---

[1] The ordering of the domains here is different than in earlier publications on this framework (Mahboob 2014/2015). The mode dimension has been reversed here to reflect the primacy of oral language over written language.

Table 1   Eight domains of language variation based on the 3D framework

	Domains	Areas of linguistic study	Examples
1	Local, oral, everyday	Dialectology, World Englishes	Family members planning their vacation
2	Local, written, everyday	Dialectology, World Englishes	Old school friends exchanging e-mails with each other
3	Local, oral, specialised	Need more attention	Members of an Aboriginal community talking about the local weather system
4	Local, written, specialised	Need more attention	Newsletter produced by and for a rural community of farmers in rural Australia
5	Global, oral, everyday	ELF (English as a Lingua Franca)	Casual conversations amongst people from different parts of the world
6	Global, written, everyday	Genre studies, traditional grammar	International news agencies reporting on events
7	Global, oral, specialised	ELF, language for specific purposes; genre studies	Conference presentations
8	Global, written, specialised	Language for specific purposes, genre studies	Academic papers

The model of language variation presented above has a number of implications for educational contexts. It shows us how language varies based on who the participants are, what the purpose of language use is, and what modality(/ies) is(/are) being used. Thus, it predicts what type of language we might find in what context and also puts into perspective the various areas of studies that prioritise different types of variations in language (e.g., 'use' based for genre pedagogy; 'user' based for dialect studies and World Englishes). The framework also contextualises language in terms of how we may use it in our everyday lives and how it relates to educational dimensions. The 3D framework draws significantly on Systemic Functional Linguistics (SFL) (Halliday & Matthiessen 2004) in that it uses the three register variables to develop the three dimensions of language variation. So, *field* is projected as *use*; *tenor* as *users* and *mode* as *mode*. However, this is where the similarity ends. The fourth dimension, time, while it is not mapped onto the framework (Figure 1), is also very relevant in understanding language variation but is not a register variable in SFL. Furthermore, the actual language within each domain does not vary only in terms of any one of the three field variables, but all three. So, within a particular domain, e.g., domain 1, actual language samples would still be analysed based on the three register variables: how they realise field, tenor, and mode through a metafunctional analysis.

As individuals—whether we are native speakers or non-native speakers of a language, our use of language for everyday purposes typically falls in domains 1 & 2—we use language orally or in writing with people whom we are familiar with and about everyday topics. The 'local' language that we use in such contexts reflects the norms of our local communities. When we shift our context and use language with people that we do not know well or about things that are technical/specialised, then our language shifts too. While most of us develop the language that we use in domains 1 & 2 naturally in our contexts, the language we need to communicate successfully in domains 5 & 6, or 7 & 8 does not come naturally. We need to learn this language—and, typically, we do this at school. Thus, the job of (English language) teachers is to help students develop an ability to understand and use language which can be used in globally oriented and/or specialised contexts. This is an important observation and has implications for ELTs. As ELTs, we need to help our students use language that allows them mobility and an ability to use language successfully beyond their immediate surroundings, with people that they do not know, and for specialised and technicalised purposes.

The language that students bring to school from their home—language in domain 1 (and, perhaps, 2)—may or may not share features with globally oriented language (domains 5 & 6). In some cases, for various historical and sociolinguistic reasons, students who come from urban middle-class Anglo families, have a higher chance that the local language that they speak and write shares features with the language in domains 5 & 6 (note that they have a higher chance, but that it is not a given). For all other students— including monolingual speakers of other dialects/varieties of English— access to domains 5 & 6 is through education. This is true for whether the local dialect spoken by a child is Aboriginal English, Afro-American English, Anglo-American English from a working-class or regional background, Chicano English, Jamaican English, or Pakistani English, etc. In all such cases, kids have to be taught global ways of using language (domains 5 & 6). When teachers are aware and attuned to the differences between 1 & 2 and 5 & 6 (see, for example, Martin & Matthiessen 2014; Derewianka 2014), they are better able to help students understand these differences and give them resources that will enable them to develop proficiency in using language in new domains. If the teachers (or the curriculum) are not aware of or fail to recognise these differences, or if teachers do not succeed in teaching the students globalised ways of using language (for everyday as well as technical/specialised uses), then the students are left to their own devices to learn about and use appropriate language. In such cases, while a few students may be able to understand and learn appropriate ways of using the language of domains 5 & 6 (and even fewer the language of domains 7 & 8), a large number of them fail to do so and are thus unable to succeed in and through education.

While domains 5 & 6 allow us to use language for a range of everyday purposes with people who come from all parts of the world, the language of domains 7 & 8 is highly specialised and/or technicalised and is something that needs to be learnt by everyone. One can perhaps even argue that the global orientation of the language of domains 7 & 8 comes through their specialisation/technicalisation. No one is a 'native-speaker' of domains 7 & 8. The language of domains 7 & 8 evolves as people come together to focus on a particular specialised/technicalised issues; the backgrounds of the people who come together are not important here, but rather the focus is on what needs to be done through language. The language of domains 7 & 8 is first introduced to children in schools (most commonly in subject areas, such as science, math, etc.) and then expanded and developed in college (through specialised degrees in subject areas). As teachers—whether NESTs or NNESTs—we need to note that none of us are 'native speaker' of the language in domains 7 & 8 and that we need to learn (about) it ourselves before we are able to teach (about) it. Access to knowledge production typically happens through language in domains 7 & 8 and this knowledge is then recontextualised for the wider audience through domains 5 & 6 and/or 1 & 2.

To understand this better, let us consider the following example. Expert knowledge in medicine is published in highly technical medical journals (domain 8) or presented at professional conferences (domain 7). This knowledge, even though it is in English, is not accessible to an average user of the English language (regardless of whether they are native or non-native users of English). Medical practitioners (who may be native or non-native users of English), who specialise in and understand medical discourse, make sense of this expert knowledge and use it to communicate with other medical practitioners (domains 7 & 8). However, when doctors talk to patients, they avoid this highly technical language and explain things in ways that are accessible to their patients. Typically, doctors translate the technical work into the language of domain 1 or 5, depending on where and with whom they are interacting. When doctors translate from domain 7 or 8 to domain 1 or 5, a lot of the technicality is lost. This is a compromise that has to be made for the doctors to communicate successfully with their patients; however, when communicating with other doctors, they maintain domains 7 & 8. This shows how important these variations/domains are and how they work across the society. For most ELTs, again, regardless of whether they are NESTs or NNESTs, their goal is to help students develop language that is more appropriate for domains 5 & 6; and then, if they are teaching specialised courses to help students develop language, they will need to participate in domains 7 & 8. Being a native speaker does not help in any of this, but knowing how language works makes a big difference.

Before proceeding, it is useful to look at the nature of language in domain 1, the domain that children develop naturally at home (if they do not have any learning disabilities). Children, as they develop language, do not develop 'a particular language', i.e., they do not develop what adults see and categorise as languages, such as Arabic, English, French, or Urdu, etc. These languages/labels are adult categories and are separated out in complex ways (such as location, group identity, mutual intelligibility, nationalism etc.). For children developing language, language labels do not matter. Matthiessen (2009) points out that 'language has evolved as a learnable system: its adaptiveness and inherent variability make it easier to learn because we do not have to learn it in one fell swoop; we learn it in a cumulative way, building up the complexity gradually from texts instantiating different registers' (p. 214). As children develop language, they are not concerned by variations etc., but by learning how to mean. As Halliday (1975/2004, p. 55) describes it, once a child 'learns how to mean', they continue to develop language by making meanings, or negotiating, in more and different contexts over time. Importantly, this process happens for all users of language; children do not differentiate between languages, but learn how to make meanings. García (2009) refers to the use of multiple languages in different contexts as *translanguaging*. According to García (2009), translanguaging goes beyond code-switching to include the range of '... *discursive practices* in which bilinguals engage in order to *make sense of their bilingual worlds*' (p. 45, emphasis original). Translanguaging is an important aspect of language (specially in domains 1 & 2) and will be discussed again in the section on using local language later.

The 3D model of language variation presented above uses the NNEST lens to develop a multilingual perspective on understanding language and language variation. This work relates to, draws from, and contributes to a growing body of research in this area. For example, the 3D model relates strongly with work on complex adaptive dynamic system which points out:

> (1) The system consists of multiple agents (the speakers in the speech community) interacting with one another. (2) The system is adaptive, that is, speakers' behavior is based on their past interactions, and current and past interactions together feed forward into future behavior. (3) A speaker's behavior is the consequence of competing factors ranging from perceptual mechanics to social motivations. (4) The structures of language emerge from interrelated patterns of experience, social interaction, and cognitive processes. (Beckner et al. 2009, p. 2) (see also, Larsen-Freeman & Cameron 2008; Matthiessen 2009; Hensley 2010)

This model, as discussed earlier, also closely aligns with research on translanguaging (see, for example, García & Li 2013; Canagarajah 2014) and transculturalism (see, for example, Motha et al. 2012) that questions the traditional static models of and boundaries between languages. These works have also led to the questioning of the notion of 'language proficiency' in recent years; for example, Mahboob and Dutcher (2014) argue that models of language proficiency need to respond to criticisms of the static nature of language and engage with dynamic models. Presenting their Dynamic Approach to Language Proficiency (DALP), they posit that 'being proficient in a language implies that we are sensitive to the setting of the communicative event, and have the ability to select, adapt, negotiate, and use a range of linguistic resources that are appropriate in the context' (p. 117).

This discussion of language has numerous implications for applied linguistics and TESOL research and practice in general. For example, rethinking the nature of language and language policy has implications for work in the areas of language assessment, identity research, and second language development studies. Canagarajah (2006) argues that static models of language proficiency are anachronistic and that we need a new generation of tests which 'should be performance based; they should feature social negotiation; and they should demonstrate pragmatic competence. We need tests that are interactive, collaborative, and performative' (p. 240). Extending this work, Mahboob and Dutcher (2014) discuss the implications of DALP on language assessment. They suggest that tests of language proficiency should investigate an individual's (both native and non-native speakers') ability to negotiate meaning in diverse contexts rather than responding to discrete test items based on a static model of language.

All these aspects of language, language variation, and grammar along with the implications of this work in different aspects of research and theory in TESOL and applied linguistics need to be integrated in teacher education programs. This work, which adopts an NNEST lens, avoids a monolingual orientation and is therefore more reflective of the needs and practices of teachers (both NESTs and NNESTs). Below, we will look at one particular area where this work can help classroom teaching practices.

Using Local Languages

One of the most consistent findings in the NNEST literature is that students and teachers find proficiency in the students' local language as a positive and useful resource (see, for example, Mahboob et al. 2004; Moussu & Llurda 2008; Braine 2010; Selvi 2014). Given these findings, it is striking that TESOL and applied linguistics programs do not explicitly train teachers in judicious and pedagogically appropriate uses of local languages (domains 1 & 2) in the classrooms. Mahboob and Lin (2016) discuss a number of issues that have led to the current situation. They point out that one of the key reasons that led to a development of negative attitudes towards the use of local languages in English language classes is related to the history of English language teaching and teacher education. English language teaching evolved from practices in foreign language teaching. In early days, the dominant approach to language teaching was the grammar translation approach. This approach gave primary position to a (dominant) local language and used it extensively in building knowledge of and about the target language. Many of the teachers of languages in these contexts were non-native speakers of the target language and shared the dominant local language with the students. The grammar translation approach was used to teach not only English but also a range of other foreign languages. However, over time, the demographics of who was involved in teaching and learning of English (and where) changed and these changes had a major effect on the development of theory and practice in TESOL and applied linguistics in the 20th century.

During the British colonial period, a large number of people from the colonies moved to the UK. In this context, the ESL (English as a sceond language) student population came from a number of different countries and language backgrounds, and the teachers as well as teacher educators/ researchers did not share languages with students. Given these contextual factors, the role of local languages was not really considered as a factor in the development of pedagogical material or training of teachers. Howatt and Smith (2014) in reviewing the history of ELT, state:

> ... translation into the language being learnt was, in general, firmly rejected within the Reform Movement as well as by Berlitz. With hindsight, it is a pity that this distinction between L2 to L1 and L1 to L2 translation did not survive the adoption of 'Direct Method' as a blanket term and that the many techniques and procedures developed by non-native speaker school teachers ('Reform Methods') have remained under-acknowledged. The Direct Method—in all its forms—was set, however, to strongly influence the subsequent era. (p. 84)

In addition to being the context of development of some of the major approaches to language teaching in the 20th century, academics and researchers in inner-circle countries also published key textbooks for preparing English language teachers. These textbooks, which excluded and/or critiqued the use of local languages in English language teaching, were not only used in the inner-circle countries, but also in outer and expanding circle countries. Thus, methods and approaches that were designed for particular contexts were marketed as being 'global' and used to train teachers around the world. One result of this has been a negative attitude towards the use of local languages in schooling.

Another major factor that has resulted in the non-use and non-recognition of local languages in ELT is the monolingual bias associated with describing and theorising languages—as discussed in detail in the previous section. Language, as was pointed out earlier, has traditionally been taught as a set of rules that are abstracted from monolingual native speaker intuitions about language. In doing this, language is seen as a discrete entity and separated from other languages and meaning-making systems and modalities. Recent literature (Canagarajah 2007) has critiqued the essentialist views of language as discrete systems that are pervasive in the language policy and TESOL methodology discourses. The official discourses of language-in-education policy makers in many postcolonial societies, however, still tend to project and assert the view of languages as stable, monolithic (uniform), reified (concrete) entities with clear-cut boundaries. The job of the language planner is seen as lying in the prescription and standardisation of linguistic systems, culminating in the production of authoritative dictionaries, grammars, and teaching manuals for the national and official languages to be spread among the population. These standard languages are put forward as educational targets, and the state's acquisition planning aiming at designing the most effective approaches for achieving these targets usually results in the recommendation of monolingual immersion approaches: total use of the target language is supposed to be the best way to achieve target language proficiency.

However, such thinking and theorisation of language has been questioned in recent times—as discussed in the previous section. Recent work on language has questioned the limitation of studies based on their focus on a single semiotic (meaning-making) mode and ignoring how meanings are construed and represented multimodally (using more than one mode, e.g., by using images and text together, as in children's story books) (see Canagarajah 2005; Bezemer & Kress 2014) in different contexts. The 3D model of language variation described in the previous section is also a response to this gap. Similarly, work on translanguaging (García 2009) and language as a complex adaptive dynamic system (Beckner et al. 2009) also looks into this issue. This body of work can help us theorise and develop ways that can be used by classroom teachers to help their students develop the language of domains 5 & 6 and eventually 7 & 8.

Mahboob and Lin (2016) drawing from Lin (2010) discuss the *Multimodalities/Entextualisation Cycle* as one way in which classroom teachers can draw on and use students' existing language knowledge (domains 1 & 2) and help them to develop domains 5 & 6. Mahboob and Lin (2016) identify three stages in the Multimodalities/Entextualisation Cycle:

Stage 1: Create a rich experiential context to arouse students' interest, and immerse the students in the topic field (e.g., festivals in the students' country), using multimodalities such as visuals, images, YouTube videos, diagrams, demonstrations, actions, inquiry/discovery activities, etc. In this stage, the familiar local languages of students (e.g., domains 1 & 2 as well as everyday language from domains 5 & 6) can be used to help the students to grasp the main gist of the experience.

Stage 2: Engage students in reading a coherent piece of TL (target language) text on the topic introduced in Stage 1, and then engage students in note-making or mind-mapping tasks that require some systematic 'sorting out' or re-/presentation of the target language textual meaning using different kinds/combinations of *everyday* local/target language spoken/written genres and multimodalities (e.g., bilingual notes, graphic organisers, mind maps, visuals, diagrams, pictures, oral description, story-boards, comics); these activities help students to *unpack* the target language academic text using local/target everyday language and multimodalities.

Stage 3: Engage students in *entextualising* (putting experience in text) the experience using target language spoken/written genres (e.g., poems, short stories, descriptive reports) with language scaffolds provided (e.g., key vocabulary, sentence frames, writing/speaking prompts, etc.)

These three stages form a curriculum genre, which Lin (2010; 2016) calls the Multimodalities/Entextualisation Cycle. The Multimodalities/ Entextualisation Cycle (see Figure 2) can be reiterated until the target language learning goals have been achieved. The key principle is to use students' local languages (domains 1 & 2) to scaffold students into TL everyday languages (domains 5 & 6) and genres together with multimodalities.

Mahboob and Lin (2016) argue that when we adopt a balanced and open-minded stance towards the potential role of local languages in English language

Figure 2   The Multimodalities/Entextualisation Cycle
Adapted from Lin (2010) (Key: Ss = students; LL = local language; TL = target language)

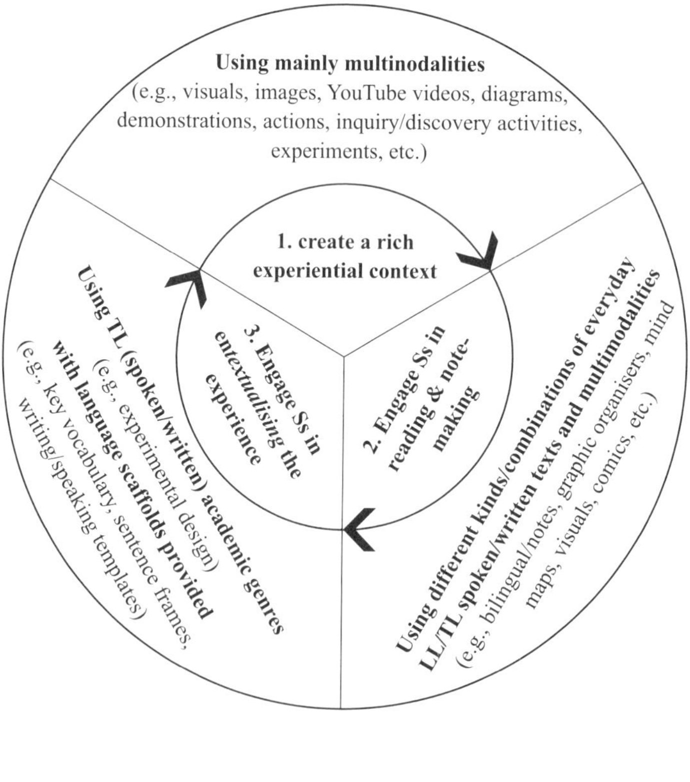

classrooms, there is a lot of systematic planning and research that we can do to figure out how and when we can use language of domains 1 & 2 to help students develop the language needed to successfully participate in domains 5 & 6 and then eventually domains 7 & 8. We need additional research to explore these areas and to provide us with guidelines that can be used to train and empower teachers and students in the future.

Conclusions

This chapter aimed to discuss the implications of the NNEST lens in the context of teacher education programs in TESOL by looking at two issues: avoiding the monolingual bias in describing languages and language variation; and, avoiding a monolingual bias in developing teaching methods. In discussing the first issue, the chapter identified some of the limitations in how many ELTs (and others) see language and grammar in limited ways and how this can be expanded by using an NNEST lens. The chapter described the 3D framework of language variation in some detail and discussed its implications for language teaching. In the following section, the chapter discussed why local languages are not included in much of the theorisation and practice of TESOL. The chapter argued that there are historical as well as theoretical reasons why local languages have been excluded in TESOL. The chapter then shared Lin's (2010) Multimodalities/Entextualisation Cycle as one way in which teachers can consider integrating local languages in their classrooms. The section ended by suggesting that teachers and researchers need to experiment and try out different ways in which they can integrate local languages in their classrooms and share notes on what combinations work best.

In concluding, this chapter provides a discussion of some of the directions that TESOL teacher education programs can develop in if they use the NNEST lens in developing their programs. Programs that draw on the NNEST lens will challenge the monolingual bias in the field and provide ways to move our research and practice forward in a responsible manner.

References

Beckner, C., Blythe, R., Bybee, J., et al. (2009). Language is a complex adaptive system: Position paper. *Language Learning*, 59 (Suppl. 1), 1–26.

Bezemer, J., & Kress, G. (2014). Touch: A resource for making meaning. *Australian Journal of Language and Literacy*, 37(2), 78 85.

Braine, G. (2010). *Nonnative Speaker English Teachers: Research, Pedagogy, and Professional*

Growth. New York: Routledge.

Bruthiaux, P. (2003). Squaring the Circles: Issues in Modeling English Worldwide. *International Journal of Applied Linguistics*, 13(2), 159–178.

Canagarajah, A. S. (2005). *Reclaiming the Local in Language Policy and Practice.* Mahwah, NJ: Lawrence Erlbaum Associates.

Canagarajah, A. S. (2006). Changing communicative needs, revised assessment objectives: Testing English as an international language. *Language Assessment Quarterly*, 3(3), 229–242.

Canagarajah, A. S. (2007). Lingua Franca English, multilingual communities, and language acquisition. *The Modern Language Journal*, 91(5), 923–939.

Canagarajah, A. S. (2014). In search of a new paradigm for teaching English as an international language. *TESOL Journal*, 5(4), 767–785.

Derewianka, B. (2014). Supporting students in the move from spoken to written language. In Ahmar Mahboob & Leslie Barratt (Eds.) *Englishes in Multilingual Contexts—Language Variation and Education.* Dordrecht: Springer.

García, O. (2009). Education, multilingualism and translanguaging in the 21st century. In Ajit Mohanty, Minati Panda, Robert Phillipson & Tove Skutnabb-Kangas (Eds.) *Multilingual Education for Social Justice: Globalising the Local.* New Delhi: Orient Blackswan.

García, O., & Li, W. (2013). *Translanguaging: Language, Bilingualism and Education.* New York: Palgrave Macmillan.

Halliday, M. A. K. (1975/2004). Learning how to mean. In Jonathan Webster (Ed.) *The language of early childhood. Vol. 4 in the collected works of M. A. K. Halliday.* London: Continuum. [Reprinted from Eric Lenneberg and Elizabeth Lenneberg, (Eds.) *Foundations of Language Development: A Multidisciplinary Perspective*, 1975, London: Academic Press.]

Halliday, M. A. K. (2009). Language and Society. London: Continuum.

Halliday, M. A. K., & Matthiessen, C. M. (2004). *Introduction to Functional Grammar*, 3rd edition. London: Edward Arnold.

Hartford, B., & Mahboob, A. (2004). Models of discourse in the letter of complaint. *World Englishes*, 23(4), 585–600.

Hensley, J. (2010). A brief introduction and overview of complex systems in applied linguistics. *Journal of the Faculty of Global Communication*, 11, 83–96.

Howatt, A. P. R., & Smith, R. (2014). The history of teaching English as a foreign language, from a British and European perspective. *Language and History*, 57(1), 75–95.

Jenkins, J. (2015). *Global Englishes: A Resource Book for Students*, 3rd edition. London: Routledge.

Kachru, Y. (1994). Monolingual bias in SLA research. *TESOL Quarterly*, 28(4), 795–800.

Kirkpatrick, A. (2010). *Routledge Handbook of World Englishes.* London: Routledge.

Krishnaswamy, N., & Burde, A. (1998). *The Politics of Indians' English: Linguistic Colonialism and the Expanding English Empire.* Delhi: Oxford University Press.

Larsen-Freeman, D., & Cameron, L. (2008). *Complex Systems and Applied Linguistics.* Oxford: Oxford University Press.

Lin, A. M. Y. (2010). How to teach academic science language. Keynote speech given at the Symposium on Language & Literacy in Science Learning, organized by Hong Kong Education Bureau (Curriculum Development Institute, Science Education Section), 24 June 2010, Hong Kong.

Lin, A. M. Y. (2016). *Language Across the Curriculum & CLIL in English as an Additional Language (EAL) Contexts*. Singapore: Springer.

Mahboob, A. (2010). English as an Islamic language. *World Englishes*, 28(2), 175–189.

Mahboob, A. (2014). Understanding language variation: Implications for EIL pedagogy. In Roby Marlina & Ram Giri (Eds.) *The Pedagogy of English as an International Language: Theoretical and Practical Perspectives from the Asia-Pacific*. Switzerland: Springer.

Mahboob, A. (2015). Identity management, language variation, and English language textbooks. In Dwi Djenar, Ahmar Mahboob & Ken Cruickshank (Eds.) *Language and Identity Across Modes of Communication*. Boston: Mouton de Gruyter.

Mahboob, A., & Dutcher, L. (2014). Dynamic approach to language proficiency: A model. In Ahmar Mahboob & Leslie Barratt (Eds.) *Englishes in Multilingual Contexts: Language Variation and Education*. Dordrecht: Springer.

Mahboob, A., & Liang, J. (2014). Researching and critiquing World Englishes. *Asian Englishes*, 16(2), 125–140.

Mahboob, A., & Lin, A. (2016). Using local languages in English language classrooms. In Handoyo Widodo & Willy Renandya (Eds.) *English Language Teaching Today: Building a Closer Link Between Theory and Practice*. New York: Springer International.

Mahboob, A., & Szenes, E. (2010). Construing meaning in world Englishes. In Andy Kirkpatrick (Ed.) *Routledge Handbook of World Englishes*. London: Routledge.

Mahboob, A., Uhrig, K., Newman, K. L., et al. (2004). Children of lesser English: Status of nonnative English speakers as college-level English as a second language teacher in the United States. In Lia Kamhi-Stein (Ed.) *Learning and Teaching from Experience: Perspectives on Nonnative English-Speaking Professionals*. Ann Arbor, MI: University of Michigan Press.

Martin, J. R. (1985). Language, register and genre. In Frances Christie (Ed.) *Children Writing Course Reader*. Geelong: Deakin University Press.

Martin, J. R., & Matthiessen, C. M. I. M. (2014). Modelling and mentoring: Teaching and learning from home through school. In Ahmar Mahboob & Leslie Barratt (Eds.) *Englishes in Multilingual Contexts—Language Variation and Education*. Dordrecht: Springer.

Matthiessen, C. M. I. M. (2009). Meaning in the making: Meaning potential emerging from acts of meaning. *Language Learning*, 59(Suppl. 1), 206–229.

Motha, S., Jain, R., & Tecle, T. (2012). Translinguistic identity-as pedagogy: Implications for language teacher education. *International Journal of Innovation in English Language Teaching*, 1(1), 13–27.

Moussu, L., & Llurda, E. (2008). Non-native English-speaking English language teachers: History and research. *Language Teaching*, 41(3), 315–348.

Pennycook, A. (2002). Turning English inside out. *Indian Journal of Applied Linguistics*, 28(2), 25–43.

Selvi, A. F. (2014). Myths and misconceptions about nonnative English speakers in the

TESOL (NNEST) movement. *TESOL Journal*, 5(3), 573–611.

Wolfram, W. (2014). Integrating language variation into TESOL: Challenges from English globalization. In Ahmar Mahboob & Leslie Barratt (Eds.) *Englishes in Multilingual Contexts: Language Variation and Education*. Dordrecht: Springer.

Annotated bibliography

Braine, G. (2010). *Nonnative Speaker English Teachers: Research, Pedagogy, and Professional Growth*. New York: Routledge.

This book traces the origins and growth of the NNEST movement and summarises the research that has been conducted on the issue. It highlights challenges faced by NNESTs as well as promotes their professional development.

Mahboob, A. (2015). Identity management, language variation, and English language textbooks. In Dwi Djenar, Ahmar Mahboob & Ken Cruickshank (Eds.) *Language and Identity Across Modes of Communication*. Boston: Mouton de Gruyter.

This paper introduces the Identity Management framework and discusses how using inappropriate models of local language in educational context can impact students' semiotic development and their identities.

Mahboob, A., & Barratt, L. (2014.). *Englishes in Multilingual Contexts: Language Variation and Education*. Dordrecht: Springer.

These contributions to this edited volume first look at the importance of studying English language variation in the context of education and then identify pedagogical possibilities that respect language variation and empower English language learners in diverse contexts.

Selvi, A. F. (2014). Myths and misconceptions about nonnative English speakers in the TESOL (NNEST) movement. *TESOL Journal*, 5(3), 573–611.

This paper provides a concise review of myths and misconceptions about NNESTs and discusses some of the key purposes and achievements of the NNEST movement.

Questions for reflection and discussion

1. How does the definition of grammar presented in this chapter differ from common-sense understandings of the term? How is an understanding of grammar, as discussed in this chaper, relevant to your context of language learning/teaching?
2. The 3D model presented in this chapter argues that both native and non-native speakers develop their language in domains 1 & 2. How does this view differ from or is similar to traditional approaches about nativeness? What are some of the implications of this in the context of education?
3. The chapter states, 'No one is a "native-speaker" of domains 7 & 8.' What are some reasons behind this claim?
4. The chapter argues that there is a role for local languages (domains 1 & 2) in language teaching/learning. Do you agree with this suggestion? Provide evidence/arguments to support your position.

Chapter 12

Researching and Critiquing World Englishes

Mahboob, A., & Liang, J. (2014). Researching and Critiquing World Englishes. *Asian Englishes, 16*(2), 125–140.

Introduction

Research on World Englishes has mushroomed over the last few decades with descriptions of 'newer' varieties of Englishes being written and published from around the world. A large body of this work presents syntactic features of these varieties of Englishes as representing features of these varieties. These features are typically identified by contrasting local patterns of language use with 'standard' British or American Englishes. Any variations found are marked and those that have more than a few tokens are typically included in descriptions of the 'new' variety. While interesting, there seems to be little effort made to understand the semiotics of these variations, how widely they are used in that particular variety, in what contexts are they usually found, and/or how they relate to other varieties of English. As a result of this, we now have a large number of descriptions of Englishes, which, arguably, have little application or use. In an important, but under-cited paper, Lavandera (1978: 171) points out that variation studies deal primarily with morphological, syntactic and lexical variation and 'suffer from the lack of an articulated theory of meanings'. She problematises this lack of attention to meaning in sociolinguistics research and argues that different forms mean different things and therefore should be studied as such. Without such consideration, a study of these variables 'can only be heuristic devices, in no sense part of a theory of language' (Lavandera 1978: 179). This is a severe criticism of variation studies that do not consider meaning to be an essential aspect of their study. Unfortunately, much current research on World Englishes falls into this category and this is perhaps one reason why research on World Englishes has not had much impact on language theory and why there are few applications of this work.

The purpose of this chapter is to critique the research methods used in current studies in World Englishes by addressing the limitations of this work and identifying strategies that can help in future work. In order to do so, this chapter critically reviews the literature on the syntactic features of China English. The findings indicate that the features described as China English might fail to index the variety itself. This is partly a consequence of the limitations of the research methods that were adopted in these studies. One of the main methodological problems identified in this chapter is the failure of the researchers to account for the sociolinguistic contexts and the demographic background of the participants. The results of the meta-analysis of syntactic features of China English presented in this chapter also suggest that much of the current work on World Englishes has ignored the similarities between different varieties and overlooked the sociolinguistic context(s) in which these varieties are used. The implications drawn from this chapter can help us in reconsidering the methodological requirements for work in this area; they can also help address the country-based naming practices in the field an issue that will be discussed in a later section of this chapter.

Problems in Researching World Englishes: A Focus on Syntactic Features

After reviewing the existing literature concerning the syntactic features of different varieties, we note that many of the features that are identified as features of a particular variety might not necessarily index this variety itself. What we mean by this is that although the presence of particular syntactic features in a particular variety of English, China English in this chapter, as described in the literature, is not questioned, their mere presence cannot imply the existence of a distinct (national) variety of English. This is because the features that are described as features of one variety of English are also found in other varieties of English—as will be demonstrated in this chapter. In addition to problematising the controversial descriptions of English varieties, we also critically review the foci and research methodologies of these studies. One exemplification of the problematic research focus is the overlooking of the sociolinguistic context in which the variety is used. In much of previous research on China English, too much focus is placed on the 'users' of a language instead of the 'uses' of a language (Mahboob 2010); in other words, this literature focuses on how people use a certain variety rather than how the variety is used in particular contexts and for specific functions. This chapter will also show how a) grammars of written English are used to analyse data based on oral texts; and b) the difference between register variations is ignored. The descriptions of China English based on these research practices are therefore rather limited and do not necessarily imply or index the variety. This also leads us to re-examine the current nation-based approaches to naming varieties of Englishes (Mahboob & Szenes 2010; Saraceni 2010).

Problems with Studies of Syntactic Patterns in China English

Research on China English, beyond any doubt, has made a significant contribution to the recognition and development of this variety of English. Since Ge (1980) first put forward the concept of China English, a number of papers concerned with China English have been published. Most of these papers can be generally categorised into three groups: 1) general introduction of China English (e.g., Ge 1980; Li 1993; Zhang 1995; Zhang 1997; Lin 1998; Du & Jiang 2001; Pan 2002; Yan 2002; Zhang 2002a; Pan 2005; Cheng 2007; He & Li 2009; Wang 2011; Shi 2012; Zhang 2012); 2) linguistic features of China English (e.g., Jia 1990; Jiang 1995; Pinkham 2000; Jiang 2002; Kirkpatrick & Xu 2002; Zhang 2002b; Chen 2005; Yang 2005; Cao 2006; Deterding 2006; Poon 2006; Li 2007; Xu 2008, 2010; Shen 2011; Yu 2013); and 3) perception and attitude of China English (e.g., Luo 1998; Hu 2004, 2005; Cui 2006; Chen & Hu 2006; Wang 2012; Tan 2013). In this study, examples from papers that describe the syntactic features of China English are critically reviewed. The studies analysed in this chapter were collected from some of the leading journals in the field, such as *World Englishes*, *Asian Englishes*, *English Today*, as well as chapters in certain representative books, for instance, the *Routledge Handbook of World Englishes* (Kirkpatrick 2010), and the *World Englishes, Implications for International Communication and English Language Teaching* (Kirkpatrick 2007).

A critical review of the syntactic features of China English found in the literature on China English leads us into identifying six issues undermining the validity and useability of these descriptions. One of these issues is related with the uniqueness of features being described and therefore questions the ability of these features to index a particular text as China English. The other five issues are about problematic research methodology. Each of these six issues is discussed below.

Issue One: Uniqueness

Many of the syntactic features described as features of China English are not unique to China English but are also shared by other varieties of Englishes, implying that the presence (or absence) of these features might not necessarily imply that a given text is China English (or not). We will briefly discuss five syntactic features described in literature on China English to exemplify this issue.

Inversion in subordinate finite wh-clause

Xu (2010) includes the inversion of subject-operator in subordinate finite wh-clauses as a feature of China English. An example of this feature can be observed in Xu (2010: 291) as follows:

> I really don't know what is International English.

This feature fails to index China English because it is widely shared by other varieties of Englishes. It can also be attested in Outer circle varieties, for example, South African Indian English (Mesthrie 1996, cited in Melchers & Shaw 2003: 158) and Pakistani English (Mahboob 2004: 1063). In addition, as Xu himself mentions, Quirk et al. (1985: 1051–1052, cited in Xu 2010) state that 'such inversion may occur particularly when the clause functions as complement and the superordinate verb is BE or when it functions as appositive'.

Word order

Xu (2010) points out that China English does not consistently use an SOV word order. While Standard English is commonly described as a 'fixed-word-order language', China English, influenced by Chinese, has a more variable word order and attests a presence of OSV word order. For example,

> Yes, I think many many easy words we have forgotten. Xu (2010: 291)

This feature is again not only found in China English, but is also attested in Singapore English. A typical example of object preposing of Singapore English is: '*To my sisters sometimes I speak English*' (Wee 2004: 1063). The 'free word order' (Kirkpatrick 2007: 110) is also common in African English.

Co-occurrence of connective pairs (CCP)

CCP refers to an utterance or a sentence where a main clause and a subordinate clause are connected with two conjunctions, for example, *because* and *so*, or *although/though* and *but* are both used (Xu 2010). For instance,

> *Yes, although it's not as big as Beijing, but I like it, because I was born in it.* Xu (2010: 290)

The use of double conjunctions is also attested in Nigerian English, for example, *'Although he is rich but he is stingy'* (Alo & Mesthrie 2004: 819). The feature is also attested in India English *'Though the farmer works hard, but he cannot produce enough'* (Mesthrie, Swann, Deumert, & Leap 2000: 300).

Yes/No response

Xu (2008, 2010) points out that while Yes/No responses are based on the truth-value of the corresponding statement in most native varieties, China English users tend to treat them as agreement or disagreement to the question itself. The following example given by Xu (2010: 290) illustrates this feature:

> *A: You don't want to make a living by playing guitar on the street.*
> *B: Yes. Of course not.* (ibid)

This feature is not only found in China English, but also in other varieties of World Englishes. For example, Kirkpatrick (2007: 110) points out that in African English, 'negative yes/no questions are confirmed by responding to the form of the question so that the answer to "he isn't good?" becomes "yes (he isn't)"'. This feature, as pointed out by Zhang (2002b), is also shared by South Asian English and Far-Eastern varieties of English.

Arranging sentences according to time sequence

Jia (1990) points out that the time sequence of English is from the present to the past, while Chinese prefers to start with the past and then come to the present. The following sentence is an example of Standard English accommodated:

> *He had flown in just the day before from Georgia where he had spent his vocation basking in the Caucasian sun after the completion of the construction job he had been engaged in the South.* (Jia 1990: 14)

In China English, in contrast, one would prefer:

> *He had been engaged in a construction job, and after he completed it he went*

to Georgia to spend his vocation basking in the Caucasian sun, and now he just flew back the day before. (ibid)

Both of the structures are attested in Standard English and the choice of one over the other is a tendency rather than a feature of the language itself. The choice of the structure is determined by what meanings need to be foregrounded in a particular context; however, current literature on China English does not discuss the context or semantics of these choices.

In concluding our discussion of the first issue, we need to note that while these individual syntactic variations do not index China English, it is possible that they may co-occur in certain patterns which may be characteristic to China English. However, the current work on China English does not explore collocations of this type and therefore is unable to provide us with any (sets of) indexical features of China English syntax. Furthermore, it is also possible that there are differences in how (what context and what register) these features are distributed across different varieties of English. Again, the current descriptions of these features don't allow us to carry out such analyses. Finally, one may argue that the features and examples discussed in this section are only examples of features that are attested in China English and are not meant to index China English. While this is possible, it is unlikely given that these features and examples are used in papers that are written to describe China English (as opposed to papers describing features of English in China).

Issue Two: Register Variation

Some of the syntactic features that are identified as features of China English appear to reflect register variation in English and are perhaps not features of China English per se. One feature that exemplifies this issue is nominalisation. Xu (2008: 16) claims that nominalisation is a feature of China English and the following sentence is an example extracted from his paper:

The Central Committee of the Communist Party of China (CPC) and the State Council have decided to increase investments in the sectors of education, health, and culture in rural areas. (ibid)

While a higher proportion of nominalisation might be found in China English (this needs to be confirmed through research), nominalisation is not necessarily a feature of China English. Nominalisation is a feature of particular registers (Halliday 1994). Certain registers—especially formal and written registers—tend to use more nominalisation than casual and oral registers. A large number of examples used to exemplify this feature of China English typically come from formal written texts. Thus, finding examples of nominalisation in these texts reflect features of formal and/or written texts rather than China English per se.

If there is indeed a higher proportion of use of nominalisation in China English, it might be a consequence of English language teaching/learning practices. A majority of users of China English learn the language in formal educational settings and through written material. Nominalisation is more common in written and formal language, such as the language used in textbooks. Thus, users of China English might be influenced in their use of nominalisation because of the context in which they learnt the language. However, these observations need to be further investigated with support from appropriate research and descriptions before any claims are made.

Issue Three: Using Norms or Writing for Describing Oral Language

A number of syntactic features of China English described in the literature are actually based on data collected from oral interviews (e.g., in Xu 2008, 2010); however, researchers tend to use the grammar of written language to analyse these data. This creates a mismatch between the nature of the data and the analytical tools used. One example of this issue is the description of Adjacent Default Tense (Xu 2008, 2010). This feature indicates that if the context of the utterance marks the overall tense, then the 'adjacent' finite verbs in the utterance can be set in their 'default' forms (Xu 2010: 289). For example,

> *When I was 7 years old, I first came here and lived with my relatives. So, maybe at that time, I think Beijing is a good city as a child.* (ibid)

However, instead of being a syntactic feature of China English, this is a feature of 'unplanned' conversation (Tannan 1982). One of the characteristics of informal spoken discourse summarised by Ochs (1979, cited in Tannan 1982: 7) is that the speakers have a 'tendency to begin narrative in past tense and switch to present'. Thus, the use of oral data without reference to grammars of oral/conversational English can lead to questionable descriptions of World Englishes.

Issue Four: Insufficient Sociolinguistic Information

In several of the previous studies on the linguistic features of China English, the sociolinguistic context in which particular features are found is not presented, and/or the features listed are not supported by any examples. For example, Yan (2002: 231) identified several features as syntactic features of CE, such as the tendency 'to avoid using articles, especially definite articles', 'often mix Adverbs with Adjectives and use "very" indiscriminately' and 'do not use third personal singular form'. However, there is no discussion of the sociolinguistic context in which these features are found and no examples of these features are provided in Yan's work. A lack of the description of the sociolinguistic distribution of particular features supports our argument that previous works on World Englishes tend to focus too much on how people use a certain variety ('users' language) whereas the context in which the variety is used is usually not described. Furthermore, many of the features listed in Yan's work are also found in other varieties of English. Because there are no discussions of the context of use in these descriptions, there are no ways of ascertaining whether these features differ from their use in other varieties of Englishes.

Issue Five: Stability and Extent of Use

The literature that describes the syntactic features of China English does not include information about the extent of use of that feature or the stability of the described features. Furthermore, features listed by different scholars are not similar to each other. Based on our analysis of published literature, we found that the identified features in different studies by different scholars are to a large extent different from each other. Table 1 below presents a summary of features of China English presented in Jia (1990), Xu (2008, 2010), and Yan (2002). The Table shows how most of the features identified in these three studies don't overlap with each other. This, again, shows us the importance of why it is essential to give contextual information when studying World Englishes; otherwise, the features described may not be shared across different studies/contexts and lead to confusion and weak descriptions.

Issue Six: Problematic Sources of Data

A review of the relevant literature also shows that previously identified features of China English are mainly based on interviews with students or

Table 1 Summary of the syntactic features of China English in three academic works

	Jia (1990)	Xu (2010)	Yan (2002)
Feature		Regard the Yes/No response as agreement or disagreement to the question itself	Regard the Yes/No response as agreement or disagreement to the question itself
Feature	The nuclear meaning of a sentence is placed at the end		
Feature		Null Subject/Object Co-occurrence of connective pairs	
Feature			Often mix Adverbs with Adjectives and use 'very' indiscriminately. Avoid using passive voice
Feature	The sentence order is Subject ^ Adverbial ^ Predicate ^ Object		
Feature		Adjacent default tense	Tense within a sentence is incongruent
Feature	The sentence is ordered chronologically, from the past to the present		
Feature		Unmarked sentence order: Object ^ Subject ^ Verb	
Feature			Tendency to avoid using articles, especially definite articles

(continued)

(*Table 1 continued*)

	Jia (1990)	Xu (2010)	Yan (2002)
Feature	Do not prefer using 'it' if the subject is aerial. For example, CE prefers 'The clock struck nine' than 'it struck nine o'clock'		
Feature		Subject pronoun copying	
Feature			Do not use third personal singular form
Feature	The position of privative is different from SE		
Feature		Topic comment	
Feature			Most people are reluctant to use tag questions
Feature		Co-occurrence of connective pairs	
Feature			Subjunctive Mood is overlooked when necessary
Feature		Inversion in subordinate finite wh-clause	
Feature			Tense within a sentence is incongruent
Feature		Nominalisation	
Feature		Parallel structure of two or more conjoins within a sentence	
Feature		Modifying-modified sequence	

newspaper texts (Xu 2008, 2010). The use of these sources as the primary sources to describe a particular variety of English is highly problematic. Student texts represent learner language and therefore are not reliable sources of how proficient users of China English may use the language. Studying learner language might fail to reach the goal of describing a variety because of their limited language proficiency on managing the linguistic code as well as the contextual knowledge (Mahboob & Dutcher 2013). Apart from the inappropriate use of learner data, it is also worth reconsidering the appropriateness of looking at data from newspapers, such as China Daily. Newspaper texts in English language undergo editing before being published. In addition, a number of 'Standard English' users are involved in editing such newspapers: the mission of China Daily is to satisfy readers from all over the world through using 'standard and idiomatic' English (China Daily 2012). As a result, using texts from China Daily might not be representative of the features of China English.

Discussion

In the previous section we identified and exemplified six issues in the current work on China English. These issues focussed on the failure of the described syntactic features to index China English; problems with the methodology, which ignored the sociolinguistic context; and the use of inappropriate data sources. In addition to identifying these issues, we need to consider ways in which to avoid these problems in future work in this area. Foremost amongst the issues that need to be resolved is the urgent need to take the sociolinguistic context into consideration. As Kachru (1992) points out, descriptions of English need to be based on an understanding of both sociocultural and educational contexts (p. 49). In addition, Kachru further points out that the English-speaking community must be seen in a framework in which a linguistic activity is under analysis within a specific sociocultural context (p. 57), which supports our stress that language should be studied in a particular context. In doing so, it is recommended that descriptive studies of World Englishes should be situated within a particular context (or domain or register) and that a description of this context be provided in some detail. They should look at how the variety is used in that specific context and avoid generalisations.

In addition to a description of the context, detailed information about the sources of data and participant demographics should also be provided and taken into account in the discussion of the findings. For example, studies should clearly include information about at least the following variables: age, location, profession, years spent studying English, self/other-evaluation of English language skills, age at which participant first started learning English, social class, other languages/dialects spoken, duration of use of English, context of language learning, etc. The significance of considering this information lies in that the variation of these aspects may lead to different results; and such results will allow for better comparison across studies of particular features in the same variety (across contexts, sources, and participants). Thus, having appropriate demographic and contextual information can help researchers in developing more detailed and context-sensitive descriptions of the variety. Issue five identified above supports this position—that the instability of the features identified by different scholars is potentially a result of the neglect of including participants' demographic information. This finding is further corroborated by Mahboob's (2013) work on Pakistani English, in which he argues that the differences in demography of the participants do result in a difference in attitudes towards specific linguistic features of Pakistani English. Mahboob hence suggests that future studies of World Englishes should be sociolinguistically responsible, and demographic and other information about the source of data be taken into consideration.

In terms of the sources of the data, researchers also need to avoid their dependence on learner data (unless the research purpose of a particular paper explicitly requires these). This is because the linguistic features reflected in learner texts might be features of learner language and not a particular variety of the language. The selection of the source of data needs to be planned carefully. Using only newspaper or fiction is also insufficient because of their edited and/or stylised language.

Another issue in need of being addressed is the "uniqueness" of a certain feature. Current descriptions of World Englishes are not always able to index a variety. There might be many reasons for this. One that we will consider here is the use of nation states as the main criteria for labeling varieties of World Englishes. Mahboob and Szenes (2010) and Saraceni (2010) have also discussed this issue in detail. Here we will look at this issue from the perspective of using the label 'China' in defining and describing China English. If China English is treated as a single variety that represents how English is used in China, then we might easily ignore the various social and demographic factors identified earlier and thus end up with descriptions of China English that have the kind of problems that were identified in this chapter. In addition, based on Mahboob and Szenes (2010), we can identify at least two problems in using nation states as a way of labelling and categorising China English. The first problem is the ignorance of the linguistic diversity that is presented within China and that may influence local varieties of Englishes. There are more than 200 languages and dialects spoken in China (Ethnologue, n.d.), and these languages may result in variations within China English that are rarely reflected in current descriptions of China English. For example, the dialects spoken in the multiethnic areas such as Yunnan and Xinjiang, are quite different from other dialects of Chinese that are spoken in other parts of China. However, descriptions of China English rarely differentiate or describe mother-tongue (dialect) influenced variations in China English in a systematic manner. This is true for even some of the more recent literature such as Ao and Low (2012), which studies the (pronunciation) features of English spoken in Yunnan province, a multiethnic and multilingual area in Southwest China. The second problem is that nation states or boundaries are not based on natural boundaries but emerged as a process of decolonisation or a product of a series of complicated historical events. In the case of China, English spoken in Guangzhou is very similar to English spoken in Hong Kong because of the shared Cantonese language and culture. In contrast to this, English spoken in Beijing is markedly different from that spoken in Guangzhou. However, the Englishes spoken in Beijing and Guangzhou are both labelled as 'China English' with little discussion of the differences between them. Therefore, we suggest that using the national variety as a singular unit which is defined and labelled based on the notion of a nation state needs to be problematised and perhaps abandoned; instead, we need studies that are more contextually sensitive. Finally, descriptions based on such studies should not be generalised, until and unless we have sufficient data and research to document how widely (both in the sense of region and context) a particular feature (or a set of features) is used. In order to do this, we need descriptive studies that do not simply draw on data that is convenient to access, but studies that are systematic and thorough in their identification, collection, and analysis of the data. One useful framework for doing this work is the three-dimensional model (see Figure 1) presented in Mahboob (2014). The three-dimensional model of language variation considers language variation based on: 1) users of Englishes, 2) uses of Englishes, and 3) modes of communication. Each of these dimensions forms an

Figure 1   Language variation framework

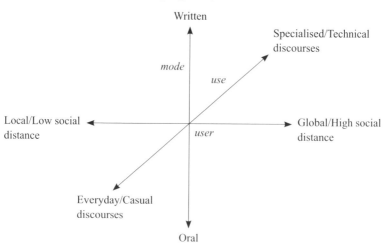

independent cline or continuum that influences language choices. These three clines can be mapped onto each other to give us a three-dimensional model of language variation.

This three-dimensional model helps us in identifying eight domains that represent different ways in which language varies based on who is using it, for what purpose, and in which mode. The eight variables and examples of the types of texts we will find in each domain are introduced in Table 2 below.

Table 2   Eight domains of language variation

	Domains	Examples
1	Local, written, everyday	Friends writing letters to each other
2	Local, oral, everyday	Friends talking to each other about their plans for the holidays
3	Local, written, specialised	Texts written by and for a local group of farmers
4	Local, oral, specialised	Farmers discussing specifics about their crops
5	Global, written, everyday	International news agencies reporting on events
6	Global, oral, everyday	Conversations amongst people from different parts of the world
7	Global, written, specialised	Academics writing research papers
8	Global, oral, specialised	Conference presentations

In understanding this framework, it needs to be noted that there is considerable language variation within each of the domains. This variation relates to the particular users, uses, and modes at play in a communicative event. One of the strengths of the framework presented here is that it provides an overview of how language variation can be modeled in a global context and therefore allows us to map these variations out and study them systematically. The model is not based on 'native-speaker' norms and can also help in our studies of translanguaging.

In operationalising this model, we need to track information on at least 5 facets: users, uses, mode, register, text type, and language strata for the data used in each study. Researchers in World Englishes should share information about each of these facets in their work so that their work can be appropriately tagged and categorised. Below, we will identify some of the key foci that need to be identified for each of the facets.

User facet

The following information about the 'users' needs to be identified:

Authors/participants
Age
First language
Location
Observants/others present, if any
Other languages
Relationship between participants
Sex
Social status

If additional user information is available and/or is relevant to a particular context, then it should also be explicitly stated.

Use facet

The 'use' facet includes three main foci: themes and issues, register, and text type. Each of these foci can be identified from the context of language use. Below, we will list some of the key areas/aspects that can serve as a starting point for descriptions of particular varieties of English.

Themes and issues foci

This focus deals with the categorising of the orientation/focus of the project. Some of the main themes and issues that are researched in the literature on World Englishes are listed in Table 3.

Table 3　Some key themes and issues discussed in the literature on World Englishes

Acculturation and deculturation in world Englishes	Code mixing in World Englishes
English as a lingua franca	English language teaching and learning
Hybrid Englishes	Intelligibility
Key and specialist terms (the 'circles' of English, endonormative vs exonormative models etc.)	Language policy and Language planning
Literatures in World Englishes	Models and theories of the development of world Englishes
Pidgins and creoles	Pragmatics and World Englishes
The role(s) of English as a lingua franca (local, regional, international)	World Englishes and academia
World Englishes and commerce and industry	World Englishes and computer mediated communication
World Englishes and education (including, but not limited to English language teaching/learning)	World Englishes and identity
World Englishes and 'local' languages	World Englishes and local, regional and international communication
World Englishes and law	World Englishes and media
World Englishes and bi-/multilingualism	World Englishes and popular culture
World Englishes and religion	World Englishes and translation
World Englishes in social media	World Englishes in the workplace

Register foci

Since language varies based on its register, we need to identify the register for the texts being analysed. Based on Matthiessen (2006), we can categorise all texts as belonging to one of the following socio-semiotic registers:

Expounding: general knowledge—explaining or classifying or documenting. Texts used for analysis of this may include examination scripts, research/ academic essays, and conference presentations, etc.

Reporting: on sequences of particular events, or regions of places—recording (events)/surveying (places). Texts used for analysis of this may include news reports—written and oral.

Recreating: aspects of socio-semiotic life, typically particular, personal and imagined experiences—narratives and/or dramatizing. Texts used for analysis of this may include fiction, lyrics, etc.

Sharing: typically personal and particular experiences and values. Texts used for analysis of this may include conversations, telephone calls, e-mails, and anecdotes, etc.

Doing: social action, with semiotic processes facilitating. Texts used for analysis of this may include business letters, meetings, auctions, etc.

Recommending: a course of action; advising/exhorting (promoting). Texts used for analysis of this may include advertisements, and tour guides, etc.

Enabling: a course of action—empowering somebody to undertake it, or regulating their behaviour. Texts used for analysis of this may include procedures, instructional texts.

Exploring: positions and values; arguing/evaluating. Texts used for analysis of this may include administrative writing, editorials, sermons, social letters, etc.

Text type foci

This focus identifies the type of texts used to collect data for a particular study. Table 4 is a list of some sources of text that can serve as a starting point for collecting and studying context specific language variation:

Table 4　Some key sources/context of data for researching World Englishes

Administrative writing	Advertisements	Advice	Anecdotes
Auctions	Blogs	Business letters	Classroom lectures
Computer mediated communication	Conference talks	Conversations	Court proceedings
Creative works	Diary	E-mails	Editorials
Instructional texts	Legal texts	Letters to the editor	Manuals
Meetings	Menu	Narratives	News reports
Obituaries	Office communication	Parliament/ constitutional texts	Political speeches
Procedures	Research/ academic essays	Seminar/workshop presentations	Sermons
Service encounters	Shop signage	Social letters	Social media
Songs/lyrics	Street signage	Student texts: exams, essays	Telephone calls
Textbooks	Tour guides	Warnings	Websites

The text types listed above are not exhaustive. Furthermore, there might be considerable variation between texts included in each text type. Therefore, any relevant information about the texts used should also be included in the descriptions.

Mode facet

The mode facet should tell us about the source of the data, including information such as when, where, and how it was collected. In addition, it should document whether the text used in the study was oral, written, signage, gesture, image, or multimodal.

Strata facet

The strata facet can help categorise descriptions of World Englishes based on whether they focus on: phonetics, phonology, morphology, syntax, semantics, pragmatics, or discourse/text.

Using this model can help in producing descriptions of World Englishes that go beyond nation-state-based labels and provide descriptions of language as it is used in different contexts for different functions and therefore generate descriptions of language variation that can be used for various purposes—for example, in producing textbooks, context relevant texts, and other resource material etc.

Conclusion

This chapter identified and exemplified six issues in current studies in World Englishes. While we have drawn examples for this chapter from literature on China English, the issues that have been discussed here are more widely applicable and have implications for descriptive work on World Englishes in general. This chapter has shown how descriptions of a variety of English that are based on nation states result in a number of limitations and issues. These limitations include the neglect of the sociolinguistic context in which the variety is used, overlooking of demographic/source information of the texts used, as well as not considering registerial features of the data. To address these limitations, it is suggested that future study on World Englishes should consider relevant social and demographic factors and avoid making generalisations. The chapter adopted the three-dimensional model of language variation to identify key facets and foci that need to be considered in studies and descriptions of World Englishes. Paying close attention to the research methodology will result in more focused descriptions of World Englishes that will be both more robust and more useable than the current broad-brush descriptions found in the literature.

References

Alo, M. A., & Mesthrie, J. (2004). Nigerian English: Morphology and Syntax. In B. Kortmann et al. (Eds.), *A Handbook of Varieties of English, Volume 2: Morphology and Syntax*. 813– 827. Berlin and New York: Mouton de Gruyter.

Ao, R., & Low, E. (2012). Exploring Pronunciation Features of Yunnan English. *English Today*, 28(3). 27–33.

Cao, N. (2006). Ye Lun Zhongguo Yingyu he Zhongshi Yingyu [Discussion on China English and Chinglish]. *Journal of Hunan Institute of Humanities*, *Science and Technology*, 2. 128–130.

Chen, J. (2005). *Studies of EFL Learning in China*. Beijing: Higher Education Press.

Chen, M., & Hu, X. (2006). Towards the Acceptability of China English at Home and Abroad. *English Today*, 22 (4), 44–52.

Cheng, Y. (2007). Zhongguo Yingyu de Tedian Ji Yu Zhongshi Yingyu de Qubie [Features of China English and its Differences with Chinese English]. *Journal of Shiyan Technical Institute*, 20(2). 76–78.

China Daily (2012). *Brief Introduction of China Daily*. Retrieved October 26, 2012, from http://www.chinadaily.com.cn/static_c/gyzgrbwz.html.

Cui, X. (2006). An Understanding of "China English" and the Learning and Use of the English Language in China. *English Today*, 22(4). 40–43.

Deterding, D. (2006). The Pronunciation of English by Speakers from China. *English World Wide*, 27(2), 175–198.

Du, R., & Jiang. Y. (2001). Jin Ershi Nian Zhongguo Yingyu Yanjiu Shuping [China English in the Past Twenty Years]. *Waiyu Jiaoxue yu Yanjiu [Foreign Language Teaching and Research]*, 33(1), 37–41.

Ethnologue (n.d.). *Languages of China*. Retrieved October 28, 2012, from http: //www.ethnologue.org/show_country.asp?name=CN.

Ge, C. (1980). Mantan You Han Yi Ying Wenti [Talks on the Problems of Translation from Chinese to English]. *Fanyi Tongxun [Translation Newsletter]*, 2. 3–10.

Halliday, M. A. K. (1994). *Introduction to Functional Grammar*. London: Arnold.

He D. Y., & Li. D. C. S. (2009). Language Attitudes and Linguistic Features in the 'China English' Debate. *World Englishes*, 28(1), 70–89.

Hu, X. (2004). Why China English Should Stand Alongside British, American, and Other 'World Englishes'. *English Today*, 20(2), 26–33.

Hu, X. (2005). China English, at Home and in the World. *English Today*, 21(3), 27–38.

Jia, D. (1990). Siwei Moshi yu Xianxing Xulie—Hanshi Yingyu Yuxu Tese [Thinking Pattern and Linear Sequence—the Sentence Sequence Characteristics of Chinese English]. *Journal of Foreign Language, 69*(5), 12−16.

Jiang, Y. (1995). Chinglish and China English. *English Today, 11*(1), 51−53.

Jiang, Y. (2002). China English: Issues, Studies, and Features. *Asian Englishes, 5*, 4−23.

Kachru, B. (1992). Models for Non-Native Englishes. In B. Kachru (Eds.), *The Other Tongue: English across Cultures.* 48−74. Urbana and Chicago: University of Illinois Press.

Kirkpatrick, A. (2007). *World Englishes: Implications for International Communication and English Language Teaching.* Cambridge: Cambridge University Press.

Kirkpatrick, A. (ed.) (2010). *Routledge Handbook of World Englishes.* London: Routledge.

Kirkpatrick, A., & Xu, Z. C. (2002). Chinese Pragmatic Norms and China English. *World Englishes, 21*(2), 269−279.

Lavandera, B. R. (1978). Where Does the Sociolinguistic Variable Stop? *Language in Society, 7*(2), 171−182.

Li, W. (1993). Zhongguo Yingyu he Zhongshi Yingyu [China English and Chinese English]. *Waiyu Jiaoxue yu Yanjiu [Foreign Language Teaching and Researching], 96*(4), 18−24.

Li, Y. (2007). Cong Yuyan he Wenhua Shijiao Tanxi Dangdai Zhongguo Yingyu Zhengzhi Cihui [Research on the Political Lexical Item of China English from the Perspective of Language and Culture]. *Journal of Chifeng University, 33*(5), 170−171.

Lin, Q. (1998). Zuowei Waiyu De Yingyu Bianti: Zhongguo Yingyu [China English: An English Variety as a Foreign Language]. *Waiyu yu Waiyu Jiaoxue [Foreign Language and Foreign Language Teaching], 110*(8), 16−17.

Luo, Y. (1998). Zhongguo Yingyu Qianjingguan [Prospect of China English]. *Waiyu yu Waiyu Jiaoxue [Foreign Language and Foreign Language Teaching], 107*(5), 24−26.

Mahboob, A. (2004). Pakistani English: Morphology and Syntax. In B. Kortmann et al. (Eds.), *A Handbook of Varieties of English, Volume 2: Morphology and Syntax.* 1045−1057. Berlin and New York: Mouton de Gruyter.

Mahboob, A. (2010). World Englishes and higher education. *Kritika Kultura, 15*, 5−33.

Mahboob, A. (2013). Pakistani English. In B. Kortmann & Lunkenheimer, K. (Ed.), *World Atlas of Varieties of English.* 531−539. Berlin: Mouton de Gruyter.

Mahboob, A. (2014) Language Variation and Education: A Focus on Pakistan. In S. Buschfeld, T. Hoffmann, M. Huber & A. Kautzsch (Eds.), *The Evolution of Englishes.* Amsterdam: John Benjamins.

Mahboob, A., & Dutcher, L. (2013). Towards a Dynamic Approach to Language Proficiency. *Asian English Studies, 15*, 5−21.

Mahboob, A., & Szenes, E. (2010). Constructing Meanings in World Englishes. In A. Kirkpatrick (Ed.), *Routledge Handbook of World Englishes.* Oxford: Routledge.

Matthiessen, C. M. I. M. (2006). Educating for Advanced Foreign Language Capacities: Exploring the Meaning-Making Resources of Languages Systemic-Functionally. In H. Byrnes (Ed.), *Advanced Instructed Language Learning: The Complementary Contribution of Halliday and Vygotsky.* London & New York: Continuum.

Melchers, G., & Shaw, P. (2003). *World Englishes: An Introduction*. New York: Oxford University Press.

Mesthrie, R., Swann, J., Deumert, A., & Leap, W. (2000). *Introducing Sociolinguistics*. Edinburgh: Edinburgh University Press.

Pan, Z. (2002). Zhongguo Yingyu Bianti de Yanjiu—Huigu yu Zhanwang [Research on Chinese Variety of English: Retrospect and Prospect]. *Waiyu Yanjiu [Foreign Language Research]*, 76(6), 24–27.

Pan, Z. (2005). *Linguistic and Cultural Identities in Chinese Varieties of English*. Beijing: Peking University Press.

Pinkham, J. (2000). *The Translator's Guide to Chinglish*. Beijing: Foreign Language Teaching and Research Press.

Poon. F. K. C. (2006). Hong Kong English, China English and World English. *English Today*, 22(2), 23–28.

Saraceni, M. (2010). The Relocation of English: Shifting Paradigms in a Global Era. Basingstoke: Palgrave Macmillan.

Shen, Y. (2011). Cong Wenhua Renzhi Jiaodu Fenxi Zhongguo Yingyu [Analysis of China Engish from the perspective of Cultural Recognition]. Master Thesis. Suzhou Univerisity. Retrieved February 18, 2014, from www.wanfangdata.com.cn.

Shi, M. (2012). Zhongguo Yingyu ji qi zai Zhongguo de Yingyong [China English and its Application in China]. *Journal of Hubei University of Science and Technology*, 32(11), 140–141.

Tan, H. (2013). The prospect of China English. *Shangqing, 17*, 262–263.

Tannen, D. (1982). Oral and Literate Strategies in Spoken and Written Narratives. *Language*, 58(1), 1–21.

Wang, J. (2012). Cong Fanyi Shiying Xuanzelun Kan Zhongguo Yingyu Cunzai de Helixing [Discussion on the Rationality of China English from the Perspective of Translation]. Master Thesis. Tianjin Commercial University. Retrieved February 19, 2014 from www.wanfangdata.com.cn.

Wang, L. (2011). Zhongguo Yingyu he Zhongshi Yingyu [China English and Chinese English]. *Theory and Practice of Contemporary Education*, 3(12), 129–133.

Wee, L. (2004). Singapore English: Morphology and Syntax. In B. Kortmann et al. (Eds.), *A Handbook of Varieties of English, Volume 2: Morphology and Syntax*. 1058–1072. Berlin and New York: Mouton de Gruyter.

Xu, Z. (2008). Analysis of Syntactic Features of Chinese English. *Asian English, 11*(2), 4–31.

Xu, Z. (2010). Chinese English—A future power? In A. Kirkpatrick (Eds.), *Routledge Handbook of World Englishes*. Oxford: Routledge.

Yan, Z. (2002). *Shijie Yingyu Gailun* [Introduction of World Englishes]. Beijing: Foreign Language Teaching and Research Press.

Yang, J. (2005). Lexical Innovations in China English. *World Englishes*, 24(1), 425–436.

Yu, J. (2013). Wenhua Renzhi Shijiao Xia de Zhongguo Yingyu Tanxi [Research on China English from the perspective of Cultural Recognition]. *Yushuwai Xuexi, 7*, 63.

Zhang, A. (1997). China English and Chinese English. *English Today, 13*(4), 39–41.

Zhang, H. (2002a). Chinese Englishes: History, Contexts, and Texts. Doctoral Dissertation. University of Illinois at Urbana-Champaign.

Zhang, H. (2002b). Bilingual Creativity in Chinese English: Ha Jin's "In the Pond". *World Englishes, 21*(2), 305–315.

Zhang, P. (1995). Shiyong Mudi yu Guobie Bianti [Use Purposes and Englishes—or China English]. *Xiandai Waiyu [Modern Foreign Language], 69*(3), 16–21.

Zhang, Y. (2012). From Chinglish to China English—An Analysis on the Possibility and Feasibility. Master Thesis. Ocean University of China. Retrieved February 19, 2014, from www. wangfangdata.com.cn.

Chapter 13

Dynamic Approach to Language Proficiency—A Model

Mahboob, A., & Dutcher, L. (2014). Dynamic approach to language proficiency: A model. In A. Mahboob, & L. Barratt (Eds.), *Englishes in multilingual contexts: Language variation and education.* London: Springer.

Introduction

Traditionally, language proficiency has been treated as a monolingually oriented static entity that does not change when a person moves between different situations or modes of use. We argue that such views are outmoded in a world where multilingual contexts are the norm, even in countries that acknowledge only one official language (García 2009, p. 44). We respond to this gap by offering an alternate conception of proficiency that is framed and exemplified by the use of Englishes in multilingual contexts. The need for this Dynamic Approach to Language Proficiency (DALP) is highlighted in the reviews of current models; for example, according to Widdowson (2003, in Leung and Lewkowicz 2006), even a model such as Bachman's (1990) useful multicomponential view of language is divided into static features which "cannot account for the dynamic interrelationships which are engaged in communication itself" (p. 214).

Amongst other things, this static notion of language is used in developing tests of linguistic ability such as the International English Language Testing System (IELTS), which often act as gate-keeping measures to workplaces and educational institutions. This is quite problematic because their set of tasks and assessment rubric do not incorporate the range of situations that people will encounter if they are successful in passing the test and do not consider the dynamic nature of language. Furthermore, current measures of proficiency are based upon standard, native speaker norms (McNamara 2012, p. 199), showing a monolingual bias that does not account for the complex nature of language proficiency in multilingual contexts. In this chapter, we present a new model of language proficiency that responds to these issues by recognizing the dynamic nature of language proficiency in multilingual and multicultural contexts. This model resonates with Johnson's (2008) "dialogically based philosophy of second language acquisition" (p. 271), in which language is viewed as "speech embedded in a variety of sociocultural contexts" (Johnson 2003, p. 179). To theorize and operationalize this model, we draw upon work in language variation, including the areas of World Englishes (WE) and English as a Lingua Franca (ELF), and language as a social semiotic as described in the theory of Systemic Functional Linguistics (SFL).

Kachru (2006) summarizes the tension between language variation and traditional monolingual views as follows:

> The concept World Englishes, then, emphasizes the pluricentricity of the language and its cross-cultural reincarnations. This conceptualization about the functions and multi-identities of English, therefore, has become a loaded weapon for those who view the spread of the language exclusively in terms of the celebration of the Judeo-Christian mantras of the language—the view that the "global," "international," and "world" presence of the language is essentially a victory of what is perceived as a monocultural Western medium, and that the language is the English-using West's weapon in the clash of civilizations ... That view ... does not represent the current global state of the language or the multiple identities English has created across cultures. (p. 447)

In this view, English is not the property of native speakers from the so-called Inner Circle countries, but is deployed by its users around the world to "reflect and incorporate local ... philosophies, idioms and cultures" (Mahboob 2009, p. 181; cf. Kachru 1992; Canagarajah 2005). If this is the reality of language use today, then a new model of proficiency which accounts for linguistic expertise in these multilingual contexts is sorely needed.

To develop such a model, a compatible theory of language is needed that focuses on language in use rather than a speaker's adherence to ideal forms. Systemic Functional Linguistics (SFL) provides one such theory of language because it views language as a social semiotic system, where language is seen as a system of choices made by its users. Language is also viewed in this theory as being inextricably linked to context. As Halliday (1978) explains, "language as a social semiotic" means "interpreting language within a sociocultural context, in which the culture itself is interpreted in semiotic terms—as an information system, if that terminology is preferred" (p. 2). SFL's view of language in context originates with the work of Firth (1935), who drew upon the work of Malinowski (Goodwin & Duranti 1992, p. 16) to argue that *context of situation* consists of "the human participant or participants, what they say, and what is going on" and that each person "carries his [sic] culture and much of his social reality about with him [sic] wherever he [sic]goes" (Firth 1935, p. 64). As Nelson (2011) explains, "Context [as described by Firth] may be determined more narrowly, as in differentiating different types of social situations, or more broadly, as in the usages of speakers who are from a particular culture and those who are not" (p. 4). Therefore utterances in a language—words, phrases, and sentences—do not occur in isolation but are the product of interactions that take place within a broader cultural setting (Johnson 2008, p. 271). That is, language is a resource that is used to make meaning in a particular culture; at the same time, this culture creates the set of meaning-making potentials in a language (Painter 1989, p. 19).

Hasan (2009) links context and linguistic proficiency by describing language use and communication as changing "along the context line, whereby during one and the same socio-historical age the content and structure of one verbal interaction will vary from another according to variation in the social context relevant to that interaction; this is what forms the basis for perceptions of degrees of *appropriateness* of behaviour in interactive practices" (p. 9; emphasis original). In other words, the success of communication is inextricably linked to the context in which it takes place, which includes the location and the people involved, among other factors. Accordingly, the model presented in this chapter defines context in terms of the two elements: use and users (Halliday 1978, p. 35). *Use of language* includes the purpose of the communicative event and the location in which it takes place, while *users of language* refer to the key interlocutors in an event, including their relative status and power. Together, these variables have an effect upon the socio-cultural practices of a particular context.

Use of language has been examined extensively in genre theory, which is a branch of SFL that investigates the way language varies according to the purpose for which it is used and the ways users of a language learn how to effectively make meaning in these different contexts. As a whole, it examines the way certain valued ways of making meaning emerge in particular cultures, and the nature and meaning of these genres. A genre is defined as a "staged, goal-oriented social process", where staged means that genres unfold in a certain order with particular steps and goal-oriented means that they are incomplete if the stages are not finished; the term social refers to the fact that these genres take place within interactions (Martin & Rose 2007, 2008; Martin 2009). Genre is significant to this model because it means that a person's proficiency in one genre does not account for their whole proficiency in a language. For example, a person may be able to write a friendly thank-you note proficiently in a certain language but may not be able to write a business report in that same language. In order to do so, this person would need to learn the conventions of this new genre to use the linguistic code in this way.

According to Matthiessen (2009), "Language has evolved as a learnable system: its adaptiveness and inherent variability make it easier to learn because we do not have to learn it in one fell swoop; we learn it in a cumulative way, building up the complexity gradually from texts instantiating different registers" (p. 214). The model therefore accounts for an individual's varying proficiency in different genres and the way this proficiency changes over time as he or she learns to negotiate these genres successfully (Johnson 2008, p. 275). One branch of SFL examines this ontogenetic development of language, a process which is defined by Matthiesson (2009) as "the learning of a personalized meaning potential" (p. 206) that happens throughout one's lifetime, "from birth, through infancy and childhood, and on through adolescence into adult life" (Halliday 1993, p. 93). As Halliday (1975/2004) describes it, once a child "learns how to mean", he or she continues to develop language by making meanings in, or negotiating, more and different contexts over time (p. 55). Importantly, this process happens for all users of languages, regardless of which mother tongue is learnt initially. The model presented in this chapter uses the process of ontogenesis to account for a speaker's changing ability to communicate in a range of contexts over the course of his or her lifetime.

Language users are one factor considered in language variation studies, which investigate how people of different backgrounds, including age, social class, region, and educational level, among other factors, use language differently. In these studies, the use of the linguistic code is shown to change significantly in the hands or mouths of different users in the creation of complex and meaningful interactions. Furthermore, such studies have examined and critiqued the way power and status are attached to these different ways of using language. The way language changes according to its user is an important part of the contextual element of this model because one's understanding of the linguistic practices of his or her interlocutors impacts the ability to communicate with them. This aspect of language variation is also salient in work on English as Lingua Franca (ELF). ELF is defined by Seidlhofer (2011) as "any use of English among speakers of different first languages for whom English is the communicative medium of choice, and often the only option" (p. 7). Researchers in this area and World Englishes critique the privileging of native-speaker norms by observing that non-native users of English "can be, and usually are, characterized as incompetent when their performance does not conform to standard native speaker norms" (Widdowson 2012, p. 8). Studies of ELF interaction have revealed the inherent variability of such contexts of use and do not view ELF as "a variety" but instead recognize "its diversity and interactive character" (Seidlhofer 2007, in Schneider 2012, p. 60). As Firth (2009) argues, "If there is a 'lingua franca factor' it resides ... between its variability of form and action, and what ELF entails metatheoretically" (p. 162). This adaptation of language for negotiating different communities and identities is seen as a process that is a part of the human experience of learning to make meaning in different contexts, a view which is compatible with the SFL concept of ontogenetic development described previously.

The Dynamic Approach to Language Proficiency (DALP) is a model of proficiency that responds to the issues the studies in SFL and language variation raise. Because the appropriate use of linguistic code changes lexically, syntactically and stylistically based on its use in context, depending on the use and users, the DALP model considers shared linguistic code and shared contextual knowledge as the two core dimensions of proficiency. These two elements are represented as intersecting clines; when this is done, four quadrants emerge which are considered as four different zones of proficiency. DALP is dynamic in the sense that any user's language proficiency can move from zone to zone in a non-linear fashion, depending on changes in the myriad variables within the context of the interaction and/or the linguistic code required (Larson-Freeman & Cameron 2008, p. 2).

This chapter begins with the theoretical background of the terminology that will be used throughout to describe elements of proficiency, followed by a description and exemplification of the core elements and zones of proficiency. We then use data from ELF/WE literature to show how the DALP model can be operationalized to describe the nature of proficiency in written and spoken contexts of communication.

Finally, we discuss the potential implications of this model in three areas: assessment, language teaching, and migration research.

Theoretical Background

In this section, we set out some concepts from Systemic Functional Linguistics and World Englishes and show how these concepts relate to each other to form a theoretical framework for the DALP model.

According to SFL, language as a system is comprised of three sub-systems, called strata: the grapho-phonology stratum, or meaning at the sound and sign level; the lexicogrammar stratum, or meaning at the word level; and the semantics stratum, or meaning at the sentence level (Halliday 1978, p. 38). These strata together comprise language as a semiotic system, which is a "system of potential, a range of alternatives" for making meaning. These strata are configured together in a realization hierarchy, so that the individual sounds or orthographic figures together realize what a speaker or writer can say, which in turn realizes what a speaker or writer can mean. Therefore, in SFL "... we see the text as actualized potential ... so that any text represents an actualization (a path through the system) at each level: the level of meaning, the level of saying ..., and of course the level of sounding or writing" (Halliday 1978, p. 40). Taking this tristratal view of the language system makes it possible to describe aspects of language use from the perspective of each of these strata. For example, they allow us to discuss previously described distinctions between use and users as follows. Halliday refers to linguistic variations in language use as register and the linguistic variations between users of a language as dialect. The dialects of a given language "differ from each other phonologically and lexicogrammatically, but not ... semantically" (p. 185); by contrast, registers differ semantically. Furthermore, lexicogrammatical differences occur as an "automatic consequence" (p. 185) of these semantic differences because meaning is realized by this stratum.

The description of language presented above corroborates work on intelligibility in World Englishes as well. For example, the three dimensions of intelligibility described below, which are presented in the Smith Framework (Smith & Nelson 1985), can be aligned with an understanding of strata shared above. Smith and Nelson (1985) and Nelson (2011) provide useful working definitions of the commonly used terms intelligibility, comprehensibility, and interpretability in the following way:

1. *intelligibility*: word/utterance recognition,
2. *comprehensibility*: word/utterance meaning (locutionary force),
3. *interpretability*: meaning behind word/utterance (illocutionary force)
(Smith and Nelson 1985, p. 334).

We argue that these levels correspond to the strata of SFL theory, so that intelligibility is mutual understanding at the level of phonology, the sound/orthographic system; comprehensibility is mutual understanding at the level of lexicogrammar, meaning at the word/phrase level or what a person says; and interpretability is understanding at the level of discourse semantics or what a person means by what he or she says. Like the strata of the language system, these terms allow for a more precise description of proficiency in terms of mutual understanding in communicative contexts. Conversely, when a misunderstanding occurs, these terms allow the description of the stratum at which it is perceived to have occurred.

Some researchers, such as Rajagopalan (2010, in Nelson 2011, p. 76), have critiqued Smith's definition of terms as being highly subjective and dependent upon the hearer and speaker, or reader and writer, in a given situation. However, as Nelson argues, this is precisely the point: an utterance's intelligibility, comprehensibility and interpretability are dependent upon the people engaged in it because "... linguistic communication is an interactive enterprise" (p. 76). That the communication may not be appropriate in all contexts is irrelevant to the fact that successful communication has occurred in its given context. For the purposes of the DALP model, these terms allow us to discuss the nature of proficiency in different texts to show how an interaction or text in a particular register may be incomprehensible to a reader or interlocutor who is perfectly proficient in another; likewise, this same interaction or text may be comprehensible or not to a different reader or interlocutor who uses (a) different dialect(s).

The Dynamic Approach to Language Proficiency

The DALP model consists of two core elements: shared linguistic code and shared contextual knowledge (Figure 1). Shared linguistic code is the user's control of the myriad features of a given language such as mode of communication (written or spoken), syntax, lexicogrammar, morphology, phonology, discursive practices, and realization of politeness. Shared contextual knowledge is the familiarity with, and ability to successfully negotiate, the setting, purpose, socio-cultural practices, participants, and turn-taking organization of an event. These two elements are not viewed as absolutes in this model, but instead as continuums, so that the abilities of a person can be placed along a line of having relatively more or less proficiency in a certain area. In the model, these two clines intersect to form four Zones of Proficiency (see Figure 1); a person's Zone of Proficiency can change in a non-linear fashion depending on his or her knowledge of the linguistic code and/or contextual features of a situation. Furthermore, it models the ontogenetic development of language for all individuals over time because a person's proficiency is shown to increase as he or she develops the ability to communicate at a high level of competence in a wider range of situations. This development is not based upon the person's adherence to an outside norm but rather their flexibility in negotiating communication in different contexts. Placing the basis of proficiency on communicative flexibility rather than solely on norm-adherence means that multilingualism is valued, as is the ability to negotiate different contexts within the same linguistic code.

The following hypothetical examples will show how this model relates to the linguistic development of both native and non-native speakers of English. The purpose of these two examples is to show how both native and non-native speakers of English adapt to different contexts of language use in similar ways as they are exposed to different contexts and must adapt linguistically to communicate. They show how the core elements of proficiency, shared

Figure 1   The dynamic approach to language proficiency (DALP) model

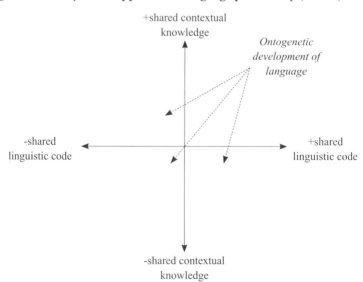

linguistic code and shared contextual knowledge, combine in different ways to create a more nuanced description of proficiency.

The first example that we will discuss here is that of Christine, an American who learns English by growing up in a home where it is spoken by her parents and extended family and becomes aware of a wider range of genres and written forms of English during primary school and high school. When she enters university in the USA, she is asked to write a literature review as an assignment. On her first attempt, she produces what her lecturer calls a summary rather than building an argument and does not receive a high mark for the assignment. In this situation, Christine has knowledge of the required linguistic code but is not able to deploy it appropriately to achieve the requirements of this register until she finds a way to learn the competencies required to become proficient in this genre. Later in her university career, Christine decides to study abroad for a year in Australia. When she goes to the pub with her new Australian friends, she finds that she is unable to understand or participate in the jokes that make reference to local cultural experiences and jargon; in this situation, she also at times finds their utterances unintelligible and incomprehensible due to differences in dialect. However, in her university lectures she is able to draw upon shared contextual knowledge of registers that she has encountered in the past, which enables her to negotiate communication more readily. By the end of her year abroad, she is able to negotiate both the informal and academic settings much more effectively.

The second example is Zainab from Pakistan. She speaks Urdu at home and has learnt English formally throughout her schooling. She attends university in Pakistan, where she studies biology; for medical school, she decides to study in Singapore in an English-medium university. Because she studied British English in school, the conventions of spelling and pronunciation are familiar to her. However, her lecturers come from a range of linguistic and cultural backgrounds, so in the beginning, she finds their accents and use of language difficult to understand. But by the end of her first semester, helped by her background in the field of biology, she is able to understand lectures in a range of varieties of English, such as Chinese and Singaporean Englishes. When she completes her degree, she moves to a small town in the United States to practice medicine at a hospital. In the hospital setting, she finds that it is at times difficult to make herself understood by the staff and patients; likewise, when topics other than medicine are discussed, she finds it difficult to make out what they want to say because of their use of cultural references with which she is not familiar. Over time, she is increasingly able to understand and be understood as both she and her colleagues and patients become more familiar with the other's dialect and cultural references.

As Christine and Zainab move through different contexts, their control of the linguistic code and familiarity with the context changes so that they also move through different Zones of Proficiency. The following sections will describe these four Zones through the introduction of metaphors that serve as archetypes of each quadrant.

Zainab and Christine are in the Zone of Expertise when they use Urdu and American English, respectively, to communicate about everyday matters in the home because in this context they are in full control of the linguistic code and the conventions of appropriate contextual use. This zone is represented by the metaphor of the local, who could be someone who was born in a particular city and is a native speaker of the local dialect, or could be someone who has migrated to a city from another place and who has lived there long enough to learn the conventions of the local culture and language use. Therefore the local archetype represents all persons who are able to negotiate communication in a wide range of familiar contexts in (a) certain language(s) as a result of their previous experience. The criteria for the Zone of Expertise are not what one's mother tongue is, but rather one's ability to negotiate contexts successfully through control of the linguistic code and the associated conventions. Therefore, after Zainab has adapted to the variety of English used in small-town USA, she is in the Zone of Expertise for this context even though she may not consider herself to be a native speaker.

When Christine moved to Australia and Zainab moved to the USA, the linguistic code was familiar but the context was not, particularly in informal settings where many unfamiliar cultural references were made. In these situations, they are considered to be in the Zone of Expanding Experience. In this zone, the user is familiar with the language that is being used in a particular context, but the context itself is unfamiliar. The metaphor used for this zone is a visitor, which represents someone who has linguistic knowledge but is unfamiliar with, or visiting, a new context. As a result, this person uses the linguistic code in a way that marks him or her as being new to this particular context. In order to move to the Zone of Expertise for this context, the user would need to learn how to use the language he or she already knows in a new way as well as learn new language appropriate in the context. To do this, he or she would need to expand his or her experience through some means of education (formal or not), but would not have to learn an entirely new linguistic code in order to do this. Both Christine and Zainab made this transition through a combination of asking direct questions and making inferences through other resources than language and slowly building up a broader repertoire over time.

When Zainab moved from Pakistan to Singapore to study medicine at an English-medium university, the context and subject matter were familiar but the linguistic code used by her lecturers was unfamiliar. Therefore she was in the Zone of Expanding Code. The metaphor used for this zone is migrant because it typifies the language user who must learn to operate in a new linguistic code in order to negotiate familiar contexts in a new community. The linguistic code could be unfamiliar because it is an entirely new language or variety for the user (e.g. Spanish versus Chinese, or Indian English versus Australian English), because the mode is unfamiliar (e.g. written or spoken), or because the appropriate register is unfamiliar (e.g. formal or informal). In this zone, the user has experience in this context but is not in control of the favoured or socially appropriate use of language for this context.

If either Christine or Zainab were to go on holiday to a new country where a completely unfamiliar linguistic code is used, they would be unfamiliar with both the contextual elements and the linguistic code of a situation. This is described in the DALP model as being Zoned Out. The metaphor for this zone is a foreigner, someone who has recently arrived to a new place where a different language is spoken and new cultural contexts are being encountered regularly. This person has not yet learnt to negotiate the situation at hand and also does not have control of the linguistic code required. As the speaker becomes more familiar with either the contextual or linguistic elements, he or she moves toward the other Zones of Proficiency (Figure 2).

In the following section, we examine data from the literature in World Englishes (WE) and English as a Lingua Franca (ELF) to further operationalize the DALP model in diverse contexts. The analytical framework we have established will be used to describe the Zones of Proficiency for interlocutors in each sample, including speakers/writers and listeners/readers. Written and spoken data will be used to exemplify the Zones of Expertise, Expanding Experience, and Expanding Code.

Figure 2 Zones and metaphors of the DALP model

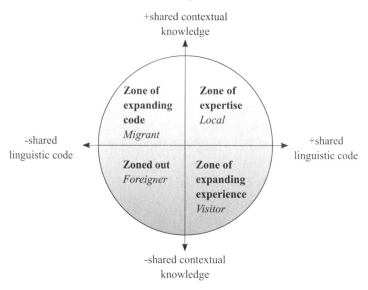

Operationalizing the DALP Model

In the following section, we will show how the DALP model can be used to describe and analyze spoken and written data. To do this, we draw upon selected data and analyzes from the literature in World English and English as a Lingua Franca to show how the concepts of intelligibility, comprehensibility, and interpretability from the Smith Framework can be deployed to place written and spoken interactions in the corresponding Zone of the DALP model. In this way, we will show how the model can be used in analysis of naturally occurring data.

The first sample comes from Firth (2009), which is an excerpt of a business interaction by telephone between an Egyptian cheese wholesaler (B) and a Danish cheese producer/seller (A):

According to Firth, though some of the utterances in this excerpt may not conform to the norms of an ENL (English as a Native Language) context, there is no evidence of difficulty with comprehensibility or interpretability in this interaction. Therefore Firth argues that these speakers demonstrate the ability to communicate in ELF contexts, which "entails not so much mastery of a stable and standardized code or form, but mastery of strategies for the accomplishment of accommodation of diverse practices and modes of meaning" (Firth 2009, pp. 162–163). Based on this analysis, according to the DALP model, these speakers are operating in the Zone of Expertise. This conception of proficiency differs considerably from traditional conceptions of proficiency, which would view these interactions as a deviation from the standard norm.

1	B:	uh (.) I 'ave asked this uh for one single thing that (.) I want (.)
2		to 'ave uh an exclusive brand in
3		order to maintain my prize ((price)) (.) in the market, I can-
4		nobody can compete (.) with my price, if
5		I will maintain a good price, and the other one has the same
6		brand and the same product (.) he can sell
7		less, and he can just (.) play with the market
8		(0.3)
9	A:	that's (.) yeah
10	B:	the brand, always, which is in the hand of so many people (.)
11		cannot have a good way
12	A:	no I am uh: (0.5) uh (.) I fully understand your p- point of view
13		because when there is more than one importer of a brand (.) uh
14		there can always (.) be price uh: problems
15		(0.7)
16		becau: se if one is- is holding a big- big stock he will sell at
17		that low price
18		(0.7)
19	B:	yes
20		(0.5)
21	A:	an' that's destroy the brand
22	B:	an' that's why ... ((continues))

(Firth 2009, p. 157)

The following written excerpt from Nelson (2011), by the Indian novelist Anita Desai, exemplifies a writer operating in the Zone of Expertise. As an accomplished creative writer, she shows control of a range of lexicogrammatical forms used to create rich descriptions:

Arun was a Vegetarian.
Papa was confounded. A meat diet had been one of the revolutionary changes brought about in his life, and his brother's, by their education. Raised

amongst traditional vegetarians, their eyes had been opened to the benefits of meat along with that of cricket and the English language: the three were linked inextricably in their minds. They had even succeeded in convincing the wives they married of this novel concept of progress, and passed it on to their children. Papa was always scornful of those of their relatives who came to visit and insisted on clinging to their cereal- and vegetable-eating ways, shying away from the meat dishes Papa insisted on having cooked for dinner. Now his own son, his one son, displayed this completely baffling desire to return to the ways of his forefathers, meek and puny men who had got nowhere in life. Papa was deeply vexed.

(from *Fasting, Feasting*, Desai 1999, p. 32; in Nelson 2011, p. 62)

To a reader who can understand English and who is familiar with the contextual setting of this text, understanding this passage is likely to be unproblematic in terms of intelligibility, comprehensibility and interpretability. However, to an English-speaking reader who is unfamiliar with the cultural references in this text, this may not be the case. The text is intelligible and comprehensible to those readers who share the linguistic code, but it may not be interpretable to all of these readers because the concepts of vegetarianism and eating meat have different connotations in different cultures. In this text and according to the character of Papa, "Vegetarianism" is seen as traditional and associated with "ignorance", whereas meat-eating is modern and associated with "education" (Nelson 2011, p. 62). In other contexts, for example in the United States where Nelson is from, the situation is quite the reverse: vegetarianism is commonly associated with politically liberal, modern views while meat-eating is associated with more traditional, conservative outlooks. Therefore, readers from these cultural backgrounds may be in the Zone of Expanding Experience when reading this text if they are not already aware of these cultural differences.

A sample of spoken data from Kirkpatrick's (2007) textbook on World Englishes shows how speakers in the Zone of Expanding Experience can experience misunderstanding due to a lack of shared contextual knowledge that results in a lack of interpretability. The excerpt is taken from a conversation between EO, an expatriate police officer, and CPC, a Chinese police constable, in Hong Kong. This data was collected as part of a project conducted when Hong Kong was under British colonial rule. In the excerpt, CPC is approaching EO to make a request for leave; in Chinese culture, reasons are given before the request, often in the hopes of a superior anticipating what will be requested. In English culture, the request is made first, followed by the reasons. Since these are often considered to be private, they are only given if needed. Kirkpatrick argues that these cultural differences in communication result in the following interaction:

CPC:	My mother is not well, sir
EO:	So?
CPC:	She has to go to hospital
EO:	Well?
CPC:	On Thursday, sir

(Kirkpatrick 2007, p. 25).

Even though CPC is speaking perfectly intelligible and comprehensible English, there is evidence of an issue of mutual understanding at the level of interpretability. Kirkpatrick argues that "the reason for the misunderstanding is that the Chinese speaker, while speaking standard English in terms of grammar, is using Chinese cultural norms and these influence the schema he adopts" (p. 25). Traditional native-speaker-based conceptions of proficiency would put the onus on CPC to adjust his awareness of Inner Circle cultural norms in order to facilitate mutual understanding (Lindemann 2006); however, the DALP considers both speakers to be in the Zone of Expanding Experience in this interaction because both are negotiating new cultural terrain.

Spoken data presented in Deterding's (2012) work on intelligibility in ELF interactions exemplifies speakers in the Zone of Expanding Code. A participant in the data collected for the Asian Corpus of English (ACE) was asked to transcribe some of the recorded interactions in which she participated. The participant/transcriber is from Brunei, and her co-interlocutor is from Nigeria. When the Bruneian participant was doing the transcription, she was unable to decipher some words spoken by her Nigerian co-interlocutor. The researchers contacted this participant, who clarified the lexical items that are bolded in the excerpt below. "B" is the participant/transcriber from Brunei; "N" is her co-interlocutor from Nigeria; the bolding of the lexical items in question has been added to the original and all other notation is identical to the source: "<1> ... </1>indicates overlapping speech, (.) shows a short pause, and ':' marks lengthening" (p. 187).

B	so what what- what kind of punishment<1>how far</1>
N	<1>yeah the punishment</1>will be (.) giving you **portion** go there you
	have to go and **weed** the something with **cutlass** or: you have to kneel
	down inside the sun for some hours
B	under the hot sun
N	yeah that is it

(Deterding 2012, p. 187)

As stated previously, it was revealed after this interaction that these three key lexical items (portion, weed and cutlass) were not understood due to issues understanding at the sound level; therefore there was an issue of intelligibility because the sounds heard could not be interpreted into words by B. However, the interaction does not break down because B is familiar with the context of "some kind of punishment under the hot sun" (p. 187). Deterding goes on to argue:

> the failure of B to understand portion and cutlass seems to be mostly lexical: the use of portion to refer to a kind of punishment is unusual outside of West Africa; and in Brunei, a long knife would generally be called a parang rather than a *cutlass*. (p. 187)

Therefore the lack of intelligibility is due to a lack of familiarity by B with the linguistic code used by N rather than a lack of familiarity with the broader context, which situates her proficiency in this micro-interaction in the Zone of Expanding Code. As a result of this interaction and subsequent clarification, it is likely that her awareness of linguistic code now includes the lexical items used by N.

The following data sample shows the Zone of Expanding Code in written form. In New Zealand, lexical items from Maori are often borrowed by English speakers in written and spoken forms. Maori is an indigenous language which has the status of an official language in New Zealand (MacAlister 2007, in Grant 2012, p. 166). In the following newspaper headlines, the italicized lexical items are originally from the Maori language.

> It's *kapat* that every English chat is peppered with *te reo*.

'Kiwi speak' isn't *pakaru*, despite the mutterings of some *waka-jumpers* who *korero* on the *kumara vine*.
(New Zealand Herald, 16 May 2005; Degani and Onysko 2010, in Grant 2012)

Grant argues that because these items are untranslated in a context where writers aim to be understood as clearly as possible by their readers, this indicates "the general understanding of many Maori lexical items in NZE [New Zealand English] and also of the increasing acceptance of the bicultural nature of New Zealand society ..." (p. 166). Proficient users of NZE would be in the Zone of Expertise when reading these headlines; however, proficient users of English who are not familiar with these Maori lexical items would be in the Zone of Expanding Code as readers of these texts because these words and phrases are incomprehensible to them and their meanings are not readily accessible from the surrounding text.

Discussion

The DALP model presented in this chapter responds to our understanding that language proficiency varies across different dimensions in the contextual setting, which are the uses to which language is put and the users of the language. It is a response to standard models which show proficiency as a linear progression and do not cohesively account for this variation in proficiency across various dialects and registers. So far in this chapter, the model has been grounded in use of English. However, the same principles apply for use of other languages together with English, as shown in the previously described example of the use of code-switching in New Zealand English. Therefore the principles of the dynamic nature of proficiency apply to use across multiple languages as well as within languages. García (2009) refers to the use of multiple languages in different contexts as translanguaging, building upon Cen Williams' use of the term in the description of pedagogical practice. According to García, translanguaging goes beyond code-switching to include the range of "... *discursive practices* in which bilinguals engage in order to *make sense of their bilingual worlds*" (p. 45, emphasis original). Furthermore, within different languages including English, speakers experience changes in dialect and register that cause fluctuations in their proficiency and contribute to the "continuous developmental process" of language learning (p. 59).

Use of the DALP model could have a range of implications for pedagogy, assessment, and migration research. In English language teaching, the native-speaker model, e.g. British or American English, is often given as the standard norm regardless of the teaching context. As Jenkins (2006) argues, in these cases, English is treated as a Foreign Language (EFL) in the tradition of Modern Foreign Languages rather than as a Lingua Franca. While there may be contexts where the English as a Foreign Language approach is appropriate, there are others where it is not. In the case of Firth's (2009) example of ELF speakers' interaction, a teacher taking the EFL approach would likely deem it necessary to "correct" the variations from native-speaker norms, and this may be appropriate if the speakers, for example, wish to study in an English-speaking university. However, in this particular contextual setting, the linguistic code is appropriate for the users and therefore the EFL approach would not necessarily be useful for these speakers. As Firth argues, the focus in these kinds of interactions is "getting the work done with the available—and known-in-common communicative resources" (p. 156). Seidlhofer (2011) describes language learning from a lingua franca perspective as a process of learning "to language" rather than "a language" (p. 198). Learning to language means developing the ability to negotiate meanings in context rather than learning a set of isolated forms. The DALP model provides a way to conceptualize proficiency that is compatible with this ELF approach.

Just as the DALP model can be used to analyze one's proficiency based on familiarity with the linguistic code and the context, it can also be used to assess student needs. Most teachers know that they need to "try to take into account what [learners] want the language for and who they will use it with" (Nelson 2011, p. 81), and the DALP model provides a framework that can help to define these parameters more clearly. In the case of the previously described example of American students who have recently arrived at university, proficiency in the linguistic code is often conflated with contextual familiarity, and at some institutions teachers are not prepared to address these needs sufficiently. Analyzing their competencies and needs and placing these students in the Zone of Expanding Experience may help teachers identify the language needs of these students. They may realize that even local students can benefit from the competencies that are presented explicitly to newly arrived international students, such as planning and writing a research paper or incorporating and citing academic sources.

The DALP model can also be used to clarify issues in some of the other dominant views of language proficiency. For example, it can be used to respond to some of the criticisms of the Common European Framework of Reference (CEFR), which is widely used in language education settings to describe linguistic proficiency. The CEFR has been adapted for many languages, including English, and consists of adaptable competencies that are grouped together in descriptions of what a speaker is able to do in a language at a particular proficiency level. Many versions for English have been critiqued for citing the native speaker as the standard for the highest levels (e.g. McNamara 2012; Seidlhofer 2011). Progression through the CEFR levels shows a linear development from simpler to more complex competencies. However, as Graddol (2012) points out, the CEFR was intended to be adapted to different contexts and therefore if native speaker norms are not appropriate for a particular context, the user of the framework should adapt it for the setting (cf. Council of Europe 2001; University of Cambridge ESOL Examinations 2011). In terms of the DALP model, the competencies in the CEFR could be seen as contexts that the speaker is able to negotiate successfully using the linguistic code. Therefore, the DALP model can account for this progression through the CEFR levels by showing the way interlocutors build a repertoire of contexts that can be negotiated successfully using a particular language. The DALP model can also provide more nuanced insights into what is needed to develop a specific competency.

The DALP approach to language proficiency could also have implications for the current widely used methods of language assessment. Standardized tools for language assessment such as the Test of English as a Foreign Language (TOEFL) and the International English Language Testing System (IELTS) (Leung & Lewkowicz 2006) hold "powerful positions" as gatekeeping measures to institutions and countries (McNamara 2012, p. 199). For example, in Australia, successful completion of an IELTS test is a requirement for immigration and entry into educational institutions from overseas. The Academic version of the test is used to assess language proficiency for undertaking a university course, while the General test is used as a prerequisite for entry to vocational and technical institutions. However, since 2001 the General test has also been used for immigration purposes (Ahern 2009).

Furthermore, as Ahern (2009) points out, because an overseas student can apply for an onshore visa which allows him or her to apply for residency following the completion of the university degree, the Academic version of the test also functions as a gatekeeper for immigration. Just as the Academic test does not incorporate the range of situations a university student will encounter, such as making formal presentations or writing lengthy essays, neither test accounts for unique contexts of different types of workplaces. This is not a critique of the IELTS test itself, but rather its application to broader contexts for which it was not initially designed and is therefore ill-suited to assess.

As in Australia, such standardized tests are used as gate-keeping measures for the immigration of students and workers to many English-speaking countries, yet their frameworks of proficiency and methods of test design do not take into account "... a world with accelerating movements of peoples from diverse ethnolinguistic backgrounds" (Leung & Lewkowicz 2006, p. 229). As Canagarajah (2005, in Leung & Lewkowicz 2006) points out, a Sri Lankan university student moving to New York City will encounter more varieties and languages than standard American English in his or her day-to-day life both inside and outside the university. Though it would be difficult to include the complete range of contexts encountered by these individuals in standardized tests, Leung and Lewkowicz argue that "the case for maintaining a universal English proficiency in assessment has been weakened" (p. 230). We posit that the DALP model is a useful tool in leading to this re-consideration of how language proficiency interacts with migration.

Furthermore, such tests are often based upon native-speaker standards which are often cited in the upper levels of proficiency descriptors, even though the term itself may be omitted (p. 201). For example, the IELTS 9-band scale describes Band 8, a Very Good User, as someone who, "has fully operational command of the language with only occasional unsystematic inaccuracies and inappropriacies. Misunderstandings may occur in unfamiliar situations. Handles complex detailed argumentation well" (p. 12). In practice, these "occasional unsystematic inaccuracies" are not based upon contextual variables but instead upon a standard norm which is unnamed in the document. In addition, the hierarchy of band scores in the IELTS tests presents language proficiency as a sort of ladder to be climbed by the test-taker, a view which does not reckon with the often non-linear progression of language development. Johnson (2008) proposes that a new framework for proficiency which accounts for changing language use in different contexts would assess the "learner's potential development" rather than focussing on "the learner's actual level of development" (p. 282). This type of assessment would involve direct engagement between the assessor and the speaker to ascertain the speaker's ability to adapt their use of language to different situations and their "responsiveness to assistance or feedback" (p. 282). As Poehner and Lantolf (2003, in Johnson 2008) point out, "potential development varies independently of actual development, meaning that the latter, in and of itself, cannot be used to predict the former" (p. 282). Such a method of assessment would more accurately describe a person's potential ability to engage in new communities and situations using the language knowledge they already possess.

The re-conception of proficiency presented through the DALP model could have a significant impact on the institutions of teaching and assessing language. Though there have been some adjustments to the way language is treated in these contexts as a response to the changing use of English, and indeed language, worldwide, these changes have been made to existing models rather than to core components of these institutions. That is, there has not yet been a model or consolidated framework that could change the basis of the way policies are executed by these institutions. Though further testing and refinement of the DALP model would be necessary for it to be used in this way, it is proposed as a first step in this process of change.

Summary and Conclusion

In this chapter, we presented and described the Dynamic Approach to Language Proficiency (DALP) model which views language proficiency as a non-static phenomenon that changes in a non-linear fashion as a person encounters different contextual settings. To do this, we argued that proficiency consists of two main dimensions, shared contextual knowledge and shared linguistic code, which operate as two intersecting continuums. These intersecting clines result in the emergence of four quadrants, or Zones of Proficiency. These include the Zone of Expertise, where both contextual knowledge and the linguistic code are shared resources for communication, the Zone of Expanding Experience, where only the linguistic code is a shared resource, the Zone of Expanding Code, where only contextual knowledge is a shared resource, and Zoned Out, where neither of these resources is shared. We then described how this model views proficiency through the lens of the Systemic Functional approach to language, which sees language as a set of strata that operate in a realization hierarchy, and argued that these strata link to the Smith Framework from World Englishes, so that phonology correlates to intelligibility, or understanding at the level of sound/orthography, lexicogrammar correlates to comprehensibility, or understanding at the level of words and phrases, and semantics correlates to interpretability, or understanding at the level of underlying meaning.

Using this theoretical framework, we gave hypothetical and metaphorical examples of how speakers move through different zones of proficiency as they encounter different situations. By selecting written and spoken data excerpts and analyzes from World Englishes and English as a Lingua Franca literature, we showed how the model can be operationalized to describe the zones occupied in different contexts by a range of interlocutors. Finally, we discussed some possible implications of this new model for language teaching, assessment, and migration by problematizing the static view of language proficiency that prevails in the current frameworks of language competency and assessment, and showed how this model could interact with and refine these frameworks.

Possible future research directions include the operationalizing of the model in different contexts by analyzing longitudinal data which shows how users move across the Zones over time. This would provide insights into how the model operates on both micro and macro levels, from the turn-taking level of interaction all the way up to the negotiation of different registers over time. The presentation of this model is a call for such research to be carried out which can support the development of a viable alternative to existing frameworks that reflects language use in an increasingly globalized, multicultural, multilinguistic world.

References

Ahern, S. (2009). 'Like cars or breakfast cereal': IELTS and the trade in education and immigration. *TESOL in Context*, 19(1), 39–51.

Bachman, L. (1990). *Fundamental considerations in language testing*. Oxford, England: Oxford University Press.

Canagarajah, S. (Ed.). (2005). *Reclaiming the local in language policy and practice*. Mahwah: Lawrence Erlbaum Associates, Inc.

Council of Europe. (2001). *Common European framework of reference for languages: Learning, teaching, assessment*. Cambridge: Cambridge University Press.

Deterding, D. (2012). Intelligibility in spoken ELF. *Journal of English as a Lingua Franca*, 1(1), 185–190.

Firth, A. (1996). The discursive accomplishment of normality: On 'lingua franca' English and conversation analysis. *Journal of Pragmatics*, 26(2), 237–259.

Firth, A. (2009). The lingua franca factor. *Intercultural Pragmatics*, 6(2), 147–170.

Firth, J. R. (1935). The technique of semantics. *Transactions of the Philological Society,* 34(1), 36–73.

García, O. (2009). *Bilingual education in the 21st century: A global perspective.* Malden: WileyBlackwell Pub.

Goodwin, C., & Duranti, A. (1992). Re-thinking context: An introduction. In A. Duranti, & C. Goodwin (Eds.), *Re-thinking context: Language as an interactive phenomenon* (1–42). Cambridge: Cambridge University Press.

Graddol, D. (2012, May). *How economic change can shape the future of ELF.* Symposium paper presented at The Fifth International Conference of English as a Lingua Franca, Istanbul, Turkey.

Grant, L. E. (2012). Culturally motivated lexis in New Zealand English. *World Englishes,* 31(2), 162–176.

Halliday, M. A. K. (1978). *Language as social semiotic: The social interpretation of language and meaning.* Maryland: University Park Press.

Halliday, M. A. K. (1993). Towards a language-based theory of learning. *Linguistics and Education,* 5, 93–116.

Halliday, M. A. K. (2004). Learning how to mean. In J. Webster (Ed.), *The language of early childhood. Vol. 4 in the collected works of M.A.K. Halliday* (28–59). London: Continuum. [Reprinted from E. Lenneberg & E. Lenneberg (Eds.), *Foundations of language development: A multidisciplinary perspective* (239–265), 1975, London: Academic Press.]

Hasan, R. (2009). *Semantic variation: Meaning in society and sociolinguistics.* London: Equinox.

IELTS. (2013). *Guide for educational institutions, governments, professional bodies and commercial organisations.* http://www.ielts.org/PDF/Guide_Edu-20Inst_Gov_2013.pdf. Accessed April 7 2014.

Jenkins, J. (2006). Points of view and blind spots: ELF and SLA. *International Journal of Applied Linguistics,* 16(2), 137–162.

Johnson, M. (2003). *A philosophy of second language acquisition.* New Haven: Yale University Press.

Johnson, M. (2008). Local and dialogic language ability and its implications for language teaching and testing. In R. Hughes (Ed.), *Spoken English, TESOL, and applied linguistics: Challenges for theory and practice* (271–286). Basingstoke: Palgrave Macmillan.

Kachru, B. B. (2006). World Englishes and culture wars. In B. B. Kachru, Y. Kachru, & C. L. Nelson (Eds.), *The handbook of World Englishes* (446–471). Malden: Blackwell.

Kachru, B. B. (Ed.). (1992). *The other tongue: English across cultures* (2nd ed.). Urbana and Chicago: University of Illinois Press.

Kirkpatrick, A. (2007). *World Englishes: Implications for international communication and English language teaching.* Cambridge: Cambridge University Press.

Larson-Freeman, D., & Cameron, L. (2008). *Complex systems and applied linguistics.* Oxford: Oxford University Press.

Leung, C., & Lewkowicz, J. (2006). Expanding horizons and unresolved conundrums: Language testing and assessment. *TESOL Quarterly*, 40(1), 211–234.

Lindemann, S. (2006). What the other half gives: the interlocutor's role in non-native speaker performance. In R. Hughes (Ed.), *Spoken English, TESOL and applied linguistics: Challenges for theory and practice* (23–46). Basingstoke: Palgrave Macmillan.

Mahboob, A. (2009). English as an Islamic language: A case study of Pakistani English. *World Englishes*, 28(2), 175–189.

Martin, J. R. (2009). Genre and language learning: A social semiotic perspective. *Linguistics and Education*, 20, 10–21.

Martin, J. R., & Rose, D. (2007). *Working with discourse: Meaning beyond the clause* (2nd ed.). London: Continuum.

Martin, J. R., & Rose, D. (2008). *Genre relations: Mapping culture*. London: Equinox.

Matthiessen, C. M. I. M. (2009). Meaning in the making: Meaning potential emerging from acts of meaning. *Language Learning*, 59(Suppl. 1), 206–229.

McNamara, T. (2012). English as a lingua franca: The challenge for language testing. *Journal of English as a Lingua Franca*, 1(1), 199–202.

Nelson, C. L. (2011). *Intelligibility in World Englishes: Theory and applications*. New York: Routledge.

Painter, C. (1989). Learning language: A functional view of language development. In R. Hasan & J. R. Martin (Eds.), *Language development: Learning language, learning culture. Meaning and choice in language* (18–65). Norwood: Ablex Publishing Corporation.

Schneider, E. (2012). Exploring the interface between World Englishes and second language acquisition—and implications for English as a lingua franca. *Journal of English as a Lingua Franca*, 1(1), 57–91.

Seidlhofer, B. (2011). *Understanding English as a lingua franca*. Oxford: Oxford University Press.

Seidlhofer, B., & Widdowson, H. (2009). Accommodation and the idiom principle in English as a lingua franca. In K. Murata & J. Jenkins (Eds.), *Global Englishes in Asian contexts* (26–39). Basingstroke: Palgrave Macmillan.

Smith, L. E., & Nelson, C. L. (1985). International intelligibility of English: Directions and resources. *World Englishes*, 4(3), 333–342.

University of Cambridge ESOL Examinations. (2011). Using the CEFR: principles of good practice. October 2011. http://www.cambridgeenglish.org/images/126011-using-cefr-principlesof-good-practice.pdf. Accessed November 4 2013.

Widdowson, H. G. (2012). ELF and the inconvenience of established concepts. *Journal of English as a Lingua Franca*, 1(1), 5–26.

Chapter 14

Understanding Language Variation: Implications for EIL Pedagogy

Mahboob, A. (2014). Understanding language variation: Implications for EIL pedagogy. In R. Marlina & R. Giri (Eds.), *The pedagogy of English as an international language: Perspectives from scholars, teachers, and students.* London: Springer.

Introduction

The Pedagogy of English as an International Language: Perspectives from Scholars, Teachers, and Students have looked at the pedagogical implications of using English as an International Language (EIL) as a model for language education in diverse ways. Each of the chapters in the volume makes a unique and important contribution in exploring issues related to this. While the individual papers take slightly different approaches, the volume is unified by what Marlina (2014) refers to as a shared belief in 'the importance of recognising the pluricentricity of English and the equal treatment given to all varieties of English and its speakers'. However, one might ask what we mean by 'all varieties of English'? How many are there? How are they identified? How are they classified and categorised? How do they relate to educational, academic, and professional contexts? In the introductory chapter to this volume, Marlina refers to work on World Englishes, English as a Lingua Franca (ELF) and EIL to point out how people in different parts of the world use English to communicate with each other and with others and how all of these varieties of the language can be considered legitimate varieties of English. While linguistic evidence is clearly present to support this position as well as the positions taken by scholars working in World Englishes, ELF, and EIL, I believe that this body of work is missing a broader framework that provides coherence to studies of language variation. By looking at only certain populations and contexts, the current work in these areas tends to give a somewhat narrow and limiting view of English language variation. As such, while the use of these descriptions for pedagogical purposes may help in creating a more positive attitude towards language variation, they do not necessarily allow people who use 'non-standard' varieties to engage with and contribute to academic and professional materials. To do this, we need a model of language variation that reflects different dimensions in which language varies—and not just the location, background and ethnicity etc. of the people using the language.

In this chapter, I will unpack the notion of 'pluricentricity of English' in the hope that it clarifies some of the dimensions across which language varies. In doing so, I will describe a model of language variation that helps us to situate various ways in which language varies in relation to each other. The purpose of developing this model is to provide a broad understanding of how different Englishes relate to each other and how different ways of studying them can be seen as complementary approaches to studying language variation (rather than as being in any inherent conflict or turf war). In doing so, I will also suggest that the notion of EIL perhaps needs to be expanded to look at all the domains identified in a holistic approach to language variation, rather than placing different types of Englishes in separate (and sometimes conflicting) positions. I will then conclude the chapter by briefly discussing how these variations relate to educational contexts.

To start with, it will be useful to briefly consider the development of the field of World Englishes. Traditionally, the English language used by 'native' speakers was considered the appropriate model for language description, language acquisition, and language teaching. However, over the last 20 years or so, as linguists document how the English language varies around the world, there has been a growing acceptance of language variation and of World Englishes. There are two main bodies of research that have contributed to this work. The first thread of research that looks at World Englishes examines the language (and its politics and uses) in different parts of the world. This work on World Englishes focuses on language divergence—i.e., how local/regional varieties of English differ from other varieties of Englishes. The second thread of research looks at ELF and focuses on language convergence—i.e., what happens when people who use different varieties of Englishes interact with each other. In addition to these two threads of research, recent work on EIL also looks at how English has evolved and 'recognises the international functions of English and its use in a variety of cultural and economic arenas by speakers of English from diverse lingua-cultural backgrounds who do not speak each other's mother tongues' (Marlina, 2014).

Typical research on World Englishes describes the linguistic features of particular varieties of Englishes. Research on ELF, on the other hand, looks at: (1) features of language that are shared by different varieties of Englishes, (2) features of language that can impede communication between users of different varieties, and (3) strategies that people use to accommodate for language variation. World Englishes and ELF research focus on different aspects of the same global phenomenon: global spread of English. In doing so, World Englishes examines how language changes as it spreads; whereas ELF researchers look at how language variations are negotiated or accommodated in order to achieve a communicative goal. In both of these approaches to looking at English language in a global context, the focus is on the language as used by people in diverse contexts and not on an abstract notion of a 'standard' language that is based on 'native' speaker norms. There are several reasons for linguists to go beyond the 'native' model of English.

Descriptions of 'native' Englishes tend to be based on English as spoken by middle-class White speakers of the language. Being the politically dominant group in BANA (Britain, Australia, and North America) countries, their dialect is used to 'codify' and 'standardise' the language. Other speakers of English are marginalised. For example, the English spoken by Afro-Americans or the Chicano speakers in the United States is not used for the purposes of codification of Standard American English. One example of the difference between Standard English and Afro-American English is in the use of double negatives. Double negatives such as 'I ain't gonna do nothing' are considered inappropriate in Standard English; however, this linguistic feature is quite common in Afro-American English. Scholars researching World Englishes are aware of this and note that using only 'Standard English' models in diverse settings (e.g., education) can have negative implications for people who speak divergent varieties of English (as highlighted in the previous chapter). Their work is, thus, a tool to help give 'legitimacy' to the local uses of English and to empower these varieties (and the speakers of these varieties).

Another thing that linguists have noted is that there is no single 'standard' English. Native speakers of English show a lot of language variation. As a result of this, grammar books that are based on the 'native' speakers are not always accurate in their description of English. For example, while many (prescriptive or pedagogical) grammar books decree that we should not split infinitives, i.e., we should not insert an adverb in between a word group such as 'to conclude', there is plenty of evidence that people [even native speakers] do so quite frequently. If we look at how language is actually used, we will note that this rule cannot be supported by actual language data. We often come across constructions such as: 'to quickly conclude', 'to boldly conclude', and 'to finally conclude'. In all three of the examples just cited, the to-infinitives are broken up by an insertion of an adverb. Grammar books prohibit this; however, users of the language still do it. This shows that (native) speakers of a language show considerable variation and that grammar books that are used to describe the language do not always capture this variation. Thus, linguists go beyond the 'standard' models and look at how language is actually used by people from different backgrounds and in different contexts. These studies of language variation can help us in identifying factors that play a role in language variation and thus help us in developing a model for understanding language variation.

Modeling Language Variation

English, or more appropriately *Englishes*, diverge from each other along a number of dimensions. They reflect the variations in the use, meanings and structures of the language as they have evolved in different parts of the world to achieve different goals and purposes over a period of time. As such, we need to take account of the various types of variations that are intrinsic here and use this understanding to set up a model of language variation that allows us to identify the key aspects in which the context and use of language shapes these variations. An understanding of these variations allows us to build a 'bigger picture' of how language variation relates to the use of language across different contexts.

There are three key dimensions that need to be considered in modeling language variation: (1) users of Englishes, (2) uses of Englishes, and (3) modes of communication (see Halliday et al. 1964, for a discussion of language variation across the dimensions of use and users). Each of these dimensions can be understood as independent clines or continuums that influence language choices and can then be brought together as a three-dimensional model that allows us to 'situate' various aspects of language variation (see Hasan 2009, for a discussion of language context and language variation). These three dimensions are first briefly described below and then brought together to form a coherent model of language variation.

One dimension of variation in language relates to who we are as 'users' of the language and with whom we are interacting. This is the kind of language variation that is studied in the broad research on sociolinguistics and intercultural communication studies; including research that focuses on World Englishes (see for example, Kirkpatrick 2010) and other dialect studies (see Wolfram 2014). In the context of World Englishes, we typically look at how people in one location (country/speech community) use language for local purposes. The social distance between these participants is typically low in terms of their geographic location. However, the social distance might vary within these contexts based on social class, age, gender and other such variables. Each of these factors impacts how similar or different the language of various speakers is. People who are based in the same geographical region and are related (close friends/family etc.) may have unique ways of using language that reflect their close relationship and this language may not always be transparent to others (see for example, Wolfram 2014). For example, couple talk, sibling talk, or friend talk can be seen as language that is used between people who have low social distance (and thus is localised) and may not be interpretable to an outside audience. On the other hand, when interacting with people with whom one has a higher social distance, one tends to use a more 'standard' or 'international' or 'global' language— one that minimises local references, idioms, forms, and features and is thus less prone to miscommunication. Thus, one cline of language variation can be based on 'low' vs. 'high' social distance. The indicator 'low social distance' helps us understand why people use 'local' forms of language, with their local denotations and connotations. The indicator 'high social distance' helps us understand why people use 'international' forms of language, minimising local forms and features, and allowing for communication with people who do not share their local features. In developing a model of language variation, we need to identify and understand these variables in order for us to be able to provide fine-tuned analyses and discussions of how Englishes vary based on the users of the language.

A second dimension of variation in language is related to the purpose or 'use' of the language. This kind of language variation is typically studied in research on genres and English for Specific Purposes (ESP). This body of work looks at how language varies based on the purpose it is used for (see for example, Martin & Rose 2008). For example, the language used in a biology research paper is different from the language used in a movie review. In terms of operationalising this dimension of language variation, a key factor to consider is whether the language is about 'everyday/casual' discourses or about 'specialised/technical' discourses. The difference between 'everyday/casual' and 'specialised/technical' discourses is not necessarily about the topic of the discourse, but rather about its purpose. For example, one could talk about the weather using specialised/technical language—the purpose of which might be to engage with an informed audience of environmental scientists at a conference; or one could talk about the weather in everyday/casual language—the purpose of which would perhaps be to serve as an ice breaker at a social event. In both the cases the topic remains the same; however, the choice of language will vary based on the purpose of the exchange. In linguistic terms, this variation is understood as register variation and is used extensively in literature in genre and ESP studies. Currently, there is limited work on register variation in multilingual contexts; however, there is no theoretical reason to assume that such variations do not exist in and across different varieties of Englishes. In fact, it is quite necessary to understand if and how language varies in different parts of the world while being 'used' for similar purposes. For example, an understanding of how registers are similar/different across World Englishes can help in developing educational material and resources.

The third dimension of language variation, which will inform our model, is 'mode' (Martin 1985; Derewianka 2014; Kirkpatrick, 2014). Modes of communication include aural, visual, and mixed channels of communication. The way we use language varies based on whether we are speaking, writing, or—as is becoming common today—combining these two modalities (for example, in online chats, blogs, etc.). The mode of communication impacts the language choices that we make and therefore needs to be studied. For example, if we keep the 'use' and 'users' of language constant, the language might still vary based on whether we are writing or speaking. For example, an academic/researcher will draw from different sets of linguistic resources based on whether they are presenting their work at a conference or writing up the paper for publication.

The three dimensions of language variation identified above are not mutually exclusive. They interact with each other in myriad ways. Some of these dimensions are captured in the three-dimensional model below (see Figure 1)—which is the result of mapping the three dimensions described above into a single model.

Among other things, this model gives us eight different possibilities or domains of mapping language variation (see Table 1). These are listed below, along with examples of where we can find such languages. It should be noted that language varies within each domain too and not just across domains. These variations may happen across the various strata of language and reflect changes in the register variables of field, tenor, and mode.

Figure1   Language variation framework

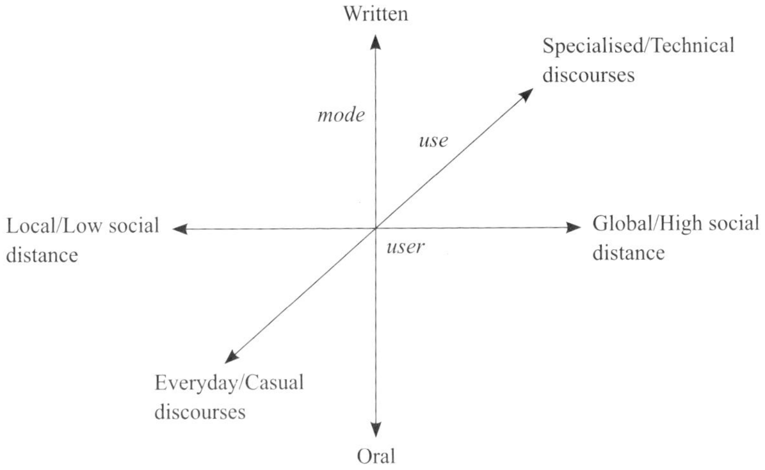

Table 1   Eight domains of language variation

	Domains	Examples
1	Local, written, everyday	Friends writing letters to each other
2	Local, oral, everyday	Friends talking to each other about their plans for the holidays
3	Local, written, specialised	Texts written by and for a local group of farmers
4	Local, oral, specialised	Farmers discussing specifics about their crops
5	Global, written, everyday	International news agencies reporting on events
6	Global, oral, everyday	Conversations amongst people from different parts of the world
7	Global, written, specialised	Academics writing research papers
8	Global, oral, specialised	Conference presentations

One strength of the framework presented here is that it provides an overview of how language variation can be modeled in a global context and therefore allows us to map these variations out and study them systematically. At the moment, these eight domains of language variation tend to be studied under a range of different traditions. For example, domains 1 & 2 are typically studied by people focusing on dialects, pidgin and creoles, and/or World Englishes; domain 6 is the focus of research on English as a Lingua Franca (ELF); and domains 7 & 8 are covered by studies on genre and English for Specific Purposes (ESP). Domains 3 & 4 are rarely studied within a World Englishes framework at the moment—something that needs to be addressed. Domain 5 is perhaps the most commonly studied in English linguistics and is the main source of the traditional (and pedagogical) grammars. This use of a single domain to provide pedagogical grammars is quite problematic since it does not reflect how language is used differently in the other contexts—especially in domains 7 & 8, which serve as gatekeepers to higher strata of academic and technical knowledge. It also raises questions about the exclusion of other Englishes from the educational context and raises questions about the implications of such exclusion of other Englishes.

The framework presented here also helps us to see that the variations in language are not just about 'nativeness' or 'ownership' of a variety, but about the community (of practice) that uses a particular variety. Each community, either user- or use-oriented, negotiates its own linguistic norms and practices. These norms are not static, but change as the community membership changes. So, for example, the language of a discipline does not remain constant, but changes with time: research papers in biology today are not written in the same language as they were 100 years ago; similarly, the language of research articles in a journal such as *TESOL Quarterly* is not the same today as it was 25 years ago. The changes in the language reflect the shift in the community membership over time and space as well as the development of the field. This implies that even in inner circle countries, not all students who go to school have access to the language of domains 7 & 8— this is something that they have to develop through schooling. By promoting local varieties of English (domains 1 & 2) in and through education at the cost of international Englishes, the students will not be taught how globally oriented language works. Without appropriate teaching of the global specialised discourses (both written and spoken), students who only have control of local varieties of English will have a difficult task in reading, writing and participating in a globally oriented knowledge community that falls in domains 7 & 8 of the framework. Thus, it is important to expose students to a range of language varieties and variations and to give them access to globalised norms of language use in specialised domains.

Language Variation and Education

The framework presented above raises a number of questions in terms of the use of local dialects for educational purposes. Some World

Englishes scholars have been advocating for utilising local varieties for educational purposes in the outer and expanding circle countries (see for example, contributions to Matsuda 2012). This advocacy acknowledges the local varieties of English and assumes that if students are taught a local variety, which is the dialect of English used in their context, they will be more empowered. While this position is well-meaning and appears to be in the interest of the students; a broader understanding of language variation—as developed through the framework presented here—would suggest that local varieties may be used in educational contexts, but this should be done without replacing access to the global norms of the language. EIL pedagogy needs to recognise and be inclusive of different ways of using language across the different domains.

In trying to understand the role of language in education, it is useful to develop an understanding of the notions of 'language allocation' and 'language affiliation'. The language that we learn in our families and learn to use in our everyday environments plays a critical role in shaping our sense of ourselves and our surroundings. As we grow older, we learn new ways of meaning and also learn about how and where to use which forms of language. This language, that we learn at home, can be seen as our language allocation—it is the language that is allocated to us based on who we are (domains 1 & 2). As time goes by, we note that different communities of practice (such as a community of scientists, historians, or people in another region) use our language differently (or use a different language). We can choose to (or be forced to) learn this language, which we can call the language of affiliation—this is the language that we learn to use based on how and with whom we want to be affiliated with. This distinction between our allocated languages and our languages of affiliation is quite important and can help us explain how individuals' repertoire of language(s) evolves and changes over their lifetime. However, keeping our focus on language and education here, we will use the notions of allocation and affiliation to understand how access to knowledge is distributed throughout the society.

Let us imagine a scenario where children learn the dialect 'X' at home. When they go to school, they can find that the language of their home serves as the foundation of the language of schooling. If this is the case, they feel affirmed in their school environment—although this does not guarantee success in school. However, if they find that their home language is not recognised within the wider school curriculum, they have to learn another language and then learn through it. This becomes a double handicap for

250 Part II Language Variation

these children and signals to them that their home language is not valued in school contexts. This can result in an unequal distribution of opportunities for children in school. When children are put into these situations, without well-developed language and literacy support frameworks, they tend to fall behind other students whose language matches that of schooling. If this process carries on for a long time, people start pointing out that students from certain 'language' (or ethnic or social) backgrounds do not perform as well as others. In these situations, people fail to question the choice of the linguistic code adopted in schooling that produces such result. They tend to overlook how the socio-economic resources that the parents can afford (and the parents' own linguistic and educational backgrounds) correlate with how children from certain backgrounds succeed or fail. It is for this reason that scholars advocate the use of a local (allocated) variety of English in schooling. However, what this advocacy fails to consider is that the language of education and knowledge production is not the same as local dialects/varieties (including many dialects and varieties used by mono-lingual speakers of English). Schools therefore need to provide language and literacy support for students (both speakers of standard and 'non-standard' dialects) in order for them to access texts and resources used in academic and professional contexts. Providing schooling in their language of allocation, without providing appropriate training in the language that they may need to affiliate with can create a barrier that may restrict these students' future opportunities.

Concluding Remarks

The work on EIL and the book *The Pedagogy of English as an International Language: Perspective from Scholars, Teachers, and Students* discuss issues of language variation and education. One of the benefits of using EIL in the context of education is that it looks at the uses of the language instead of focussing on the users. This is a step in the right direction—however, this work still needs to be developed further: it needs to be grounded not just in the functions of English as an International Language, but also in a consideration of the linguistics of language variation. It needs to consider the features of English as it is used in different contexts and use these descriptions in its pedagogical models. The chapters in this volume, individually and collectively, reflect an awareness of taking a broader pluricentric approach to language in pedagogical contexts. The present chapter has elaborated on what a pluricentric approach to language entails and recommends that language teaching should be grounded in such an understanding of language in order for it to meet the needs of learners in various contexts and who are learning English for different purposes.

References

Derewianka, B. (2014). Supporting students in the move from spoken to written language. In A. Mahboob & L. Barratt (Eds.), *Englishes in multilingual contexts—Language variation and education*. Dordrecht: Springer.

Halliday, M. A. K., McIntosh, A., & Strevens, P. (1964). *The linguistic sciences and language teaching*. London: Longman.

Hasan, R. (2009). *Semantic variation: Meaning in society and sociolinguistics*. London: Equinox.

Kirkpatrick, A. (ed.) (2010). *Routledge handbook of world Englishes*. London: Routledge.

Kirkpatrick, A. (2014). Teaching English in Asia in non-Anglo cultural contexts: Principles of the 'lingua franca approach'. In R. Marlina & R. Giri (Eds.), *The Pedagogy of English as an international language: Perspectives from scholars, teachers, and students*. London: Springer.

Marlina, R. (2014). The pedagogy of English as an international language (EIL): More reflections and dialogues. In R. Marlina & R. Giri (Eds.), *The pedagogy of English as an international language: Perspective from scholars, teachers, and students*. London: Springer.

Martin, J. R. (1985). Language, register and genre. In F. Christie (Ed.), *Children writing course reader*. Geelong: Deakin University Press.

Martin, J. R., & Rose, D. (2008). *Genre relations: Mapping culture*. London/Oakville: Equinox.

Matsuda, A. (2012). *Principles and practices of teaching English as an international language*. Bristol: Multilingual Matters.

Wolfram, W. (2014). Integrating language variation into TESOL: Challenges from English globalization. In A. Mahboob & L. Barratt (Eds.), *Englishes in multilingual contexts—Language variation and education*. Dordrecht: Springer.

Chapter 15

Language Variation and Education: A Focus on Pakistan

Mahboob, A. (2014). Language variation and education: A focus on Pakistan. In *The Evolution of Englishes*, S. Buschfeld, T. Hoffmann, M. Huber & A. Kautzsch (eds.), 267–281. Amsterdam: John Benjamins.

Language Variation and Education

English, or more appropriately Englishes (Kachru 1992), diverge from each other along a number of dimensions. These dimensions reflect the variations in the use, meanings and structures of the language (including discourse structures, lexico-grammatical features and grapho-phonemic systems) as it has evolved around the world to achieve diverse goals and purposes over a period of time. In order to understand how these various types of Englishes relate to each other, we need to consider three main dimensions: (1) users of Englishes, (2) uses of Englishes, and (3) modes of communication (see Halliday et al. 1964, for a discussion of language variation across the dimensions of use and users). Each of these dimensions forms an independent cline or continuum that influences language choices. These three clines can be mapped onto each other to give us a three-dimensional model of language variation. Below, I will first briefly discuss each of these dimensions and then introduce the three-dimensional model of language variation.

One dimension of variation in language relates to who we are as "users" of the language and with whom we are interacting and is studied in the broad research of sociolinguistics and intercultural communication studies; including research that focuses on World Englishes (see, for example, Kirkpatrick ed. 2010) and other dialect studies (see Wolfram 2014). In the context of World Englishes, we typically look at how people in one location (country/speech community) use language for local purposes. The social distance between these participants is typically low in terms of their geographic location. However, the social distance might vary within these contexts based on social class, age, gender and other such variables. Each of these factors impacts how similar or different the language of various speakers is. People who are based in the same geographical region and are related (close friends/family etc.) may have unique ways of using language that reflect their close relationship and this language may not always be transparent to others (see, for example, Wolfram 2014). For example, couple talk, sibling talk, or friend talk can be seen as language that is used between people who have low social distance (and thus is localised) and may not be interpretable to an outside audience. On the other hand, when interacting with people with whom one has a higher social distance, one tends to use a more "standard" or "global" language—one that minimises "local" idioms, forms, and features and is thus less prone to miscommunication of language variation can be based on "low" vs. "high" social distance. The indicator "low social distance" helps us understand why people use "local" forms of language, with their local denotations and connotation. The indicator "high social distance" helps us explain why people use "global" forms of language, minimising local forms and features, and facilitating communication with people who speak a different "local" variety of the language. Choosing language that reflects low or high social distance with people who do not fall into that category can also serve as a social metaphor: by choosing language that reflects high social distance with people who are close, one may be creating a distance between themselves and their interlocutors/readers; conversely, using language that reflects low social distance with people who are not close can suggest that one is trying to affiliate with them.

A second dimension of variation in language is related to the purpose or "use" of the language. This kind of language variation is typically studied in research on genres and English for Specific Purposes (ESP). This body of work looks at how language varies based on the purpose it is used for (see, for example, Martin & Rose 2008). For example, the language used in a biology research paper is different from the language used in a movie review. In terms of operationalising this dimension of language variation, a key factor to consider is whether the language is about "everyday/casual" discourses or about "specialised/technical" discourses. The difference between "everyday/casual" and "specialised/technical" discourses is not necessarily about the topic of the discourse, but rather about its purpose. For example, one could talk about the weather using specialised/technical language—the purpose of which might be to engage with an informed audience of environmental scientists at a conference; or one could talk about the weather in everyday/casual language—the purpose of which would perhaps be to serve as an ice breaker at a social event. In both cases, the topic remains the same; however, the specific linguistic choices will vary based on the purpose of the exchange. In linguistic terms, this variation is understood as register variation, a concept used extensively in literature in genre and ESP studies. Currently, there is limited work on register variation in World Englishes contexts; however, there seems to be no theoretical reason to assume that such variations do not exist in and across different varieties of Englishes. In fact, it is quite necessary to understand if and how language varies in different parts of the world while being "used" for similar purposes. For example, an understanding of how registers are similar/different across World Englishes can help in developing educational materials and resources.

The third dimension of language variation, which will inform our model, is "mode" (Martin 1985; Derewianka 2014). Modes of communication include aural, visual, and mixed channels of communication. The way we use language varies based on whether we are speaking, writing, or—as is becoming common today—combining these two modalities (for example, in online chats, blogs, etc.). The mode of communication impacts the language choices that we make and therefore needs to be examined. If we keep the "use" and "users" of language constant, the language might still vary based on whether we are writing or speaking. For example, an academic/researcher will draw from different sets of linguistic resources based on whether they are presenting their work at a conference or writing up the paper for publication.

The three dimensions of language variation identified above are not mutually exclusive. They interact with each other in myriad ways. Some of these dimensions are captured in the three-dimensional model below (Figure 1)—which is the result of mapping the three dimensions described above into a single model. In addition to these three dimensions, a fourth dimension, time, also plays an important role in language variation. This factor is not considered here in detail, but will be included as this model of language variation is further developed.

The three-dimensional model helps us in identifying eight domains that represent different ways in which language varies based on who is using it, for what purpose, and in which mode. It should be noted that language varies within each domain too and not just across domains.

The first four domains include language variations that reflect their

Figure 1 Language variation framework

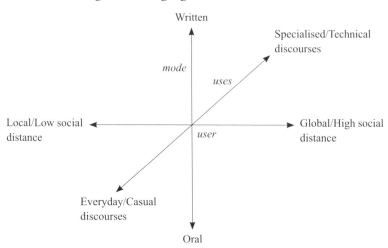

local usage. This local usage does not differentiate between mother tongue or non-mother tongue varieties of the language. Thus, while the language used by locals in a bar in Alabama might be different from that used by a group of Singaporeans at a restaurant, they are similar in that both these variations reflect ways of using the language in the local community. These same people, when they interact with each other, will need to shift towards a more global variety of the language and accommodate each other if they were to communicate with each other successfully. The globally oriented language which allows for communication to succeed between people who come from different backgrounds is not necessarily stable or static. However, it does include recognisable patterns that emerge from repeated interactions between and within such communities. Below, I will briefly describe each of the eight domains.

The first domain includes locally oriented language that is written and relates to everyday or casual goals. Examples of such language use include letters or e-mails written by friends to each other. They may also include notes left by couples on the refrigerator and other written communications between friends and family or other members of the local community. The second domain, like the first one, is locally oriented and relates to everyday or casual uses of language. However, unlike the first domain, the mode of communication here is oral, not written. This kind of language is observed in most oral interactions between people who share strong connections (including their place of origin, age, gender, etc.).

Examples of such language include couples talking privately to each other; or friends chatting about sports at a local pub.

The third domain includes the use of language which, like domain 1, is locally oriented and written but serves specialised purposes. These texts would include things like information sheets and guidelines etc. written for or by local farmers for local use. The fourth domain will also include examples of language use that are locally oriented and serve specialised purposes, but are oral. This would include oral interactions between farmers talking about farming, crops, etc.

The next four domains differ from the previous ones in that they refer to the use of language in contexts where the participants in the exchange need to communicate with people who do not share their local ways of using language. Thus, the fifth domain includes language that, while written and serving everyday goals, is globally oriented. Examples of this language can be found in international editions of newspapers, which avoid local colloquialisms and references to make the text more accessible to a wider community of readers. The sixth domain, unlike the fifth one, includes oral interactions between people who have different local orientations to language; but, like the fifth domain, it serves everyday and casual purposes. Examples of such language use are quite common and would include casual conversations between people from different parts of the world.

The seventh domain includes language that is written and globally oriented, but serves specialised and/or technical purposes. This globally oriented written language for specialised purposes evolves as a community of practices interacts across local geographical boundaries. The members of this community may come from different parts of the world, but they are interested in and exchange information that is specialised. Published academic research papers would be one example of such language. This language shares patterns of usage which are not native to any one community but evolve as the community develops its understanding of particular subjects and ways of exchanging that information with regularised patterns of writing. The final domain is similar to the seventh one, but differs in that it is oral. Examples of such use of language can be found in lectures at international universities or at international conferences, etc.

In understanding this framework, it needs to be noted that there is considerable language variation within each of the domains. This variation relates to the particular users, uses, and modes at play in a communicative event. One of the strengths of the framework presented here is that it provides an overview of how language variations can be modeled in a global context and therefore allows us to map these variations out and study them systematically. At the moment, these eight domains of language variation are studied under a range of different traditions. For example, domains 1 & 2 are typically studied by people focusing on dialects, pidgins and creoles, and/ or World Englishes; domain 6 is the focus of research on English as a *Lingua Franca* (ELF); and domains 7 & 8 are covered by studies on genre and ESP. Domains 3 & 4 are rarely studied within a World Englishes framework at the moment—something that needs to be addressed. Domain 5 is perhaps the most commonly studied in English linguistics and is the main source of the traditional (and pedagogical) grammars. This use of a single domain to provide pedagogical grammars is quite problematic since it does not reflect how language is used differently in the other contexts—especially in domains 7 & 8, which serve as gatekeepers to higher strata of academic and technical knowledge. It also raises questions about the exclusion of other Englishes from the educational context and raises questions about the implications of such exclusion of other Englishes.

This framework also raises a number of questions in terms of the use of local dialects for educational purposes. Some World Englishes scholars have been advocating for utilising local varieties for educational purposes in the outer and expanding circle countries (see, for example, contributions to Matsuda 2012). This advocacy acknowledges the local varieties of English and assumes that if students are taught a local variety, which is the dialect of English used in their context, they will be more empowered. While this position is well-meaning and appears to be in the interest of the students, a broader understanding of language variation—as developed through the framework presented here—would suggest otherwise. The framework helps us to see that the variations in language are not just about "nativeness" or "ownership" of a variety, but about the community (of practice) that uses a particular variety. Each community—either user- or use-oriented—negotiates its own linguistic norms and practices. These norms are not static, but change as the community membership changes. So, for example, the language of a discipline does not remain constant, but changes with time: research papers in biology today are not written in the same language as they were a hundred years ago; similarly, the language of research articles in a journal such as *TESOL Quarterly* is not the same today as it was 25 years ago. The changes in the language reflect, among other things, a shift in the community membership over time and space as well as the development of the field. This implies that even in inner circle countries, not all students who go to school have access to the language of domains 7 & 8—this is something that they have to develop through schooling. By only promoting local varieties of English (domains 1 & 2) in and through education, the students may not be taught or given access to how globally oriented language works. Without appropriate teaching of the global specialised discourses (both written and spoken), students who only have control of local varieties of English will have a difficult task in reading, writing and contributing to globally oriented knowledge bases that fall in domains 7 & 8 of the framework.

In the case of the Pakistani textbooks, the authors use a local variety of English: most of the language choices in these textbooks reflect the language choices relevant to domain 1. These include both variations in discourse structures and lexico-grammatical resources. In this chapter, we will focus on variations in the discourse structure and not on the lexico-grammatical resources used (although there are a number of these present in the texts analysed). The reason for focussing on the text structure here is to show how shifts in discursive practices in Pakistani English do not only signal localisation, but may also reflect how particular meanings are prioritised in the text. Looking at only lexico-grammatical features exemplifies language localisation but is not equally amenable to a study of the ideological and political meanings that are projected through the text. A study of the genre structure of the texts shows how the stages of a text as well as what is included in these stages can be localised to create and promote particular worldviews.

Pakistani English is a widely recognised and researched variety of English and reflects patterns of localisation (Mahboob 2009). It is the variety of English that most students in Pakistan are exposed to in their everyday life—in local media, newspapers, lectures, etc. However, Pakistani English is quite distinct from the varieties of English in domains 7 & 8, which, as pointed out earlier, are the varieties of English in which higher learning and knowledge production typically takes place at a global level. Thus, one consequence of the choice of model in textbooks is that students taught through only locally oriented textbooks find it difficult—if not impossible— to continue higher education in English. One main reason for this, as will be seen in this chapter, is that the genre structure of texts is often changed to project an ideological position. This shift of the genre structure in the local textbooks withholds opportunities for the students to read and learn about how the same genres are used in more globally oriented communities (domains 7 & 8). One consequence of this is that they have difficulty in reading and writing globally oriented texts once they enter university. Most public and private universities in Pakistan use English as the medium of instruction. Students graduating from government schools and who have had English language instruction only through the government approved textbooks find it difficult to meet the entrance criteria for these universities; and if they do make their way in, they struggle to meet the English language and literacy requirements expected of them at the university level. One result of this is that students coming from elite private schools, who have been exposed to and taught global varieties of English, are able to do well in these tertiary institutions while the government school graduates struggle at best. This further perpetuates the social class distinctions in the society and reflects the role of educational institutions in managing the distribution of knowledge and cultural capital in a way that maintains the socio-economic status quo (Apple 1990).

Language of the Textbooks

The language of the government-issued English language textbooks reflects Pakistani discursive practices. This is evident not only in some of the lexico-grammatical choices, but (particularly) in the discourse structure. To examine this, let us look at one biography from the grade 10 textbook.

Biographies are a core genre in English language textbooks in Pakistan: for example, 25% of the texts in the grade 10 textbook are biographies. Biographies, as a text type, tend to begin with a discussion of key aspects of the person being talked about (these can be personal details or a description of their key achievements etc.). In terms of genre, Rose & Martin (2012: 111) categorise biographies as a type of historical recount. A typical biography written for a global audience (domain 5 for mass consumption; domain 7 for specialised audiences) starts with an Orientation, followed by a series of Record of stages, and may include a Coda. In terms of lexico-grammatical features, biographies tend to be written in past tense; include specific references to time, place, and events; and tend to be chronologically ordered. Biographies also typically have an objective stance and focus primarily on the person and their close associates.

However, the discourse structure of the biographies included in textbooks published by the Government Textbook Boards in Pakistan does not follow this trend. Instead, they reflect a Pakistani English orientation to writing such texts. Biographies included in textbooks published by the government for public schools often start with a paragraph (or two) that does not directly relate to the focus of the biography. In many cases, as in the Shah Abdul Latif biography (Figure 2 below), the first paragraph tends to discuss Islamic themes.

This biography of Shah Abdul Latif starts with a reference to Islam instead of starting with an introduction to the person. The opening sentence of the text is "Islam is the religion of peace". This unambiguous reference to Islam in this text contributes to the normalisation of beliefs about Islam and its history in the community and leads to the creation of "shared knowledge" in the Pakistani community. It needs to be noted that Islam is not only presented as "a" religion of peace, but defined exclusively as "the" religion of peace—implying that other religions do not have the same claim to this. In this particular example, the choice of the article does not only reflect structural variation, but carries meaning. While there is literature on Pakistani English (Rahman 2011; Mahboob 2013) that shows how articles are used in divergent ways in Pakistani English, this work does not take the semantics associated with articles into consideration. Thus, it is not just that Pakistani English chooses articles that are different from British/American Englishes, but, as in the example above, may project particular meanings.

The rest of the first paragraph then builds on this theme and focuses on Islam and Islamic personalities—without any specific reference to Shah Abdul Latif. The second paragraph builds on the first one, but focuses on national personalities and contains specific references to all the four provinces of Pakistan (Lahore & Multan in Punjab, Peshawar in the North West Frontier Province, Quetta in Baluchistan, and then finally Sindh—the province in which the textbook was published)—thus fostering a "national" identity. It is only in paragraph three that we first see a description of Shah Abdul Latif—the focus personality for this biography.

Even in paragraph three, Shah Abdul Latif is not the main agent/actor in the text. Instead, paragraph three provides only skeletal information about the poet. Most of the paragraph still focuses on the history and the influence of Muslims in the region. It is noteworthy that Aurangzeb has been appraised positively as the "good Mughal Emperor Aurangzeb". This is a reflection not of historical accounts of Aurangzeb per se, but of General Zia-ul-Haq's admiration for this particular Mughal Emperor. General Zia, the Islamicist military dictator who ruled Pakistan from

Figure 2   Shah Abdul Latif biography—grade 10 textbook
(Sindh Textbook Board)

Shah Abdul Latif

Islam is the religion of peace. God sent the Prophet as blessing to mankind. He won people's hearts by his kind nature and gentle ways. His noble example was followed by many of his followers, in all ages, all over the world. It was through the efforts of these saintly men that Islam spread far and wide. These holy men were, extremely successful in bringing non-Muslims to the fold of Islam.

In every part of our country, there are shrines of such saints. In Lahore, are the shrines of Data Ganj Bukhsh and Mian Mir Sahib. In Pak Pattan lived and died Baba Fareed. In Multan, is the shrine of Ghous Bahaul Haq. In Peshawar, in Quetta, and in countless other towns and cities there are the tombs of these men of God. In Sindh are the tombs of two great saints, Shah Abdul Latif and Qalandar Lal Shahbaz.

The great saint Shah Abdul Latif, who is lovingly called Lal Latif by his devotees, was born in 1689, in a small village called "Hala Haveli". The good Mughul Emperor Aurangzeb then ruled the country. Shah Abdul Latif's ancestors had migrated to Sindh during the days of Tamerlane. They had come from Hirat. Sindh was then a centre of Muslim culture and Shah Abdul Latif's ancestors liked it so much that they decided to make it their home. But no one would have remembered their names or learnt about them, if many centuries later one of their descendants, Sayed Habib Shah, had not been blessed with a son who grew up to be saint Lal Latif.

Shah Latif had a very sensitive mind. His heart was soon filled with the love of God. The beauty of nature aroused his feelings strongly. While he was only a boy, he started composing poetry. He was also keen on acquiring knowledge and he grew up to be a scholar of Arabic and Persian. When he was twenty, he married a noble and good lady. He showed great kindness to his wife and lived at home for many years. His heart, however, tuned more and more towards religion and devotion, and he felt restless in living a normal domestic life.

When his father died, Shah Latif left his home and went to live on a mound at some distance from his village. A mound of sand is called "Bhit" in Sindhi. Due to the fact that he lived on this mound for the rest of his life, Shah Latif came to be known as "the Saint of Bhit". To this day, he is famous all over the country as Shah Abdul Latif Bhitai or Shah Latif of the Mound.

As days passed, Latif's love of God grew, until he found pleasure only in devotion and spent most of his time in prayer and deep thinking. His spiritual power grew stronger with prayer and devotion, so much so that people began to be attracted towards him. Any one who came to him was strongly impressed by his gentle ways and his followers increased day by day. Close to the mound on which Lal Latif came to live is a natural lake. His poetic nature loved the calm atmosphere. He would spend much of his time sitting on the bank of this lake. As he sat there, he prayed to God and sometimes composed verses in His praise.

(To be continued)

Shah Latif was not only a saint and a poet, but also a musician. He found great comfort in music. His skill in this art enabled him to make many improvements and changes in the difficult music of his time. As in everything else, he loved simplicity in music and musical instruments. He did not agree with the idea that music should be difficult. So he made it simple. He also invented a simple musical instrument used by the Arabs but the number of strings was different. To this day the "Tambooro" is popular all over Sindh. Old and young play it and sing the songs of Latif to its simple but moving tunes.

Lal Latif died in 1752 on the mound where he had lived and was buried there. A famous king of Sind, Ghulam Shah Kalhoro, was so devoted to him that he built a shrine over his grave. Latif's devotees collected his poetry and this collection came to be called the Risalo of Shah Abdul Latifi. He was a poet of the people, so he wrote poetry in the language of the common man. This collection of his poems is so valued that it has been translated into many languages. One great quality of Latif's poetry, besides its simplicity, is its moving music. When you listen to it, even if you do not understand a word of it, you will be moved by its melody.

Latif's "urs" is held at his shrine every year on 14th Safar, the second month of the Muslim calendar. Many thousands of people gather, listen to the Saint's songs sung to the "Tambooro" and offer their prayers. Many learned men read papers that tell about Latif's life and his poetry. Recently a library, a rest house and a museum have been built. The shrine itself has been rebuilt and connected with the main road. Its lovely white dome representing the purity and dignity of Latif, can be seen from many kilometers.

Latif's message is the message of love. He believed in the brotherhood and equality of men and in pleasing God by good deeds. This according to him is the goal of life.

1977 till his death in 1988 in a plane crash, followed a strong right-wing conservative Muslim agenda. Amongst other things, he was responsible for having the educational curricula and textbooks rewritten. The textbook being examined here, although still used, was produced under the directive of General Zia. The prioritisation of Islamic references and personalities in the text was a deliberate act carried out on government directives to create a more "Islamic" culture in the country (Mahboob 2009). As such, the shift in the genre structure of these texts reflects deliberate efforts to manage the identities of the students being educated through them.

It is also worth noticing that by the time Shah Abdul Latif is introduced in the text in the third paragraph, he has been raised to the status of a "great saint". This is done through a gradual shift in the meaning of the word "saint" across the first two paragraphs of the text. We first see a reference to "saintly men" in the first paragraph where "saintly men" refers to the followers of Prophet Muhammad, who spread Islam. "Saintly" here becomes associated with someone who spreads Islam. "Saintly men" are then replaced by "these holy men" in the following sentence, where the merit of these "saintly" or "holy" men is to convert non-Muslims to Islam. Then, the following paragraph starts by introducing various shrines of saints across Pakistan. This normalises the understanding that the people who are being referred to, including Shah Abdul Latif, were "saints" because they spread the word of Islam. However, this is not necessarily historically accurate. Shah Abdul Latif, like the other people mentioned in paragraph two of the text, was a Sufi poet. Sufis represent a mystical interpretation of Islam and transcended the Muslim-Hindu divide (Gidvani 2009 [1992]). As such, their beliefs and practices were contrary to those of General Zia, who endorsed a conservative and literal interpretation of Islam. Thus, the purpose of the inclusion of a text on Shah Abdul Latif, a Sufi poet, placed a number of challenges to the textbook writers. Shah Abdul Latif is recognised as one of the greatest Sufi poets of Sindh—there is even an annual provincial holiday dedicated to him in the province of Sindh. Thus, excluding/removing Shah Abdul Latif from the curriculum in Sindh could have raised political risks. Instead, the textbook authors used a range of linguistic maneuvers to recreate an image of Shah Abdul Latif. For example, the text does not once use the word *Sufi*; instead, it projects Shah Abdul Latif as a "saint" who was devoutly religious, someone whose goal in life was to spread Islam, and subtly affiliated him with Aurangzeb—a conservative Islamicist—through a textual reference.

The first two paragraphs of this text, in addition to foregrounding a religious and national identity, also serve as a tool for resignification. Bucholtz (2015) refers to resignification as a process where "semiotic forms acquire new meanings through the purposeful recontextualising acts of stylistic agents". In this text, the shift in the genre structure and the purposeful change in the meaning of "saint" allows the authors to recreate a new image and persona of Shah Abdul Latif: from being a Sufi poet, he becomes a "great saint", where "sainthood" is resemanticised (Mahboob 2009) as referring to a person who spreads Islam and converts non-Muslims. By doing this, the authors of the text use the authority of textbooks to create and endorse a different character portrayal of Shah Abdul Latif. And students, especially those who do not have access to other information about Shah Abdul Latif, may develop an understanding of Shah Abdul Latif only as a religious poet. In doing so, the authors of the textbook attempt to manage the identity and positions of the students, instead of giving them access to historical facts and/or giving them models of how biographies are written in global contexts.

In addition to the shift in the genre structure, this text also differs from the expected language features of a biography in terms of references to time, place and events. There are hardly any circumstances of time present in the text. There are only two years mentioned: (a) Shah Abdul Latif's year of birth and his death—but no specific dates are provided; and (b) there is one reference to "14th Safar", the day his Urs is celebrated. This last date is given according to the Islamic calendar. Since the students reading the text in Pakistan would know what *Safar* refers to, the inclusion of an explanation of *Safar*, "the second month of the Muslim calendar", is also noteworthy. The purpose of using a non-restrictive relative clause to explain what *Safar* can perhaps be interpreted as modeling ways in which local and religious terms can be introduced to non-locals in English. Furthermore, in the absence of specific dates, it is also not clear whether the text is chronologically ordered or not.

In addition to the religiously oriented slant of the text, it also projects other socio-cultural beliefs and practices as the norm. For example, in the fourth paragraph of the text, Shah Abdul Latif's wife is positively appraised (Martin & White 2005) as being "noble" and "good". These appraisals project a sense of the kind of "lady" one should marry. The text does not give us any specific details about his wife or marriage: the text does not mention her name nor does it give us the year of their marriage (it also includes no information about their children or if they had any). The author then goes on to state that Latif "showed great kindness" to his wife and "lived at home for many years"—these, at first read, appear to be an odd thing to say: for example, why would one expect that a husband would not live at home? The purpose of including this information becomes clearer as the text unfolds: staying at home might be acceptable in youth ("when he was twenty"), but what needs to happen is that a person should turn "more and more towards religion and devotion" in time. The text then continues to show how this devotion implies giving up a "normal domestic life". This example of the use of appraisal in this text shows how the readers are positioned to appraise the qualities of a marriageable woman as well as what a person is expected to do in their youth and then as they become older.

The coda, or the last paragraph of the text, once again directly relates to religious themes. Instead of highlighting Shah Abdul Latif's major achievements or things that he is most remembered for, the text ends with a reminder that one of his key contributions was to "please God by good deeds". This again reinforces the image of Shah Latif as a religious poet who believed that the key goal of life was to serve and "please" God. The analysis of the genre structure and discourse semantic resources in writing this text shows how the text projects the beliefs and attitudes of the authors and approvers of the textbook as normalised ways of being. By using such language in this textbook, as well as in other approved textbooks, the Ministry of Education attempts to position the readers to view the world in particular ways—ways that are approved of by the powerful. It provides models of texts that serve a particular political purpose and reflect local practices; not globally oriented ways of creating meaning that are required for engaging with knowledge and people from around the world.

Discussion and Conclusion

As (English language) teachers, researchers, and teacher educators, many of us assume that the ultimate goal of any government, organization, or institution involved in developing or using language in education policy is to ensure that students are able to use the language with the proficiency required to enhance their prospects in accessing better opportunities in education, community membership and employment within their own contexts and/or globally. This assumption is quite necessary for us to believe in because it makes us feel that we are making a positive change in the lives of our students. However, this chapter has shown that in some contexts the content and the language of the textbook in government-endorsed textbooks do not provide access to globalised ways of using language for knowledge production to the students who are educated through these texts. The texts used to teach particular academic genres can be structured not with regards to the norms of the genre (as used in global contexts or domains 7/8), but are rather locally oriented to achieve ideological purposes (domains 1/2). The content and the language of the texts may be designed to manage students' identities and to promote and reinforce particular sociocultural beliefs and positions. These sociocultural positions are promoted by the ruling elite, who, ironically, send their own children to elite private schools instead of government schools (Rahman 1997).

In attempting to show how Pakistani English is used for ideological goals, this chapter presented a three-dimensional model of language variation. This model shows how language variation is studied across a number of sub-disciplines in (applied) linguistics. One of the implications of this model is that it indicates that the language of academia and global knowledge construction is different from that of local communities. These variations run across the various strata of language (including discourse semantics, lexico-grammar, and grapho-phonology). The choice of using local variations in English language textbooks can limit students' ability to access and engage with globally oriented language. These local variations are not only structural variations (as described in mainstream work on World Englishes), but carry and project specific meanings (which may not be visible to outside readers). By using a local variety of English in textbooks, the government is able to project worldviews and beliefs that it holds and makes it difficult for students to interact with and access global networks. Thus, the choice of language here is not simply a reflection of local uses of English; but serves to maintain the socio-political and economic interests of the dominant groups. In order to fully understand and challenge these hegemonic practices, we need to look beyond studying only particular types of language variation, and need to consider models of language variation that provide a more holistic representation of how language varies across different contexts and domains (and across various strata of language).

As pointed out above, using locally oriented content and language in mainstream government schools serves a number of purposes. In terms of socio-political agendas, it promotes a particular (conservative) reading of Islam, history and personalities. These texts normalise particular interpretations as mainstream beliefs and therefore influence the religio-political identities of the students. By promoting a specific set of views and practices through educational texts, these views develop a cultural capital and become something that the students aspire to believe in, do, and become like. Since a large proportion of Pakistani school students do not go to universities, the understanding of the world that they develop in school can become their worldview for life. This can limit their ability to understand, engage with, or appreciate other sociocultural practices and positions (both from other parts of the country and from around the world) and may isolate them from having meaningful interaction with others. Perhaps, the current state of religious and ethnic violence in Pakistan is related to the language that the population has been taught for over 35 years now.

In his extensive work on language and curriculum, Michael Apple has argued that schools serve a primary function of promoting and projecting the ideologies of the dominant and the powerful. He argues that one consequence of this is to maintain the status quo between the powerful and the powerless. In his seminal work, *Ideology and Curriculum*, he writes:

> Schools do not only control people; they also help control meaning. Since they preserve and distribute what is perceived to be "legitimate knowledge"—the knowledge that "we all must have", schools confer cultural legitimacy on the knowledge of specific groups. But this is not all, for the ability of a group to make its knowledge into "knowledge for all" is related to that group's power in the larger political and economic arena. Power and culture, then, need to be seen, not as static entities with no connection to each other, but as attributes of existing economic relations in a society. They are dialectically interwoven so that economic power and control is interconnected with cultural power and control.
>
> (Apple 1990: 61)

Amongst other things, Apple here discusses the use of educational institutions and materials by the dominant in terms of "the ability of a group to make its knowledge into 'knowledge for all'" (ibid.). This ability of the dominant group to demarcate certain kinds of knowledge as desirable knowledge and embed it within educational contexts relates to Bourdieu's (1986) notion of cultural capital, and, more specifically, to the notion of institutionalised forms of cultural capital, which are objectified through educational qualifications and credentials. Cultural capital, like economic capital and social capital, is not equally distributed. By controlling the content and the language of the textbooks used in schools, the government can control access to this cultural capital. In the case of the Pakistani textbook examined in this chapter, we see how a particular set of beliefs is projected on to the students and how the semiotic and linguistic resources allocated to these students do not reflect the globally oriented language resources that they need to succeed in specialised domains.

In terms of socio-economic aspects, these localised textbooks reinforce and maintain the socio-economic hierarchies in favor of the dominant groups. By limiting the linguistic and semiotic resources that students in government schools are exposed to, the approved curriculum does not prepare them to read or write texts that are globally oriented. This limits the chances of students educated in government schools to access higher education and therefore to better jobs and prospects. The use of globally oriented English in the higher education context, as opposed to the locally oriented English in the approved school textbooks, also contributes to the cultural capital of "good" English. Since the students graduating from government schools do not have access to the English that is needed to succeed in higher education or for socio-economic mobility, they develop a belief that "good" English is essential for a successful professional career.

This social capital associated with English further allows educated middle-class families who send their children to private schools to maintain their privileges.

In terms of cultural practices, the representation of women, of minorities, of people with disabilities etc. in strongly evaluating language influences how students view these people and their role and position in society. In addition, a lack of inclusion of minorities, alternative lifestyles, other religions, etc. in the textbook makes invisible other possible beliefs, practices and ways of being. This allows—and in some cases encourages—uninformed and discriminatory practices to exist at a larger societal level.

In concluding, this article aimed to show how different traditions of studying language variations need to be understood in relation to each other and to what types of variations they prioritise. This modelling can be used to understand how localisation of language, e.g. in the case of World Englishes, relates to other types of language variations. This work can then be used to explore how different types of Englishes are used in educational contexts, how they relate to the norms of the genres being represented, what meanings are they prioritising, and the potential implications of this. In doing so, it is important that we look beyond formal/structural variations in World Englishes and also focus on variations in the discourse structures and semantics. By doing so, we can extend the implications of studying language variation and give it an "appliable" orientation (Halliday 2006)—one where theories and descriptions of language serve to address real-life problems and issues.

References

Apple, M. W. (1990). *Ideology and Curriculum*. London: Routledge.

Bourdieu, P. (1986). The forms of capital. In *Handbook of Theory and Research for the Sociology of Education*, J. G. Richardson (ed.), 242–258. New York: Greenwood.

Bucholtz, M. (2015). The elements of style. In *Language and Identity across Modes of Communication*, D. Djenar, A. Mahboob & K. Cruichkshank (eds), 27–60. Berlin: Mouton de Gruyter.

Derewianka, B. (2014). Supporting students in the move from spoken to written language. In *Englishes in Multilingual Contexts: Language Variation and Education*, A. Mahboob & L. Barratt (eds.), 165–182. Dordrecht: Springer.

Gidvani, M. M. 2009 [1992]. *Shah Abdul Latif*. Charleston: Bibliolife.

Halliday, M. A. K, McIntosh, A., & Strevens, P. (1964). *The Linguistic Sciences and Language Teaching*. London: Longman.

Halliday, M. A. K. (2006). Working with meaning: Towards an appliable linguistics. *Inaugural lecture to mark the launch of the Halliday Centre for intelligent applications of language studies at the City University of Hong Kong,* Hong Kong.

Kachru, B. (1992). *The Other Tongue: English across Cultures.* Urbana-Champaign IL: University of Illinois Press.

Kirkpatrick, A. (ed.). (2010). *The Routledge Handbook of World Englishes.* London: Routledge.

Mahboob, A. (2009). English as an Islamic language: A case study of Pakistani English. *World Englishes* 28(2): 175–189.

Mahboob, A. (2013). Pakistani English. In *World Atlas of Varieties of English,* B. Kortmann & K. Lunkenheimer (eds), 531–539. Berlin: Mouton de Gruyter.

Mahboob, A., & Barratt, L. (eds.). (2014). *Englishes in Multilingual Contexts: Language Variation and Education.* Dordrecht: Springer.

Martin, J. R. (1985). Language, register and genre. In *Children Writing Course Reader,* F. Christie (ed.), 21–30. Geelong: Deakin University Press.

Martin, J. R. & Rose, D. (2008). *Genre Relations: Mapping Culture.* London: Equinox.

Martin, J. R., & White, P. R. R. (2005). *The Language of Evaluation: Appraisal in English.* Houndmills: Palgrave Macmillan.

Matsuda, A. (2012). *Principles and Practices of Teaching English as an International Language.* Bristol: Multilingual Matters.

Rahman, T. (1997). *Language and Politics in Pakistan.* Karachi: Oxford University Press.

Rahman, T. (2011). *Pakistani English: The Linguistic Description of a Non-Native Variety of English.* Islamabad: National Institute of Pakistan Studies Quaid-i-Azam University.

Rose, D., & Martin, J. R. (2012). *Learning to Write, Reading to Learn: Genre, Knowledge and Pedagogy in the Sydney School.* London: Equinox.

Wolfram, W. (2014). Integrating language variation into TESOL: Challenges from English globalization. In *Englishes in Multilingual Contexts: Language Variation and Education,* A. Mahboob & L. Barratt (eds.), 15–32. Dordrecht: Springer.

Chapter 16

Identity Management, Language Variation and English Language Textbooks: Focus on Pakistan

Mahboob, A. (2015). Identity management, language variation, and English language textbooks. In D. Djenar, A. Mahboob & K. Cruickshank (eds.), *Language and Identity Across Modes of Communication*, 153–177. Boston: Mouton de Gruyter.

Introduction

Bucholtz and Hall (2005: 586) define identity as "social positioning of self and other" and see it as emergent: i.e., it is construed, realized and negotiated in and through discourse. More recently, Bucholtz (2015) relates identity to elements of style, where "style" is defined as "a system of sociocultural positioning through modes of semiotic action". One key aspect of this work is the focus on style as semiotic action—actions that construe and realize meaning. These actions can be both linguistic and non-linguistic and are therefore open to multimodal discourse analysis. In focussing on the semiotic dimension of style, Bucholtz's work encourages linguists to look beyond the description or distribution of formal features of language and consider how language makes meaning in context. This chapter is one attempt to operationalize such an approach. Drawing on Systemic Functional Linguistics (SFL), particularly genre theory, it examines how English language texts used in Pakistani schools are written to project, shape, and normalize particular sociocultural positioning of the students. In doing so, such texts in effect limit the students' discursive ability to access cultural capital. I have adopted SFL as my conceptual orientation because it is interested in how meanings are construed and represented. In this approach, language is considered to be a semogenic system; that is, as a meaning-making system. SFL also considers multimodality to be an important aspect of understanding meaning, hence it is particularly amenable to a study on identity.

This chapter analyzes sections of English language textbooks written and used in a World Englishes context. World Englishes can broadly be defined as Englishes that have emerged and evolved in different parts of the world over time to suit local contexts, needs and purposes. For this reason, the chapter also includes a consideration of how language variation relates to educational practices and identity. In order to explore the relationship between language variation, education, and identity, this chapter introduces two frameworks to help develop a comprehensive understanding of relevant issues. These two frameworks are: 1) a framework for studying identity management, and 2) a framework for studying language variation. The chapter locates the role of mainstream education in relation to these frameworks and shows how texts included in the school curricula can use local varieties of English to project particular ideological positions. In doing so these texts shape and influence students' identity and reinforce dominant sociocultural positions, hence they impact students' control of and access to semiotic resources and maintain socio-economic and socio-political hierarchies. In order to do this, this chapter will focus on textbooks used in Pakistan. However, it needs to be noted that the frameworks and issues introduced in this chapter can be applied to other contexts as well.

In his extensive work on language and curriculum, Apple (1978) argues that schools serve a primary function in promoting and projecting the ideologies of the dominant and the powerful. He stresses that one consequence of this is to maintain the status quo between the powerful and the unpowerful (Apple 1978: 63). He writes, for example, that

> Schools do not only control people; they also help control meaning. Since they preserve and distribute what is perceived to be 'legitimate knowledge'—the knowledge that 'we all must have,' schools confer cultural legitimacy on the knowledge of specific groups. But this is not all, for the ability of a group to make its knowledge into 'knowledge for all' is related to that group's power in the larger political and economic arena. Power and culture, then, need to be seen, not as static entities with no connection to each other, but as attributes of existing economic relations in a society. They are dialectically interwoven so that economic power and control is interconnected with cultural power and control.

Amongst other things, Apple here discusses the use of educational institutions and materials by the dominant group "to make its knowledge into 'knowledge for all'". The ability of this group to demarcate certain kinds of knowledge as desirable knowledge and embed it within educational contexts relates to Bourdieu's (1986) notion of cultural capital, and more specifically, to the notion of institutionalized forms of cultural capital. Such forms are objectified through educational qualifications and credentials. Cultural capital, like economic capital and social capital, is not equally distributed. In the context of Western societies, cultural capital may be gained through education, where educational materials provide access to the semiotic and discursive resources that embody that capital. This is not to say that all students in the West have equal opportunities to acquire or transfer cultural capital into economic capital or to achieve socio-economic mobility. In fact, the truth is far from this—children from the working classes have little chance to access the cultural capital available through schooling. Part of the reason for this, as Bernstein (1996) argues, is that children from working-class and middle-class background have different linguistic orientations, which themselves are a reflection of the cultural capital that they gain by being born into particular social classes. The difference in children's linguistic orientation impacts their ability to engage in school environments and results in differentiated life prospects (see, for example, Hasan and Williams 1996).

While equal access to cultural capital through mainstream education is already difficult to achieve, the issue becomes even more complex in the context of the developing world, especially in countries that use English for educational purposes even though it is not the mother tongue of the majority of the local population. Pakistan is a good case in point. In Pakistan, the elite educational institutions teach English and teach through English; however, the medium of instruction in the majority of government schools is either Urdu or one of the sanctioned provincial languages (e.g., Sindhi in the province of Sindh). In these government schools, English is only taught as a subject for a few hours a week, whereas students in elite private schools study all their subjects in English (see Rahman 1997 and Mahboob 2002, for a detailed discussion of English language education in Pakistan). The situation in which the government school students find themselves stand in stark contrast to that of students from private schools in which English is the medium of instruction. The use of English in elite and other private schools reflects the considerable cultural capital that it carries. Children of the rich and the educated middle class are exposed to the language and literacy practices expected from them in schools at home from early on in their lives so that they are ready for private schools. By contrast, children coming from a working-class background do not have the privileged early home education and hence struggle with the English language throughout their school life (Martin and Matthiessen 2014).

Children who attend government schools learn through Urdu, or in some limited contexts in a sanctioned provincial language (e.g., Sindhi in the case of certain areas of Sindh). Urdu, while being the national language of Pakistan, is spoken by less than 10 % of the population as a mother tongue. This means that many of the students attending Urdu medium schools have to develop literacy in Urdu as well as learn English. Privileging Urdu and English adds to the social capital of these two languages and relegates other regional and ethnic languages and dialects to the periphery.

In addition to the challenge of learning English in a multilingual context, where the students' mother tongues have limited cultural capital, the educational material used in government schools uses non-standard English at all strata of language, including discourse structure and genre, and locally oriented content. By using non-standard forms of English in the textbooks, the curriculum and textbooks manipulate the limited English language exposure that the students have and hence also limit the semiotic resources that the language potentially affords. Access to only local variants of English and not to the English of knowledge production, which is globally oriented, limits the chances of the students to acquire the kind of English that carries cultural capital. As a consequence, students have a limited opportunity to access cultural capital through education and to have equal opportunities in life. Apple (1978: 376) is also aware of this, referring to Bourdieu, and states:

> Cultural capital ("good taste," certain kinds of prior knowledge, abilities, and language forms) is unequally distributed throughout society, and this is dependent in large part on the division of labor and power in that society. By selecting for such properties, schools serve to reproduce the distribution of power within the society.

This chapter aims to show how educational materials in Pakistani government schools maintain the socio-economic status quo by controlling both what is included in the curriculum and the language in which it is presented. It identifies the ideological loadings of the textbooks that form part of the habitus in which the children are educated and which attempts to manage their identities into conformist positions. In order to study this, I will next introduce the "identity management" framework.

Identity Management

For the purposes of this chapter, identity management is defined as any institutionalized or localized effort to shape or direct individual or group identities. The key idea here is that an individual's sociocultural positioning is shaped through discourse and is done either locally (micro-level), by individuals or groups of people that a person interacts with, or through institutionalized (macro-level) processes. The sociocultural positions being promoted can be norm-conforming or contesting of the norms. These two dimensions of identity management can be plotted on a Cartesian plane as shown in Figure 1.

Figure 1 places the sociocultural positioning that is being projected on the x-axis and the level at which this is done on the y-axis. Identity management can occur along any of the domains that emerge along these lines. If identity management is aimed at promoting a conforming sociocultural position through institution processes, i.e., at a macro level, then it tends to be done through policy work and its implementation. The role of mainstream education is typically such—it uses policy, curricula, educational materials and resources, as well as teaching approaches to promote a conformist position. By "conformist" I mean that the students' identities are shaped in relation to the dominant and powerful sociocultural beliefs and practices. The focus of this chapter is on this type of identity management. It provides an analysis of textbooks that promote the ideological position of the politically dominant group.

Figure 1   Identity management framework

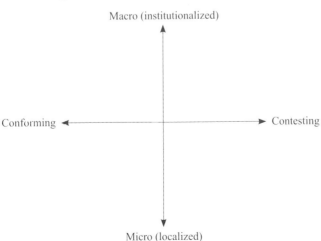

Macro-level identity management can also promote contesting identities. For example, this can be done through large-scale political movements, where political parties use institutional resources (such as various types of media) to project sociocultural positions that counter the dominant positions. In educational contexts, for example, critical pedagogy can be used to position students to question the norms of the powerful elites.

When identity management promotes a conforming sociocultural position at a micro level (e.g., locally by parents, siblings, extended family, or community groups), it tends to be done through interactive discourse. For example, weekend language schools tend to be locally organized by members of a community to teach their heritage language to the children in the community. This kind of schooling imposes a conforming sociocultural position (see, for example, Cruickshank 2015). In this context, the conforming position is one that reflects the positions of the people and community in question (and may or may not conform to mainstream positions).

Micro-level identity management can also promote a contesting sociocultural position. Examples of this can be found in peer group discourses, where peers may discursively position others and themselves in a contesting position.

Such positions are contesting in that they reject mainstream positions and open up space to create counter-cultures. Micro-level contesting identity management can also, at times, take on an educational discourse through local workshops and summer camps, etc. As these are typically not institutionalized, they tend not to have access to the same resources as macro-level projects and are also often more difficult to access or study.

This chapter, as pointed out earlier, focuses on identity management that is carried out through mainstream educational institutions. Such institutions tend to be funded and administered by governmental agencies. In the context of Pakistan, the government regulates the production and distribution of textbooks and other curricular materials through provincial textbook boards. The content and the language of textbooks have to be approved by the relevant provincial textbook board and/or the ministry of education before the books can be used in schools. In regulating the content and the language of the textbooks, the government can influence what material students will have access to and in what language this material will be presented. In fact, in Pakistan, the only prescribed textbooks used in government schools are those produced by the Textbook Boards. Private schools are permitted to use other books; however, school exit exams are set and regulated by the government. These exams are based on the prescribed textbooks only. By basing exams on the prescribed texts, the government makes sure that all students sitting the exams have been exposed to the state-approved curriculum. This in effect is a form of identity management; it requires all students to be familiar with the texts and contents prescribed by the government and to be able to report on these in the examinations.

It needs to be noted here that the notion of "identity management" does not discount the role of agency. The possibility is open to teachers and students to have different interpretations of the mainstream educational curriculum. Teachers, students, and parents do resist the position being projected by the government by responding to it in various ways. However, given space constraints we will not focus on this in this paper. The focus of this chapter is on understanding how the school curriculum tries to manage conforming identities of the students through government-endorsed textbooks.

In addition to content, the language used in these textbooks is also crucial for identity management. Language, as one of the primary semiotic resources, construes meaning through a selection of linguistic choices. These linguistic choices can either be in accord with the global ways of writing/speaking similar texts or can be different. In choosing a different set of resources, as in the English language textbooks analyzed later in this chapter, the texts not only reflect a local orientation but also impact students' ability to engage with more globally oriented discourse practices. In order to understand how language relates to this, we need to understand how language varies across contexts. This understanding of language will help us in identifying ways in which Pakistani students in government schools are disenfranchised and left with few opportunities to have access to the academically sanctioned cultural capital that is available to the children in elite private schools.

Understanding Language Variation

Variations across Englishes can be studied by identifying a set of dimensions that influence linguistic choices and behaviours. In this section of the chapter, we identify some of these key dimensions of language variation. The framework proposed below helps us explain how textbooks in Pakistan use locally oriented linguistic practices to shape students' beliefs and practices and potentially exclude them from accessing more globally oriented discourses.

In modelling language variation, we consider three dimensions: 1) users of the language, 2) uses of the language, and 3) modes of communication (see Halliday, McIntosh, and Strevens 1964, for a discussion of language variation across the dimensions of use and users). Each of these dimensions can be understood as independent clines or continuums that influence language choices and can then be brought together as a three-dimensional model (Figure 2) that allows us to "situate" various aspects of language variation (see Hasan 2009, for a discussion of language context and language variation). These three dimensions are first briefly described below and then brought together to form a coherent model of language variation. Given that the focus of this chapter is on English, we will discuss the model in relation to English. However, the model itself can be applied to examine patterns of variations in other languages as well.

Figure 2   Language variation framework

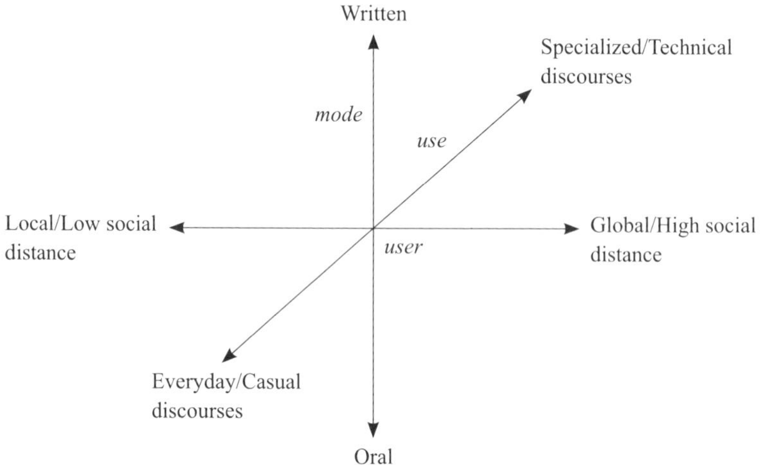

One dimension of variation relates to who we are as "users" of the language and with whom we are interacting. This is the kind of language variation that is studied in sociolinguistics and intercultural communication studies, including research that focuses on World Englishes (see, for example, Kachru 1992 and Kirkpatrick 2010) and other dialect studies (see Wolfram and Schilling-Estes 2006). In the context of World Englishes, one typically looks at how people in one location (country/speech community) use language for local purposes. The social distance between these participants is typically low in terms of their geographic location (i.e., they tend to live in the same region). However, the social distance between these users may vary based on social class, age, gender, and other such variables. Each of these variables impacts how similar or different the language of various speakers is. People who are based in the same geographical region and are related (close friends, family, etc.) may have unique ways of using language that reflect their close relationship and this language may not always be transparent to others. For example, couple talk, sibling talk, or friend talk can be seen as language that is used between people who have low social distance (and thus is localized) and may not be interpretable to an outside audience. On the other hand, when interacting with people with whom one has higher social distance, one tends to use a more "standard" or "global" language—one that minimizes "local" idioms, forms, and features and is thus less prone to miscommunication. Thus, one cline of language variation can be based on "low" vs. "high" social distance. The indicator "low social distance" helps us understand why people use "local" forms of language, with their local denotations and connotations. The indicator "high social distance" helps us understand why people use "global" forms of language, minimizing local forms and features, and allow for communication with people who do not share their local features. In developing a model of language variation for our purposes, we need to identify and understand these variables in order for us to be able to provide fine-tuned analyses and discussions of how Englishes vary based on the users of the language.

A second dimension of variation in language is related to the purpose or "use" of the language. This kind of language variation is typically studied in research on genres and English for Specific Purposes (ESP). This body of work looks at how language varies based on the purpose it is used for (see, for example, Martin and Rose 2008). For example, the language used in a biology research paper is different from the language used in a movie review. In terms of operationalizing this dimension of language variation, a key factor to consider is whether the language is about "everyday/casual" discourses or about "specialized/technical" discourses. The difference between "everyday/casual" and "specialized/technical" discourses is not necessarily about the topic of the discourse, but rather about its purpose. For example, one could talk about the weather using specialized/technical language—the purpose of which might be to engage with an informed audience of environmental scientists at a conference; or one could talk about the weather in everyday/casual language—the purpose of which would perhaps be to serve as an ice breaker at a social event. In both cases, the topic remains the same; however, the choice of language will vary based on the purpose of the exchange. In linguistic terms, this variation is understood as register variation and is used extensively in literature in genre and ESP studies. Currently, there is limited work on register variation in multilingual contexts; however, there seems to be no theoretical reason to assume that such variations do not exist in and across different varieties of Englishes.

In fact, it is quite necessary to understand if and how language varies in different parts of the world while being "used" for similar purposes. For example, an understanding of how registers are similar/different across World Englishes can help in developing educational materials and resources.

The third dimension of language variation, which will inform the model, is "mode" (Martin 1985; Derewianka 2014). Modes of communication include aural, visual, and mixed channels of communication. The way we use language varies based on whether we are speaking, writing, or—as is becoming common today—combining these two modalities (for example, in online chats, blogs, etc.). The mode of communication impacts the language choices that we make and therefore needs to be studied. For example, if we keep the "use" and "users" of language constant, the language might still vary based on whether we are writing or speaking. For example, an academic/researcher will draw from different sets of linguistic resources based on whether they are presenting their work at a conference or writing up the paper for publication.

The three dimensions of language variation identified above are not mutually exclusive. They interact with each other in myriad ways. Some of these dimensions are captured in the three-dimensional model above (Figure 2)—which is the result of mapping the three dimensions described above into a single model.

Among other things, this model gives us eight different possibilities or domains of mapping language variation. These are listed below (Table 1) along with examples of where we can find such languages. It should be noted that language varies within each domain too and not just across domains. These variations may happen across the various strata of language and reflect changes in the register variables of field, tenor, and mode.

One area of strength that the framework offers is that it provides an overview of how language variations can be modelled in a global context and therefore allows us to map variations out and study them systematically.

This framework also raises a number of questions in terms of the use of local dialects for educational purposes. Some World Englishes scholars have

Table 1   **Eight domains of language variation**

	Domains	Examples
1	Local, written, everyday	Friends writing letters to each other
2	Local, oral, everyday	Friends talking to each other about their plans for the holidays
3	Local, written, specialized	Texts written by and for a local group of farmers
4	Local, oral, specialized	Farmers discussing specifics about their crops
5	Global, written, everyday	International news agencies reporting on events
6	Global, oral, everyday	Conversations amongst people from different parts of the world
7	Global, written, specialized	Academics writing research papers
8	Global, oral, specialized	Conference presentations

been advocating for the utilization of local varieties for educational purposes in the outer and expanding circle countries (see, for example, Matsuda 2012). This advocacy acknowledges the local varieties of English and assumes that if students are taught a local variety, which is the dialect of English used in their context, they will be more empowered. While this position is well-meaning and appears to be in the interest of the students; a broader understanding of language variation—as developed through the framework presented here— would suggest otherwise. The framework helps us to see that the variations in language are not just about "nativeness" or "ownership" of a variety, but about the community (of practice) that uses a particular variety. Each community, either user- or use-oriented, negotiates its own linguistic norms and practices. These norms are not static, but change as the community membership changes. So, for example, the language of a discipline does not remain constant, but changes with time: research papers in biology today are not written in the same language as they were a hundred years ago; similarly, the language of research articles in a journal such as *TESOL Quarterly* is not the same today as it was twenty-five years ago. The changes in the language reflect the shift in the community membership over time and space as well as the development of the field. This implies that even in inner circle countries, such as Australia, Canada, England, Ireland, New Zealand, the United States, not all students who go to school have access to the language of domains 7 and 8 in Table 1—this is something that they have to develop through schooling. By promoting local varieties of English (domains 1 and 2) in and through education, the students may not be taught or given access to how globally oriented language works. Without appropriate teaching of the global specialized discourses (both written and spoken), students who only have control of local varieties of English will have a difficult task in reading, writing, and contributing to globally oriented knowledge bases that fall in domains 7 and 8 of the framework.

In the case of the Pakistani textbooks, the authors use a local everyday variety of English (domains 1 and 2). This choice of a locally oriented and everyday English in the textbooks limits students' ability to engage with global specialized texts and consequently to higher education and better employment prospective. Pakistani English is a widely recognized and researched variety of English and reflects patterns of localization (Mahboob 2009). It is also the variety of English that most students in Pakistan are exposed to in their everyday life—in local media, newspapers, lectures, etc. However, Pakistani English is quite distinct from the varieties of English in domains 7 and 8, which, as pointed out, are the varieties of English in which higher learning and knowledge production typically take place at a global level. Thus, one consequence of the choice of model in textbooks is that students taught through only locally oriented textbooks find it difficult—if not impossible— to continue higher education in English. Most public and private universities in Pakistan use English as the medium of instruction. Students graduating from government schools and who have had English language instruction only through the government-approved textbooks find it difficult to meet the entrance criteria for these universities; and if they do make their way in, they struggle to meet the English language and literacy requirements expected of them at the university level. One result of this is that students coming from elite private schools, who have been exposed to and taught global varieties of English, are able to do well in these tertiary institutions while the government school graduates struggle, at best. After graduation (and if they do graduate at all), this difference in English language proficiency impacts their job prospects. Thus, by regulating the language of these textbooks, the curriculum helps in maintaining the socio-economic status quo. This further perpetuates the social class distinctions in the society and reflects Michael Apple and Pierre Bourdieu's positions about the role of educational institutions in managing the distribution of knowledge and cultural capital in a way that maintains socio-economic status quo. Furthermore, and as will be exemplified in the following section, the choice of adopting a local everyday discourse in English language textbooks helps in identity management.

Identity Management Through Textbooks in Pakistan

Identity management in government-approved textbooks can be studied in at least two ways. One way of examining the complexities of how language and ideology work together would be to conduct a content analysis of textbooks printed in English as well as the layout and presentation of the texts. Another way would be to examine the language of the textbooks. Both content and language are considered in the discussion below.

Content Analysis of Textbooks

An analysis of the content and presentation of the textbooks can provide us with an overview of the kind of topics and readings that textbook writers choose to include. In the context of Pakistani government-approved textbooks, examining the text in Figure 3 below can help identify the relationship between curriculum and identity management. This text is the preface to the grade 1 English language textbook published and endorsed by the Sindh Textbook Board.

There are two things that we want to notice here. First, the text begins with the Arabic phrase "بِسْمِ اللهِ الرَّحْمٰنِ الرَّحِيمِ" which translates to: "I begin in the name of Allah who is the most gracious and the most merciful". This statement in Arabic is a shared feature of all textbooks published and authorized by the government. It reflects the Islamic tradition of starting all things in the name of Allah. The use of Arabic—and not its English translation—shows the iconic power of Arabic and its indexical relationship with Islamic values and systems. Second, I want to note the stated aims of the English language textbook: "[...] inculcating the ingredients of universal Islamic brotherhood [sic.] and to reflect the valiant deeds of our forebears and portray the illuminating patterns of our rich cultural heritage and traditions". This statement suggests that Arabic and other Islamic markers in the textbook are perhaps systematically incorporated into the texts and have a clear function of indexing and projecting an Islamic identity. The Islamic "ideology" can be seen throughout all the textbooks published by the Textbook Board. In using term "ideology", I follow Bernstein (1996: 31), who argues that ideology "is not a content but a way in which relationships are made and realized". This view of ideology as a way of making meaning is important in understanding how the use of Islamic phrases, images, and traditions in the English language textbooks is used to construct an Islamic identity in and through English.

**Figure 3   Preface to the grade 1 English language textbook
(Sindh Textbook Board)**

PREFACE

The Sind Textbook Board, is assigned with preparation and publication of the textbooks to equip our new generation with knowledge, skills and ability to face the challenges of new millennium in the fields of Science, Technology and Humanities. The textbooks are also aimed at inculcating the ingredients of universal Islamic brotherhood and to reflect the valiant deeds of our forebears and portray the illuminating patterns of our rich cultural heritage and traditions.

To accomplish this noble task, a team of educationists, experts, working teachers and committee of friends has been constituted which incessantly endeavours to develop, test and improve content and design of the textbooks on the basis of the horizontal and vertical flow of informational feed back. The preset intellectual product has been presented with joint efforts of the team to project the aforementioned assignment in its true perspective.

It is expected that the discerning parents, learned teachers and concerned citizens will go through it and offer their valuable opinion to the Board for brining about improvement in the next edition.

Khalid Mehmood Soomro
Chairman
SINDH TEXTBOOK BOARD,
JAMSHORO, SINDH

The implementation of the policy stated in the preface for the grade 1 textbook is evident through the choice of content and the use of language in all government-sanctioned school textbooks. For example, Figure 4 is an image of the table of contents page for the grade 10 textbook published by the Sindh Textbook Board.

This book is the only prescribed text for the province-wide government grade 10 exit exams (known as the Matric exams, a high stake test in Pakistan) that all students have to pass before they can enrol in the last two years of high school (known as Intermediate College). This textbook includes twenty texts in all. The first text is a summary of the key points that were made in the last sermon of Prophet Muhammad; five texts are

Figure 4   Table of contents for the Grade 10 text book
(Sindh Textbook Board)

CONTENTS

Page

1.	The Last Sermon of the Holy Prophet	2
2.	Shah Abdul Latif	7
3.	*The Neem Tree* (Poem)	17
4.	Moen-jo-Daro	19
5.	Helen Keller	28
6.	*The Daffodils* (Poem)	33
7.	Allama Iqbal	37
8.	The Role of Women in the Pakistan Movement	45
9.	*Children* (Poem)	55
10.	What the Quaid-i-Azam Said	59
11.	Health is Wealth	66
12.	*Stopping by Woods on a Snowy Evening* (Poem)	71
13.	The Great War Hero	74
14.	Nursing	80
15.	*The Miller of the Dee* (Poem)	85
16.	Responsibilities of a Good Citizen	87
17.	The Village Life in Pakistan	92
18.	*Abou Ben Adhem* (Poem)	97
19.	The Secret of Success	99
20.	The Guddu Barrage	106

biographies; two texts are about places in Pakistan; four texts are about social issues; one text is a summary of some of the key sayings of the first Governor General of Pakistan; one text is about a profession; and six texts are poems. One salient feature that emerges in this review of the Table of Contents is the emphasis on the local places, people, heroes, and practices. Another noticeable element is the large proportion of biographies: while there are five units on biographies, the actual number of biographies included in the textbook is higher because one of the texts, "The Role of Women in the Pakistan Movement", includes biographies of four female political leaders. The large proportion of biographies raises the question of their purpose in the textbook. Biographies celebrate heroes and create role models for students. Hero building is an important aspect of identity management and projects models that the students are expected to aspire to follow (Tann 2010). As such, it is noteworthy that of the five biographies, two are of national heroes ("Allama Iqbal" and "Women in the Pakistan Movement"), one a folk poet who is projected as a religious poet (Shah Abdul Latif), and one a war hero (The Great War Hero). There is also one biography about a non-Pakistani, Helen Keller, which we will discuss later in this section. The choice of including mostly national, religious, and military heroes—and not, for example, artists, authors, or scientists—is noteworthy. It reflects the emphasis on projecting an Islamic and patriotic identity instead of (or in addition to) intellectual or academic identities. In addition to the selection of texts to be included, the linguistic features used are also managed. To exemplify this, we will focus on the biographical text on Shah Abdul Latif in the following section.

The one biography of a non-Pakistani, Helen Keller, in this textbook is a telling example of how the texts attempt to carry out identity management. This text is supposed to be a biography, but it does not follow the genre structure of one. Biographies, as we will discuss in more detail later on, tend to begin with highlighting some aspect (personal or professional) of the person whose life is being reviewed and celebrated. However, this is not the case with the biography of Helen Keller. The first paragraph of the text can be seen in Figure 5.

Figure 5   First paragraph of the text *Helen Keller*

Helen Keller

How fortunate are those who are born into this world with two eyes to see all its beauty! But there are some unfortunate people who can neither see nor hear. This world, which is so full of beautiful colours and sweet sounds, appears colourless and dull to these poor souls. What a misfortune! They cannot see the lovely flowers blooming in the gardens and hear the birds singing sweet songs. They indeed feel very sad, for their fate is so hard. Worse is the fate of those who can see and hear once and then no more. But they are so courageous and bold that they do not look unhappy. They accept the challenge of their fate and try to live cheerfully.

The chapter starts not with a detail about Helen Keller, as one would expect, but with an exclamatory sentence which evaluates people who can see as "fortunate". This sets up a dichotomous relationship between people who can see and who are fortunate and people who cannot see (or hear) and are "unfortunate". This opposition is created in the first two sentences of the text. It then goes on to list the things that fortunate people can do, e.g., being able to see "beautiful" colours and hear "sweet" sounds. Notice here that the colours and sounds are presented with positive attributes. This appraisal highlights the contrasts between the fortunate and the "poor souls" who have met with "misfortune". The text further creates pity for the "unfortunate" by specifying things that people with no physical challenge take for granted and goes on to project the feeling of sadness to people who cannot see or hear. The text then proceeds to claim that the fate of those who have lost sight or the ability to hear is even worse because they know what they miss. In doing this, the text ascribes a prosody of negative attitude towards those with physical disabilities. The paragraph concludes by suggesting that these people may look happy only because they are "courageous and bold" and they accept the "challenge of fate". This whole paragraph does not mention Helen Keller, the focus of the biography, but instead does identity management by projecting a particular stance towards people with physical disabilities. The content and the prosody of the text create a feeling of pity towards people who cannot see or hear and cast these people as less than normal. After this preamble, the text moves into talking about Helen Keller. But this biography is now shadowed by the reader being positioned to believe that anything that a person with a disability achieves should be seen as a great achievement and their happiness judged not in the sense of a "fortunate" person who can see or hear, but rather in terms of them facing the "challenge of their fate". This example shows how the content of a biography is managed to project particular attitudinal positions and thus to manage identities and positions.

This biography of Helen Keller is radically different from one that would be found in a globally oriented textbook. While one may argue that the way of writing this biography in the Pakistani textbook reflects Pakistani discursive practices and should therefore be permitted, this is not really correct. Other biographies in the textbook, such as that of Allama Iqbal, do follow the norms of a globally oriented biography. Figure 6 presents the first paragraph of this biography in the same textbook.

As can be seen in Figure 6, the biography starts off with an orientation to the person and then outlines his major achievements. This raises the question of why certain biographies follow globally oriented patterns and others locally oriented ones. An analysis of all the biographies in the textbook for the grade 9 and 10 suggests that biographies of people who

Figure 6   First paragraph of the text *Allama Iqbal*

> **Allama Iqbal**
>
> Allama Mohammad Iqbal, the poet of the East, was born in Sialkot, a town in the Punjab, on 9th November, 1877. He received his early education in his home town. In 1895, he went to Government College, Lahore. He passed his M.A. in 1899, from the University of the Punjab. In the same year, he was appointed Professor of Arabic at the Oriental College, Lahore. He held this job till 1905. In that year, he left for England for higher studies. In London he received a law degree. In 1908, he was awarded a degree of Ph. D. by Munich University, for his work on Persian philosophy. That is why, he is also known as Dr. Mohammad Iqbal.

are well-recognized in Pakistan tend to follow a globally oriented pattern, while those who may not be local or may be seen as controversial figures have an altered pattern. This altered pattern, as in the case of Helen Keller, tends to set up an ideological perspective in the orientation stage (or the introduction) of the text that shapes the reading of the rest of the text. An analysis of Shah Abdul Latif's biography presented in the following section provides a more detailed exemplification of how this is done. It further exemplifies how identity management is attempted through texts through linguistic choices that project a certain set of opinions and beliefs and provide little, if any, space for alternative interpretations or understandings.

Language of the Textbooks

The language of the government-issued English language textbooks incorporates and projects a Pakistani Islamic identity as well as political attitudes of the dominant, conservative political parties. To examine this, we will look at one biography from the grade 10 textbook in some detail.

Biographies are a core genre in English language textbooks in Pakistan. For example, as shown earlier, they comprise 25 % of the texts in the grade 10 textbook. Biographies, as a text type, tend to begin with a discussion of key aspects of the person being talked about (these can be personal details or a description of their key achievements). In terms of genre, they are a type of historical recount (Rose and Martin 2012). A typical biography written for a global audience (see Table 1, domain 5 for mass consumption, and domain 7 for specialized audiences) starts with an Orientation, followed by a series of Record of stages, and may include a Coda. In terms of lexico-grammatical features, biographies tend to be written in past tense, include specific references to time, place, and events, and tend to be chronologically ordered.

Biographies also typically have an objective stance and focus primarily on the person and their close associates.

However, the discourse structure of the biographies included in textbooks published by the government textbook boards in Pakistan does not always follow this trend. Like the Helen Keller biography that we looked at earlier, some of the other biographies included in textbooks published by the government for public schools also start with a paragraph (or two) that does not directly relate to the focus of the biography. In many cases, as in the Shah Abdul Latif biography (Figure 7) the first paragraph tends to discuss Islamic themes.

This biography of Shah Abdul Latif starts with a reference to Islam instead of an introduction to the person. The opening sentence of the text is "Islam is the religion of peace". This unambiguous reference to Islam contributes to the normalization of beliefs about Islam and its history in the community and leads to the creation of "shared knowledge" in the Pakistani community. It needs to be noted that Islam is not only presented as "a" religion of peace, but is defined exclusively as "the" religion of peace—implying that other religions do not have the same claim to this. The use of this biography to highlight the merits of Islam is not only a Pakistani or an Islamic trait. As one of the editors of Language and Identity Across Modes of Communication pointed out, this echoes claims in early Christian texts as well. Cruickshank noted that the role of historical writing in medieval Latin Christian homilies was not a factual biography but to exemplify a sermon exemplum highlighting Christian traits and virtues.

The rest of the first paragraph in Shah Abdul Latif's biography builds on this theme and focuses on Islam and Islamic personalities, without any specific reference to Shah Abdul Latif himself. The second paragraph builds on the first one, but focuses on national personalities and includes specific references to all the four provinces of Pakistan (Lahore and Multan in Punjab, Peshawar in the North West Frontier Province, Quetta in Baluchistan, and then finally Sindh—the province where the textbook was published)—thus fostering a "national" identity. It is only in paragraph three that we first see a description of Shah Abdul Latif—the focus personality for this biography.

Even in paragraph three, Shah Abdul Latif is not the main agent/actor in the text. Instead, paragraph three provides only skeletal information about the poet. Most of the paragraph still focuses on the history and the influence of Muslims in the region. It is noteworthy that Aurangzeb has been appraised positively as the "good Mughal Emperor Aurangzeb". This

**Figure 7   Shah Abdul Latif biography—grade 10 textbook
(Sindh Textbook Board)**

Shah Abdul Latif

Islam is the religion of peace. God sent the Prophet as blessing to mankind. He won people's hearts by his kind nature and gentle ways. His noble example was followed by many of his followers, in all ages, all over the world. It was through the efforts of these saintly men that Islam spread far and wide. These holy men were, extremely successful in bringing non-Muslims to the fold of Islam.

In every part of our country, there are shrines of such saints. In Lahore, are the shrines of Data Ganj Bukhsh and Mian Mir Sahib. In Pak Pattan lived and died Baba Fareed. In Multan, is the shrine of Ghous Bahaul Haq. In Peshawar, in Quetta, and in countless other towns and cities there are the tombs of these men of God. In Sindh are the tombs of two great saints, Shah Abdul Latif and Qalandar Lal Shahbaz.

The great saint Shah Abdul Latif, who is lovingly called Lal Latif by his devotees, was born in 1689, in a small village called "Hala Haveli". The good Mughul Emperor Aurangzeb then ruled the country. Shah Abdul Latif's ancestors had migrated to Sindh during the days of Tamerlane. They had come from Hirat. Sindh was then a centre of Muslim culture and Shah Abdul Latif's ancestors liked it so much that they decided to make it their home. But no one would have remembered their names or learnt about them, if many centuries later one of their descendants, Sayed Habib Shah, had not been blessed with a son who grew up to be saint Lal Latif.

Shah Latif had a very sensitive mind. His heart was soon filled with the love of God. The beauty of nature aroused his feelings strongly. While he was only a boy, he started composing poetry. He was also keen on acquiring knowledge and he grew up to be a scholar of Arabic and Persian. When he was twenty, he married a noble and good lady. He showed great kindness to his wife and lived at home for many years. His heart, however, tuned more and more towards religion and devotion, and he felt restless in living a normal domestic life.

When his father died, Shah Latif left his home and went to live on a mound at some distance from his village. A mound of sand is called "Bhit" in Sindhi. Due to the fact that he lived on this mound for the rest of his life, Shah Latif came to be known as "the Saint of Bhit". To this day, he is famous all over the country as Shah Abdul Latif Bhitai or Shah Latif of the Mound.

As days passed, Latif's love of God grew, until he found pleasure only in devotion and spent most of his time in prayer and deep thinking. His spiritual power grew stronger with prayer and devotion, so much so that people began to be attracted towards him. Any one who came to him was strongly impressed by his gentle ways and his followers increased day by day. Close to the mound on which Lal Latif came to live is a natural lake. His poetic nature loved the calm atmosphere. He would spend much of his time sitting on the bank of this lake. As he sat there, he prayed to God and sometimes composed verses in His praise.

(To be continued)

Shah Latif was not only a saint and a poet, but also a musician. He found great comfort in music. His skill in this art enabled him to make many improvements and changes in the difficult music of his time. As in everything else, he loved simplicity in music and musical instruments. He did not agree with the idea that music should be difficult. So he made it simple. He also invented a simple musical instrument used by the Arabs but the number of strings was different. To this day the "Tambooro" is popular all over Sindh. Old and young play it and sing the songs of Latif to its simple but moving tunes.

Lal Latif died in 1752 on the mound where he had lived and was buried there. A famous king of Sind, Ghulam Shah Kalhoro, was so devoted to him that he built a shrine over his grave. Latif's devotees collected his poetry and this collection came to be called the Risalo of Shah Abdul Latifi. He was a poet of the people, so he wrote poetry in the language of the common man. This collection of his poems is so valued that it has been translated into many languages. One great quality of Latif's poetry, besides its simplicity, is its moving music. When you listen to it, even if you do not understand a word of it, you will be moved by its melody.

Latif's "urs" is held at his shrine every year on 14th Safar, the second month of the Muslim calendar. Many thousands of people gather, listen to the Saint's songs sung to the "Tambooro" and offer their prayers. Many learned men read papers that tell about Latif's life and his poetry. Recently a library, a rest house and a museum have been built. The shrine itself has been rebuilt and connected with the main road. Its lovely white dome representing the purity and dignity of Latif, can be seen from many kilometers.

Latif's message is the message of love. He believed in the brotherhood and equality of men and in pleasing God by good deeds. This according to him is the goal of life.

is a reflection not of historical accounts of Aurangzeb *per se*, but of General Zia-ul-Haq's admiration for this particular Mughal Emperor. General Zia, the Islamicist military dictator who ruled Pakistan from 1977 until his death in 1988 in a plane crash, followed a strong right-wing conservative Muslim agenda. Amongst other things, he was responsible for having the educational curricula and textbooks rewritten (Mahboob 2009). The textbook being examined here, although still used, were produced under his directive. The prioritization of Islamic references and personalities in the text was a deliberate act carried out on government directives to create a more "Islamic" culture in the country. As such, the genre structure of these texts reflects deliberate efforts to manage the identities of the students being educated through them. It also reflects the priorities of the textbooks as stated by the Chairman of the Sindh Textbook Board (see Figure 3 above).

It is also worth noticing that by the time Shah Abdul Latif is introduced in the text in the third paragraph, he has been raised to the status of a "great saint". Sainthood in a religious sense relates to Catholicism and requires a certain set of characteristics in the person and its canonization requires a formal religious process. Shah Abdul Latif was never canonized, yet he is given the status of a saint in this text. This is done through a gradual shift in the meaning of the word "saint". We first see a reference to "saintly men" in the first paragraph where "saintly men" refers to the followers of Prophet Muhammad, who spread Islam. "Saintly" here becomes associated with someone who spreads Islam. "Saintly men" are then replaced by "these holy men" in the following sentence, where the merit of these "saintly" or "holy" men is to convert non-Muslims to Islam. Then, the following paragraph starts by identifying the various shrines of saints across Pakistan. This normalizes the understanding that the people that are being referred to, including Shah Abdul Latif, were "saints" because they spread the word of Islam. However, this is not necessarily historically accurate. Shah Abdul Latif, like the other people mentioned in paragraph two of the text, is a Sufi poet. Sufis represent a mystical interpretation of Islam and transcended the Muslim-Hindu divide (Gidvani 2009 [1922]). As such, their beliefs and practices were contrary to those of General Zia, who endorsed a conservative and literal interpretation of Islam. Thus, the purpose of including a text on Shah Abdul Latif, a Sufi poet, placed a number of challenges to the textbook writers. Shah Abdul Latif is recognized as one of the greatest Sufi poets of Sindh—there is even an annual provincial holiday dedicated to him in the province of Sindh. Thus, excluding Shah Abdul Latif from the curriculum in Sindh could have raised political risks. Instead, the textbook authors used a range of linguistic manoeuvres to recreate an image of Shah Abdul Latif. For example, the text does not once use the word "Sufi"; instead it projects Shah Abdul Latif as a "saint" who was devoutly religious, someone whose goal in life was to spread Islam, and subtly affiliates him with Aurangzeb—also a conservative Islamicist—through a textual reference.

The first two paragraphs of this text, in addition to foregrounding a religious and national identity, also serve as a tool for resignification. Bucholtz (2015) refers to resignification as a process where "semiotic forms acquire new meanings through the purposeful recontextualizing acts of stylistic agents". In this text, the shift in the genre structure and the purposeful change in the meaning of "saint" allows the authors to recreate a new image and persona of Shah Abdul Latif: from being a Sufi poet to a "great saint", where "sainthood" is resemanticized (Mahboob 2009) as referring to a person who spreads Islam and converts non-Muslims. By doing this, the authors of the text use the authority of textbooks to create and endorse a different character portrayal of Shah Abdul Latif. And students, especially those who do not have access to other information about Shah Abdul Latif, may develop an understanding of Shah Abdul Latif only as a religious poet. In doing so, the authors of the textbook attempt to manage the identity and positions of the students, instead of giving them access to historical facts and/or giving them models of how biographies are written.

In addition to the shift in the genre structure, this text also differs from the expected language features of a biography in terms of references to time, place, and events. There are hardly any circumstances of time present in the text: there are only two years mentioned (Shah Abdul Latif's year of birth and his death—but no dates given), and there is one reference to "14th Safar", the day his Urs is celebrated. This last date is given using the Islamic calendar. Since the students reading the text in Pakistan would know what Safar refers to, the inclusion of an explanation of "Safar" is noteworthy as well. The purpose of using a non-restrictive relative clause to explain what Safar is can perhaps be interpreted as modelling ways in which local and religious terms can be introduced to non-locals in English. Furthermore, in the absence of specific dates, it is also not clear whether the text is chronologically ordered or not.

The text also does not appear to take an objective stance. This was already evidenced in our discussion of the genre structure of text and its contribution to the resignification of Shah Abdul Latif. In addition, instead of documenting facts and events, the text is full of appraisals. For example, the text consistently includes Judgements (Martin and White 2005) to assess and evaluate the character and behaviour of various entities. While Judgements can be both positive and negative, in this text, it is noticeable that there are only positive Judgements included. The targets of the positive Judgement are the "Prophet", "saintly men", "Shah Abdul Latif", "Mughal Emperor Aurangzeb", "Latif's ancestors", and "lady" (referring to Shah Abdul Latif's wife). The dominant use of positive Judgements in the text creates an attitudinal slant in the text and subtly influences the readers' position in relation to the targets of the appraisal. It projects and directs particular stances towards the targets of the appraisal. Given the absence of specifics about the life and events of Shah Abdul Latif on the one hand, and the extensive use of Judgement on the other, we can begin to see how the language of this text is used for the purpose of identity management, instead of helping students build their linguistic resources to read and write objective biographies. As discussed earlier, not providing appropriate models and access to globally oriented linguistic resources to the students impacts their ability to develop the semiotic resources that they need in order to engage with and write the kind of texts that are expected in higher education. This places the students in a disadvantaged position in relation to their ability to build their cultural capital through education and limits their life prospects.

In addition to the religiously oriented identity management, the text also projects other sociocultural beliefs and practices as the norm. For example, in the fourth paragraph in Figure 7, Shah Abdul Latif's wife is positively appraised as being "noble" and "good". These Judgements of Propriety and Normality project a sense of the kind of "lady" one should marry. The text does not give us any specific details about his wife or marriage; it does not mention her name nor does it give us the year of their marriage (it also includes no information about their children or if they had any). The author then goes on to state that Latif "showed great kindness" to his wife and "lived at home for many years"—these, at first read, appear to be odd things to say: why, for example, would one expect that a husband would not live at home? The purpose of including this information becomes clearer as the text unfolds: staying at home might be acceptable in youth ("when he was twenty"), but what needs to happen is that a person should turn "more and more towards religion and devotion" in time. The text then continues to show how this devotion implies giving up a "normal domestic life". A brief analysis of this text shows how the readers are positioned to appraise the qualities of a "marriageable" woman as well as learn about what a person can do in their youth and what they should do as they become older.

The analysis of the genre structure as well as the use of lexico-grammatical and discourse semantic resources in this text shows how the text projects the beliefs and attitudes of the authors and approvers of the textbook as normalized ways of being. By using such language in this textbook, as well as in other approved textbooks, the Ministry of Education attempts to position the readers to view the world in particular ways—ways that are approved of by the powerful.

Conclusion

As (English language) teachers and teacher educators, many of us assume that the ultimate goal of any government, organization, or institution involved in developing or using language in education policy is to ensure that students are able to use the language with the proficiency required to enhance their prospects in accessing better opportunities in education, community membership, and employment within their own contexts and/or globally. This assumption is necessary for us to believe in because it makes us feel that we are making a positive change in the lives of our students. However, this chapter has questioned the universality of this assumption. It has shown that in some contexts the content and the language of the textbook in government-endorsed textbooks do not provide access to globalized ways of using language for knowledge production for students. The texts used to teach particular academic genres are structured not with regard to the norms of the genre (as used in global contexts) or by making expected linguistic choices, but rather are locally contextualized to achieve ideological purposes. The content and the language of the texts—as exemplified above—are designed to manage students' identities and to promote and reinforce particular beliefs and practices. These sociocultural positions are promoted by the ruling elite, whose children attend elite private schools and hence are not exposed to these positions (Rahman 1997).

Using locally oriented content and language in mainstream government schools serves a number of purposes. In terms of socio-political agendas, it promotes a particular (conservative) reading of Islam, history, and personalities. These texts present particular interpretations as norms and therefore influence the religio-political identities of the students. They are also developed as a cultural capital for students to aspire to. Since a large proportion of Pakistani school students do not go to universities, the understanding of the world that they develop in school can become their worldview for life. This condition limits their ability to understand, engage with, or appreciate other sociocultural practices and positions (both from other parts of the country and from around the world) and isolates them from having meaningful interaction with others. Furthermore, by including a large number of biographies of national, religious, and military personalities, the students are provided with only a limited set of heroes and models. The exclusion of scientists and other (contemporary) social leaders from the textbooks provides no alternative models for the students. This influences the kind of futures that the students can imagine for themselves. It helps in building support for conservative positions to dominate in society, and for the military—the largest institution in the country—to be valorized as the saviour of the country at the cost of civil institutions.

In terms of socio-economic aspects, these localized textbooks reinforce and maintain the socio-economic hierarchies in favour of the dominant groups. By limiting the linguistic and semiotic resources that students in government schools are exposed to, the approved curriculum does not prepare them to read or write texts that are globally oriented. This limits their chances of accessing higher education and better job prospects. The use of globally oriented English in higher education contexts, as opposed to the locally oriented English in the approved school textbooks, also contributes to the cultural capital of "good" English. Since students graduating from government schools do not have access to the English that is needed to succeed in higher education or for socio-economic mobility, they develop a belief that "good" English is essential for a successful professional career. This social capital associated with English further allows educated middle-class families to maintain their privileges.

In terms of cultural practices, the representation of women and people with disabilities in strongly appraised language influences how students view these people and their role and position in society. In addition, the absence of references to minority groups, alternative lifestyles, and other religions from the textbook makes invisible other possible beliefs, practices, and ways of being. This allows—and in some cases encourages—uninformed and discriminatory practices to exist at a larger societal level.

In concluding this chapter, I would like to point out that while this chapter has exemplified how identity management works in mainstream education by providing examples from Pakistan, Pakistan is not the only country where this happens. The choice of focusing on Pakistan is based on my familiarity and understanding of Pakistan and the Pakistani educational context. The main purpose here is to identify issues involved in identity management and exemplify ways of studying it. By doing so, I hope to encourage further work in this area.

References

Apple, M. W. (1978). Ideology, reproduction, and educational reform. *Comparative Education Review*, 22(3), 367–387.

Bernstein, B. (1996). *Pedagogy, symbolic control and identity: Theory, research, critique.* London: Taylor & Francis.

Bourdieu, P. (1986). The forms of capital. In J. Richardson (ed.), *Handbook of theory and research for the sociology of education*, 242–258. New York: Greenwood.

Bucholtz, M. (2015). The elements of style. In D. Djenar, A. Mahboob & K. Cruickshank (eds.), *Language and Identity Across Modes of Communication*, 27–60. Boston: Mouton de Gruyter.

Bucholtz, M., & Hall, K. (2005). Identity and interaction: A sociocultural linguistic approach. *Discourse Studies*, 7(4–5), 585–614.

Cruickshank, K. (2015). Community languages schools: The importance of context in understanding hybrid identities. In D. Djenar, A. Mabboob & K. Cruickshank (eds.), *Language and Identity Across Modes of Communication*, 83–106. Boston: Mouton de Gruyter.

Derewianka, B. (2014). Supporting students in the move from spoken to written language. In A. Mahboob & L. Barratt (eds.), *Englishes in Multilingual Contexts: Language Variation and Education*, 165–182. Dordrecht: Springer.

Gidvani, M. M. 2009 [1922]. *Shah Abdul Latif*. Charleston: Bibliolife.

Halliday, M. A. K., McIntosh, A, & Strevens, P. (1964). *The linguistic sciences and language teaching*. London: Longman.

Hasan, R., & Williams, G. (eds.). (1996). *Literacy in society*. London: Longman.

Hasan, R. (2009). *Semantic variation: Meaning in society and sociolinguistics*. London: Equinox.

Kachru, B. (1992). *The other tongue: English across cultures*. Urbana-Champaign: University of Illinois Press.

Kirkpatrick, A. (ed.) (2010). *Routledge handbook of World Englishes*. London: Routledge.

Mahboob, A. (2002). No English, no future! Language policy in Pakistan. In S. Obeng & B. Hartford (eds.), *Political independence with linguistic servitude: The politics about languages in the developing world*, 15–39. New York: NOVA Science.

Mahboob, A. (2009). English as an Islamic language: A case study of Pakistani English. *World Englishes*, 28(2), 175–189.

Martin, J., & Matthiessen, C. (2014). Modelling and mentoring: Teaching and learning from home through school. In A. Mahboob & L. Barratt (eds.), *Englishes in Multilingual Contexts: Language Variation and Education*, 137–163. Dordrecht: Springer.

Martin, J. (1985). Language, register and genre. In F. Christie (ed.), *Children writing course reader*. Geelong: Deakin University Press.

Martin, J., & Rose, D. (2008). *Genre relations: Mapping culture*. London & Oakville: Equinox.

Martin, J., & White, P. (2005). *The language of evaluation: Appraisal in English*. New York: Palgrave Macmillan.

Matsuda, A. (2012). *Principles and practices of teaching English as an international language*. Bristol: Multilingual Matters.

Rahman, T. (1997). *Language and politics in Pakistan*. Karachi: Oxford University Press.

Rose, D., & Martin, J. (2012). *Learning to write, reading to learn: Genre, knowledge and pedagogy in the Sydney School*. London: Equinox.

Tann, K. (2010). *Semogenesis of a nation: An iconography of Japanese identity*. Sydney, Australia: University of Sydney thesis.

Wolfram, W., & Schilling-Estes, N. (2006). *American English: Dialects and variation*. Malden/Oxford: Blackwell.

Chapter 17

The Power of Language in Textbooks: Shaping Futures, Shaping Identities

Mahboob, A. (2017). The power of language in textbooks: Shaping futures, shaping identities. *Asian Englishes* 19(3), 259–272.

Introduction

Previous research on Pakistani English language textbooks has shown how these textbooks promote a particular interpretation of Islam and how they adapt language to embed certain socio-cultural and religious beliefs (Mahboob 2009, 2015). This work has several implications: it shows how people in power can influence the curriculum and textbooks by infusing their ideologies into the textbooks; it exemplifies one way in which a government attempts to influence the beliefs and knowledge of citizens; and it demonstrates how this is done by appropriating and changing language. By studying this work, we can see how educational structures and curricula, instead of empowering students with power language, may limit their abilities by giving them limited access to semiotic resources. The impact of a weak education, in the context of Pakistan, can be seen in its low and falling involvement in the global knowledge economy[1], its poor socio-economic development[2], and its susceptibility to violence and non-tolerance[3]. In this chapter, I argue that, amongst other things, it is the infusion of conservative religious ideologies in the curriculum

---

[1] While Pakistan has been investing substantially in higher education, most graduates, including those with PhDs, are often unable to publish or contribute to their respective fields in a global context. I argue that this is partly a consequence of their limited knowledge (procedural and declarative) of discipline-specific language.

[2] According to World Bank reports, the Gross National Income (GNI) per capita for Pakistan was only $1410 in 2014, the lowest in South Asia. Current reports suggest that Pakistan has failed to meet most of the Millennium Development Goals (MDGs).

[3] Overseas Security Advisory Council (OSAC) states that the crime level in Pakistan is high; and many countries have travel advisories against travelling to Pakistan given the high rate of violence and terrorism.

and the accompanying shifts in language of the curriculum that has led to these consequences. The textbook examined here has been used for over 35 years, with minimal or no changes. Many of the textbooks used in government schools in key academic years (grades 9 and 10, also known as Matric) in Pakistan today were written in the late 1970s under the directive of the then military leader of Pakistan, General Zia-ul-Haq, who was a conservative Muslim. After taking power, the General ordered that the curriculum of Pakistan needed to be aligned with his interpretation of Islam (Rahman 1997).

Many of the textbooks developed as a result of this policy are still in use and have been used to educate generations of students. As pointed out earlier, and as will be demonstrated in this chapter, these textbooks limit students' access to semiotic resources and thus create a context where peoples' understanding of the world may be limited and they may become targets of being manipulated into intolerant and extremist positions. This paper, then, will extend the current work on textbooks in Pakistan and illustrate how students' semiotic resources may be restricted and how they are immersed in conservative religious and pro-military ideologies.

Theoretical Concerns

Before proceeding, there are a number of issues that need to be discussed in relation to this chapter. These include building a shared understanding of 'language', 'language variation', and 'identity management'. Following Halliday (2009), this project takes language to be a semogenic system: a system that construes and represents meanings. Language is one of several semogenic systems and works with these other systems (e.g. image, color, music, etc.) to create and represent meanings (see, for example, Kress and van Leeuwen 2006). As such, language helps create our 'realities' and allows us to share and negotiate them with others. Adopting a social semiotic orientation to language has implications for our understanding of grammar as well. Firstly, grammar is not 'a set of rules', where things are right or wrong; but rather 'a system of choices', where the choices that we make relate to the context of language use and impact the meanings that are created and understood. So, while a traditional, rule-based, orientation to grammar might suggest that a statement such as 'Islam is the religion of peace' is grammatically incorrect and that the definite article is being used inappropriately, we can look at this as a deliberate choice made to construe a particular meaning, a meaning where other religions are not seen as being 'peaceful'. As we will discuss later in this chapter, such choices made in the textbooks (attempt to) create a particular representation of the world and religion in the minds of the students.

The difference in the use of articles, as already exemplified, is often identified as a feature of Pakistani English (e.g., in Rahman 2011). Such descriptions of Pakistani English (as well as other World Englishes) tend to focus on how particular phonological or morpho-syntactic features vary across Englishes. These variations are typically identified and described in contrast to the use of these features in 'Standard' British or American Englishes. In doing so, the purpose of such descriptions is to show how English language varies in different countries. Krishnaswamy and Burde (1998), Pennycook (2002), Mahboob and Szenes (2010), Saraceni (2010), and Mahboob and Liang (2014) have problematised the use of national labels in describing languages and Englishes. As pointed out by Mahboob and Szenes (2010), this is problematic because it leads World Englishes researchers into describing discrete linguistic features that are used to contrast one national variety with another that do not necessarily contribute to a theory of language or of how meaning is construed or communicated in and across these varieties. For instance, as seen with the example of the use of articles cited earlier, while a traditional World Englishes approach would identify this variation in the use of articles as a feature of Pakistani English, a social semiotic approach to language can help us understand what meanings are being construed by choosing to use a particular deictic in this context.

While it is important to understand language variation, using nation-state-based understandings of language is not necessarily productive. Instead, we need to think of language variation across a range of continua (or dimensions). In my previous work (Mahboob 2014), I have identified four continua: users, uses, mode, and time that help us understand how language varies based on who is using it, for what purposes, with what resources, and when. The location of language use is not separately categorised here, but is implicit in an understanding of users and uses of language. In this work, I have also mapped the three-dimensions (users, uses, and mode) to develop a three-dimensional (3D) framework of language variation (see Figure 1). Below, I have included some of the relevant points from my previous work (Mahboob 2014, 2015) to explain the three dimensions.

Figure 1   The 3D framework of language variation

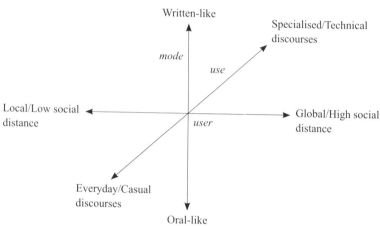

The first dimension of variation in language in the framework relates to who we are as 'users' of the language and with whom we are interacting. The user cline of language variation can be based on 'low' vs. 'high' social distance. People who have low social distance (i.e. they have shared social factors, e.g. age, gender, origin, location, socio-economic status, ethnicity, religion, family, school, etc.) may have unique ways of using language that reflect their relationship and this language may not always be transparent to others (see, for example, Wolfram 2015). For example, couple talk, sibling talk, or friend talk can be seen as language that is used between people who have low social distance (and thus is localised) and may not be interpretable to an outside audience. Anti-language (Halliday 1976) is also an example of language that is used by members of a closed community and is not transparent to other people. The indicator 'low social distance' helps us understand why people use 'local' forms of language, with their local denotations and connotations. On the other hand, when interacting with people with whom one has a higher social distance, one tends to use a more 'standard' or 'global' language—one that minimises 'local' idioms, forms, and features and is thus less prone to miscommunication. The indicator 'high social distance' helps us explain why people use 'global' forms of language, minimising local forms and features, and facilitating communication with people who speak a different 'local' variety of the language. Choosing language that reflects low or high social distance with people who do not fall into that category can also serve as a social metaphor: by choosing language that reflects high social distance with people who are close, one may be creating a distance between themselves and their interlocutors/readers; conversely, using language that reflects low social distance with people who are not close can suggest that one is trying to affiliate with them.

The second dimension of variation in language is related to the purpose or 'use' of the language. To understand this dimension of language variation, we consider whether the language being used is about 'everyday/casual' discourses or about 'specialised/technical' discourses. For example, one could talk about music using specialised/technical language; or one could talk about music in everyday/casual language. In both cases, the topic remains the same; however, the specific linguistic choices vary based on the purpose of the exchange. In linguistic terms, this variation is understood as register variation, a concept used extensively in literature in genre and English for Specific Purposes (ESP) studies.

The third dimension of language variation is 'mode' (Martin 1985; Derewianka 2015). Modes of communication include aural, visual, and mixed channels of communication. The way we use language varies based on whether we are speaking, writing, or—as is becoming common today—combining these two modalities (for example, in online chats, blogs, etc.). The mode of communication impacts the language choices that we make and therefore needs to be examined. If we keep the 'use' and 'users' of language constant, the language might still vary based on whether we are writing or speaking. For example, the linguistic choices we make will be different based on whether we are giving an oral presentation or writing a paper for publication.

These three dimensions are plotted together in Figure 1 to provide the basic framework of language variation. The framework helps identify eight domains (Table 1), with each domain including a range of variations, based on varying combinations of users, uses, and mode. Table 1 below lists the eight domains[4], identifying areas of linguistic study that focus their research on that domain, and examples of where one would find such language.

As readers would have noticed, the fourth dimension, time, is not plotted in Figure 1, nor represented in Table 1. This is because time relates to each of the other three dimensions and every one of the eight domains that emerge from the framework. Thus, for example, language varies

---

[4] The ordering of the domains here is different than in earlier publications on this framework (Mahboob 2014, 2015). The mode dimension has been reversed here to reflect the primacy of oral language over written language.

Table 1   Eight domains of language variation based on the 3D framework

	Domains	Areas of linguistic study	Examples
1	Local, oral, everyday	Dialectology, World Englishes	Family members planning their vacation
2	Local, written, everyday	Dialectology, World Englishes	Old school friends exchanging e-mails with each other
3	Local, oral, specialised	Need more attention	Aboriginal community talking about specifics of their crops
4	Local, written, specialised	Need more attention	Newsletter produced by and for a rural community of farmers in rural Australia
5	Global, oral, everyday	ELF (English as a Lingua Franca)	Casual conversations amongst people from different parts of the world
6	Global, written, everyday	Genre studies	International news agencies reporting on events
7	Global, oral, specialised	ELF, language for specific purposes, genre studies	Conference presentations
8	Global, written, specialised	Language for specific purposes, genre studies	Academic papers

across time on the user dimension: language in all communities shifts and changes over time. Thus, while the impact of time is acknowledged in this model, it is not easy to visually represent it.

Halliday and Matthiessen (2004) point out that semiotic change can be understood in relation to varying ranges of time. They identify three ways in which time can be seen to impact language change: logogenesis, ontogenesis, and phylogenesis. Logogenesis has to do with the 'ongoing creation of meaning in the unfolding of text' (Halliday and Matthiessen 2004: 43); that is, it focuses on how meanings of a text develop as a text unfolds over time. Ontogenesis looks at how language and meaning develop and change across an individual's life. And, phylogenesis looks at the evolution of language and meaning that are afforded by a culture over time. This model of time and semiotic change is crucial for our understanding of how language and curriculum relate to identity management. Martin (2005: 9) writes:

> ... logogenesis provides the material (i.e. semiotic goods) for ontogenesis, which in turn provides the material for phylogenesis; in other words, texts

provide the means through which individuals interact to learn the system, and it is through the heteroglossic aggregation of individual (always already social) systems that the semiotic trajectory of a culture evolves. Language change in this model is read in terms of an expanding meaning potential, a key feature of semiotic systems as they adapt to new discursive and non-discursive (physical and biological) environments.

As noted by Martin, the texts that a person is immersed in influence their individual system. While individuals have agency and may resist the dominant texts, the main point here is that texts (and the textbooks and curriculum that are formed by texts) have a significant potential influence on the semiotic systems that individual students develop. It is this potential influence of texts on the shaping of an individual's semiotic systems that has previously been described as 'identity management'. Identity management is any institutionalised or localised effort made to shape or direct individual or group identities (see Mahboob 2015, for a detailed discussion). The key idea here is that an individual's socio-cultural position can be influenced through discourse and can be done either locally (micro level), by individuals or groups of people that a person interacts with; or through institutionalised (macro level) processes. The socio-cultural positions being promoted can be norm-conforming (norms are established by the dominant/powerful groups) or can be contesting of these 'norms'. These two dimensions of identity management can be plotted on a Cartesian plane to give us a framework for identity management as in Figure 2 below.

Figure 2   Identity management framework (adapted from Mahboob 2015)

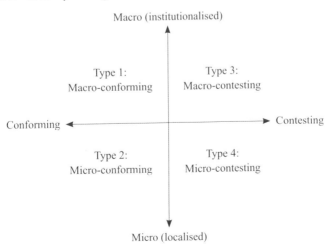

Educational curriculum and textbooks used in public schools in Pakistan are written and approved by the government. The texts included in these materials conform to the beliefs that the powerful elites (those in government) want to be projected in and through the textbooks. Thus, they are one way in which macro-conforming identity management discourses can work and normalise the beliefs of one group as the norm. This is what, as we will see in the next section, happens in the context of public school curriculum in Pakistan.

Pakistani Public School Curriculum and Identity Management

As stated earlier, textbooks used in key years—for example, grades 9 and 10—in public schools in parts of Pakistan have not been revised since the late 1970s. In this section, we will focus on the English language textbooks used in the grade 9/10 (known as Matric, and a final school year for many students in Pakistan) in the province of Sindh to see how the texts used work to manage student identities. In doing so, we will look at how this can happen at the levels of genre, discourse and lexicogrammar. We will focus on biographical recounts (Rose and Martin 2012) as the main source of texts in doing so. This is because biographies of key Pakistani national, religious and military heroes are the single largest text type in the textbooks: 25% of the texts in the grade 10 textbook are biographies. The choice of including biographies as the main text type in the English textbooks is itself worth noticing. Biographical recounts are historical texts and describe key contributions and thoughts of important personalities. The choice of selecting mostly (male) national, religious and military heroes reflects the importance given to these issues in the textbooks. Furthermore, the text structure and lexico-grammatical resources used in the texts are exploited to emphasise particular beliefs and positions.

Typical biographical texts begin with an introduction to the individual (these can be personal details or a description of their key achievements etc.). A typical biography written for a global audience (domain 6 for mass consumption) starts with an Orientation, followed by a series of Record of stages, and may include a Coda (Rose and Martin 2012). In terms of lexico-grammatical features, biographies tend to be written in past tense; include specific references to time, place, and events; and tend to be chronologically ordered. Biographies also typically have an objective stance and focus primarily on the person and their close associates. However, these linguistic characteristics of biographies are appropriated in different ways in the various biographies included in the textbook under investigation here.

Appropriating Genre Structure for Identity Management

The genre structure of the biographical recounts included in the textbook varied across the text. While, some of the texts, e.g. King Faisal or Allama Iqbal (on the surface) appear to follow the predicted organizational structure and start with an orientation followed by a description of events/accomplishments of their lives, others do not. In previous work, I have analysed the text structure of Shah Abdul Latif's biography in detail (see, for example, Mahboob 2015) and shown how that text includes two paragraphs before the first mention of Shah Abdul Latif. The first paragraph of the Shah Latif biography does not start with an introduction to Shah Latif, but discusses Islam. The second paragraph is also not about Shah Latif, but provides a national orientation to the text. It is not until the third paragraph that the text introduces Shah Latif, and even here he is not the main participant in the text. The Shah Latif text showed how Islam is prioritised in this text by appropriating the text structure. Below, we will look at another biographical text—that of Helen Keller:

Text 1   Helen Keller; grade 10 textbook (Sindh Textbook Board, Pakistan)

Helen Keller

How fortunate are those who are born into this world with two eyes to see all its beauty! But there are some unfortunate people who can neither see nor hear. This world, which is so full of beautiful colours and sweet sounds, appears colourless and dull to these poor souls. What a misfortune! They cannot see the lovely flowers blooming in the gardens and hear the birds singing sweet songs. They indeed feel very sad, for their fate is so hard. Worse is the fate of those who can see and hear once and then no more. But they are so courageous and bold that they do not look unhappy. They accept the challenge of their fate and try to live cheerfully.

Among such brave and courageous persons, the name of Miss Helen Keller tops the list. Helen Keller was born in 1880 in a little town in the United States of America. Up to age of two, she was quite a normal child. She could see and hear every thing. In February 1882, little Helen fell dangerously ill. All felt sorry for her, because she

---

(To be continued)

became blind and deaf. Her parents looked sad. Everybody was unhappy and the little child felt miserable.

When she was seven years old, her life suddenly changed. Helen's father asked a lady named Miss Sullivan to come and look after his blind child. Miss Sullivan had herself, become blind, when she was a child but afterwards she got her eyesight back. She thanked God for His kindness to her by helping other blind people and making them happy and content. She started teaching Helen. One day, she took Helen to the river bank and put her hand in the water. Slowly she made her write the word 'w-a-t-e-r' on the sand. She made her do it several times and thus Helen learnt how to spell the word 'water'. She felt very excited, because she knew that at last there would be some light in her dark world.

The work was very slow and difficult, but Miss Sullivan was very kind and patient. Little by little, she taught Helen about mountains and rivers and about history and geography. She even taught her how to count and do sums.

When she was eight, she was sent to a school for blind children. She had forgotten how to speak, but her teacher helped her. She would put Helen's hand on her own lips and let her feel the movements of the lips at the time of speaking. Helen did many exercises like this and at last at the age of ten she was able to speak again. "What a joy!" she exclaimed. By and by, she learnt to read books. These books were printed with raised points instead of letters and she read them by touching with her fingers. In this way, she was able to learn as much as other people could. She passed all her examinations easily. She went to college and then to Harvard University. She studied at the University and graduated without difficulty. She proved to be a better student than many others. Her teachers loved and admired her.

In 1956, this wonderful lady visited Pakistan. She was seventy-six, but still very active. Pakistani people gave her a warm welcome. She came to our country to help the blind and the deaf. She addressed many gatherings in Karachi and visited the School for the Blind, Deaf and Dumb. "What a nice school!" she exclaimed. "How wonderful it is to be with you, my dear sons and daughters! Always be happy and cheerful. Never curse your fate. You can do everything in this world", she said to the students of the school and admired heartily all the ladies who were working and teaching there voluntarily with so much zeal and selfless affection.

This text, like the Shah Latif one, does not start with an introduction to Helen Keller. Instead, the first paragraph starts with an evaluation of people who can see as 'fortunate'. This sets up a contrast between people who can see (fortunate) and those who cannot (unfortunate). The paragraph then goes on to list the things that fortunate people can do, e.g. being able to see 'beautiful' colours and hear 'sweet' sounds in contrast to the 'poor souls' who have met with 'misfortune'. This paragraph sets up a prosody of negative attitudes towards people with physical disabilities and suggests that the appropriate feelings towards these people is that of pity and sadness. In doing so, this paragraph does identity management by projecting a particular stance towards people with physical disabilities, including Helen Keller. When Helen Keller is introduced in the text, we notice that the text continually attempts to control our emotions and attitude towards Helen and other people with disabilities instead of providing factual information. For example, instead of providing specifics about her birth (the text does not include her birthday) or her parentage, it states that she was 'normal' for the first two years of her life before falling ill—the disease that she contracted is not mentioned. Instead, the text projects feelings that may have been experienced by people at that time (without any references or citations), 'All felt sorry for her ... Her parents looked sad. Everybody was unhappy and the little child felt miserable.' There are no images accompanying the text, so the reference to 'parents looked sad' does not appear to be based on or referring to any specific image or situation, but rather draws a broad brush picture which extends the prosody set up in the first paragraph: feel sad and have pity towards people with disabilities.

Adapting Lexico-Grammatical Resources for Identity Management

In addition to a prosody of pity that builds across the text, the text lacks specifics and details about Helen Keller and her life. Similar to the Shah Latif biography, the text does not provide specific details about the people being portrayed, but includes evaluations and appraisal. The Helen Keller text does not mention her birthday, her death, or cite any other major events in her life—other than her illness and her visit to Pakistan. The text does not include any information about her politics, her contributions, or her work; it does not mention that Helen Keller was an internationally acclaimed author and speaker, was a strong feminist and an active member of the socialist party. Instead, the text suggests that Helen Keller, like her teacher Anne Sullivan, helped other people with disabilities in order to thank 'God for His kindness'.

By changing the text structure and the lexico-grammatical features of a biographical text to serve identity management purposes, the students are exposed to model texts that are not appropriate for or reflect global orientation to writing. For example, while there are a number of direct quotes included in the Helen Keller text, the text includes no references or citations and it is not clear where the quoted material is sourced. As a model text, it therefore does not serve as a good example for the students. Instead of exemplifying how globally oriented biographical texts are written, this text shows the students that they can include quoted material without any references or citations and write a biographical text without necessarily citing or providing detailed information about the person in focus.

The Helen Keller text, as pointed out earlier, is not dissimilar from the Shah Latif text in terms of its linguistic features. The Shah Abdul Latif text also adapts lexico-grammatical resources for identity management. The opening sentence of the text is 'Islam is the religion of peace' (we discussed this example earlier as well). This unambiguous reference to Islam in this text contributes to the normalisation of beliefs about Islam and its history in the community and leads to the creation of 'shared knowledge' in the Pakistani community. It needs to be noted that Islam is not only presented as 'a' religion of peace, but defined exclusively as 'the' religion of peace—implying that other religions do not have the same claim to this. In this particular example, the choice of the article does not only reflect structural variation, but carries meaning. While there is literature on Pakistani English (Rahman 2011) that shows how articles are used in divergent ways in Pakistani English, this work does not take the semantics associated with articles into consideration. Thus, it is not just that Pakistani English may use articles differently from British/American Englishes, but, as in the example above, the choice is made to project particular meanings.

In addition to the religiously oriented slant of the text, the text also projects other particular socio-cultural beliefs and practices as the norm. For example, in the fourth paragraph of the text, Shah Abdul Latif's wife is positively appraised (Martin and White 2005) as being 'noble' and 'good'. These appraisals project a sense of the kind of 'lady' one should marry. The text does not give us any specific details about his wife or marriage: the text does not mention her name nor does it give us the year of their marriage; it also does not include any information about their children, or if they had any. The author then goes on to state that Latif 'showed great kindness' to his wife and 'lived at home for many years'—these, at first read, appear to be odd things to say: for example, why would one expect that a husband would not live at home? The purpose of including this information becomes clearer as the text unfolds (logogenesis): staying at home might be acceptable in youth ('when he was twenty'), but what needs to happen is that a person should turn 'more and more towards religion and devotion' in time. The text then continues to show how this devotion implies giving up a 'normal domestic life'. This example of the use of appraisal in this text shows how the readers are positioned to appraise the qualities of a marriageable woman as well as exemplify what a person is expected to do in their youth and then as they become older.

Discussion

Above I provided evidence to show how textbook writers in Pakistan appropriate language to promote particular beliefs and carry out identity management. By varying language use and creating local ways of writing biographical recounts, the texts withhold access to language that is used to create global ways of writing biographical recounts. In addition, the extensive use of biographical recounts in an English language textbook implies that students are not given access to other genres or how they are used in global contexts. These decisions by the textbook writers influence what linguistic and semiotic resources the students are offered in school. While some students, for example, those from educated or economically stable backgrounds, may be able to supplement these texts with additional resources, others may not.

In a country where the majority of the population does not enter university, school textbooks play a major role in the knowledge about the world and about language that they will be exposed to. By limiting access to control of a range of (globally oriented) semiotic resources, textbook writers, in essence, shape the futures of these populations. Without appropriate language and literacy skills, graduates from schools that use these textbooks, which are primarily state-run schools, have a difficult (if not impossible) time accessing higher knowledge. This implies that a large proportion of the population is essentially unable to participate in higher education or contribute to knowledge production or reflective literacy. The limited (and identity-managing) semiotic resources can also make these people more prone to being manipulated into conservative socio-political and religious positions (including those that are not very tolerant of diversity or otherness).

In her work on semantic variation, Hasan (2009) painstakingly illustrates in detail how groups of people do not only show linguistic variation in terms of morpho-syntactic or phonological patterns, but that the variations in language can also reflect semantic variation. Hasan (2011: 186) states,

> ... while most people might do the same thing, their ways of meaning by way of carrying out these activities could be critically different. Speakers

are oriented towards different ways of saying and meaning depending on the material conditions of their social existence ... There is, thus, a good deal of semantic variation across social strata; different social segments of a community develop different predispositions for meaning making, different ideological stances, so that given the same social process, they will tend to say and mean somewhat different sorts of things.

We accumulate and develop linguistic and semiotic repertoires in particular social contexts and while engaging in different activities. While our repertoires develop and expand throughout our lives (ontogenesis), the language and discourses that we are immersed in our childhood greatly impact what language we use and what meanings we create with such language. One important source of language for children is through schooling. As seen in the last section, the linguistic choices and the meanings emphasised in the grade 9/10 textbooks used in public schools in Sindh, Pakistan, are used not just to teach language or teach students how to do things with language, but to prioritise a particular set of beliefs. A detailed reading of the Helen Keller and Shah Abdul Latif texts shows how these texts, as they unfold (logogenesis) tell us little about the life, events or contributions of the people in focus and instead attempt to shape our attitudes, positions, and identities. While, as single texts, these might not have been worth discussing in detail, it is the accumulation of such texts across the curriculum that raises concerns and which limits graduates' participation in other literacy practices.

An analysis of the texts included in the textbook as well as the activities and exercises built around these texts suggests that the goal of these textbooks is 'recognition literacy'. Recognition literacy is one of the three types of literacies education identified in Hasan (2011); the other two being 'action literacy' and 'reflective literacy'. Hasan notes that each of these types of literacy practices are grounded in particular assumptions about the nature of language and pedagogy and that they produce qualitatively different abilities in the students educated through them.

Recognition literacy, according to Hasan, puts an emphasis on the expression plane of language: on the mechanics of spelling, pronunciation, vocabulary, and grammar. It does not consider semiotics or language as 'a mode of social action' (Hasan 2011: 178). This is observable in the textbook examined here by considering the kind of notes and exercises included in the book. For example, the Shah Abdul Latif text is immediately followed by exercises. Figure 3 shows parts of the first exercise.

Figure 3   Image of the textbook with exercises for the Shah Abdul Latif text. Source: Grade 10 Sindh Textbook Board, Pakistan.

> ### Exercises
>
> **Study of Structures**
>
> 1. Of
>
>   *Examples:*
>
>   1. Islam is a religion *of* peace.
>   2. Latif came to be known as the Saint *of* Bhit.
>   3. Please give me a cup *of* water.
>   4. The box *of* matches is in the kitchen.
>
> 2. With
>
>   (a) *Examples:*
>
>   1. His heart was soon filled *with* the love of God.
>   2. He was blessed *with* a son.
>   3. She is *with* me.
>   4. She goes to school *with* her brother.
>
>   *With* is a Preposition. It shows the relationship of a Noun or Pronoun to some other word in the sentence.
>
>   (b) Some more uses of *with*.
>
>   *Examples :*
>
>   1. He is writing *with* a pen.
>
> **11**

Almost as if on cue from Hasan, the exercises focus on structural features and on requiring students to memorise definitions and demonstrate 'correct' use of isolated morphological/lexical items. This shows how, as Hasan (2011: 178) points out:

> in the absence of an approach to language which sees it as a mode of social action, the nature and function of these aspects of language is badly conceived, and worse still, these unfounded conceptions have often become the very end of literacy teaching in the pedagogic context.

Furthermore, in relation to identity management, we note that the exercise includes clauses based on the main text which includes direct references to Islam. Of special interest here is example 1.1 in Figure 3: 'Islam is *a* religion of peace' [emphasis added]. This clause shows a contrast with the opening sentence of the main text, 'Islam is *the* religion of peace' [emphasis added]. This contrasting use of articles exemplifies the variation in use of articles in Pakistani English and potentially opens up space for a discussion of articles and the meanings that they help create. However, while it is possible, I have not found any evidence (based on hours of classroom observations) that teachers use these examples to discuss the meaning-making resources of language and grammar. Instead, and as the exercise requires, teachers focus on prepositions and work on these exercises to help students in passing their exams, which also focus on isolated linguistic features. These exercises thus project an understanding of language and grammar in terms of rules that need to be followed and not of language and grammar as a resource for meaning.

A focus on language as a set of rules that need to be followed, without an understanding of language variation or of how language creates meaning in context, has a number of implications. By focusing on the structural features of language and on what is 'correct' and 'incorrect', students (and teachers) develop an understanding of language as a set of rules that need to be followed. Rules and standards of language are seen as fixed and given, something to be accepted by the students without question and replicated in their exams. Students learn/memorise the 'rules' and expected 'answers' that they are required to reproduce in their homework, assignments and exams in order to pass exams without necessarily focusing on the appraisals and other meanings. What this suggests, at a deeper level, is that learning and education is about memorising and reproducing facts and norms that are included in the curriculum. While this is very far from an understanding of how language varies in context and how language is a semiotic tool, it does serve the purposes of recognition literacy. It controls the language and belief structures of the students educated through this curriculum. It limits their access to globally oriented texts by projecting particular beliefs: beliefs that prioritise a conservative view of Islam, a view which sees Islam as 'the' religion and 'the' purpose of life, resulting in a negative bias towards other religions, cultures, and communities. This potentially limits the students' opportunities to engage with and participate in knowledge construction in a global setting.

Furthermore, limiting the semiotic resources of students from the lower spectrum of social economic classes limits the educational and professional opportunities that children in public schools can access (and succeed in). This serves a secondary goal of recognition literacy; that is, to maintain and reinforce the social class systems, which provides more opportunities for children from middle and higher social classes and marginalises those from the lower and working classes.

Concluding Thoughts

This chapter illustrates how textbooks used in public schools in one province of Pakistan limit students' semiotic resources by withholding access to global ways of using language for particular purposes (in this case, biographical recounts). The appropriation of linguistic resources in this case highlights how textbooks attempt to manage students' identities. In addition, the chapter argued that controlling access to semiotic resources and limiting their understanding of language as a meaning-making system (of choices) influences their opportunities in life. One important conclusion to draw from this chapter is that if we are serious about changing the current social, economic, and political conditions in Pakistan and about making it a more tolerant society which values and contributes to global knowledge construction, then textbook boards need to carry out a thorough revision of the educational curriculum and rewrite the textbooks and the tests used in the country.

This chapter also has implications for research on World Englishes. It demonstrates how a focus on the structural features of a variety fails to look at the semantics of the variety, or the possibility of semantic variation. The chapter exemplifies how taking a social semiotic approach to language (and language variation) can help us in understanding the meanings that are construed, represented and negotiated in different varieties of Englishes. Studies of World Englishes that are couched in a broader understanding of language variation can help us move beyond simply identifying surface-level similarities and differences between different varieties of a language and look at how these varieties use various linguistic resources to create meaning (and what meanings they create).

As we conclude this chapter, it needs to be pointed out that although the focus of this chapter has been on Pakistan, the issues raised and the implications drawn are not restricted to Pakistan. However, it would not be surprising to find similar concerns in other parts of the world. For example: are there any differences in the language of science when one shifts from an evolution perspective to an intelligent design in textbooks used in some parts of the United States? If and how do commercially produced (international) English as a Second Language (ESL) textbooks project particular consumerist and market economy positions as global norms?

Finally, while this chapter has focused on the language of textbooks in Pakistan, we also need to look at classrooms (and other) teaching practices using such books (in Pakistan and around the world). We need to explore if teachers conform to the positions projected in the textbooks or resist and challenge them. We need to learn if and how teachers (may) take a critical orientation within conservative contexts and what the outcomes of such practices are. We need to consider the role of technology and the Internet; so, while the textbook might provide limited information and bad models, are the students and teachers using additional web-based resources to supplement the textbooks? If not, can these be used to create alternatives to provide students in public schools with access to better models and texts? Can these additional resources be used to help students develop the kind of semiotic resources that they will need to interact with and contribute to the wider world? In short, if the governments do not act to change the textbooks, what can the people do to take control of the situation and create/access resources that will help the younger generation have access to both the local and global orientations to language and knowledge?

References

Derewianka, B. (2015). Supporting students in the move from spoken to written language. In A. Mahboob & L. Barratt (eds), *Englishes in Multilingual Contexts: Language Variation and Education*. Dordrecht: Springer.

Halliday, M. A. K. (1976). Anti-languages. *American Anthropologist* 78(3), 570–584.

Halliday, M. A. K. (2009). *The Essential Halliday*. London: Continuum.

Halliday, M. A. K., & Matthiessen, C. M. I. M. (2004). *An Introduction to Functional Grammar* (3rd edn). London: Hodder Arnold.

Hasan, R. (2009). *Semantic Variation: Meaning in Society and in Sociolinguistics*. London: Equinox.

Hasan, R. (2011). *Language and Education: Learning and Teaching in Society*. London: Equinox.

Kress, G., & van Leeuwen, T. (2006). *Reading Images: The Grammar of Visual Design*. London: Routledge.

Krishnaswamy, N., & Burde, A. (1998). *The Politics of Indians' English: Linguistic Colonialism and the Expanding English Empire*. Delhi: Oxford University Press.

Mahboob, A. (2009) English as an Islamic language. *World Englishes* 28(2), 175–189.

Mahboob, A. (2014). Language variation and education: A focus on Pakistan. In S. Buschfeld, T. Hoffmann, M. Huber & A. Kautzsch (eds), *The Evolution of Englishes* (Vol. 2). Amsterdam: John Benjamins.

Mahboob, A. (2015). Identity management, language variation, and English language textbooks. In D. Djenar, A. Mahboob & K. Cruickshank (eds), *Language and Identity Across Modes of Communication*. Boston: Mouton de Gruyter.

Mahboob, A., & Liang, J. (2014). Researching and Critiquing World Englishes. *Asian Englishes* 16(2), 125–140.

Mahboob, A., & Szenes, E. (2010). Construing meaning in world Englishes. In A. Kirkpatrick (ed), *Routledge Handbook of World Englishes*. London: Routledge.

Martin, J. R. (1985). Language, register and genre. In F. Christie (ed), *Children Writing Course Reader*. Geelong: Deakin University Press.

Martin, J. R., & White, P. R. R. (2005). *The Language of Evaluation: Appraisal in English*. London & New York: Palgrave Macmillan.

Pennycook, A. (2002). Turning English inside out. *Indian Journal of Applied Linguistics* 28(2), 25–43.

Rahman, T. (1997). *Language and Politics in Pakistan*. Karachi: Oxford University Press.

Rahman, T. (2011). *Pakistani English: The linguistic description of a non-native variety of English*. Islamabad: National Institute of Pakistan Studies Quaid-i-Azam University.

Rose, D., & Martin, J. R. (2012). *Learning to Write, Reading to Learn: Genre, Knowledge and Pedagogy in the Sydney School*. Sheffield: Equinox.

Saraceni, M. (2010). *The Relocation of English: Shifting Paradigms in a Global Era*. Basingstoke: Palgrave Macmillan.

Wolfram, W. (2015). Integrating language variation into TESOL: Challenges from English globalization. In A. Mahboob & L. Barratt (eds), *Englishes in Multilingual Contexts: Language Variation and Education*. Dordrecht: Springer.

Part III

Moving Forward

Chapter 18

Moving Forward with Education ... *

Leaving the promises behind
I choose to retreat into the woods
To listen, to learn, to unlearn

I wrote this short response to Robert Frost's 'Stopping by Woods on a Snowy Evening', which was part of my high school English curriculum in Pakistan, while working on this chapter and living in the Bom Bom Forest in Northern New South Wales, Australia.

Having only lived in desert climates at the time when I first read Frost's poem, the idea of stopping by the woods on a snowy evening was very attractive and romantic. And, it painted a picture of a dream for not just me but for most of my friends and classmates. Frost's poem, like most other texts in our syllabus, had little relationship with our environment or our lives—but, they were beautiful visions of paradise, which was in England, of course.

In Frost's poem, the protagonist is attracted by the beauty of nature. The woods in Frost's poem are not wild or free: they are owned by a person, who does not live on the land, and may be harvested for private profit. Regardless of this, the woods are beautiful, and one empathises with the protagonist as they leave in order to fulfil their responsibilities and commitments.

And, as with all things included in our curriculum, there was a moral lesson to be learnt from Frost's poem: it is essential to fulfils one's promises—no matter what the distractions.

Frost's poem continues to be taught across schools in Pakistan today—as are most of the other poems I was taught in the 1980s. Children today are still made to memorise texts that are designed to make them fall in love with the natural beauty and wonders of England and the 'West'—while most students and teachers in Pakistan and other exploited

---

* With contributions from *Amna Anwar*, *Hafiz Nauman Ahmed*, *Mujahid Shah* and *their students.*

communities live in polluted environment themselves.

It is this contrast between the texts taught and the real-life environment that many people across Pakistan—as in other exploited contexts—find themselves in that led me to ask these questions: if our education was supposed to help us develop and improve, why is it that our lands, our environment, and our people keep getting poorer and weaker? Is it really true that leaving the harmony of nature in order to support a 'global' economy and fulfil other peoples' needs, as Frost and schools teach us, is the best way forward? Should one abandon one's local language and ecologies and ways of being and doing in order to learn and be like the English? Is it really true that all solutions to our problems lie in the 'English' language, science, and ways of doing? Have we not observed the environmental destruction and social injustices that are committed in the name of modernisation, globalisation, development, science, and security? Is it not perhaps time for us to retreat: to listen, to learn, and to unlearn?

The promotion of English language and knowledge, specially through English medium instruction, at the expense of local socio-semiotics has been harmful to the local populations across the non-English speaking world, which includes much of the exploited world. In addition, one of the primary goals of education in exploited contexts, e.g., Pakistan, the country where I will draw most examples from, is literacy, which is seen as a doorway to getting jobs. Such goals require the educational curriculum, pedagogy, and material to be framed in particular ways, which often ignore minorities, and, indigenous, and local forms of knowing, doing, and being. Furthermore, current educational practices do not help students, teachers, or others to develop skills or knowledge that can be used to improve their local living conditions—since the educational system is geared towards generating graduates who can go overseas and support a remittance economy or work for others in-country. Current education in Pakistan—not unlike other exploited contexts—it appears, sells students, parents, and others dreams of a future abroad or of working for others, while they continue to live in the harsh realities of today.

In this chapter, after briefly discussing one key issue in education, we will outline alternative ways in which to conceptualise and practice education. It will include real-life examples of projects where students and teachers have experimented with some of the ideas shared in this chapter. While the examples and discussion in this chapter will focus on Pakistan, they are relevant to other exploited contexts as well.

The Trap of Modern Education

A key trap of modern education—and the only one that I will focus on in this chapter—is its dependency on literacy.

Literacy, in a traditional view, is seen as the ability to read and write. The goal of education in Pakistan, as in most other exploited communities, is to teach students to read and write and then assess them on their ability to remember bits of information provided through texts in a dominant language (often not the mother tongue/dialect of many/most students). Current assessment practices evaluate an individual's grasp of literacy practices and open up or close down life opportunities for each person based on their performance on specified tests and assessments. Those who succeed in demonstrating skills and ability in an 'other' defined set of literacy measures may be given options to progress and get employed by local or multinational corporations. In doing so, dominant forms of education—with literacy development as their goal—enable the conditions that allow the elites to retain their power and authority.

The problem with literacy, it needs to be stressed, is NOT with its use of one form of visual symbols to develop, share, or preserve meanings. The problem with literacy is in its use as a key measurement of education and ability—people with low or no literacy, one will observe, are discriminated against in most contexts.

Literacy, it needs to be noted, is not primary to human learning and development. If it were, all human communities would have evolved literacy for this purpose. Again, observation tells us that most indigenous communities did not use literacy for education. This does not mean that communities around the world did not have literacy before modern education: literacy evolved and was used by different groups of people for different purposes at various times in history. However, literacy was not used as the dominant medium of education and assessment across the world.

In contrast, all humans—like other biological species—primarily use non-literacy-based forms of communication and engagement. For humans, regardless of their location, oral language, or 'boli', as it is lexicalised in my tongue, is a shared resource for meaning making and communicating. 'Boli', as technicalised in my work, is dynamic: it represents, informs, responds to, and evolves in relation to the needs and geographical contexts of her users. 'Boli' shifts and changes continuously. 'Boli' is a socio-semiotic inheritance we receive from our ancestors (this can be contrasted with DNA, which is our biological inheritance). 'Boli' is not restricted to humans: non-humans also have 'boli', e.g., 'bakri ki boli' (a goat's oral language), 'chirya ki boli' (a bird's oral language). While there is little evidence to claim that other species and life forms use sounds to interact, it is possible that other biological species use different sensory systems or a combination of these to do what we do through a limited range of sound waves.

'Boli' was the primary medium of education in pre-colonial South Asia, as in most parts of the world before European colonisation. Literacy existed in many places and was primarily used by the trading classes, who needed it for record keeping and other trading needs. Other communities—many of whom were nomadic and lived across regions of South Asia, did not have a need for literacy, and hence did not develop it. This includes religion: religion was essentially an oral practice before the use of printing press and mass-literacy-based education. Once religion was tied to published and static texts, its ability to serve people by being fluid and re-interpretative stagnated. This stagnation of religion, based on particular sanctioned interpretations of static texts, is one cause of intra-religion and inter-religion conflict.

Pre-colonial South Asia used 'boli' as the primary modality for education. Education was based on an apprenticeship model, not literacy. Students learnt by observing, listening, and participating. While most traditional forms of education have been dismantled across South Asia in favour of literacy-based models marketed by exploitative powers, we still find some remnants of this practice in certain professions. For example, even today, if one wants to learn music in South Asia, one can enter into an apprenticeship and learn from an 'Ustad' (an expert teacher). The same practice of apprenticeship also operates in most unregulated local industries, such as auto-mechanic work, plumbing, carpentry across the region.

Education in the pre-colonial period was designed to serve the needs of the people. Through education, one developed ability (not literacy) in areas needed for the well-being of the community. This required education to be based on understandings of the local context and needs, not necessarily texts written in (or translated from) foreign languages, which are often reflective of different socio-economic and geographical settings. In addition, skills were distributed in a community, where people apprenticed—either formally or informally—and developed skills in areas where they excelled. As we now know from recent work, intelligences are multiple, and different people have different things that they are better at. For example, I would be terrible at most sports, partly because I lack the kind of intelligence needed to be good at sports. Literacy, if it did exist in a community, for example, the trading communities, would be passed on to those who took an interest in it. For others, there were plenty of other things that they could do and contribute. Literacy was not needed for such a distribution of skills and forms of education.

Current dominant forms of education in Pakistan (and other exploited communities), in contrast, are based on written texts; and, these texts are often about things that are non-present in the students' immediate environment. This use of written text as the main source of knowledge in education implies that students (and others) need to put their trust in educational material used in schooling. Given that most of the information included in educational texts and curricula is not within the observable environment of students and teachers, they have to believe what they are reading and learning/teaching: they have to trust that the material they are using is unbiased, that it is not written to misguide or mislead them, and is designed to enable them.

The content and language of educational material is a major problem with literacy and education in Pakistan: educational material—which is propagated through written language—is often biased and/or false (fake news), and is written by and in the interest of the dominant powers (locally, regionally, and/or internationally). One implication of this observation, which can be verified by reading through textbooks used in Pakistani schools, is that we have to question almost everything that is normalised through colonial models of education, literacy, and knowledge production.

For example, in English language and linguistics, we see language as including three primary modalities: oral, written, and sign (Braille, which operates through touch, is not included in a study of linguistics; and, even sign language is minimally studied within proper *linguistics*). The three modalities are seen as inter related, where one can convey linguistic meaning either through sound, writing, or signage (notice that both writing and sign operate through our visual system). Language, in English and in English-influenced linguistics, is further used as a way of differentiating between humans and all other life forms. For example, pretty much any introductory textbook on linguistics will separate out human *language* and non-human *communication*, often based on a set of features that differentiate the two (such as 'displacement', 'arbitrariness', or 'discreteness'). In doing so, linguists privilege human language and often study it to:

- show how languages are genealogically related to each other; and/or,
- provide structural and/or functional descriptions of language, which are based on contrastive features.

And, it needs to be noted, that they often draw on structural/functional variations to do genealogical work. Dominant approaches in linguistics separate out language (langue) from its use and application (parole) and then study them in isolation. As such, there is little actual use or application of such abstract descriptions of language.

Taking 'boli' as a starting point, instead of 'language', leads us to understandings that are quite different from those promoted in English-based linguistics. For example, the concept of 'boli', which is only oral, does not conflate two different sensory systems: sound and sight. 'Boli' operates through sound only; writing systems are not required for a 'boli'. This contrasts with the English notion of a language, which has two primary modalities: speech and writing. In English, writing is given the same importance as oral language; and, in exploitative education, reading-writing is given more importance than listening-speaking, e.g., formal and summative assessments tend to be literacy-based. This leads to marginalisation of people from non-privileged backgrounds. In addition, educational and other policies do not recognise 'boli' that does not have a writing system—so, for a large number of people in Pakistan and around the world, their 'boli' is invisible from education, governance, economy and other domains of life. This leads to people dropping their 'boli' for a more powerful 'language'. And, with that shift, 'boli'—the socio-semiotic inheritance and a repository of local knowledge and science—starts to wane and potentially die out. While linguists and others regret the loss of 'boli', nothing substantial is done to support the well-being of the people who speak/spoke this 'boli'. It is ironic that these linguists tend to forget that it is not the language that suffers, it is the people who speak the language who are suffering. Instead of just documenting languages, our work needs to support the people. If the people are well and strong, they will have a strong 'boli' or language; if the people are weak and defeated, their 'boli' will deteriorate too.

On a different but related note, we need to note that most new writing systems promoted by colonial or colonial-trained linguists are phonetic (i.e., characters represent individual sounds, as in English). Phonetic writing systems, as will be discussed next, are amongst the worst forms of writing systems. To understand this, we need to understand what writing systems are and how they operate.

Writing systems use visual symbols to create and represent meanings (in contrast to sound symbols, which is how 'boli' operates). As such, visual symbols can be more or less independent of sounds. A purely visual writing system would carry linguistic meaning without any correlation with sound. Observe that the only extant writing system that does so to a degree is Chinese. All other writing systems use symbols that denote particular sounds or combinations of sounds. Amongst these, some writing systems use symbols for a syllable (e.g., Cherokee, Katakana, and several pre-colonial indigenous languages across the Philippines), while others use symbols to mark phonemic contrast (e.g., English, Urdu, and almost all scripts created by linguists). Syllable-based writing systems, because they focus on syllables and not phonemes, can accommodate to a larger variation of phonemic realisations of a symbol. In contrast, a phonemic writing system is highly sensitive to variations in peoples' dialects, sociolects, and idiolects. This is one reason that people spell the same words in different ways based on the dialect they speak. One job of literacy-based education is to suppress these deviations and variations; literacy-based education promotes and evaluates people based on pre-defined (and often non-dialectally appropriate) sets of spellings, words, and grammars. Deviations from expected norms are often marked as mistakes and errors and looked down upon. Evidence for this can be found by looking at students' notebooks from almost any school across Pakistan.

Another issue with literacy is that it attempts to restrain and 'standardise' a system that is inherently dynamic. Trying to restrain the dynamicity of 'boli' or oral language through the adoption of one (or selected) forms of 'language', 'grammar', and 'literacy' disempowers people who do not come from certain backgrounds as well as restricts what people are allowed to *do* with language. The restrictions imposed on language and literacy in exploitative education impact what and how people learn. In the context of Pakistan at the moment, most students—regardless of their grade level—learn stuff that is not directly relevant to their local needs and context and is not designed to enable people to meet their needs.

'Boli', furthermore, is a socio-semiotic inheritance. 'Boli' is learnt from one's caretakers and encapsulates the essence of what one's ancestors learnt about and from their environment; along with information about what to do, how, when, where, why, and with whom. This local and contextual learning, which is encapsulated in 'boli', evolves over generations in large· geographical regions and is passed on from one generation to the next. In many ways, 'boli' is the only socio-semiotic inheritance that we receive from our ancestors—and can be compared to DNA, which is our biological inheritance. Notice how, when we deny other people's language or 'boli', we deny them the right to use and benefit from their socio-semiotic inheritance. By replacing local and indigenous 'boli' with non-local languages, education in Pakistan—as in most other exploited locations—has and continues to destroy indigenous and local knowledge, sciences, and peoples.

At this point, readers might validly ask: how is a replacement of 'boli' a destruction of local science? To understand this, we need to first understand what science is. At the most fundamental level, without methodologies and applications, science is a way of sorting things, i.e., of categorising or classifying things. All languages sort the world around them, i.e., they create taxonomies. And, in doing so, they show us how 'boli' is the fundamental of all sciences. Furthermore, each 'boli' carves up the world in a slightly different way: this is observed in the variations in meanings and things that different types of 'boli' represent and do. Each 'boli', in a nutshell, is its own science: it presents a unique and geographically embedded way of seeing and understanding the world; and, in extension, relating to that world. One reason why the variety of 'boli' or 'languages' are different from each other—and some have wider currency than others—is because of the way they are spread across different geographical settings/range and across varying human populations.

The reason why English is the language of global dominance is because the English empire controlled very large parts of the world, forced their language and practices on the local populations, and integrated terms and concepts from those places into the English language. At the same time, they encouraged the borrowing of English terms and concepts into local 'boli'. The English (not unlike other European colonisers) rewarded locals who learnt their language and ways by giving them jobs, resources, and prestige—not unlike what English offers to individuals from poor countries today. By doing so, English language and English ways of knowing and doing are given preference over other languages and ways—and, slowly, the local populations, their ways of knowing, of being, and of supporting local communities, economies, and ecologies wane. And this loss of our socio-semiotic inheritance, coupled with economic, social, and political suppression, contributes to ecological and social disaster.

Mapping a Way Forward

In order to address the deep problems with current forms of education, which were established and are marketed by exploiting powers, we need a decolonised and decolonising education.

Decolonisation of education requires a study and reformation of all social, educational, economic, legal, defence, political, religious, cultural, environmental, and linguistic policies of an exploited region and then realign them to support the well-being and prosperity of all residents—humans and non-humans—and neighbours. And, this process can begin with education and academia. There are two main reasons for this:

- All members of legislature, judiciary, military, media and other professions are required to be educated. So, if education is strong and independent, graduates will be strong and independent; and, in time, institutions will become stronger and more independent.
- Educators are responsible for caring for the socio-semiotic well-being of students. If they are unaware of the damage that the current practices are causing, then they can contribute to the perpetuation of fractals that will continue to undermine our well-being.

Fractals are patterns that repeat themselves at different scales in natural systems. Fractals can be observed in both material and socio-semiotic systems. At present, in the exploited world, the socio-semiotic fractals are patterns of corruption, dishonesty, and exploitation—these patterns repeat themselves at various scales across most aspects of our society including, but not limited to, agriculture, education, employment, governance, healthcare, housing, industry, law, media, military, politics, science, religion, and travel. Decolonisation requires one to identify these suppressive fractals and alter them, which can allow for new patterns to emerge. The goal of decolonisation is to replace the fractals of dishonesty and exploitation with those of harmony and well-being.

Decolonisation is a complex process—and, in many ways, it is an individual and personal one; at the same time, decolonisation can also be turned into an educational outcome and goal. There are multiple ways of achieving these goals. Here are six possible features of education which do not centre on 'literacy':

- It is not consumed by the goal of spreading universal literacy.
- It is not designed only to prepare people to work for others for (petty) wages.
- It considers the needs of the community and then trains citizens to learn to address those needs.
- It values all forms of knowledge and skills, not just ones included in colonial textbooks/languages.
- It is designed to make people independent and able to manage their own needs and resources.
- It involves all stakeholders in its development and management.

Ways out of colonisation will require both integrity and an understanding of how symbolic (or socio-semiotic) systems work; and, the ability to apply these understandings to improve the material and non-material conditions that people find themselves and others in. There is no single way in which these reforms and transitions can be made; nor is there a predictable way of knowing what the outcomes of such reforms will be. These will depend on context. However, one thing is for sure, if these reforms are led with integrity (and not ego, or greed, or personal gains), then humans and non-humans in the region will be much better off than they are under regimes of exploitation and colonisation.

In order to achieve some of these goals, we can consider adopting a CREDIBLE approach for both teaching and research purposes. The acronym CREDIBLE is briefly explained in Figure 1.

Figure 1   The CREDIBLE approach

CREDIBLE Project/research

Contextually relevant {think locally}

Responds to practical needs {not driven by theory}

Engages stakeholders {not just collecting 'data'}

Draws on an understanding of local knowledge and practices {pay attention to beliefs, practices, and expressions of the locals}

Informed by diverse approaches and experiences {not just western}

Benefits local communities {without benefit, there is little credibility of a project}

Leads the field/discipline and contributes to the larger (global) theories {there is no one way of doing things}

Ethical {responsible and respectful; not just having consent forms signed}

The CREDIBLE approach, one should note, focusses on doing community-beneficial things and draws on diverse forms of knowledge and sources. In doing so, the CREDIBLE approach encourages interdisciplinarity: one should draw on all sources and disciplines that may be required to achieve the goals of the project. Literacy in such projects is one resource amongst many; and, NOT the goal.

In the following section, I will share some examples of how three educators in Pakistan have tried to adopt the CREDIBLE approach.

Examples from the Classroom

The ideas shared in Figure 1 can be turned into concrete educational practices across all strata of education. In order to do so, we should consider starting our work with a goal that will contribute to our own needs and contexts (not a goal that contributes to or evaluates the learning of only literacy-based *knowledge*).

Our community-beneficial educational goals require us—along with our students and others—to create things, not just read and write about them. What people create and how they create whatever they do will depend on context. The goal of making things can be enhanced by taking an interdisciplinary orientation; and by drawing on translingual sources, including:

- Academic and non-academic sources
- Oral sources
- Observations of nature and non-human life forms

Over the last year, I have collaborated with a number of educators and researchers in different parts of the world in developing alternative practices that meet and supersede institutional requirements. By meeting or superseding institutional requirements, we satisfy administrative requirements and avoid conflict. In addition, by engaging other community members, we bring community and educational interests into alignment and harmony.

Below, I will introduce three colleagues from Pakistan, their work and some of their students. These examples—from schools, universities, and higher education research contexts—inform us of ways in which teachers or researchers can draw upon and adapt the ideas shared in this chapter into their own settings.

Amna Anwar teaches in the Department of English at Government Women University, in the city of Rawalpindi in Pakistan. Amna and her community has been concerned about how the Punjabi language is in decline because it is not used in education and sometimes carries a negative social attitude. In addition, she also observed how some of the schools in her community currently teach science and maths in very abstract and theoretical ways, without engaging students or making them understand how science relates to their lives. In order to address this, Amna along with her students collaborated with local schools and set up a series of workshops. During these workshops, students and teachers worked together to design and create puppets and then acted out a script that was about the water cycle. They did this in their mother tongue, Punjabi. By doing so, they brought science, maths, language, and play together. In Amna's own words:

> The series of workshops is highly significant with regard to preservation of the indigenous language, i.e., Punjabi. It not only involves teachers but students as well. Reinforcement of concepts from different subjects can be conveniently done by using local language (Punjabi). This makes teaching & learning an enjoyable activity. It will also initiate the positive dialogue on preserving the local identities. It is a step forward to introducing other cultures to Punjabi culture.

Amna's activity with her students is an example of a CREDIBLE project: it addressed a local and real issue by taking action, drawing on our understandings of language, science, and development from various sources and in different languages.

Details of Amna's projects, in her own words, are included as Appendices A (project design) and B (sample script in Punjabi). In addition, a short video description of the puppet project is available on Facebook. The video transcript appears below:

> It is proved that education in mother tongue enhances the creative capacity of a child. Moreover, it is his right as well. Global Monitoring Report Education (2009) also confirms that education in mother-tongue yields more positive results. English is important but not at the cost of mother-tongue. This presentation is also in line with it. For which a lecturer along with a group of students from Rawalpindi Women's University has prepared a project to promote a project Mother-tongue and mother-tongue as a medium of instruction in schools. For this purpose, this group targeted the suburban public and private schools of Satellite Town, Rawalpindi. Under this project school kids and their teachers were taught different science projects

in Punjabi by using puppetry as an aid. Students produced few scripts in Punjabi with the help of their teachers and presented them with puppets. It aims at inculcating creative abilities, promoting mother tongue and bringing theoretical concepts and experiential concepts closer to mother tongue. It is the need of hour to ensure the promotion of education in mother tongue.

In looking through this material, one can observe how Amna provided models of all things that needed to be made or done and demonstrated how these were made before working with others to make more things. This approach, which is similar to the idea of scaffolding or the teaching-learning cycle, can actually be observed across species. Parents and caretakers across numerous species follow the same approach in helping their young ones develop new abilities and skills: modelling, elaborating, and jointly doing, and then, over time, the young gain confidence in their new abilities and become independent. And, later, once they are experts, they repeat the same pattern with their young ones.

Hafiz Nauman Ahmed, like many teachers/academics in Pakistan and around the world, works at three institutions in order to make a living: Riphah International University, University of the Punjab, and University of Management and Technology (UMT), in Lahore. Nauman has been experimenting with numerous projects drawing on the CREDIBLE approach. Here I will highlight one recent project carried out at Riphah International University, where he and his students made a number of short videos and other material highlighting the dangers of fake news and ways of identifying it in multiple languages. They posted this material on social media, which has been widely watched and shared.

Nauman carried out this project with the undergraduate students of BS English (Literature & Linguistics) in courses such as *Modern Drama, English Prose, Semantics & Pragmatics,* and *Morphology & Syntax.* Since these courses traditionally focus on the explanation and understanding of literary texts, in case of literature, and definitions, explanations, word and sentence analyses, in case of linguistic courses, Nauman had to explain how his activities were related to the courses. Here are some of the things that he pointed out:

In response to the question, I tried to create a link between the two, mentioning the following points:
- Different disciplines of education are interlinked with each other. There is no subject/study discipline which is completely independent from others. For example, Pragmatics is the study of language in use; to study language

in use, we need to study the context, e.g., verbal, non-verbal, formal, informal, social media, news chapter etc. Hence, the one who is more skillful at analyzing different contexts, can do a better pragmatic analysis.

- One of the key objectives of studying the courses of English literature/ linguistics is to develop critical thinking (for example, we are often asked questions with a word 'critical' in them, and, especially this is common in our literature exams). This critical thinking should be used in developing any practical project like identifying fake news.
- The purpose of any course (education) is to solve the problems of the society we live in. If we are not using our knowledge to solve the societal issues, our knowledge may be useful (if to any extent) only for us not for the others.
- Fake news is a language related issue which has grown to a great extent in Pakistani society, especially with the emergence of COVID-19. Therefore, to get understanding about such issues through developing some projects and spread these learnt ideas further are very important for the society.

Nauman's interdisciplinary approach and use of local languages in English literature courses, while not typical, was appreciated by his students and colleagues. This can be observed in the videos that they produced as part of their activity, and also from the 56 responses of a questionnaire administered by Nauman to his students who participated in the activity (See Appendix C).

In looking through the information provided in Appendix C, one will note how students draw on multiple languages and locally relevant examples and sources. It is also worth noting that while the students' videos and sources might have been in any language, they were guided to write project reports for their work in English. By doing so, the many languages found in Nauman and his students' context, which are usually left out of education, were included in and used for education and project work. By engaging in translingual practices, Nauman is able to help boost the prestige and use of local languages, something ignored by the current educational policies and curriculum. In addition, in using the CREDIBLE approach, Nauman observed an increase in the motivation, participation, and performance of students who participated in the project.

Through this experience, Nauman realised that if a teacher is willing to give the CREDIBLE approach a try, they will find that their students and colleagues will join them in working to make their communities stronger. While, as in his experience, there may be some people who resist or create problems; the majority appreciate and support such work.

Mujahid Shah teaches at Abdul Wali Khan University in the city of Mardan in Peshawar. Of the three colleagues that I have introduced, Mujahid is the only one who has a PhD degree and trains research students in higher education. Mujahid has been drawing on the CREDIBLE approach in training research students at his institution to carry out projects that will bring direct benefits to their communities. In order to do so, Mujahid incorporates the CREDIBLE approach as part of his coursework teaching and encourages students to work on a range of social and health issues, including, for example, diet (Appendix D) and drug addiction (Appendix E). This work gives Mujahid's students some experience in how the CREDIBLE approach works and how they can adapt it for their own purposes, including in their MPhil and PhD projects.

I will briefly share below the projects of two of Mujahid's students' (the full reports are available in Appendices D and E). Once the students in Mujahid's course identified a real-world issue in their localities, they carried out a broad review of that topic—drawing on academic and non-academic sources in multiple languages. They then carried out a brief informal survey on the topic to get a better understanding of the issues in a local context and used this information and their review to set the direction of their project.

Project 1: You are what you eat.

The pre-survey shows that adults in Mardan have little awareness regarding healthy eating habits and they maintain a balanced/portioned diet. The project can be significant in changing their attitude towards their eating habits, helping them to maintain a healthy weight, enhancing their energy and making them feel better which in turn can affect their studies positively. The project is aimed at making a model of 'my nutritious plate' (زمه صحت بخش خورال) using the local language, i.e., Pashto, and is based on the 'Healthy eating plate' devised by nutrition experts at the Harvard T.H. Chan School of Public Health and editors at Harvard Health Publications. This was designed originally to address deficiencies in the U.S. Department of Agriculture (USDA)'s MyPlate and can be used by anyone for further study or awareness campaign.

Project 2: Reducing drug use, specially ICE, in Khyber Pakhtunkhwa.

The pre-survey shows that adults in the Khyber Pakhtunkhwa province of Pakistan have little awareness about ICE (a highly addictive drug), and the extent to which it can endanger them. Through this project, we will create awareness of the harmful impact of ICE and be able to influence participants' attitudes towards good health.

Mujahid's students developed resources in Pashto and other local languages and share these on social media. Examples of this material are included in Appendices D and E. Students documented the completed projects in English (since the course is part of the English Language Department) and submitted these as part of their course requirements. Mujahid's students are continuing to build on their projects even after the study and are self-motivated in doing their work. In addition, he observed that he did not have many cases of plagiarism, which is a major problem in many educational institutions across Pakistan. Following this study, Mujahid's students are now working on CREDIBLE projects, and looking into ways of finding funding and other resources to make their work stronger.

Summary and Conclusions

We started this chapter with these lines:

Leaving the promises behind
I choose to retreat into the woods
To listen, to learn, to unlearn

Metaphorically speaking, in this chapter, we left the promises marketed by exploitative education behind to retreat and evaluate our circumstances, and to consider ways forward. To do this, we *listened* and observed things, instead of using copious references; *learned* about how colonial models of education contrast with our indigenous ones; and, *unlearned* that 'literacy' should be the key goal of education.

In specific, this chapter critiqued the use of literacy as a key goal of education identifying underlying problems in using literacy as a major tool and goal of education. One reason for this is that writing systems are visual representations of linguistic meanings; they are not the same as oral language, which I technicalised as 'boli' in this chapter. Writing systems are (and were) not used frequently or widely across most of the indigenous and pre-European colonial world. By using a visual semiotic system that is not indigenous to people, literacy can influence local language and other socio-semiotic systems. This, especially when education and literacy are engineered for malicious purposes (such as taking over other people's lands and rights; or, maintaining their own status and power), can lead to a degradation of local socio-semiotics and, hence the people. And, when the people are weak, other creatures and the environment suffer as well.

In concluding this chapter, as in starting it, I will share a poem. This poem, 'Splendid! Simply splendid!' tells the story of our ancestors and us. If we want to stop and reverse the actions and goals described in this poem, then, I suggest, that we stop arguing over literacy- and reference-based thinking, and, instead create projects that address our local concerns and needs.

Image 1   Splendid! Simply splendid! (The image in the background is the flag of East India Company.)

Splendid! Simply splendid!
Ahmar Mahboob

1850s

"Sir, the danger is increasing,
The natives are resisting."

How ignorant! How savage!
They don't appreciate our attempts to salvage?

How can they know what's best for them?
Let's save them — in our God's name!

Burn their books, destroy their past;
Let us teach them what we want

Introduce money, buy us friends
Give some wealth and lots of lands

Teach people religion, to hate each other
Break their union into different nations

Create new symbols, build new systems
Change the ways they think and function

When this is done, come back to me
And I will tell you what next can be.

1940s

"Sir, I am pleased to report our progress
Your directives have brought us success:
The natives are divided and broken
They are killing each other in dozens."

Splendid! Simply splendid!
And now for the next bits:

Let us retire to our beautiful estate
Let our friends govern their new states

With our stories to guide their future
We can relax and let them suffer

Sell them books and let them know
If they want progress, they can come for more

Invite some natives, give them means
Turn them into posters for the rest to dream

When this is done, it will be seen:
Those who fought us, now fight in-between.

Splendid! Simply splendid!

Appendix A

Reinforcing/Localizing concepts with indigenous languages: Workshop on using puppetry as a learning & teaching technique (*Amna Anwar and team at Government Women University, Rawalpindi*)

Objectives/outcomes of the workshop:

- Preservation of the Punjabi language and culture by making it a medium of instruction
- Making teaching & learning a more enjoyable and convenient activity by using the mother tongue (Punjabi)
- Use of puppetry & other creative ideas for teaching & learning in the

Punjabi language
* Reinforcement of concepts in different subjects, i.e., Physics, Chemistry etc., by using the local language

Significance of the workshop: The series of workshops is highly significant with regard to preservation of the indigenous language, i.e., Punjabi. It not only involves teachers but students as well. Reinforcement of concepts from different subjects can be conveniently done by using the local language (Punjabi). This makes teaching and learning an enjoyable activity. It will also initiate a positive dialogue on preserving the local identities. It is a step towards introducing other cultures to the Punjabi culture.

Audience selection criteria: Participants were selected based on immediate availability and on the basis of being Punjabi-speaking students and teachers. The city of Rawalpindi in Pakistan is multi-ethnic and multilingual, and there are certain areas which have a majority of Punjabi-speaking population. These are the areas in focus.

Teachers who participated in the project were first convinced to use Punjabi and made to practice puppet shows as part of their teaching design with both children and adults as target audience in mind.

Participating schools:
* Government Girls High School, Shimla Islamia, B-Block
* Government. M.C High School (Girls) B-Block
* Government. M.C High School (Boys) B-Block
* Government. Elementary School (Girls) Dhoke Paracha
* Government. Elementary School (Boys) Dhoke Paracha

Group 1. Faculty   **Group 2.** Students of grade 5 & above

Resource persons: Two groups from Rawalpindi Women University, Rawalpindi Pakistan will initially target the 5 elementary & secondary schools of the suburban area of Rawalpindi Women University. These groups will conduct a series of workshops in the target schools, interacting with both faculty and students.

Group In-charge: Ms. Amna Anwar   **Co-In charge:** Roma Altaf

Group 1: Ms. Amna Anwar, Umme Ammarah, Shanzeh Farooq

Group 2: Rooma Iltaf, Farah Yasmine, Raima Arooj

Materials required: Foam, scissors, polystyrene sphere, cardboard pattern, foam craft, cutter, marker, spray paint, contact cement, colored knee-high socks & wool

Sample design: Puppet show based on the topic 'Water cycle'

Script of sample: (see Appendix B)

Selected subject: Science subject

Assignment: The groups of teachers and students will be asked to produce their own scripts based on a sample provided. Participants are expected to come up with varied and exciting new scripts incorporating creative ideas.

Reinforcement tools: Puppets, placards, foaming sheets, chart papers, hardboard, etc.

Medium of instruction: Punjabi

Limitations: Certain limitations are likely to be experienced in planning the series of workshops. These include:

- Reluctance of teachers to use Punjabi in their classes
- Lack of awareness of the Punjabi script among students and teachers
- Problems with writing Punjabi
- Unwillingness of parents to let their children use Punjabi in the school environment
- Lack of resources to help with large classes
- A strong inclination towards using English language
- Discouraging students from localising their ideas
- Reluctance of students to translate exciting ideas into their indigenous languages due to social pressure

Appendix B

Script of the water cycle project (*Amna Anwar and team at Government Women University, Rawalpindi*)

سکرپٹ آف واٹر سائیکل:

بچیو ایں اگ زمین تے میرے اتے ڈھیر سارا پانی وی ہندا اے۔ آج میں تہانوں سناواں گی ایس پانی دی کہانی کہ کیساں میرے اوتوں اے پانی اڈ کے تے واپس فیر میرے اتے آ جاوندا اے۔ اونج تے تسی بڑی وار اپنیاں کتاباں وچ اے واٹر سائیکل دا سبق پڑھیا ہووے گا پر آج تہاڈے سامنے اے واٹر سائیکل اک انوکھے تے مزےدار جیے انداز وچ پیش کراں گے تے چلو فیر اج دا اے سبق شروع کریے۔

(Water and Sun both enter from right)

سورج: (سخت گرمی)

پانی: آج تے بہت تیز دھوپ پین ڈئی اے۔۔ ہائے آج میرا کی بنے گا۔۔۔ میں تے ہوا بن کے ای اوڈ جانا اے۔۔ ((تھوڑی دیر بعد پانی بھاپ بن کے ہوا نال رل جائے گا ہائے میرے تے نکے نکے ٹوٹے ہون ڈے نیں۔۔۔ او میرے تے اتے نوں جان ڈیا ایں ہون کی کراں او کوئی تے بچا لو۔۔۔ او کوئی تے سورج بھائی نوں روکو مینوں اوڈاں توں۔۔ ہائے۔۔۔۔۔۔

سورج: لو جی اک نواں سیاپا۔ بھلا میں کیویں روک سکنا ایں پانی نوں اڈن توں۔۔ اے دے تے ڈرامے ای نئی مکدے۔۔

(بادل بنن گے)

سردار قطرہ: ویکھو بھائی میں تے آکھنا ایں کہ آﺅ سارے جنے مل کے بادل بن جائیے.. او سارے جنے رل کے سورج نوں دسیے کہ او سانو زمین توں الگ نئی کر سکدا.. چلو آﺅ سارے..
(قطرے آپس وچ رلنا شروع ہو جان گے)
ویکھو ہون اسی ساریاں نے مل کہ کنا وڈا بادل بنا لیا اے. ہون ساڈی سہیلی ہوا سانوں ٹھنڈا کر کے واپس زمین تے بھیج دے گی.

نکا قطرہ: ابا جی! ہوا ساڈی دوست کیویں اے بھلا؟ او ہی تے سانوں زمین توں چک کے اتے لیائی اے.

سردار قطرہ: آبو پتر لیائی تے بے سانوں اتے پر او ایس واسطے کہ اسیں سارے فیر واپس زمین وچ جا ملیے. ہون اے ہوا سانوں ٹھنڈا کر کے فیر پانی بنا دے گی تے اسی بارش یا برفباری بن کے زمین تے چلے جاواں گے تے فیر ندی نالیاں وچوں ہندے ہوئے دریا تے سمندر وچ جا ملاں گے.

نکا قطرہ: ابا جی اسیں ساریاں نے سمندر وچ چلے جانا اے ؟

سردار قطرہ: نہیں پتر اسیں ساریاں نے سمندر وچ نہیں ملنا جا کے. سارا پانی سمندراں وچ نہیں جاندا بلکہ تھوڑا جنا زمین دے اندر جذب ہو جاندا اے تے فیر او پانی اندرونی زمین دے پانی دے طور تے استعمال ہندا اے.
(بارش شروع)

نکا قطرہ: موجاں... ہون اسی فیر زمین تے واپس چلے آں... ہون میں سورج نوں سڑاواں گا کہ ویکھ اسیں فیر واپس آ گئے.. بڑا مزہ آئے گا.

سردار قطرہ: ہسنا شروع کر دہندا اے...

Appendix C

A   Project details: Identifying Fake News (*Hafiz Muhammad Nauman at University of the Punjab, Riphah International University, and University of Management and Technology, Lahore*)

I started teaching CREDIBLE Projects on 'identifying fake news' to my students, taking help from the sources you shared. I have taken a few classes on the fake news projects and can share the following ideas that were discussed in my classes:

The question of relevance of a project like 'identifying fake news' with the courses like 'Modern Drama', or 'English Prose' was asked by the students.

In response to the question, I tried to create a link between the two, mentioning the following points:

- Different disciplines of education are interlinked with each other. There is no subject/study discipline which is completely independent from others. For example, Pragmatics is the study of language in use; to study language in use, we need to study the context, e.g., verbal, non-verbal, formal, informal, social media, news chapter etc. Hence, the one who is more skillful at analyzing different contexts, can do a better pragmatic analysis.

- One of the key objectives of studying the courses of English literature/ linguistics is to develop critical thinking (for example, we are often asked questions with a word 'critical' in them, and, especially this is common in our literature exams). This critical thinking should be used in developing any practical project like identifying fake news.

- The purpose of any course (education) is to solve the problems of the society we live in. If we are not using our knowledge to solve the societal issues, our knowledge may be useful (if to any extent) only for us not for the others.

- Fake news is a language related issue which has grown to a great extent in Pakistani society, especially with the emergence of COVID-19. Therefore, to get understanding about such issues through developing some projects and spread these learnt ideas further are very important for the society.

Teaching of 'identifying fake news' through TLC

Modeling: In this phase, news taken from WhatsApp groups, Facebook, and other media was analysed. I first generated a 'fake text' and shared it with students (Figure 1).

Then similar 'fake news' in form of a text (Figure 2) was shared with students. The pragmatic meaning of both texts was almost the same, and the only difference between the two was that of language (language type and language style).

Figure 1   Fake news created by the teacher

The upcoming 2 weeks are very critical for Pakistan. The number of cases can reach 500,000 and death rate can touch 1000 per day. #StayHomeSatysafe

Figure 2   Fake news shared by a friend

پاکستان کورونا وائرس کی وباء کا پیک ٹائم دو ہفتے آج سے بغتے ہو رہا ہے ہے

کسی بھی چیز کے خریدنے کے لئے گھر سے مت نکلیں کیوں کہ بدترین وقت آج سے شروع ہو رہا ہے۔

آج سے "انکیوبیشن" تاریخ ختم ہوجائے گی اور بہت سے پازیٹو کیس سامنے آئیں گے۔ زیادہ تر لوگ انفیکشن کے خطرے میں ہیں۔ لہذا گھر میں رہنا بہت ضروری اور ضروری ہے۔ ہمیں اس مدت کے درمیان زیادہ سے زیادہ احتیاط برتنی چاہیے۔ کیونکہ ہم وائرس وباء کے اوپری حصے پر ہوں گے ، عام طور پر تمام انفیکشن ان دو ہفتوں میں ظاہر ہوں گے ، پھر اگلے دو ہفتوں میں سکون ہو جائے گا - امید ہے کہ اور اگلے دو ہفتوں سے زیادہ وقت میں یہ ختم ہوجائے گا.

اٹلی میں رونما ہونے والی خوفناک بات یہ ہے کہ اس متعدی وقت کو وہاں نظرانداز کیا گیا تھا اور اسی طرح وہاں پر سارے کیسز سامنے آ گئے تھے۔

کسی سے بھی نہیں ملنا ، قریبی خاندان میں بھی نہ جانا۔ یہ آپ سب کے فائدے کے لیے ہے۔

اس وقت کے آپ وائرس منتقلی کے زیادہ سے زیادہ خطرناک مرحلے پر رہیں گے یہ پیغام اپنے تمام رشتہ داروں اور دوستوں کو بھیجیں جن کی آپ کو پرواہ ہے

5:10 PM ✓✓

Later, I discussed a tweet made by a famous Pakistani journalist (Figure 3). It had some figures which upon verification revealed a slight exaggeration in them.

Figure 3   Tweet by a famous Pakistani anchorman

The analysis of another excerpt (Figure 4), from a local newspaper in Faisalabad, Pakistan, revealed that the assumption made in the news "وائرس کی طاقت بھی (the virus strength is also weakening)" was actually based on a single day COVID-19 statistics, and that it could not be used to predict further situations.

Figure 4   A news from a local newspaper from Faisalabad

Joint construction: In this phase, students researched some fake news (Figure 5a, Figure 5b, Figure 6) and discussed it in class.

Independent construction: Lastly, I have assigned students some projects on 'identifying fake news' which they have to submit by June 10 (following this

Figure 5a   **A web news from**   Figure 5b   **A web news from Pakistani news**
Pakistani news website   **website**

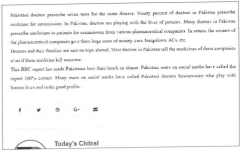

Pakistani doctors prescribe seven tests for the same disease. Ninety percent of doctors in Pakistan prescribe medicine for commission. In Pakistan, doctors are playing with the lives of patients. Many doctors in Pakistan prescribe medicines to patients for commission from various pharmaceutical companies. In return, the owners of the pharmaceutical companies give them huge sums of money: cars, bungalows, ACs, etc

Doctors and their families are sent on trips abroad. Most doctors in Pakistan sell the medicines of these companies even if these medicine kill someone.

This BBC report has made Pakistanis bow their heads in shame. Pakistani users on social media have called the report 100% correct. Many users on social media have called Pakistani doctors businessmen who play with human lives and make good profits.

f   y   ⓞ   G+   ✉

Today's Chitral

Figure 6   **A floated news on social media which is the**
translation of Figure 5a and 5b

study). These projects will be used in their final evaluation at the end of the semester.

B   Hafiz Nauman Ahmad's questionnaire

Language Learning through the Identification of Fake News

This questionnaire has been designed to know the effectiveness of fake news identification in learning many skills especially a language. Your response may help the researcher/teacher to improve or develop such more projects for the students or do research. Thanks in advance.

Language Learning

1. Do you think that you had to read the news carefully to identify it fake or real?

Strongly agree	Agree	Neutral	Disagree	Strongly disagree

2. You critically thought about the idea presented in the news.

Strongly agree	Agree	Neutral	Disagree	Strongly disagree

3. You read the news more than once.

Strongly agree	Agree	Neutral	Disagree	Strongly disagree

4. Did you translate the news either from Urdu to English or English to Urdu?

Strongly agree	Agree	Neutral	Disagree	Strongly disagree

5. Did you search for how to identify the fake news?

Strongly agree	Agree	Neutral	Disagree	Strongly disagree

6. Do you think it is a good activity for any language learning?

Strongly agree	Agree	Neutral	Disagree	Strongly disagree

7. Do you think recording audio is a good way to improve oral communication skills if you have recorded your own audio with the video or will record your voice in future?

Strongly agree	Agree	Neutral	Disagree	Strongly disagree

Critical mind development

8. Before this project, you did not have a good idea of identifying fake news.

Strongly agree	Agree	Neutral	Disagree	Strongly disagree

9. You needed to remain very critical while declaring any news fake.

Strongly agree	Agree	Neutral	Disagree	Strongly disagree

10. You searched many resources for knowing whether the news was fake.

Strongly agree	Agree	Neutral	Disagree	Strongly disagree

11. Now, you can easily identify a fake news.

Strongly agree	Agree	Neutral	Disagree	Strongly disagree

12. You are able to use your fake news identification skills in recognizing any

text, post, picture etc. fake or real.

Strongly agree	Agree	Neutral	Disagree	Strongly disagree

13. You are able to use your fake news identification skills in recognizing any text, post, picture etc. fake or real.

Strongly agree	Agree	Neutral	Disagree	Strongly disagree

Learning Technology

14. Is this your first video?

Strongly agree	Agree	Neutral	Disagree	Strongly disagree

15. Do you think that you have learnt some IT skills in developing the project?

Strongly agree	Agree	Neutral	Disagree	Strongly disagree

16. You have tried many software to develop the project?

Strongly agree	Agree	Neutral	Disagree	Strongly disagree

C   Please contact the author for online links to the work created by Nauman & his students.

Appendix D

Positive Discourse Analysis: My Nutritious Plate (*A group project by Ayesha Bashir, Marwa Munir and Nayab Huma, M. Phil. Scholars at English Department, Abdul Wali Khan University, Mardan, under the supervision of Dr. Mujahid Shah*)

Project title: You are what you eat

Goal/Outcomes of the project: The project is intended to develop a model of 'my nutritious plate' based on 'Healthy Eating Plate' (Figure 7) by nutrition experts at Harvard School of Public Health and editors at Harvard Health Publications, which in turn was designed to address deficiencies in the U.S. Department of Agriculture (USDA)'s MyPlate. The purpose of using this model along with other resources such as posters, realia and PowerPoint presentations is to bring awareness regarding proportionate diet and healthy eating habits among adults of Mardan.

Project implementation and context detail: Since the purpose of the project is to develop awareness among adults in Mardan, it is expected that the project will be eventually implemented in colleges and universities of Mardan.

Figure 7   **Healthy Eating Plate**

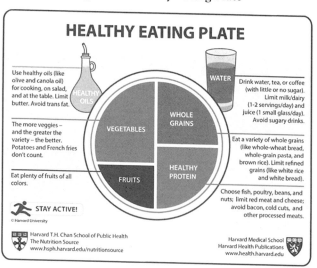

Mardan is a growing industrial city of the Khyber Pakhtunkhwa province in Pakistan. It has three universities, two post graduate colleges and many schools that are providing education to adults.

As far as the cuisine of Mardan is concerned, people of the city have regional traditional food of ethnic and cultural diversity with a blend of foreign fast foods. They have a regular pattern of three meals a day, i.e., breakfast, lunch and dinner. Roti/chapatti is common in all the three meals. Often with one or two dishes of *Salan* (curry) with vegetable, lentils, meat or the combination of them. Salad is often taken during lunch. Tea, an evening beverage of almost all locals, is often accompanied with French fries, *samosas,* or *pakoras (local snacks that are fried foods).* Based on the pre-survey we have come to know that adults going to schools, colleges or universities have the following eating habits besides their regular three meals.

- Students often have *pakora, samosa* (both are local versions of fried fritters) or fried rolls as snacks at their institutes.
- The consumption of soft drinks and chips is very common.
- Often students avoid eating anything from breakfast to lunch which makes it nearly 7–8 hours of fasting.

Significance of the project: The pre-survey shows that adults in Mardan have little awareness about healthy eating habits or a balanced diet. This project can be significant in changing their attitude towards eating habits, helping them to maintain a healthy weight, enhancing their energy and making them feel better which in turn can positively affect their studies. The project aims at having participants make a model of 'my nutritious plate' (زمه صحت بخش خورال) using the local language, i.e., Pashto, and it is based on 'Healthy Eating Plate' as devised by nutrition experts at the Harvard School of Public Health and editors at Harvard Health Publications.

Figure 8   Model for my nutritious plate

Material/Activity development: In this project a model (see, for example, Figure 8) related to a proportionate diet will be developed based on 'Healthy Eating Plate' where participants will be shown the model containing real fruit, vegetables and lentils. Through this model they will be able to recognise the nutritious value of different food items in their plate. This plate will consist of four portions (consisting of fruits, vegetables, proteins and grains), all written in Pashto.

The major purpose of this activity is to use language which participants will be more familiar with, irrespective of their education. This will help them to bring a positive improvement in their eating habits. Most participants may not be aware of the names used for local food items in English. Therefore, using Pashto language will be more helpful to make them understand.

Analyses of 'Healthy Eating Plate': We analysed the 'Healthy Eating Plate' model and came to realise that this model only provides a portioned diagram which is difficult for lay persons to understand. In order to bring some improvement in that model we decided to develop our own model of 'the nutritious plate' with real food items as it would be more helpful for people to understand the dietary portions. The use of local food items is expected to help improve eating habits.

Discussion: Several oral discussions will be organised with participants on the issue of maintaining a healthy diet and the problems associated with unhealthy food and/or imbalanced diets.

Multimedia presentations will be prepared to show the effects of malnutrition with the help of visual graphics, charts and pictures so as to make it more effective.

Questionnaires based on both open- and close-ended questions will be designed to analyse the background knowledge of the participants regarding issues associated with improper and imbalanced diets as well as the impact of the project.

Realia: The most important part of the project is the practical manifestation of balanced diet through the model, 'my nutritious plate', using proper portions of different nutrients required for good health. This model will help participants to understand the concept very easily and in a very effective manner.

Total cost of the project including printing the questionnaires and making copies of the model is around 4 lacs.

Alignment between design and goals: The main goal of this project is to spread awareness of a healthy diet and understand how to achieve this balanced diet through a properly proportioned *Healthy Plate*. Participants will be engaged in different kinds of activities so as to expose them to the knowledge of a healthy and balanced diet.

Challenges: Unhealthy eating habits have entered our life to such an extent that it has really become very difficult to get rid of them. There are several factors that makes this project challenging to implement this project. For example,

- *Advertisement and marketing.* Junk food such as burgers and soft drinks are advertised in such an attractive manner that our teens find it hard to avoid making these foods part of their lifestyle. They find it trendy and in vogue. It is really a challenge to convince them about the hazards of these unhealthy foods.
- *Fast food and fast life.* Modern life is fast and busy. The number of working women in Pakistan is increasing day by day. Students and working people find less time and stamina for cooking healthy food themselves. It is very easy to eat fast food which is readily available in the market. In addition, the culture of dining out is also getting popular among people, especially the youth. It makes the task of the project more challenging.

Negative consequences: The only negative consequence of this project seems to be the fact that participants who are under-privileged and can hardly afford taking any food may experience an inferiority complex by participating in a project that emphasises taking fruits and milk and other such items which are hard to afford. It is expected that the organisers will try to discuss the easily available items and will try to include several alternatives that are healthy but cheap and can be part of a proportioned plate of healthy diet.

Appendix E

Positive Discourse Analysis: Khyber Pakhtunkhwa cracks up the warmth on ICE drugs (*A group project by Sayed Sikandar Shah and Zabrdast Khan, M. Phil. Scholars at English Department, Abdul Wali Khan University, Mardan, under the supervision of Dr. Mujahid Shah*)

Project title:

د اعتیاد مخالف ښه حالی نه ده د اعتیاد مخالف ربط ورکونکي دی

The opposite of addiction is not sobriety; the opposite of addiction is connection!

Goal/Outcomes of the project:

- To discourage people from ICE
- To raise awareness

This project intends to raise awareness about ICE, with the help of Positive Discourse Analysis.

Project implementation and context detail: The purpose of this project is to bring the awareness among adult residents in the province of Khyber Pakhtunkhwa in Pakistan.

Meth was introduced in Khyber Pakhtunkhwa in 2010. It is usually in the form of crystals. The 'Drug use in Pakistan-2013' report was to set up by the United Nations Office on Drug and Crimes (UNODC) and Ministry of Interior and Narcotics Control. The report states that roughly 6.7 million individuals utilised controlled substances including physician recommended drugs. Sharing the key discoveries of the report, Mohammad Shahid said that the age of most of the drug clients was somewhere in the range of 25 and 39 years. He said that 860,000 individuals in the nation utilised heroin normally and 320,000 were opium clients while 1.06 million individuals between 15 to 64 years, were utilising sedatives. "Khyber Pakhtunkhwa is on the course of the drug pushers, so natural accessibility is one noteworthy reason for the high commonness of the drug (ICE) use," Mr. Shahid said.

Ladies were additionally utilising hashish, he stated, including that 45,000 ladies in Khyber Pakhtunkhwa were utilising medications and painkillers. He said that understudy inns everywhere throughout the nation were getting to be center points of medication misuse. As indicated by the report, 22 percent of ladies in the nation are medicate clients. It is said that 32 percent of ladies, who utilised medications and painkillers were uneducated.

Significance of the project: The pre-survey shows that adults in Khyber Pakhtunkhwa have little awareness regarding ICE or its associated dangers. Our project intends to create awareness and highlight the dangers associated with ICE. It is expected that this will develop positive attitudes towards health.

Material/Activity development: In this project a model (see, for example, Figure 9a and 9b) related to ICE (drug) will be developed on the Basis of one slogan (د اعتیاد مخالف خه حالی نه ده د اعتیاد مخالف ربط ورکونکي دی) and few points. Through this model they will be able to see how ICE patients will recover.

The major purpose of this activity is to use the language which participants will be more familiar with, irrespective of their education. This will help them bring a positive improvement towards ICE drug addicted patients, Therefore, using Pashto language will be more helpful to make them understand.

Analyses of

د اعتیاد مخالف خه حالی نه ده" د اعتیاد مخالف ربط ورکونکي دی

This sentence in Pashto means: *The opposite of addiction is not sobriety; the opposite of addiction is connection!*

We analysed this sentence in the views of some experts, like Johann Hari, a Swiss-British writer and journalist. He has written for publications including

Figure 9a   Model for ICE drug addicts   **Figure 9b**   Model for ICE drug addicts

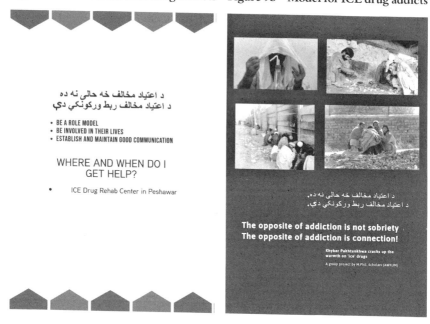

The Independent and *The Huffington Post* and has written books on the topics of depression, the war on drugs, and the monarchy. But what we realised is that these arguments need to be in a model, so that it can give a perspective to people and help them understand the dangers of drugs.

Alignment between design and goals: The main goal of this project is to spread awareness regarding ICE addicts, and how people deal with them. There will be different kinds of activities to help people deal with sick individuals.

Discussion: Several oral discussions will be organised with participants on the issue of drug addicts and the problems of ICE ADDICTS will be highlighted.

Multimedia presentations: Different multimedia presentations will be prepared to show the impact of drugs.

Challenges: Drug addiction, or more specifically, ICE addiction, is the biggest problem here in Khyber Pakhtunkhwa. According to the researchers in Khyber Pakhtunkhwa most ICE addicts are young adults, and this ratio is getting higher day by day. And like in universities it is easily available through drug dealers who have a vast connection in Pakistan. It is really a challenge to convince them of the hazards of these drugs.

References

There are no references in this chapter.

There are multiple reasons for not using any references, here I will list five (in no particular order):

– References have to be trusted, as not everyone has or can do the same readings (and with the same interpretations).

– References relate to other written texts (often in English), which exclude other forms of knowledge (specially in languages that don't have a writing system or don't use it in academia).

-- Selecting references can be a political act through which certain people and work are promoted and others dismissed.

– References, when used instead of observations/evidence to make/support a point, have to be taken at face value as there is little that readers can do to verify them.

– References can make reading difficult, especially for those uninitiated in the field; others can search to find relevant references quite easily in today's 'tech' world.

Given these and other issues with references, I choose not to include any references in this chapter. Instead, I have shared my observations and/or have pointed to things that you can locate and observe yourselves. By doing so, in many ways, I am delegating the authority and expertise typically reserved for 'the author' to you, the reader: I have shared examples and observations and you have the agency to verify them—my arguments are not protected by a 'reference wall'.

Similarly, instead of providing a specific set of guidelines or procedures to follow, I have shared some broad principles and examples of ways in which teachers and students have and can adapt and use them in their own contexts.

By reading through the chapter and the examples (including the appendices), you will note that there is no one way in which we can or should move forward with education. Instead, in moving forward with education, what we need to do is to set up goals and projects that are:

- achievable,
- respectful of all living and non-living things, not just groups of humans,
- contributing to your community building and welfare.

And, finally, just as I have not referred to any work in this chapter, please do feel free to use this work without citation or reference, if you like!